Sustainable Development and Resource Productivity

The fourth Factor X publication from the German Environment Agency (Umweltbundesamt, UBA), *Sustainable Development and Resource Productivity: The Nexus Approaches* explores the interdependencies of sustainable development paths and associated resource requirements, describing and analysing the necessities for a more resource efficient world.

The use of and competition for increasingly scarce resources are growing worldwide with current production and consumption patterns of industrialised economies soon to reach the point where the ecosphere will be overtaxed far beyond its limits. Against this background, this volume examines the important initiatives to monitor resource use at the international, EU and national level. The current trends and challenges related to sustainable resource use are discussed, including international challenges for a resource efficient world, megatrends, justice and equitable access to resources. In the second part of the book, contributions examine implementation strategies. They assess the concept known as circular economy and discuss the theory of growth and the role of the financial and education systems. The final section places special emphasis on practical examples. Overall, the book presents concrete ways and examples of achieving more sustainability in practice.

Discussing solutions for a more sustainable use of natural resources, this book is essential reading for scholars and students of natural resources and sustainable development and decision-makers and experts from the fields of policy development, industry and civil society.

Harry Lehmann is General Director of the Environmental Planning and Sustainability Strategies Division of the German Federal Environment Agency. He was an early member, and is now the President, of the Factor 10 Club for resource productivity and sustainable use of natural resources. He is one of the founders of Eurosolar and since 2011 he has been executive Chairman of the World Renewable Energy Council.

Factor X: Studies in Sustainable Natural Resource Management

'Factor X' promotes good and best practices to enable significant savings in natural resource use and ways to improve resource efficiency. In collaboration with the German Environmental Agency (Umweltbundesamt, UBA), and contributions from leading names in policy and academia, this book series proposes innovative strategies for implementing the 'Factor X' concept in order to build a more resource efficient world.

Sustainable Development and Resource Productivity
The Nexus Approaches
Edited by Harry Lehmann

For more information about this series, please visit: www.routledge.com/Factor-X-Studies-in-Sustainable-Natural-Resource-Management/book-series/FX.

Sustainable Development and Resource Productivity

The Nexus Approaches

Edited by Harry Lehmann

First published 2021
by Routledge
2 Park Square, Milton Park, Abingdon, Oxon OX14 4RN

and by Routledge
52 Vanderbilt Avenue, New York, NY 10017

Routledge is an imprint of the Taylor & Francis Group, an informa business

© 2021 selection and editorial matter, Harry Lehmann; individual chapters, the contributors

The right of Harry Lehmann to be identified as the author of the editorial material, and of the authors for their individual chapters, has been asserted in accordance with sections 77 and 78 of the Copyright, Designs and Patents Act 1988.

The Open Access version of this book, available at www.taylorfrancis.com, has been made available under a Creative Commons Attribution 4.0 International License.

Trademark notice: Product or corporate names may be trademarks or registered trademarks, and are used only for identification and explanation without intent to infringe.

British Library Cataloguing-in-Publication Data
A catalogue record for this book is available from the British Library

Library of Congress Cataloging-in-Publication Data
Names: Lehmann, Harry (Environmentalist) editor.
Title: Sustainable development and resource productivity : the Nexus approaches / edited by Harry Lehmann.
Description: New York : Routledge, 2020. | Series: Factor x: studies in sustainable natural resource management | Includes bibliographical references and index. |
Identifiers: LCCN 2020023831 (print) | LCCN 2020023832 (ebook) | ISBN 9780367429546 (hardback) | ISBN 9781003000365 (ebook)
Subjects: LCSH: Sustainable development. | Natural resources--Management.
Classification: LCC HC79.E5 S86188 2020 (print) | LCC HC79.E5 (ebook) | DDC 338.9/27--dc23
LC record available at https://lccn.loc.gov/2020023831
LC ebook record available at https://lccn.loc.gov/2020023832

ISBN: 978-0-367-42954-6 (hbk)
ISBN: 978-1-003-00036-5 (ebk)

Typeset in Bembo
by MPS Limited, Dehradun

Visit the eResources: www.routledge.com/Sustainable-Development-and-Resource-Productivity-The-Nexus-Approaches/Lehmann/p/book/9780367429546

In memoriam Prof. Dr Friedrich (Bio) Schmidt–Bleek

Contents

Foreword by Harry Lehmann	xi
In memoriam Friedrich Schmidt-Bleek	xii
List of contributors	xiv

PART I
Setting the scene 1

1 RESCUE the Anthropocene: Urgent action for the great transformation 3
HARRY LEHMANN

2 The world at the ultimate crossroads: Climate change, environmental impacts, population and natural resources sufficiency in the long perspective with integrated models 11
HARALD ULRIK SVERDRUP, ULLRICH LORENZ, AND
ANNA HULDA OLAFSDOTTIR

3 Reporting resource use in Germany 29
STEPHAN LUTTER, STEFAN GILJUM, CHRISTOPHER MANSTEIN, AND
GERDA PALMETSHOFER

4 The rise of e-mobility as a trade-off between social and ecological benefits and distributional injustice: How the socio-technical regime and externalisation prevent a profound transformation of the mobility sector 42
FABIAN ZIMMER AND DÖRTE THEMANN

5 The quest for the holy grail: Can smart cities lead us to sustainability? 55
IRA SHEFER

viii *Contents*

6 Sustainable development as the ultimate target of adopting a nexus approach to resources management 67

SERENA CAUCCI, LULU ZHANG, KARLA LOCHER-KRAUSE, AND STEPHAN HÜLSMANN

7 The water–energy nexus of Brazil's hydropower 80

THEODOROS SEMERTZIDIS AND RAIMUND BLEISCHWITZ

8 Education, sustainable development and resource management 90

KATRIN KOHL AND CHARLES A. HOPKINS

PART II
Core aspects of an integrated resource policy 101

9 Systemic analysis of the nexus of greenhouse gas emissions and material use in the energy sector 103

ULLRICH LORENZ

10 Wrong memes: Organic farming and battery electric vehicles 114

KAI NEUMANN

11 What's going on abroad? Monitoring international resource policies 122

MONIKA DITTRICH, ANDREAS AUBERGER, CHRISTOPHER MANSTEIN, DETLEF SCHREIBER, AND ELISABETH DÜRR

12 Pathways to a resource-efficient and greenhouse-gas-neutral Germany 135

JENS GÜNTHER, PHILIP NUSS, KATJA PURR, MONIKA DITTRICH, AND HARRY LEHMANN

13 Resource use in a post-fossil green Germany 147

MONIKA DITTRICH, KARL SCHOER, JENS GÜNTHER, PHILIP NUSS, AND HARRY LEHMANN

14 Vertical integration in a multi-level governance system using the example of the German Resource Efficiency Programme 158

MAIC VERBÜCHELN AND BETTINA BAHN-WALKOWIAK

Contents   ix

15 A strategy to increase the resource efficiency of
renewable energy technologies   172
HANS-MARTIN HENNING, SHIVENES SHAMMUGAM, ESTELLE
GERVAIS, AND THOMAS SCHLEGL

16 Governing critical infrastructure in digital futures 182
LOUIS KLEIN

17 The energy transition in Deventer: A Hanseatic
approach   193
IR. ALMAR OTTEN AND RON SINT NICOLAAS

PART III
Case studies of existing solutions   203

18 Natural resources as common goods   205
ALEXA K. LUTZENBERGER, FRANZISKA LICHTER, AND
SARAH HOLZGREVE

19 Sustainable resource output: Towards an approach to a
multidimensional environmental assessment of biomass
production   226
H. BÖTTCHER, K. HENNENBERG, K. WIEGMANN,
M. SCHEFFLER, AND A. HANSEN

20 More resource efficiency in production and products:
Digitalisation supports industry and trades   238
PETER JAHNS

21 Eight tons of lifestyle: Monitoring a sustainable material
footprint for households in Germany and the world   252
JENS TEUBLER, SEBASTIAN SCHUSTER, AND CHRISTA LIEDTKE

22 C like clever and cycle: Without a smart and systematic
conception of the metal industry, product labelling
and an indicator system, nothing will happen   262
KATHRIN GREIFF, FLORIAN FIESINGER, CHRISTA LIEDTKE, AND
MARTIN FAULSTICH

23 The nexus of procurement and sustainability:
Reflection of the limits and opportunities of product
labels, using the example of the Forest Stewardship
Council   275
UWE SAYER AND NINA GRIESSHAMMER

x   *Contents*

24 The role of biomass use in a defossilised and
    resource-efficient world   288

    HORST FEHRENBACH AND NILS RETTENMAIER

PART IV
Pioneering innovations   303

25 Big, environmentally friendly events: Sparing
    resources, respecting nature, setting limits – an attempt
    by the German Protestant Festival (Deutscher
    Evangelischer Kirchentag) at organising a big event on
    a sustainable footing   305

    OLIVER FOLTIN, CHRISTOF HERTEL, AND JOBST KRAUS

26 The Kwawu resilient entrepreneurial ecosystems:
    A complex adaptive systems approach to achieving
    the Sustainable Development Goals   317

    EBEN ANUWA-AMARH, CHRISTOPH HINSKE,

    NANA KWABENA BAMFO-DEBRAH, DAVID SEFA, SHERIFF AMARH,

    AND STEPHEN NASSAM

27 Exploring the possibility of a meat tax   329

    FLORIS DE GRAAD

28 Facilitating sustainable dietary choices for positive
    nutritional and environmental outcomes   337

    MAYSOUN A. MUSTAFA, AYMAN SALAMA, AND SAYED AZAM-ALI

29 Environmental systems innovation in ancient India
    with Factor X components as revealed in old Tamil
    Manuscripts   347

    KANNAN NARAYANAN

    Index   358

Foreword

This book is intended for anyone interested in the sustainable use of resources and circular economy, which is only possible if we drastically reduce the amount of resources needed for our lives – in the long term by a Factor of 10 (or X).

It provides insights into the actual situation and future development. It shows possible system policymaking, contains practical developments and innovations that will accompany us on the path of a transition towards a more sustainable society.

This book is the fourth in a series of Factor X books. A fifth one is in preparation.

I profoundly thank all authors for spending many hours to write the interesting articles contained in this book.

I would also like to thank the reviewers, Ms Martina Eick, Mr Christoph Hinske and Mr Eben Anuwa-Amarh, for their thoughtful and insightful comments that led to an improvement of the book.

Harry Lehmann

Note: The articles in this book do not necessarily reflect the opinion or the policies of the German Federal Environment Agency.

In memoriam Friedrich Schmidt–Bleek

This book is dedicated to the memory of Prof. Dr Friedrich Schmidt-Bleek (16 July 1932–26 June 2019), who was the original inventor of the Factor X idea (Schmidt-Bleek 1993a). Friedrich Schmidt-Bleek, or 'Bio' for his friends, researched resource productivity and dematerialisation, introduced the term 'Ecological Rucksack' and developed the 'Material Input Per unit of Service' (MIPS) as a basic measure for the assessment of environmental impact potentials (Schmidt-Bleek 1993a; Schmidt-Bleek 1998).

In the early 1990s, Schmidt-Bleek postulated an increase of resource productivity of industrialised countries by a 'Factor of 10' (minus 90%), as a response to the fact that the richest countries have a significantly higher consumption than the world's poorest countries (Schmidt-Bleek 1993b). Today the generalised term 'Factor X' is often used, as the required degree of dematerialisation needs to be decided individually from country to country, according to the prevailing levels of consumption (Lehmann, Schmidt-Bleek & Manstein 2018).

Friedrich Schmidt-Bleek was a German nuclear and physical chemist and environmental researcher. His impressive career included functions at the German Environment Agency (UBA) in Berlin, at the OECD in Paris and the International Institute for Applied Systems Analysis (IIASA) in Laxenburg/ Austria. From 1992 to 1997 he headed the Wuppertal Institute for Climate, Environment and Energy together with Ernst Ulrich von Weizsäcker. He was chairman of the international Factor 10 Club, president of the Factor 10 Institute in Carnoules/France (Schmidt-Bleek 2009) and co-founder and honorary president of the World Resources Forum (WRF 2019).

Schmidt-Bleek is the author of numerous books and publications. In 2001 he received the 'Takeda World Environment Award' for the proposal, promotion and implementation of the MIPS and ecological rucksack concept (Takeda Foundation 2011).

> I developed the MIPS and ecological rucksack concept to make sure that we can produce wealth for all the people on this planet and still live in peace with nature. Unfortunately, current economic and environmental policies will not get us to a sustainable future. The major problem today is

that we reward those who waste natural resources through old fashioned fiscal policies and punish those who hire people for work. Still, there are already today a number of forward-looking companies who increase the resource productivity of their products and services. They go in this direction because they want to be still in business in 10 or 20 years in a world that simply does not have enough resources to globalize the present western lifestyle for 8 or 10 billion people.

(Schmidt-Bleek 2001)

References

Lehmann, H., Schmidt-Bleek, F. & Manstein, C. (2018). Factor X – 25 years – 'Factor X Concept' is Essential for Achieving Sustainable Development. In H. Lehmann (ed.), *Factor X: Challenges, Implementation Strategies and Examples for a Sustainable Use of Natural Resources*. Springer, Berlin.

Schmidt-Bleek, F. (1993a). *Wieviel Umwelt braucht der Mensch? MIPS – das Maß für ökologisches Wirtschaften*. Birkhäuser Verlags, Berlin.

Schmidt-Bleek, F. (1993b). Revolution in Resource Productivity for a Sustainable Economy: A New Research Agenda. *Fresenius Environmental Bulletin*, 2(8), 485–490.

Schmidt-Bleek, F. (1998). *Das MIPS-Konzept. Weniger Naturverbrauch – mehr Lebensqualität durch Faktor 10*. Droemer Knaur, München.

Schmidt-Bleek, F. (2001). Schmidt-Bleek Receives the Takeda World Environment Award 2001. Retrieved from www.factor10-institute.org/pages/takeda_award_e.html.

Schmidt-Bleek, F. (2009). About. Retrieved from www.factor10-institute.org/about.html.

Takeda Foundation (2011). World Environmental Well-Being. Retrieved from www.takeda-foundation.jp/en/award/takeda/2001/recipient/06.html.

WRF (2019). Rest in Peace, lieber Bio Friedrich Schmidt-Bleek. Retrieved from www.wrforum.org/organisation/friedrich-schmidt-bleek-rip.

Contributors

Sheriff Amarh, National Association of Local Authorities, Ghana

Eben Anuwa-Amarh, Institute of Development and Technology Management, Ghana

Andreas Auberger, Institut für Energie und Umweltforschung (ifeu), Heidelberg, Germany

Sayed Azam-Ali, Crops For the Future Research Centre, Semenyih, 43500 Selangor, Malaysia

Bettina Bahn-Walkowiak, Wuppertal Institute for Climate, Environment, Energy, Germany

Nana Kwabena Bamfo-Debrah, Institute of Development and Technology Management, Ghana

Raimund Bleischwitz, UCL BSEER, University College London, UK

H. Böttcher, Öko-Institut e.V., Berlin/Darmstadt, Germany

Serena Caucci, United Nations University Institute for Integrated Management of Material Fluxes and Resources (UNU-FLORES), Dresden, Germany

Floris de Graad, Vegetariërsbond, Minahassastraat 1, 1094 RS Amsterdam, the Netherlands

Monika Dittrich, Institut für Energie- und Umweltforschung (ifeu), Heidelberg GmbH, Department on Resources, Im Weiher 10, 69121 Heidelberg, Germany

Elisabeth Dürr, Gesellschaft für Internationale Zusammenarbeit, Germany

Martin Faulstich, INZIN Institute for the Future of the Industrial Society, Germany

Horst Fehrenbach, Institut für Energie- und Umweltforschung (ifeu), Heidelberg GmbH, Department on Resources, Im Weiher 10, 69121 Heidelberg, Germany

Florian Fiesinger, INZIN Institute for the Future of the Industrial Society, Germany

Oliver Foltin, Protestant Institute for Interdisciplinary Research (FEST), Germany

Estelle Gervais, Fraunhofer Institute for Solar Energy Systems (ISE), Heidenhofstraße 2, 79110 Freiburg, Germany

Stefan Giljum, Vienna University of Economics and Business, Welthandelsplatz 1, AD 1020 Vienna, Austria

Kathrin Greiff, Department of Anthropogenic Material Cycles, RWTH Aachen University, Germany

Nina Griesshammer, FSC Germany, FSC Deutschland, Rehlingstr. 7, 79100 Freiburg, Germany

Jens Günther, German Environment Agency (UBA), Unit I1.1 – Fundamental Aspects, Sustainability Strategies and Scenarios, Sustainable Resource Use, Woerlitzer Platz 1, 06844 Dessau-Rosslau, Germany

A. Hansen, Leibniz Institute for Agricultural Engineering and Bioeconomy, Potsdam, Germany

K. Hennenberg, Öko-Institut e.V., Berlin/Darmstadt, Germany

Hans-Martin Henning, Fraunhofer Institute for Solar Energy Systems (ISE), Heidenhofstraße 2, 79110 Freiburg, Germany

Christof Hertel, Stabstelle Umweltprojekte 37. Deutscher Evangelicher Kirchentag, Germany

Christoph Hinske, The Engagement Company, SAXION University of Applied Sciences, Faculty of Finance, Economics and Management, the Netherlands

Sarah Holzgreve, Alrene Ingen, Germany

Charles A. Hopkins, York University Toronto, Canada

Stephan Hülsmann, United Nations University Institute for Integrated Management of Material Fluxes and Resources (UNU-FLORES), Dresden, Germany, and Sächsisches Landesamt für Umwelt, Landwirtschaft und Geologie, Dresden, Germany

Peter Jahns, Effizienz-Agentur NRW, Effizienz-Agentur NRW, Dr.-Hammacher-Strasse 49 – 47119 Duisburg, Germany

Louis Klein, European School of Governance (EUSG) GmbH, Kirchstraße 1, 10557 Berlin, Germany

Katrin Kohl, York University, Toronto, Canada

xvi *Contributors*

Jobst Kraus, Protestant Academy of Bad Böll, Germany

Harry Lehmann, German Environment Agency (UBA), Division I – Environmental Planning and Sustainability Strategies, Woerlitzer Platz 1, 06844 Dessau-Rosslau, Germany

Franziska Lichter, Alrene Ingen, Germany

Christa Liedtke, Wuppertal Institut, Doeppersberg 19, DE-42103 Wuppertal, Germany

Karla Locher-Krause, United Nations University Institute for Integrated Management of Material Fluxes and Resources (UNU-FLORES), Dresden, Germany, and Department of Conservation Biology/Department of Environmental Politics, Helmholtz-Centre for Environmental Research-UFZ, Leipzig, Germany

Ullrich Lorenz, Umweltbundesamt, Wörlitzer Platz 1, DE-06844 Dessau-Roßlau, Germany

Stephan Lutter, Vienna University of Economics and Business, Welthandelsplatz 1, AD 1020 Vienna, Austria

Alexa K. Lutzenberger, Alrene Ingen, Germany

Christopher Manstein, Umweltbundesamt/Federal Environment Agency, Germany

Maysoun A. Mustafa, Crops For the Future Research Centre, Semenyih, 43500 Selangor, Malaysia

Kannan Narayanan, Tamil Heritage Foundation, Chennai, Tamilnadu, India

Stephen Nassam, Alfa Precision Consult, Ghana

Kai Neumann, Consideo GmbH, Germany

Philip Nuss, German Environment Agency (UBA), Unit I1.1 – Fundamental Aspects, Sustainability Strategies and Scenarios, Sustainable Resource Use, Woerlitzer Platz 1, 06844 Dessau-Rosslau, Germany

Anna Hulda Olafsdottir, Industrial Engineering, University of Iceland, Hjarðarhagi 6, IS-107 Reykjavik, Iceland

Ir. Almar Otten, Deventer Municipality, the Netherlands

Gerda Palmetshofer, Vienna University of Economics and Business, Welthandelsplatz 1, AD 1020 Vienna, Austria

Katja Purr, German Environment Agency (UBA), Unit V1.2 – Energy Strategies and Scenarios, Woerlitzer Platz 1, 06844 Dessau-Rosslau, Germany

Nils Rettenmaier, Institut für Energie- und Umweltforschung (ifeu), Heidelberg GmbH, Department on Resources, Im Weiher 10, 69121 Heidelberg, Germany

Ayman Salama, Crops For the Future Research Centre, Semenyih, 43500 Selangor, Malaysia

Uwe Sayer, FSC Germany, FSC Deutschland, Rehlingstr. 7, 79100 Freiburg, Germany

M. Scheffler, Öko-Institut e.V., Berlin/Darmstadt, Germany

Thomas Schlegl, Fraunhofer Institute for Solar Energy Systems (ISE), Heidenhofstraße 2, 79110 Freiburg, Germany

Karl Schoer, Sustainable Solutions Germany, Wiesbaden, Germany

Detlef Schreiber, Umweltbundesamt/Federal Environment Agency, Germany

Sebastian Schuster, Wuppertal Institut, Doeppersberg 19, DE-42103 Wuppertal, Germany

David Sefa, Institute of Development and Technology Management, Ghana

Theodoros Semertzidis, UCL BSEER, University College London, UK

Shivenes Shammugam, Fraunhofer Institute for Solar Energy Systems (ISE), Heidenhofstraße 2, 79110 Freiburg, Germany

Ira Shefer, Research Fellow, Israel Public Policy Institute, Israel

Ron Sint Nicolaas, Deventer Municipality, the Netherlands

Harald Ulrik Sverdrup, Institute of Gamification, Inland University of Applied Sciences, NO-2300 Hamar, Norway

Jens Teubler, Wuppertal Institut, Doeppersberg 19, DE-42103 Wuppertal, Germany

Dörte Themann, Research Fellow, Freie Universität Berlin (Environmental Policy Research Centre), Germany

Maic Verbücheln, German Institute of Urban Affairs, Germany

K. Wiegmann, M. Scheffler, Öko-Institut e.V., Berlin/Darmstadt, Germany

Lulu Zhang, United Nations University Institute for Integrated Management of Material Fluxes and Resources (UNU-FLORES), Dresden, Germany

Fabian Zimmer, Researcher at Mobility Institute Berlin (MIB)/Non-Resident Fellow at Israel Public Policy Institute (IPPI), Germany

Part I
Setting the scene

1 RESCUE the Anthropocene

Urgent action for the great transformation

Harry Lehmann

The world at the ultimate crossroads!

As has been shown in the RESCUE report (Günther et al. 2018), global greenhouse gas (GHG) emissions continue to rise despite the implementation of various climate protection measures. In 2017, fossil GHG-emissions were 37 gigatons (Gt) about 63% above 1990 levels (EK 2019). Additionally, global materials extraction has accelerated in the last decades to more than 90 Gt in 2017, which is a fifteen-fold increase compared to 1900 (UNEP 2019). Currently, an estimated four out of nine planetary boundaries have now been crossed as a result of human activity, which would drive the Earth System into a much less hospitable state. The four are climate change, altered biogeo-chemical cycles (phosphorus and nitrogen), land-system change, and biosphere integrity (Rockström et al. 2009; Steffen et al. 2015).

According to Günther et al. (2018):

> the UNFCCC's1 Paris Agreement was adopted in 2015 to keep the increase in global average temperature to well below 2 °C above pre-industrial levels; and to limit the increase to 1.5 °C (UNFCCC 2015). Nevertheless, global existing policies are insufficient and projected to result in about 3.3 °C warming above pre-industrial levels (Climate Action Tracker 2019).

The use of primary materials in Germany increased by 4% from 2000 and amounted to 2.64 billion tonnes (gigatons = Gt) in 2014.

The current tragedy is that improvement or turnaround in the global trends is not in sight. On the contrary, every year it gets more dramatic. No one can currently predict whether we have already passed the 'tipping points' and reinforcing effects are already having an accelerating impact. No one can predict whether we have not already irretrievably destroyed system elements here or there.

Urgent action is needed to ensure that humanity preserves the life-giving functions of our natural environment. In order to face these challenges, a fundamental transformation across all societal groups and economic sectors is required.

And much worse, this is nothing new – this has been known since the Club of Rome report in the seventies. Already in the 1990s, targets for dematerialisation and decarbonisation were formulated (90% down or, in other words, a factor of 10 in productivity). This is the content of many conferences, publications, political declarations of intent, policies and treaties. Looking at the development since the 1990s, much knowledge has been generated but little has been achieved.

As a reminder, the 'basic requirement' of sustainable development is that the functions of the environment, i.e. the natural foundations of life in their various roles, are no longer endangered for this and future generations.

This means that our present anthroposphere must become 'SMALLER' to create space for the biosphere. That it must become 'DIFFERENT' (more productive, dematerialised, circular instead of linear) in order to meet the target of 5–8 tonnes of resource use by 2050. That it must become 'FAIR' to enable sustainable development for other regions and future generations. Also ultimately 'NEUTRAL', greenhouse gases, toxins, plastic waste must be reduced to zero as quickly as possible.

The path to this is the 'Great Transformation'

This transformation needs a broad perspective in analysis and implementation. The interactions between resource conservation, climate protection, energy supply, lifestyle, economic growth – to name just a few subsystems – require a systemic and interdisciplinary approach.

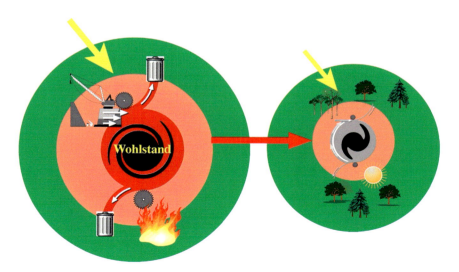

Figure 1.1 From ownership and linearity to happiness and circularity – necessary changes in our anthroposphere – the great transformation.

At this stage in history, and perhaps for all time to come, our actions must be guided by the recognition of how little we know about our planet's 'survival' system and its susceptibility. As a precautionary measure, we should therefore, attempt to minimise anthropogenic effects on this system. We should strive to prevent as far as possible any negative consequences, assuming that an undisturbed biosphere will continue to exist in a way humanity can survive and live in an agreeable manner. This precautionary principle must constitute the main guideline for all human activity if sustainable development is to be our primary aim.

RESCUE the Anthropocene

In a multi-year UBA research and cooperation project of its own, with external support based on research projects, possible solution areas for this transformation process for Germany were identified based on several scenarios. These paths and visions of the future are archetypes of sustainable development and can serve as blueprints for other regions and countries. Of course after adaptation to the general conditions in other countries.

Various studies and the results of the RESCUE ('Resource-efficient Pathways towards Greenhouse-Gas-Neutrality') project are presented in Part II of the book.

I would like to go into more detail on some of the insights that I consider important. There are plausible and sustainable pathways towards a greenhouse gas-neutral, post-fossil and resource-saving Germany in 2050 based on technologies that already exist today (technological feasibility). These paths are also possible trajectories for other regions.

Climate and resource protection complement each other. However, there are risks – decarbonisation and dematerialisation must always be achieved together (systemic approach necessary).

All sectors (consumption – housing – energy production – industry – transport – agriculture and land use) must be considered together (cross-sectoral coupling) and measured against their services (e.g. mobility).

An example of a synergy between resource protection and climate protection is the idea of 'Power to Liquid' (PTL) in aviation instead of choosing biofuels as the technological path. Since we propose a solution for aviation within the given infrastructure – we avoid building a new technological path (e.g. fuel supply, Aircrafts, engines, among others) with the associated consumption of resources. PTL is also much more resource-efficient than bioenergy. However, we need a lot of renewable energy for this and we need to start building the PTL system quickly. This path is certainly quicker to realise than a complete shift of aviation to a new technology path. This path avoids land-use competition with food and fibre (Lehmann 2017).

In all scenarios, raw material shortages (e.g. copper) are already foreseeable today if the pathways proposed in the RESCUE Study are implemented globally. This is not a shortage of quantity, it is a shortage of production quantity at a time – if everyone wants to achieve greenhouse gas neutrality – the quantity of installed renewable energies – which still need a lot of metals today – increases at a certain time. Various solutions are conceivable, the simplest solutions needing less raw materials per installed capacity and substitution by other materials. Another is to reduce the amount of energy required – here through energy efficiency and, just as importantly, resource productivity. We have no shortage of renewable energy – we have a raw material and resource limitation.

I am particularly pleased that we have succeeded in the 'GreenSupreme' scenario in taking a look at a transformation path that can be implemented globally and meets the Paris objectives. What do I understand by global implementation? Starting from an unfair distribution of materials in the different regions of the world, we end up in a world where everyone acts with his or her share of materials – greenhouse gas neutral.

This scenario would be a path for the world to achieve the sustainability goals. Not surprisingly, it would mean zero growth of the gross national product in the industrialised countries in the medium term. After a period of growth through transformation, we have frozen our 'material prosperity' at its current relatively high level. This gives other regions the chance to catch up and be carbon neutral in 2050. However, this scenario also shows that we still have a lot to do to achieve better resource use. It shows once again that the limiting factor is not renewable energies, but raw materials and resources.

One issue that has become increasingly important in the creation of scenarios and the formulation of policies is the question of lifestyle. Our private consumption, the wealth we accumulate, the way we achieve our well-being, is essential for achieving climate protection goals and a fair distribution of development opportunities in this and the next generations. It starts with food, affects the life span of products and does not stop at the number of flights per person and year. The question of 'how much is enough' is difficult to answer – without limiting our lifestyles we will not achieve the goals and global injustices will become increasingly severe.

System-Policies

> System-Policies must become the norm because policies seeking to solve individual environmental, societal, economic, and institutional problems one at a time, without taking inter-dependencies among them into account, cannot protect the environment nor can it lead to a sustained human economy.
>
> (Schmidt-Bleek et al. 2014)

'System-Policies' have several pillars and prerequisites:

- One premise – we need a more or less consistent way of measuring the 'material rucksack'.

- We need data, for example, to calculate the different solutions in retrofitting building – this data must be evolved – let us start with the indicators we have today.
- They have to be transparent, linear and easily understandable. Clearly, they will improve, through science, as in the case of greenhouse gases and will generate better and more reliable data.
- However, let us start with MIPS, COPS, TMR, RMC or whatever you like.
- Clearly we need also a land-use Indicator to lower the overall land-use of humanity.

An open question that needs to be examined very soon is how much resources we need for the various services and sectors. Just as we now set targets for the greenhouse gas emissions of a country's sectors, we must do the same for the different services and their resources use we need. Unlike greenhouse gas neutrality, it is a more complex analysis. Nevertheless, the usual policy cycle must be followed when formulating this policy. So measurement – determination of the goal – formulation of policies, measures and instruments – implementation – monitoring – and then again from the beginning.

Looking at the nexus of resource policy and biodiversity, it has been shown that resource policy approaches basically work in synergy with the goals and measures of the Biodiversity Strategy and vice versa.

All policy proposals formulated today include a very high number of individual measures. In resource protection, only 'soft' measures and instruments are currently implemented. And very few countries are starting to implement resource policies – not consistently and quickly enough in my opinion.

At present, raw materials policy, resource protection, climate policy, agricultural policy and other fields are not interlinked. The example of environmentally damaging subsidies shows that we spend a lot of money on the wrong things – even though society and politics are not prepared to reduce them (Köder et al. 2016).

Important pillars of such an integrated Policy are substitution and avoidance. Substitution is replacing of greenhouse gas- and resource-intensive technologies, services and products with decarbonised and dematerialised alternatives. Avoidance is the reduction of the consumption of products and activities through efficiency, sufficiency and consistency, leading to low greenhouse gas emissions, low primary raw material consumption and resource consumption.

I would like to mention just a few – of the many measures and instruments – along the policy cycle: Labelling – we need to know what is inside the products we buy, we use – the services we receive. Labelling, albeit crude, of the resource use of products, allows us to decide which of them is the better one. For this to be possible, we need to improve and broaden the database we have and make it available to planners and people as open source.

Even if there is no official labelling yet, information on how much land, water, biomass and non-organic materials are contained in a T-shirt, for example, is crucial for further development. Based on such labelling, it will then be possible to assess and thus control the consumption behaviour of consumers.

The calculation of a quantity in the area of material use is not as simple as for greenhouse gas emissions. The question arises to which standard should be used as a basis. The associated presumed environmental effect or a lost ecosystem service are different approaches that need to be pursued further. I think that rough figures are sufficient for an initial calculation, so that the price of metals and other materials will have to double over a decade, for example.

This can be achieved with a so-called 'material added tax' (MAT). This has the advantage that it can be levied on imports at a border, just as VAT is today, so such a system would also be an alternative for the EU. Another advantage is that this tax can be passed on from sector to sector, from company to company and that it can then be used to reflect or increase prices for consumers.

This increase in price leads to an increase in resource efficiency in production and also to substitution, as well as the use of secondary raw materials from recycling. This supports and promotes companies that work resource-efficiently. This also leads to investment in research and development, which drives the innovative strength of Germany/Europe as a business location.

It is clear to me that a precise designation of the necessary increase is a weakness of this proposal. But even at the beginning of the discussions on the implementation of renewable energies, we noticed that an increase in the price of energy led to an increase in energy efficiency both in supply and consumption. Now we cannot wait any longer until we have all sorts of scientific results, but we must act quickly and rough steering in the right direction is much more critical than any calculation of the material occurrence, cycle etc., however exact it may be. Political instruments can be readjusted. But it is more important to act at all. Regardless of how high the real prices of copper, for example, are, a relative increase in price only makes sense if we act now.

All this can be observed in the levies on primary building materials. An increase in the cost of building materials together with other policy instruments such as landfill levies, control of mining permits, legal requirements for material recovery and substitution materials, and public procurement create a steering effect. In this way, the more resource-conserving use of primary building materials can be substantially promoted through the use of recycled building materials.

A package of measures which is very important are increasing the options for *rethink, redesign, refuse, repair, reduce, remanufacture, reuse, remodel, recycle, recover* and *increase the lifetime of products*.

In order to avoid obsolescence and to enable this repair society, the following elements of a policy must be realised: the definition of product standards on minimum service life, the introduction of an obligation to provide information on the availability of spare parts and repair services, and the introduction of an obligation to state the guaranteed service life (manufacturer's warranty statement obligation). To this end, there must be improved framework conditions for repairs. This starts with access to plans and components, goes on to the question of warranty and guarantee, and extends to preferential tax treatment of repair services.

In this context, some words of agreement on the sharing economy should be said. There are examples where these contribute to dematerialisation and decarbonisation – e.g. in the field of mobility in cities. But it can also go in the wrong direction.

Agriculture will have to undergo major reforms – there are various approaches to more sustainable agriculture. Land use is one of the keys to greenhouse gas neutrality by reducing emissions of methane and nitrous oxide through other farming systems.

The removal of CO_2 already emitted from the atmosphere by carbon sinks (CDRs) to reduce greenhouse gases. Here moors, forests and sustainable land use can play an important role. Land is a scarce resource, and land use in all sectors must be lowered.

Ultimately, what remains is our approach and attitude to waste. If we want to establish a circular society, then waste is no longer waste, but a conglomerate of different recyclable materials, which are first used within the existing production chains and then finally returned to nature in various ways. It should be remembered that there can be no complete circularity, partly because there are always unavoidable dissipative losses. On the other hand, because few substances can be used completely – without degradation – again. And not to be forgotten without a design that avoids waste, that supports reuse, even the limited possibilities of the circular economy are not possible.

Urgent action needed – let's hope

As a reminder: By 2050, resource consumption must be reduced by a factor of ten, (reducing by 90 per cent) and greenhouse gas neutrality must be achieved (reducing by 100 per cent). If we analyse the policies implemented today, we still see a great many – regionally different instruments and measures – but all of them lack the impact – the transformative power.

All this is only possible if we start the transformation right now. Consistent and immediate action is necessary!

The hopes of the 1980s and 1990s that the emerging and developing countries would make a leap into the future have not been fulfilled. The hope of the turn of the millennium about the transformation to more sustainable development in the wealthy classes of the world has not been fulfilled. The implementation of the SDGs is also questioned. Lack of education, corruption, lack of transparency and the selfishness of the elites stood in the way of this. Of course an economic system that rewards those who behave greedy, selfish and unsustainable is part of the problem.

However, hope arises when I see that more and more sectors, levels, parts of society, movements, countries, cities are beginning to take a different path.

10 *Harry Lehmann*

With individual activities, with regional initiatives and with sectoral approaches. People today have recognised that quick action is necessary, and that it actually should have happened yesterday. It is necessary to implement the transformation on the different levels as quickly as possible.

References

Climate Action Tracker (2019). Climate Action Tracker. Retrieved from http://climateactiontracker.org

EK (2019). Emissions Database for Global Atmospheric Research. Retrieved from https://edgar.jrc.ec.europa.eu/

Günther, J., Lehmann, H., Lorenz, U., Pfeiffer, D. & Purr, K. (2018). Towards a Resource Efficient and Greenhouse Gas Neutral Germany 2050. In *Factor X* (pp. 417–425). Springer, Cham.

Köder, L., Burger, A. & Eckermann, F. (2016). *Umweltschädliche Subventionen in Deutschland.* Umweltbundesamt, *Fachgebiet I* 1.4.

Lehmann, Harry. (2017). Power-to-Liquids – Potentials and Perspectives. *'Greener Skies Ahead' conference, Bonn.*

Richardson, K., Crutzen, P. & Foley, J. A. (2009). A Safe Operating Space for Humanity. *Nature, 461*(7263), 472–475.

Rockström, J., Steffen, W., Noone, K., Persson, A., Chapin, III F.S., Lambin, E., Lenton, T.M., Scheffer, M., Folke, C., Schellnhuber, H., Nykvist, B., de Wit, C.A., Hughes, T., van der Leeuw, S., Rodhe, H., Sörlin, S., Snyder, P.K., Costanza, R., Svedin, U., Falkenmark, M., Karlberg, M., Corell, R.W., Fabry, V.J., Hansen, J., Walker, B.H., Liverman, D., Richardson, K., Crutzen, C. & Foley, J. 2009. A safe operating space for humanity. *Nature 461*, 472–475.

Schmidt-Bleek, F., Wilenius, M. & Lehmann, H. (2014). The Challenge of the Whole: Creating System Policies to Tackle Sustainability. In *Factor X* (pp. 137–147). Springer, Cham.

Steffen, W., Richardson, K., Rockström, J., Cornell, S. E., Fetzer, I., Bennett, E. M. … & Folke, C. (2015). Planetary Boundaries: Guiding Human Development on a Changing Planet. *Science, 347*(6223), 1259855.

UNEP (2019). UN Environment International Resource Panel Global Material Flows Database. Retrieved from www.resourcepanel.org/global-material-flows-database.

UNFCCC (2015). Paris Agreement. Retrieved from https://unfccc.int/sites/default/files/english_paris_agreement.pdf.

2 The world at the ultimate crossroads

Climate change, environmental impacts, population and natural resources sufficiency in the long perspective with integrated models

Harald Ulrik Sverdrup, Ullrich Lorenz, and Anna Hulda Olafsdottir

Introduction and background

In the last decade, many have come to the conclusion that the world has reached and transgressed the confines of the planetary capacities and boundaries, resulting in the realization that humanity may one day become limited by declining availability of food, energy and natural resources (Bardi 2013; Rockström et al. 2009, 2017; Heinberg 2011; Monbiot 2015; Sverdrup and Ragnarsdottir 2014). In addition, it has become clear that human civilization is creating pollution on such a big scale that the environment of the entire globe is affected in a substantial way.

We have gone to many meetings on sustainability over the past four decades, and in every meeting many researchers hold elaborate and compassionate talks on how everything is linked and connected. And then we all go home, and meet again the year after, and the same thing happens again, many hold elaborate and compassionate talks on how everything is linked and connected. And nothing happens to connect the aspects they talked so much about. No one connects anything for real in their models, nor in their work. They just talk about it. Again and again. One day we decided we would do those connections, for real, not just talk like everyone else seems to be doing, but actually make a model where everything was connected.

Scope and objectives

The scope and objective of this report

Each of the challenges may appear alone as to be overpowering. When the gridlock of impending natural resources exhaustion, population growth, energy transitions, continued pollution, increasing climate change, escalating environmental impacts, social challenges, the decay of governance and unstable economy, all come together, it is the largest challenge of all times. It truly calls for extraordinary thinking and truly transformative actions. We were not the first to take up the challenge of an all-connecting model. Forrester (1961, 1969, 1971) and the Meadows team (Meadows et al. 1972, 1974) had been there before. They had laid a solid foundation but met very hard challenges, one being that computers at the time were not really up to the task, as well as suffering large scale political attacks.

The purpose of the WORLD7 model

The purpose of the WORLD7 model is to assess the overall sustainability of the global civilisation and use the model for policy development in single countries and regions; Germany, Sweden, Europe. In our times, the sustainability of our societies has become challenged from a number of factors:

- Global climate change has been in progress for a long time, and now the effects are becoming visible to the layman and politician alike. The effects have substantial economic and social impacts.
- The global population has grown to levels where crowdedness and high density creates a tougher society with less margin for any type of error. Industrial and urban impacts in all aspects are substantial and global in scale. In times of economic and social stress, more extreme political forces have appeared on the arena in larger numbers than seen before, and many democracies are facing serious challenges.
- A longer period of peace and prosperity have created a growth in global wealth, but a relaxed policy towards wealth redistribution, that have allowed economical differences to grow enough in many regions to increase social tensions.

All of the issues listed above are causally linked in an intricate system, where policy becomes increasingly more difficult to develop and implement. We are in a period which will experience natural resource scarcity on a large scale across all resources, challenging economies and societies. Exhaustion does not necessarily imply that there are no resources available, but they will be harder and harder to get out of the ground, present in lower and lower quality in the materials we lift up, causing more pollution and demanding more work efforts per unit gained.

Methodology

Model development methodology

The main tool employed to build the WORLD7 model are the standard methods of system analysis and system dynamics modelling (Forrester 1961,

1969, 1971; Meadows et al. 1972, 1974, 1992, 2005; Clark and Cole 1975; Roberts et al. 1982; Senge 1990; Bossel 1998; Sterman 2000; Haraldsson and Sverdrup 2005). In 1961, Forrester created the first draft of a system dynamics model of the world's socio-economic system, World1, in response to a challenge by the Club of Rome (Forrester 1961). Forrester refined this to become World2 (Forrester 1969). World2 was published in a book titled World Dynamics (Forrester 1971) attempting to model the global economy. The Club of Rome initiated further work into this issue and Meadows et al. (1972) published the outputs from their World3 model in the book 'Limits to growth'. World models is based on system dynamics have gone through four development phases:

- 1961–1971; World1–World2; **Forrester** team (1961–1971), MIT; Industrial dynamics, urban dynamics, world dynamics, the first pioneering basic concept for how a World model may be put together. The model was very simplified and aggregated to a high level because of the limitations of the computers available at the time (Forrester 1961, 1969, 1971).
- 1972–2004; World3; The **Meadows** team (1972–2004), MIT; World dynamics and limits to growth. The model was more elaborate than World2, better parameterised and described in the book 'Dynamics of Growth in a Final World' (Meadows et al. 1972, 1974). The model had significant simplifications because of computational constraints of the computers available at the time.
- 2011–2017; WORLD4–WORLD6; **Sverdrup** team (2013–2016), University of Lund, Sweden, University of Iceland, and Inland University of Applied Science, Norway. WORLD6 has reality-based market mechanisms and simulates commodity and resource price dynamics internally. WORLD6 handles the global economic and financial development and captures economic cycles of growth, stagnation, and decline. link natural resources, economy, finances, governance, demography, society and social process dynamics (Sverdrup and Ragnarsdottir 2014; Lorenz et al. 2017; Sverdrup et al. 2013, 2014a,b, 2015a,b, 2017). WORLD6 has no software parts from the earlier models.
- 2017–2019; WORLD7 is the new, reorganized version by the **Sverdrup** team, where it all is coming together in a functioning Integrated Assessment Model (IAM) and is used operationally in European Research projects. A present social and socio-economic modules are under development.

The WORLD7 model differs from the earlier models in most aspects. Several weaknesses in the earlier World1 and World3 models were exploited as points of attack against the older model. It is important to understand that most of the attack on the World3 model and on the Meadows team, did not have much to

14 *Harald Ulrik Sverdrup et al.*

with science. The majority of the attacks were driven by the defence of political ideology and thus were deeply political in their nature. We can observe that against prejudice and fear of change, logic does not always apply (Nørgaard et al. 2014; Keegan and Laskow-Lahey 2014; Kotterer 2014). Meadows have told me later that he regretted some of those simplifications, but considering the computers he had available, there was not much choice.

1 Natural resources

    a **World3**: All resources were lumped together, (energy, fossil fuels, metals, materials, water), adding them up into one resource index R. This became a major line of attack against the World3 model, and to some degree, this was justified.

    b **WORLD7**: Reserves and resources are distinguished and the Benefit Return On Investment (BeROI, a generalized version of EROI), if a resource required more effort (energy, materials) to extract that it gives benefit, then the extraction stops.

        i The resources are treated individually. Energy is divided up into fossil energies; Hydrocarbons oil, gas and coal, uranium and thorium.

        ii Technological energy sources like wind and solar electric harvest, which have sustainable energy source but needs metals in short supply.

        iii Sustainable energy which uses abundant materials and sustainable sources of energy; hydropower and provided they are grown sustainably; biofuels.

        iv Metals and materials are treated individually, from individual resource reserves and resources and traded individually in a world market.

2 Economics:

    a **World3**: The model had a very simplified economic model, a simple cash box and total invested capital. When the cash box ran empty, the model crashed the world.

    b **WORLD7**: The model operates with several types of capital, where each stock keeps a part of society running, as well as a stock of liquid capital. Investments are solved with a mix of capital and debt. In times of societal deficits, the government can issue bonds, take up debts or print money. This is an effective way to bridge fluctuations in the economy. It will not resolve structural problems unless the debt is used for structural change. The WORLD7 model accommodates this.

3 Pollution

    a **World3**: This was generalised into something called persistent pollution, adding up all kinds of pollution into one index P for pollution of any kind. The model assumed pollution to limit the birth rate and food production, and the model came to a halt when the pollution got high enough.

b   **WORLD7**: Pollution is specified into several types, according to their characteristics and what they affect, it operates with these types:

  i CO_2 from calcination and carbon fuel combustion and CH_4 that leaks from natural gas production and use, they affect the global climate

  ii   Endocrine disruptors that drive health problems and disrupt immune systems, they affect fertility, health costs and mortality

  iii   Persistent organic pollution (POP)

  iv   Antibiotics that when lost in nature cause microbial resistance in addition to regular use, and this drives health costs and mortality

  v   SOx, NOx and particulate emissions, that drive acidification and a number of other issues. They affect health costs and mortality

  vi   Heavy metals that affect the ecology and in the end humans, with effects into health costs and mortality

4   Social aspects:

a   **World3** avoided all social aspects.

b   **WORLD7** has:

  i   Wage distribution in society and gender pay equality

  ii   Quantitative aspects of wellbeing

  iii   Rate of illness and mortality, rate of health services, medical treatment and care provision

  iv   Aspects of Quality of Governance

An important difference from World3 to WORLD7, is that the global economy and the population is not made to crash in the model when the resources become scarce. The system stability is caused by mechanisms of financing deficits in WORLD7, using monetary loans and state bonds to buffer variations in the economic system, as postulated by Keynes et al. (1932) and Keynes (1936). To balance the system, these loans need to be repaid, which can be pushed forward when the economy grows steadily. When the growth declines toward stagnation, it will become more and more difficult to repay the loans if they are too large. If total expenditures continue to grow when there is no economic growth of income, then a contraction will be unavoidable (Tainter 1987). While all the solid materials are to smaller or larger degree recyclable, all energy is in used up and dissipated within a very short timeframe (Sverdrup et al. 2014a,b, 2017). For the type of challenges facing us now, the statistical economic models used so far are not sufficient, and they do not contain required and necessary feedbacks and are unsuitable for policy development (Alexandrova and Northcott 2013; Bossel 1998; Senge et al. 2008; Falk 2017; Hamilton et al. 2015; Moosa 2017; ElSawah et al. 2017; Laniak et al. 2013).

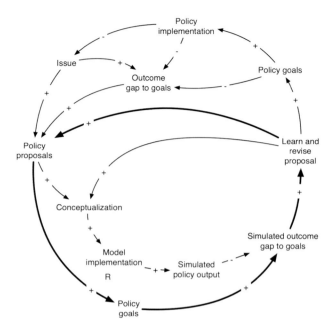

Figure 2.1 The model is used in an iterative mode in responsible performance-based policy development.

Model methodology

Figure 2.1 shows how the integrated model is used in an iterative mode in policy development. Policy proposals are made, and then the model system is used, either qualitatively or quantitatively, to estimate the effects of that policy if implemented. The outcome is evaluated on how well the goals are achieved if the side-effects are acceptable, and what kind of delays are to be expected. The iterative procedure is kept going until a satisfactory solution can be found or the proposal is rejected as unfeasible. Professional policymaking uses quantitative simulations as support. Then it is important that the models are based in real underlying principles and not just apparent correlations. WORLD7 is energy and mass balance consistent in all aspects, including the economic module. Goal conflicts may show up in the assessments from complex integrated models, so that achieving one policy goal, may actually decrease the possibility of achieving another policy goal. That may lead to hard choices, or an investigation if the system structure can be changed in order to resolve the goal conflict. When the model has been field-tested and found to be able to create the past, based on principles, without fiddling with the model to fit the desired output, then the model becomes an evidence-based assessment tool (Hamilton et al. 2015; ElSawah et al. 2017; Laniak et al. 2013).

Model description

WORLD7 operates on a global scale. Thus, there are no countries and no regions. Variables like commodity and resource prices are generated endogenously inside WORLD7 from first principles of supply and demand within the market arbitration mechanism over price. WORLD7 operates in normal mode with a daily time-step but uses yearly printouts of results. The variation in resource quality is taken care of in the ore grade classification. Figure 2.2 shows the basic units of WORLD7. Note that behind every little box in Figure 2.2, there are one or several sub-modules. Every red line is one or more links. In the model, a number of interdependencies are made between different modules and sectors. These links are:

1   Demand linkages

   a   For some energy production technologies, special materials are needed. They are included in the demand, and purchased in their extraction module and taken to the energy module.
   b   The extraction of all materials requires energy and this energy is taken from the markets in the energy module.
   c   Price feedbacks on demand, low price allow for higher demand, high price cause the demand to be lowered.
   d   Demands in some modules use input from other modules.

2   Supply linkages

   a   For the dependent materials, secondary extraction is done from mother metals, and the rate depends on the extraction rate of the mother metal.
   b   When actual supply to a module is less than demand, then the production or activity is reduced.
   c   When more energy is demanded by resource extraction, than can be supplied, then extraction is reduced.
   d   Price and supply promote profits, which promotes supply, normally supported by production.

3   Recycling linkages

   a   Recycling is done for all metals and materials, depending on the price and if there is legislation.

4   Economy

   a   Resource extraction generates income, costs and profit, a basic income in the economic model. The price is generated from supply and demand dynamics (Sverdrup and Olafsdottir 2019). This resource income makes up about half of all value generated. The rest comes from human labour, an invention of technology, technological work enhancement and knowledge input.

18 *Harald Ulrik Sverdrup et al.*

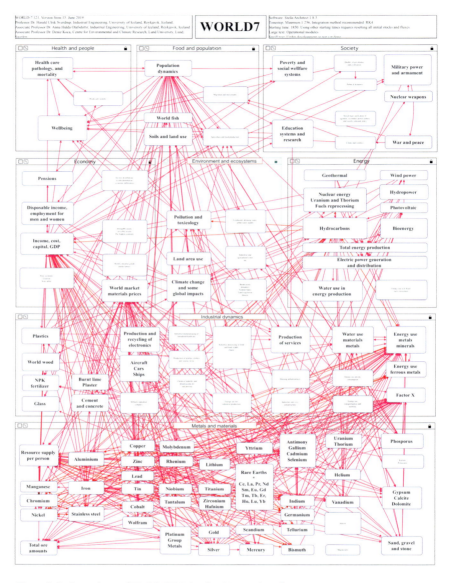

Figure 2.2 Overview of WORLD7 in the STELLA software.

5   Policy

   a   Policy decisions are automated through legislation, and some have significant impacts on many systems being managed. This depends on the institutions of society to be effective and accountable.

Results

The WORLD7 model has been tested in several ways to validate how well it performs against observed system state data. The model reproduces observed data really well. The tests were done on the extraction rates, supply rates, recycling, market prices for 40 different the materials and metals for the time 1850–2020 (Sverdrup et al. 2013, 2014a,b, 2015a,b, 2017, 2018a,b; Sverdrup and Ragnarsdottir 2014; Sverdrup and Olafsdottir 2019; Olafsdottir and Sverdrup 2018; Sverdrup 2017). The model reproduces the decline in resource quality for the materials where this can be checked (Gold, silver, copper, nickel, iron, chromium, manganese, oil, phosphorus, uranium) with equally good success. WORLD7 has a simplified climate change model based on a global carbon balance, ecosystems, land-use and use of fossil fuels. It is capable of recreating the climate trends observed for the time from 1850 to 2015 for atmospheric CO_2, average global temperature and sea-level rise. WORLD7 is capable of recreating the GDP and the GDP per capita for the period 1850–2018 with good accuracy.

Figure 2.3a shows the supply of lithium in the long term and the supply in kg per capita per year. Around 2100, lithium goes from soft scarcity to hard scarcity. That occurs when the supply becomes less that the modified demand, indicating that supply cannot meet demand. That implies that there will not be enough lithium to substitute electric vehicles for all fossil fuel vehicles presently in use. The curves for cobalt are similar but more restricting, and cobalt will be a resource that will become scarce. Figure 2.3b shows a typical output from the model for some of the strategic technology metals.

These metals are required for a number of new technologies in alternative energy production and high-performance electronics as well as the smaller of electrical motors and engines. In order to substitute fossil energy with solar panel electricity, great care must be taken in order to use the different technologies in parallel. Each individual photovoltaic technology, whether based on gallium, germanium, indium or telluride, will not have the capacity alone. And the panels must be designed in such a way that they can be recycled. Else it will run into hard scarcity and stop.

As more and more energy is required for resource extraction, and an increasing total fraction of GDP must be used for energy and materials extraction and production. The fraction of GDP used for extracting natural resources. It will go from 12% now to 25% by 2250 according to the 'business-as-usual scenario' (Figure 2.4a). Dramatic changes will be necessary in the attitude to energy use and materials use and recycling will be required to bring demand down. The fraction of all energy used for resource extraction is steadily increasing, reflecting that **Be**nefit **R**eturn **O**n **I**nvestment sinks as the resource quality decline (BeROI goes down). This fraction of all energy available is steadily increasing, reflecting that BeROI sinks as the resource quality decline (Figure 2.4b). The decline in resource quality is already being observed.

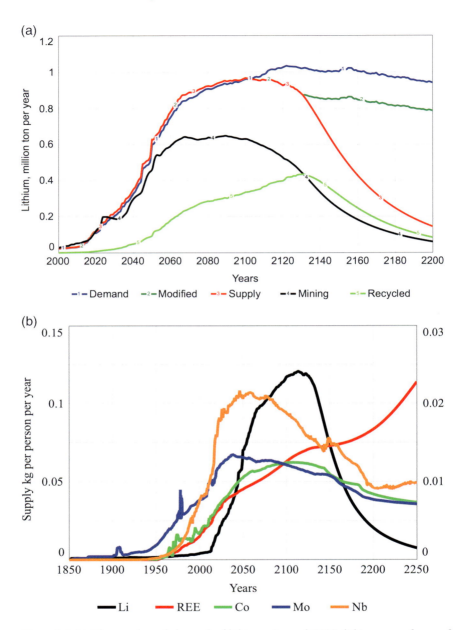

Figure 2.3 (a) The supply and demand of lithium. Around 2100, lithium goes from soft scarcity to hard scarcity. First demand separates from price modified demand. Then supply separates from price-modified demand. Supply cannot meet demand, despite willingness to pay. (b) Supply per person per year for some of the key metals for solar photovoltaic panels. The supply is sensitive to how well recycling can be managed for these elements.

The world at the ultimate crossroads 21

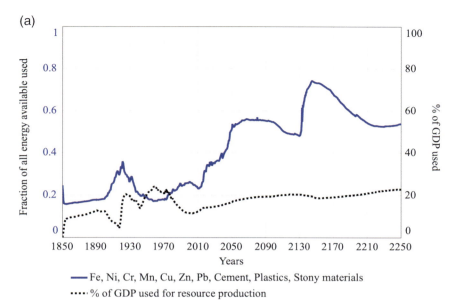

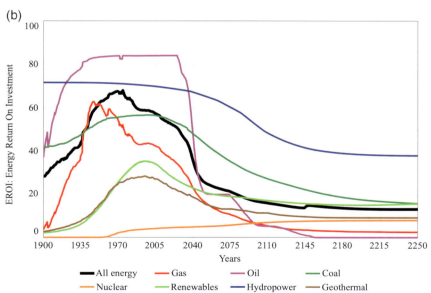

Figure 2.4 (a) Total fraction of all energy demanded by resource extraction. (b) Estimated EROI development under business-as-usual for different energy types.

22 *Harald Ulrik Sverdrup et al.*

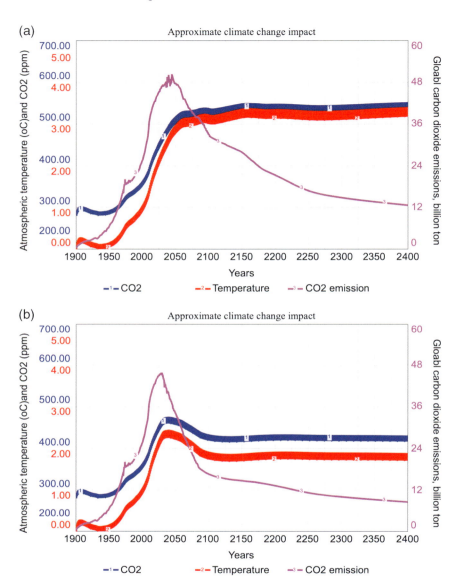

Figure 2.5 Climate change outcomes for (a) the business-as-usual case and (b) the 'Max 2°C global warming' scenario, phasing out of 90% of all fossil fuel use between 2020–2060.

Figure 2.5 shows examples from some of the assessment made for the German government where different energy scenarios were tested with respect to business-as-usual and the German 'Energiewende' policy (Lorenz et al. 2017). The results for 'business as usual' shows that the long period of growth that has lasted from 1950 to the present will stagnate after 2030. The drivers behind the economic growth are several; the increase in population, matched by un-bounded resource extraction and great improvements in work efficiency through technology and industrial organization of work.

The simulation for 'Max 2°C global warming' showed that the German 'Energiewende' policy is both possible and profitable in the long run. In order to do so, a 'Ressourcewende' would be necessary, reducing material resource losses and increase recycling. The runs suggest that a 'Energiewende' policy would be applicable on a global scale without any significant long term negative effects to the global economy. The simulation predict a positive effect on GDP development and global employment. The 'Max 2°C global warming' goal from Paris could be achieved by phasing out 90% of all fossil fuels use worldwide (Figure 2.5) 2020–2040. It will take away old jobs in the fossil industry and make old businesses that cannot change become obsolete. It will create more new companies and jobs in the new industries and services that needs to be developed.

Discussion

All of the scientific weaknesses exploited in the attempts to discredit the results from the World1, World2 and World3 models, have been amended in WORLD7. Major progress with the robustness of the model comes from adding a biophysical economic model to the integrated model. When economic deficits occur, debts and policies can be taken to bridge the gap, preventing the world from crashing. as in the earlier models. WORLD7 is based on causal links from natural resources to economic wealth, and it is capable of simulating periods of economic growth, stagnation, crisis and contraction as they come.

Table 2.1 shows a summary of policies suggested by others (Randers 2012) that we have tested with WORLD7. Many policies have been proposed with the best of intentions, but they do not always work the way it was wanted. The point is that every policy proposal needs to calculated through in order to check that it really produces the desired outcome, as well as does not produce side-effects that are unacceptable.

The problems and challenges faced by the world today are so substantial, covering so many aspects and consistently pervasive on a planetary level, that the mitigations and transformative changes needed are so large. The time window for when humanity could have stopped many of the problems may have already passed, and some damage appears to be unavoidable. But much more damage is to come, and the work must start at once, the time for long debates are long gone. Environmental pollution, climate change and resource

24 *Harald Ulrik Sverdrup et al.*

Table 2.1 A summary of policies suggested by others (see Randers 2012) that we have tested with the WORLD7 model

#	Policies suggested	Energy	Resources	Social	Works?
1.	Reduce man-made greenhouse gas emissions as soon as possible – **Global Energie-wende**	Can be done with better energy efficiency	Needs a Global **Ressouce-wende**	Depends on being socially sustainable. Limited by corruption and poor governance	**Yes**
2.	Help poor nations grow faster – by rapid industrialisation similar to Japan, Korea and China	Challenging energy supply, challenging pollution risks	High risk for hard scarcity on key technological materials	Limited by corruption and poor governance	Difficult
3.	Reduce unemployment and inequity through more jobs	Can be done with Global **Energie-wende**	Needs a Global **Ressouce-wende**	Social change stresses. Limited by corruption and poor governance	**Yes**
4	Further slow population growth – through positive incentives	Population decline reduce consumption	Population decline reduce consumption	Needs global attitude change. Limited by corruption and poor governance	**Yes**
5.	Do nothing, assume everything is to be taken care of by the markets. UN high population scenario becomes real	Energie-wende becomes far more challenging to do. Energy becomes expensive	Highest risk that resource scarcity strikes	Risk for dictatorship. Economic crisis and stresses social disruptions	No

scarcity will reach out to every corner of the world, and soon the last place to hide will be gone.

- A systemic approach is a condition for resolving the challenges.
    - Systemic changes imply that the systemic structure and systemic principles must be changed. Narrow sectorial approaches are neither systemic, nor sufficient, it is not about adjusting the parameters of the present system, feedbacks go across sectors and models that incorporate that are required.
    - A circular society for material resources is required. That creates the circular economy.

The world at the ultimate crossroads 25

- Goal conflicts will demand to be solved at a systemic level.
- Systemic changes need to be multi-sectorial, causally linked and pervasive.
    - **Energiewende** is linked to a **Ressourcewende**.
    - It involves **all fundamental systems;** industrial, economic and social dynamics. It implies **transformative changes** to existing society and power-structures.
- Transformative system change takes time.
    - Plan with at least **20 years** from start to full implementations (Ref; LRTAP protocol, IPCC progress). **Starting** is needed **at once** (2020 + 20=2040).
- Must engage all required arenas to secure a success: **Science arena, Communication and Media arena, Political arena**.

Conclusions

WORLD7 has become a powerful tool for making integrated dynamic assessments for the sustainability of nations and the global civilization. The shortcomings or earlier world models have now been overcome. WORLD7 does reconstruct the resource use, industrialization and the economy for the time from 1850 to 2015 with good success. That is a strong argument for taking the forecasts very seriously. In the scenarios for the future, the world does not crash, but many scenarios indicate economic contractions and serious challenges to things we take for granted.

References

Albin, S. (1997). Building a system dynamics model; Part 1; Conceptualization. *MIT System Dynamics Education Project* (J. Forrester (Ed)). MIT, Boston. 34pp. https://ocw.mit.edu/courses/sloan-school-of-management/15-988-system-dynamics-self-study-fall-1998-spring-1999/readings/building.pdf.

Alexandrova, A., and Northcott, R. (2013). It's just a feeling: Why economic models do not explain. *Journal of Economic Methodology*, 20, 262–267. doi:10.1080/1350178X.2013.828873.

Bardi, U. (2013) Extracted. How the quest for mineral wealth is plundering the planet. The past, present and future of global mineral depletion. *A report to the Club of Rome*. Vermont: Chelsea Green Publishing 299pp. ISBN 978-1-60358-541-5.

Bossel, H. (1998). Earth at the crossroads. Paths to a sustainable future. Cambridge: Cambridge University Press.

Clark, J., and Cole, S. (1975). *Global Simulation Models: A Comparative Study*. New York: John Wiley and Sons.

ElSawah, S., Pierce, S. A., Hamilton, S. A., van Delden, H., Haase, D., Elmahdi, A., and Jakeman, A. (2017). An overview of the system dynamics process for integrated modelling of socio-ecological systems: Lessons on good modelling practice from five case studies.

Environmental Modelling and software 93, 127–145. https://www.sciencedirect.com/science/article/abs/pii/S136481521631091X?via%3Dihub.

Forrester, J. W. (1961). Industrial Dynamics. Pegasus Communications. Boston, MA: MIT Press.

Forrester, J. W. (1969). Urban Dynamics. Pegasus Communications. Boston, MA: MIT Press.

Forrester, J., (1971). World dynamics. Waltham, MA: Pegasus Communications.

Hamilton, S. H., ElSawah, S., Guillaume, J. H. A., Jake man, A. J., and Pierce, S. A., (2015). Integrated assessment and modelling: Overview and synthesis of salient dimensions. *Environmental Modelling and software* 64, 215–229.

Haraldsson, H. (2004). Introduction to systems thinking and causal loop diagrams. *Reports in Ecology and Environmental Engineering 1*, 2004, 5th edition. Lund University, Lund, Sweden.

Haraldsson, H. and Sverdrup, H. (2005). On aspects of systems analysis and dynamics workflow. Proceedings of the systems dynamics society, July 17-21, 2005 International Conference on systems dynamics, Boston, USA. 1–10 pages. http://www.systemdynamics.org/conferences/2005/proceed/papers/HARAL310.pdf.

Heinberg, R. (2011). The end of growth. Adapting to our new economic reality. Gabriola Island, Canada: New Society Publishers.

Hoffman, R. (2015). Concepts for a New Generation of Global Modelling Tools: Expanding our Capacity for Perception. *Cadmus* 2, 134–145.

Keegan, R., and Laskow-Lahey, L. (2014). The real reason people won't change. Harvard Business Review – OnPoint 103-111. Originally published in Harvard Business review November 2001.

Keynes, J. M. (1936). The General Theory of Employment, Interest, and Money. New York: Harcourt Brace.

Keynes, J. M., Salter, A., Stamp, J., Blackett, B., Clay, H., and Beveridge, B. (1932). The World's Economic Crisis and the Way of Escape. Butterworth, London.

Kim, D. H., (1992). Toolbox: Guidelins for Drawing Causal Loop Diagrams. The Systems Thinker, 3, 5–6.

Koca, D. and Sverdrup, H. (2013). Use of Casual Loop Diagramming Methodology and Systems Thinking in Exploring Alternative Climate Change Adaptation Strategies in Seyhan River Basin, Turkey. In; Schwanninger, M., Husemann, E., and Lane, D., Proceedings of the 30th International Conference of the System Dynamics Society, St. Gallen, Switzerland, July 22–26, 2012 Model-based Management. University of St. Gallen, Switzerland; Systems Dynamics Society. 4, 3525–3538. ISBN: 9781622764143 Curran Associates, Inc.

Kotterer, J. P. (2014). Leading change; Why transformations efforts fail. Harvard Business Review – OnPoint 30–37. Originally published in Harvard Business review April 1995.

Laniak, G. F., Olchin, G, Goodall, J., Voinov, A., Hill, M., Glynn, P., Whelan, G., Geller, G., Quinn, N., Blind, M., Peckham, P., Reaney, S., Gaber, N., Kennedy, R., and Hughes, A. (2013). Integrated environmental modeling: A vision and roadmap for the future. *Environmental Modelling and software* 39, 2–23.

Lorenz, U., Sverdrup, H. U., and Ragnarsdottir, K. V., (2017). Global megatrends and resource use – A systemic reflection. Chapter 3. In: Lehman, H. (Ed). The Factor X book. 67–77. Frankfurt: Springer Verlag.

Meadows, D. H., Meadows, D. L., Randers, J., and Behrens, W. (1972). Limits to growth. New York: Universe Books.

Meadows, D. L., and Meadows, D. H., Eds. (1973). Business and Economics. Geneva, Switzerland.

Meadows, D. L., Behrens III, W. W., Meadows, D. H., Naill, R. F., Randers, J., and Zahn, E. K. O. (1974). Dynamics of Growth in a Finite World. Massachusetts: Wright-Allen Press, Inc.

Meadows, D. H., Meadows, D. L., and Randers, J. (1992). Beyond the limits: Confronting global collapse, envisioning a sustainable future. Vermont, USA: Chelsea Green Publishing Company.

Meadows, D. H., Randers, J., and Meadows, D. (2005). Limits to growth. The 30 year update. New York: Universe Press.

Monbiot, G. (2015). Consume more, conserve more: sorry, but we just can't do both. The Guardian, Tuesday 24 November 2015 19.28 GMT. http://www.monbiot.com/, https://www.theguardian.com/commentisfree/2015/nov/24/consume-conserve-economic-growth-sustainability.

Moosa, I. A. (2017). Econometrics as a Con Art: Exposing the Limitations and Abuses of Econometrics 296pp, Cheltenham: Edward Elgar Publishing Ltd. ISBN-13: 978-1785369940.

Olafsdottir, A. H., and Sverdrup, H. (2018). Modelling global mining, secondary extraction, supply, stocks-in-society, recycling, market price and resources, using the WORLD6 model; Tin. *Biophysical Economics and Resource Quality* 4, 1–32.

Randers, J. (2012). 2052, a global forecast for the next 40 years. A report to the Club of Rome. Vermont, USA: Chelsea Green Publishing.

Roberts, N., Andersen, D. F., Deal, R. M., and Shaffer, W. A. (1982). Introduction to Computer Simulation: A System Dynamics Approach. Chicago: Productivity Press.

Rockström, J., Steffen, W., Noone, K., Persson, A., Chapin, III F. S., Lambin, E., Lenton, T. M., Scheffer, M., Folke, C., Schellnhuber, H., Nykvist, B., de Wit, C. A., Hughes, T., van der Leeuw, S., Rodhe, H., Sörlin, S., Snyder, P. K., Costanza, R., Svedin, U., Falkenmark, M., Karlberg, M., Corell, R. W., Fabry, V. J., Hansen, J., Walker, B. H., Liverman, D., Richardson, K., Crutzen, C., and Foley, J. (2009). A safe operating space for humanity. *Nature* 461, 472–475.

Rockström, J., Gaffney, O., Rogelj, J. Meinhausen, M., Nakicenovic, N., and Schellnhuber, H. J. (2017). A roadmap for rapid decarbonization. *Science* 355 Issue 6331.

Senge, P. (1990). The Fifth Discipline. The Art and Practice of the Learning Organisation. New York: Century Business.

Senge, P. M., Smith, B., Schley, S., Laur, J., and Kruschwitz, N. (2008). The Necessary Revolution: How Individuals and Organisations Are Working Together to Create a Sustainable World. Doubleday Currency, London.

Sterman, J. D. (2000). Business Dynamics, System Thinking and Modelling for a Complex World. New York: Irwin McGraw-Hill.

Sverdrup, H. (2017). Modelling global extraction, supply, price and depletion of the extractable geological resources with the LITHIUM model. *Resources, Conservation and Recycling* 114, 112–129.

Sverdrup, H. U. (2019). The global sustainability challenges in the future: the energy and materials supply, pollution, climate change and inequality nexus. In: Holden, E., Meadowcraft, J. Langhelle, O., Banister, D., Linnerud, K., (Eds), Our Common Future, What Next for Sustainable Development? 30 years after the Brundtland report. Chapter 1, 7–27, Frankfurt: Springer Verlag.

Sverdrup, H., and Olafsdottir, A. H. (2019). System dynamics modelling of supply, recycling, stocks-in-use and market price for stainless steel using WORLD6. Biophysical Economics and Resource Quality. https://doi.org/10.1007/s41247-019-0056-9.

Sverdrup, H., and Ragnarsdottir, K. V. (2014). Challenging the planetary boundaries II: Assessing the sustainable global population and phosphate supply, using a systems dynamics assessment model. *Applied Geochemistry 2011*; 26, S311–S313, doi:10.1016/j.apgeochem. 2011.03.088.

Sverdrup, H., Koca, D., and Granath C. (2013). Modeling the gold market, explaining the past and assessing the physical and economical sustainability of future scenarios. In; Schwanninger, M., Husemann, E., Lane, D., Proceedings of the 30th International Conference of the System Dynamics Society, St. Gallen, Switzerland, July 22-26, 2012. Model-based Management. University of St. Gallen, Switzerland: Systems Dynamics Society. Pages 5: 4002–4023. ISBN: 9781622764143 Curran Associates, Inc.

Sverdrup, H., Koca, D., and Ragnarsdottir, K. V. (2014a). Investigating the sustainability of the global silver supply, reserves, stocks in society and market price using different approaches. *Resources, Conservation and Recycling* 83, 121–140.

Sverdrup, H. and Ragnarsdottir, K. V. (2014b). Natural Resources in a planetary perspective. Geochemical Perspectives 2: 129–341. *European Geochemical Society*. http://www.geochemicalperspectives.org/online/v3n2.

Sverdrup, H., Koca, D., and Ragnarsdottir, K. V. (2015a). Aluminium for the future: Modelling the global production, assessing long term supply to society and extraction of the global bauxite reserves. *Resources, Conservation and Recycling* 103, 139–154.

Sverdrup, H., and Ragnarsdottir, K. V. (2015b). The future of platinum group metal supply; An integrated dynamic modelling for platinum group metal supply, reserves, stocks-in-use, market price and sustainability. *Resources, Conservation and Recycling* 114, 130–152.

Sverdrup, H. U., Ragnarsdottir, K. V., and Koca, D. (2017). An assessment of global metal supply sustainability: Global recoverable reserves, mining rates, stocks-in-use, recycling rates, reserve sizes and time to production peak leading to subsequent metal scarcity. *Journal of Cleaner Production* 140, 359–372, doi:10.1016/j.jclepro.2015.06.085.

Sverdrup, H., Olofsdottir, A. H., Ragnarsdottir, K. V., and Koca, D. (2018a). A system dynamics assessment of the supply of molybdenum and rhenium used for superalloys and specialty steels, using the WORLD6 model. *Biophysical Economics and Resource Quality* 4, 1–52.

Sverdrup, H., Olafsdottir, A. H., Ragnarsdottir, K.V., Koca, D., and Lorenz, U. (2018b). The WORLD6 integrated system dynamics model: Examples of results from simulations. Proceedings from the 2018 World Resources Forum, Geneva, Switzerland. 11 pages. Matasci, C. (Ed) 'Accelerating the Resource Revolution', highlighting the importance of the Sustainable Development Goals and the Paris Climate Agreement as calls for action. World Resources Forum 2018, St. Gallen, Switzerland. https://www.wrforum.org/.

Sverdrup, H., Olafsdottir, A. H., and Ragnarsdottir, K. V. (2019). Development of a biophysical economics module for the global integrated assessment WORLD6 model. In: Cavana, R., Pavlov, O., Dangerfield, B., Wheat, D. (Eds), Modelling Feedback Economics. 47 pages. Frankfurt: Springer Verlag.

Tainter, J. A. (1987). The Collapse of Complex Societies. Cambridge: Cambridge University Press. 250pp.

Voinov, A. A. (2010). Systems science and modelling for ecological economics. London, UK: Academic Press.

3 Reporting resource use in Germany

Stephan Lutter, Stefan Giljum,
Christopher Manstein, and Gerda Palmetshofer

Resource use and sustainable development

Natural resources are the biophysical basis for any society's development (UN IRP 2017a). Consequently, the use and management of natural resources plays a very prominent role in the United Nations Sustainable Development Goals (SDGs; United Nations 2015a). SDGs 6 and 14 tackle water, Goal 7 energy, Goal 13 the climate and the atmosphere, and Goal 15 land. Raw materials are covered in two SDGs: Goal 8, with its focus on economic growth as a driver of development, formulates target 8.4 to decouple economic growth from environmental degradation. The indicators used to monitor progress stem from Material Flow Analysis (MFA) on the economy-wide level (Eurostat 2018). Goal 12 on sustainable consumption and production promotes, among other aspects, resource and energy efficiency in production and consumption activities. Target 12.2 is about the sustainable management and efficient use of natural resources and uses the same MFA-based indicators as target 8.4. These two targets are among the few, which clearly identify a methodology for how to calculate the identified indicators. Further, they are the only two targets, which include a footprint-type indicator taking into account raw materials needed along global supply chains of products and services to satisfy the final demand of a country. The indicator used is called 'material footprint' or 'Raw Material Consumption' (RMC). This indicator accounts for raw material uses, which occur abroad, but contribute to domestic final demand, are termed 'indirect flows' or 'raw material equivalents of traded goods' (Eurostat 2018; Maier 2018).

UN Environment (UNE) is the custodian for 26 environment-related indicators used to monitor the achievement of the SDGs. UNE and its sub-organisation, the International Resource Panel (IRP), regard MFA as a flagship statistical product for both the SDGs and measuring resource efficiency at the national level. The UN IRP aims to refine and harmonise the MFA methodology, to build capacity among countries and to engage with countries to foster the compilation of MFA accounts by national statistical offices. For this reason, the UN IRP commissioned the development of a global MFA database and a related manual (to be approved by the UN Statistics Division) to support countries in their efforts to compile national MFA (UN IRP 2017b; UNSD 2019). Together with the UN Lifecycle Initiative and the One Planet Network, the UN IRP also commissioned the Sustainable Consumption and Production Hotspots Analysis Tool (SCP-HAT; scp-hat.lifecycleinitiative.org). The tool illustrates a country's performance in the context of SDGs 8 and 12 and supports countries in their endeavours to design SCP-related policies.

The OECD supports countries in implementing the UN 2030 Agenda for Sustainable Development (United Nations 2015b) by contributing its strong track record in policy assessments and the development of indicators for monitoring performance. In this context, the OECD coordinates a process aiming at harmonising methods for consumption-based indicators such as the material footprint used in SDG 8 and 12, to ensure a methodologically sound monitoring process (OECD 2018).

The concept of resource efficiency as a means to achieve decoupling was also taken up in the EU Roadmap to a Resource-Efficient Europe (European Commission 2011) and its successor, the Circular Economy Action Plan (European Commission 2015). The European Environment Agency (EEA) is regularly examining strategies, instruments and targets for materials and resource efficiency and circular economy in 32 European countries (EEA 2016). According to preliminary information from the EEA, until 2018 at least eighteen European countries (including sixteen EU member states) had carried out activities to support the development of respective policies, strategies or roadmaps (EEA 2020).

The G7 countries recognise the importance of resource efficiency for environmental protection, climate protection, sustainable development and economic competitiveness. The G7 adopted its first decisions regarding resource efficiency under the German presidency in 2015. In that year, the G7 launched its Alliance on Resource Efficiency as a new forum for cooperation. At their summit in Hamburg on 7–8 July 2017, the G20 countries decided to establish the Resource Efficiency Dialogue to cooperate more closely on the efficient and sustainable use of natural resources. Also, just recently, at their meeting in Metz, in May 2019, G7 representatives strongly encouraged the UN IRP to continue its work to strengthen knowledge of resource efficiency and related topics such as the circular economy and innovative energy solutions.

Resource efficiency policies in Germany

Germany can be considered a frontrunner in recognising increased resource efficiency as a means to achieve sustainable economic development. In the early 1990s, Friedrich Schmidt-Bleek postulated an increase of resource productivity of industrialised countries by a 'Factor of 10' (minus 90%), as a response to the fact that the wealthiest countries have a significantly higher consumption than the world's poorest countries (Schmidt-Bleek 1993). Today the generalised term 'Factor X' is often used, as the required degree of dematerialisation needs to be decided individually from country to country, according to the current levels of consumption (Lehmann, Schmidt-Bleek & Manstein 2018).

In the first 'German Sustainability Strategy' (Deutsche Bundesregierung 2002), raw material productivity, calculated as GDP divided by the MFA-based indicator 'Abiotic Domestic Material Input' was included as one core indicator. Following the Factor X debate, the target for the increase in raw material productivity was set at a factor of two for the period 1994 to 2020, including a long-term improvement based on a 'Factor 4' vision.

The Resource Efficiency Programme (ProgRess), first published in 2012, made Germany one of the first countries adopting a national strategy by the federal government and identifying specific resource efficiency measures (BMU 2012). ProgRess focuses on the resource category of 'raw materials' and aims at continuously improving raw material productivity in Germany across the entire value chain, covering extraction of raw materials, production, consumption, re-use and recycling. This increased productivity shall help decoupling economic growth from resource consumption and its environmental impacts. In March 2016, ProgRess II was published (BMUB 2016), and work is currently underway for the publication of ProgRess III, which is expected for spring 2020.

In ProgRess II, an additional productivity indicator – 'Total Raw Material Productivity', which is calculated as GDP plus imports divided by the indicator Raw Material Input (RMI), complemented the indicator raw material productivity. RMI also includes raw materials that are needed abroad for the production of imported goods (see above). Closely linked to the revised German Sustainability Strategy (Federal Government 2017), ProgRess II sets a target of continuing the trend of the period 2000–2010 until the year 2030, meaning an average annual increase of 1.5% for the period 2010 to 2030.

Reporting resource use in Germany

The reporting and monitoring of resource use in Germany is framed by the two main political strategies described above – and the German Sustainability Strategy and ProgRess. Since the adoption of the UN SDGs, the German administration aimed at integrating the two national strategies and their related indicators and targets with the overarching global goals. The indicator report on sustainable development in Germany published biannually by the Germany Statistical Office (Destatis 2018) officially monitors progress. The report allocates the indicators as defined for the national Sustainability Strategy to the 17 SDGs, resulting in a very comprehensive monitoring framework. However, the applied indicators deviate considerably from the indicators agreed upon at the UN level. For example, for targets 8.4 and 12.2, the main indicator on the UN level is the consumption-based material footprint (RMC). It is used in absolute, per-capita and per-GDP terms. In contrast, Destatis reports only the input-based indicator 'Total Raw Material Productivity' (see above). Another example is SDG 6 (Water), where one of the SDG indicators is water efficiency, which is not included in the German indicator report.

The second regular publication on natural resource use in Germany is the indicator report series 'Data on the Environment' published by the German Environment Agency (UBA 2017). UBA provides a comprehensive overview of the state of the environment in Germany and identifies the actors responsible for environmental pollution as well as starting points for improving measures. To this end, 50 indicators are reported that cover all environmental areas. Where available, the indicators are backed up by existing political objectives – for example stemming from the German Sustainability Strategy, ProgRess, or from EU directives. For this reason, the system of environmental indicators also represents a balance sheet of environmental policy. The reported key indicators include raw material productivity and total raw material productivity (see above).

The research project 'Resource Use in Germany'

In addition to increasing technical efficiency in German industry and small and medium-sized enterprises (Schmidt, Spieth, Haubach & Kühne 2018), raising the awareness among important stakeholder groups such as politicians, consultants, entrepreneurs, scientists, teachers, pupils, journalists, and civil society is another one of the critical factors to achieve sustainable resource use. However, existing indicator reports often are not suitable for a broader circle of readers, as they do not analyse and interpret the complex topic of natural resources use in an appropriate manner.

To fill this existing gap, UBA launched the research project 'Resource Use in Germany' (UBA 2014). Aim of DeuRess was to develop the scientific concept and to start implementing a regular report series called 'Resource Use in Germany', which not only compiles but also analyses and interprets statistics on resource use, including comparisons over time. The series is meant to explain the causes and effects of resource use as well as the correlations between different categories of natural resources ('nexus'). By making the successes of and needs for corresponding environmental policy strategies and programmes visible, the topic shall be made more prominent to support the Resource Efficiency Programme (ProgRess) and to complement other existing reports and statistics.

The research work started with defining the specific target groups of the report series, screening similar reports on the national and international level as well as assessing available data and indicators on resource use in Germany and related methodological options. The initially broad range of target groups was narrowed down to representatives, who have a certain level of interest in the topic as well as previous knowledge, and due to their working areas can act as communication multipliers to support the transition towards a more sustainable resource use.

22 national and international reports were assessed according to a set of criteria, such as their geographical and temporal focus, the sectoral detail, the

applied data, and the graphic design. Examples for reports with a similar topic are 'The Global Resource Footprints of Nations' (Tukker et al. 2014) or the 'Decoupling Report' by the UN IRP (UNEP 2011). Reports with a similar target group but a differing topic were, for instance, the 'Living Planet Report' by WWF and partners (WWF, Zoological Society of London, Global Footprint Network & Water Footprint Network 2014) or the soil and meat atlases of the Heinrich Böll Foundation (Heinrich Böll Stiftung & FoEE 2014; Heinrich Böll Stiftung & IASS 2015). The main conclusions drawn were that the thematic focus should be set on the extraction of raw materials, their trade, the relationship between raw materials and economic performance, and their use for consumption purposes. Moreover, the main structural approach should be to present the content in small self-contained 'packages' of one double page – each with a synoptic paragraph at the beginning ('teaser'), a main graph and additional elements such as tables, boxes or additional figures.

Regarding the stocktaking on available data, publications by the Federal Statistical Office (Destatis) were identified as the main source. As part of the annual report series 'Environmental Economic Accounting (UGR)' (Destatis 2019), Destatis publishes detailed data on raw material extraction within Germany as well as on direct imports and exports of raw materials. The UGR also contains some data on water and land use of lower timeliness and detail. Besides, Destatis provides papers and publishes indicators on the indirect flows of German imports and exports (Kaumanns & Lauber 2016; Maier 2018). As part of the stocktaking, also international data sources were examined, including the Material Flow Accounts published by Eurostat (2019), OECD's Environment Statistics on material resources (OECD 2019), or the above mentioned Global Material Flows Database by the UN IRP (2017b).

Criteria used to carry out the analysis encompassed the geographical coverage of the dataset, its disaggregation regarding material categories and economic sectors, timeliness, data quality, and coverage of direct and indirect resource flows. The results showed that, apart from official data from national sources, the data sets from EUROSTAT and the IRP, as well as publicly accessible global economic-environmental models like EXIOBASE (Stadler et al. 2018) should play an important role, especially for the European and international comparison of indicators on direct and indirect material flows.

The new report series: concept and design

An important content-related decision at the very beginning of the conceptualisation process was to focus the report series on the resource category of raw materials, and to describe the use of other resources in one separate chapter only, thus following the priority setting of ProgRess.

Each report of the series consists of three main parts: (1) An introductory chapter provides the overall thematic context, a table of contents, key indicators of the report, and the methodological foundations. (2) Five main chapters cover the identified relevant topics – extraction, trade, economic use and decoupling, consumption and other resources than raw materials. (3) A separate data section summarises the numbers and data used in the report. Each of the five main chapters starts with an 'intro page' showing the key figures of each chapter in synergy with a representative thematic image. Furthermore, each chapter is divided into four to five sub-topics, each elaborated on one double page forming a closed section. This structure and design, together with an easy-to-understand guidance system, enables readers to choose between selecting one specific sub-topics of interest or flick through the whole report from the beginning to the end, always maintaining the contextual orientation.

As regards data and methods, the report series builds upon the above-explained environmental economic accounts (UGR) for the analysis of domestic extraction and direct trade of raw materials. The most recent raw material data available refer to the year 2015. With respect to indirect raw material flows, the new resource series draws upon two sources. The first is a model maintained by Destatis, which focuses on Germany and provides data for the period from 2010 to 2014 and, in an earlier version, for 2000–2010 (Kaumanns & Lauber 2016; Maier 2018). These data were used for all Germany-specific analyses. The second data source is the model EXIOB-ASE 3.3 (www.exiobase.eu; Stadler et al. 2018), which has a global coverage, distinguishing 49 countries and country groups and currently provides data for a time series from 1995–2014. Due to differences in the underlying methodologies, the figures from Destatis tend to produce lower results than those based upon the EXIOBASE calculations, and thus the two are not directly comparable. Results from the EXIOBASE calculations were therefore used primarily for analyses regarding the structure of international supply chains, for international comparisons as well as for analysing consumption areas like food or health.

Key results of the German Resource Report 2018

The report series encompasses so far two resource reports, published in the years 2016 and 2018 (UBA 2016, 2018). The following section summarises the main findings of the recent German Resource Report (UBA 2018). It is divided into the same sub-sections as the report series.

Domestic raw material extraction

In 2015, 1,040 million tonnes of non-renewable and renewable raw materials were extracted in Germany. While this represents an overall reduction since 1994, extraction of renewable raw materials increased by 28%. These are used not only for the production of foodstuffs but increasingly also as fuels and construction materials as well as in the pharmaceutical industry.

Raw materials extraction is very unevenly distributed among Germany and concentrated within a few of the larger federal states. In 2015, almost a quarter (243 million tonnes) of total domestic extraction took place in North

Rhine-Westphalia (NRW). The per-capita perspective provides an entirely different picture, however. Given its high population density, NRW was below the average federal per-capita extraction figure of 13.7 tonnes in 2015, while Saxony-Anhalt took pole position with almost 30 tonnes per capita (Figure 3.1).

Germany's share in global raw material trade

Germany is a trading nation. Raw materials and goods are imported, further processed, and a significant amount of raw materials, processed goods and final products is (re-)exported. While in 2015, Germany's imports exceeded exports by 243 million tonnes, at the same time it generated a monetary trade surplus of 265 billion Euro. This apparent discrepancy can be explained by the fact that the manufacture of higher-value products increases the value per tonne of raw materials.

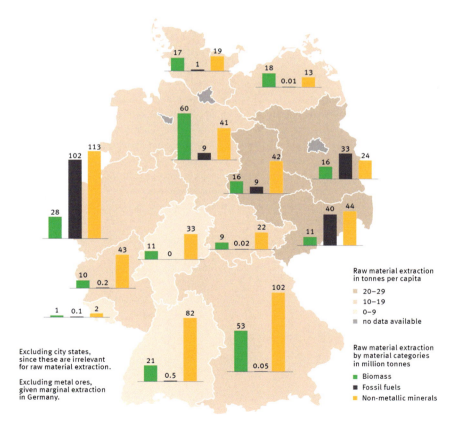

Figure 3.1 Used raw material extraction in the German federal states, 2015.
Source: UBA (2018).

As explained above, all semi-finished and finished goods imported into Germany contain indirect raw material flows. When these indirect flows are accounted for, Germany's physical trade volumes increase by almost a factor of 3. Indirect raw material flows of imports increased sharply in the past years and comprised 919 million tonnes by 2014. About 58% of the raw materials processed in the German economy were non-domestic in origin.

The role of the economy

A sustainable use of natural resources means increasing raw material productivity, hence decoupling economic growth from raw material use and its negative environmental impacts. Germany's raw material productivity, i.e. the relationship between GDP and direct material input (see above), increased by 56% during the period 1994–2015 (Figure 3.2). The indicator of total raw material productivity, which also takes account of the indirect material flows of imports to Germany, rose in recent years by an average of 1.9% per year. This is above the goal identified in ProgRess II to maintain the growth rate seen during the period 2000–2010 of around 1.5% until 2030.

Raw materials for consumption

Raw material consumption (RMC) of German final demand comprises all raw materials that are required along the supply chains of consumed products and services. In 2014, the per-capita figure was 16.1 tonnes, with an absolute amount of 1.3 billion tonnes. Although this represented a reduction since 2000

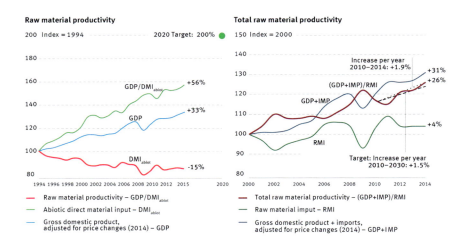

Figure 3.2 Development of raw material productivity, 1994–2015, (left) and total raw material productivity (right) in Germany, 2000–2014.
Source: UBA (2018).

by 13%, it increased again in the most recent years. Non-metallic minerals contributed the largest share to raw material consumption in 2014 (45%), followed by fossil fuels (29%) and biomass (21%).

Public and private consumption were jointly responsible for almost two-thirds of raw material consumption in Germany in 2014. With regard to private consumption, large quantities of raw materials were consumed in the areas of housing and food. The public sector's requirements for raw materials occurred primarily via the consumption of goods and services in the areas of administration, defence and health. The state's relatively high share in Germany's overall consumption reflects the key importance of the welfare state's role in the country.

Other natural resources

Since the extraction, processing and transport of raw materials and the use of products are all associated with significant energy inputs, greenhouse gas emissions occur along the entire value chain of raw materials. The use of raw materials and climate change are thus closely interlinked. It becomes evident that increasing the efficiency of raw materials use is an essential prerequisite for reaching climate goals.

When contrasting the carbon footprint and material footprint (RMC) with one another over time, it becomes evident that both curves follow a similar path. Both time series have the same downturns in 1997, 2002 and 2009, with the most accentuated in 2002, where the material footprint was at 87% of its 1995 value, and the carbon footprint at 88%. Moreover, both time series have similar peaks, especially in the year 2007. This may be explained by the fact that increased product consumption also causes higher emissions along the supply chains. At the same time, the economic crisis of 2008 produced a slump both in the RMC indicator and in the CO_2 footprint.

Résumé and outlook

The goal of the resource report series 'The Use of Natural Resources – Report for Germany' is to explain the complex topic of resource use in a generally understandable way, setting its focus on raw materials. The content-related framework fulfils this requirement by applying an innovative concept consisting of a streamlined structure (double pages) and clear figures. The 'prototype' reports 2016 and 2018 introduced the topic to a wide audience and provided relevant data and facts. Follow-up reports will present updated data in a condensed manner while treating selected aspects in more detail.

The topic of resource use is intrinsically complex and relevant for a wide range of stakeholders, making the communication of the topic a challenge. The resource reports 2016 and 2018 addressed only a part of the target groups – namely policy makers and advisors and researchers – in a meaningful way.

One conclusion drawn is that future reports should keep setting their focus on these stakeholders and that additional formats are required for ensuring targeted communication to the other groups.

Both the German Environment Agency and Destatis provide data on the use of natural resources in Germany. One challenge was to present this data without duplication and, in areas where these two institutions do not provide data, to integrate data from other sources and to deal appropriately with deviating results from different calculation models. The approach of how to deal with the observed differences was openly discussed in the method description. The results were presented in a way that clearly communicates the actual message (e.g. large differences in national per-capita or sector numbers) while at the same time avoiding confusion due to diverging absolute values.

As regards a continuation of the resource report series, a number of aspects should be taken into consideration. One refers to data harmonisation. The existing reports showed an urgent need of further harmonising the UGR provided by Destatis with the global dataset provided by the UN IRP. In this context, the main question would be how to best use the Destatis data to increase the robustness of the global dataset. Similarly, future reports should tackle the issue of how to harmonise the Destatis approach to calculate indirect material flows with other, global approaches, in order to generate more congruent results.

Future reports will certainly update the core content, such as levels of domestic extraction, trade or raw material productivity. However, in addition, future reports could aim at demonstrating the intertwining between the use of raw materials and other resources such as water, land, or greenhouse gas emissions (the so-called resource nexus), as well as the environmental impacts caused by the use of raw materials.

Finally, the resource report series aims at addressing a large number of stakeholder groups and individuals in general, to create awareness and achieve a more sustainable societal resource use. To exploit the series' full potential and increase its distribution and uptake, a thoroughly developed communication strategy targeting different stakeholders with key messages from the report could accompany the publication. Further, a comprehensive web portal with interactive elements, which provides state-of-the-art visualisations, background material and relevant links to related initiatives could accompany the publication is foreseen.

The resource report series developed by the German Environment Agency is a successful attempt to make the topic of natural resource use in Germany, which is of central relevance for global sustainable development, more tangible. Furthermore, by that means, inform and motivate readers to become responsible and active citizens. UBA will continue the research project. 'DeuRess II' will start in autumn 2019, and the third German Resources Report as a key result of this next project is expected for 2022.

Abbreviations

EEA   European Environment Agency
FoEE   Friends of the Earth Europe
G7   Group of Seven
G20   Group of Twenty
GDP   gross domestic product
MFA   Material Flow Analysis
NRW   North Rhine-Westphalia
OECD   Organisation for Economic Co-operation and Development
RMC   raw material consumption
RMI   raw material input
SCP-HAT   Sustainable Consumption and Production Hotspots Analysis Tool
UBA   German Environment Agency
UNE   UN Environment
UN IRP   United Nations International Resource Panel
UN SDG   United Nations Sustainable Development Goals
WWF   World Wildlife Fund

References

BMU (2012). *Federal Ministry for the Environment, Nature Conservation and Nuclear Safety.* German Resource Efficiency Programme (ProgRess). Berlin.

BMUB (2016). German Resource Efficiency Programme II. Berlin. Federal Ministry for the Environment, Nature Conservation, Building and Nuclear Safety (BMUB) website: www.bmu.de/en/topics/economy-products-resources-tourism/resource-efficiency/overview-of-german-resource-efficiency-programme-progress.

Destatis (2018). *Sustainable Development in Germany: Indicator Report 2018.* Wiesbaden. Retrieved from Destatis – Statistisches Bundesamt Deutschland website: www.destatis.de/DE/Themen/Gesellschaft-Umwelt/Nachhaltigkeitsindikatoren/Publikationen/Downloads-Nachhaltigkeit/indicator-report-0230002189004.pdf?__blob=publicationFile.

Destatis (2019). Umweltökonomische Gesamtrechnungen: Methode des gesamtwirtschaftlichen Materialkontos. 2019. Wiesbaden. Retrieved from Destatis – Statistisches Bundesamt Deutschland website: www.destatis.de/DE/Themen/Gesellschaft-Umwelt/Umwelt/Materialfluesse-Energiefluesse/Publikationen/Downloads-Material-und-Energiefluesse/gesamtwirtschaftliches-materialkonto-fb_5851314189004.pdf?__blob=publicationFile.

Deutsche Bundesregierung (2002). *Perspektiven für Deutschland. Unsere Strategie für eine nachhaltige Entwicklung.* Berlin.

EEA (2020). *European Environment Agency. Even more from less.* Copenhagen.

EEA (2016). *European Environment Agency. More from Less – Material Resource Efficiency in Europe.* 2015 Overview of Policies, Instruments and Targets in 32 countries. Copenhagen.

European Commission (2011). Roadmap to a Resource Efficient Europe (No. COM (2011) 571 final). Brussels.

European Commission. (2015). Closing the Loop – An EU Action Plan for the Circular Economy, COM(2015) 614. Brussels.

Eurostat (2018). *Economy-wide Material Flow Accounts: Handbook* (2018 edition). Manuals and guidelines. Luxembourg: Publications Office of the European Union. Retrieved from https://ec.europa.eu/eurostat/documents/3859598/9117556/KS-GQ-18-006-EN-N.pdf/b621b8ce-2792-47ff-9d10-067d2b8aac4b https://doi.org/10.2785/158567.

Eurostat (2019). Material Flow Accounts (Eurostat Database). Luxembourg. Retrieved from Statistical Office of the European Communities website: //appsso.eurostat.ec.europa.eu/nui/show.do?dataset=env_ac_mfa&lang=en.

Federal Government (2017). German Sustainable Development Strategy. Berlin. website: www.bundesregierung.de/breg-en/issues/sustainability.

Heinrich Böll Stiftung & FoEE (2014). Meat Atlas: Facts and Figures about the Animals We Eat. Germany. Retrieved from Heinrich Böll Stiftung; Friends of the Earth Europe website: www.boell.de/sites/default/files/meat_atlas2014_kommentierbar.pdf?dimension1=ds_fleischatlas_2014.

Heinrich Böll Stiftung & IASS (2015). Soil Atlas: Facts and Figures about Earth, Land and Fields. Germany. Retrieved from Heinrich Böll Stiftung; Institute for Advanced Sustainability Studies website: www.boell.de/sites/default/files/soilatlas2015_ii.pdf?dimension1=division_iap.

Kaumanns, S. & Lauber, U. (2016). Rohstoffe für Deutschland: Bedarfsanalyse für Konsum, Investition und Export auf Makro- und Mesoebene. Destatis im Auftrag des Umweltbundesamt (UBA Texte No. 62/2016). Dessau-Roßlau. Retrieved from www.umweltbundesamt.de/sites/default/files/medien/1968/publikationen/rohstoffe_fur_deutschland.pdf.

Lehmann, H., Schmidt-Bleek, F. & Manstein, C. (2018). Factor X – 25 Years – 'Factor X Concept' Is Essential for Achieving Sustainable Development: In: Lehmann, H. (Ed.). *Factor X. Challenges, Implementation Strategies and Examples for a Sustainable Use of Natural Resources.* Springer: Berlin.

Maier, L. (2018). *Rohstoffe weltweit im Einsatz für Deutschland: Berechnung von Aufkommen und Verwendung in Rohstoffäquivalenten* (WISTA No. 2/2018). Wiesbaden.

OECD (2018). *International Expert Workshop on Demand-Based Measures of Material Flows and Resource Productivity*: Workshop report (No. ENV/EPOC/WPEI(2017)2/REV). Paris.

OECD (2019). Environmental Statistics: Material Resources. Paris. Retrieved from Organisation for Economic Co-operation and Development (OECD) website: https://stats.oecd.org/index.aspx?r=783906.

Schmidt, M., Spieth, H., Haubach, C. & Kühne, C. (2018). 100 Pioneers in Efficient Resource Management: *Best Practice Cases from Producing Companies*: Springer. Retrieved from https://books.google.at/books?hl=de&lr=&id=5559DwAAQBAJ&oi=fnd&pg=PR5&dq=100+Pioneers+in+Efficient+Resource+Management&ots=lSTO7UMt9q&sig=pirTn02NxHrOhS3L73N-8E-OBh4.

Schmidt-Bleek, F. (1993). Revolution in Resource Productivity for a Sustainable Economy. A New Research Agenda. *Fresenius Environmental Bulletin, 2*(8), 485–490.

Stadler, K., Wood, R., Bulavskaya, T., Södersten, C.-J., Simas, M., Schmidt, S. … Tukker, A. (2018). EXIOBASE 3: Developing a Time Series of Detailed Environmentally Extended Multi-Regional Input-Output Tables. *Journal of Industrial Ecology, 22*(3), 502–515. https://doi.org/10.1111/jiec.12715.

Tukker, A., Bulavskaya, T., Giljum, S., Koning, A. de, Lutter, S., Simas, M. … Wood, R. (2014). *The Global Resource Footprint of Nations. Carbon, Water, Land and Materials Embodied in Trade and Final Consumption Calculated with EXIOBASE 2.1.* Leiden/Delft/Vienna/Trondheim.

UBA (2014). DeuRess: Resource Use in Germany. *Research project on behalf of the German Environment Agency (UBA)*. Retrieved from Umweltbundesamt website: www.umweltbundesamt.de/en/resource-use-in-germany.

UBA (2016). The Use of Natural Resources: Report for Germany 2016. *Dessau-Roßlau*. Retrieved from German Environment Agency website: www.umweltbundesamt.de/resourcesreport2016.

UBA (2017). Data on the Environment: Indicator Report. *Dessau-Roßlau*. Retrieved from German Environment Agency website: www.umweltbundesamt.de/en/data.

UBA (2018). The Use of Natural Resources: Report for Germany 2018. *Dessau-Roßlau*. Retrieved from German Environment Agency website: www.uba.de/resourcesreport2018.

UN IRP (2017a). Assessing Global Resource Use: A System Approach to Resource Efficiency and Pollution Reduction: A Report of the International Resource Panel. Nairobi. Retrieved from United Nations Environment Programme website: www.resourcepanel.org/sites/default/files/documents/document/media/assessing_global_resource_use_amended_130318.pdf.

UN IRP (2017b). *Global Material Flows Database: Version 2017*. Paris.

UNEP (2011). *Decoupling Natural Resource Use and Environmental Impacts from Economic Growth, A Report of the Working Group on Decoupling to the International Resource Panel*. Fischer-Kowalski, M., Swilling, M., von Weizsäcker, E. U., Ren, Y., Moriguchi, Y., Crane, W., Krausmann, F., Eisenmenger, N., Giljum, S., Hennicke, P., Romero Lankao, P., Siriban Manalang, A., Sewerin, S. Nairobi.

United Nations (2015a). Sustainable Development Goals: 17 Goals to Transform Our World. New York. Retrieved from United Nations website: www.un.org/sustainabledevelopment/sustainable-development-goals/.

United Nations (2015b). Transforming Our World: The 2030 Agenda for Sustainable Development: Resolution 70/1. New York. Retrieved from United Nations website: https://sustainabledevelopment.un.org/post2015/transformingourworld.

UNSD (2019). *Global Economy Wide Material Flow Accounting Manual: Draft version 2019*. New York.

WWF, Zoological Society of London, Global Footprint Network & Water Footprint Network (2014). *Living Planet Report 2014. Species and Spaces, People and Places*. Gland, Switzerland.

4 The rise of e-mobility as a trade-off between social and ecological benefits and distributional injustice

How the socio-technical regime and externalisation prevent a profound transformation of the mobility sector

Fabian Zimmer and Dörte Themann

Introduction

The global transport sector is responsible for more than 20% of the total energy-related CO_2 emissions, and this figure is expected to increase in developed as well as in emerging economies due to growing traffic volume (IPCC 2014: 603). Therefore the Intergovernmental Panel on Climate Change (IPCC) demands transport emissions to 'be strongly decoupled from GDP growth', e.g. by using less carbon-intensive technologies like the electric drives (IPCC 2014: 603). Due to these developments, many states and cities decided to support the use of electric vehicles (EV) by a broad range of means. Car manufacturers are shifting their production and research towards electric vehicles in reaction to external pressure (e.g. emission limits, driving ban for cars with combustion engine) and in expectation of increasing demand.[1] As a result of these decisions as well as of the progress in battery technology, the market share of electric vehicles is steadily growing and is expected to reach 57% of all passenger vehicle sales and over 30% of the global fleet until 2040 (BNEF 2019: 1).

As the demand for electric vehicles (especially batteries) rises, so does the demand for resources (namely for cobalt, lithium, nickel and rare earth elements) (Öko-Institut 2019; Köllner 2018). The mining of these elements (e.g. in the Democratic Republic of Congo or Chile) often leads to adverse environmental, social and human rights effects (Ali 2014; AI 2017, 2019). Despite extensive evidence on these problems, companies at the upper end of the supply chain (for example car manufacturers, battery producers) and their countries of origin take insufficient actions to ensure compliance with human rights and environmental protection standards (CNN 2018; AI 2017).

These processes, which aim to improve the quality of life and the technological progress of developed countries at the expense of emerging and developing countries can be regarded as manifestations of the 'Externalisation Society' (Lessenich 2016) or the 'Imperial Mode of Living' (Brand & Wissen 2017). While developed countries benefit from the rise of e-mobility, the resource-producing countries have to bear the social and ecological burdens.

This chapter shows that socio-technical dynamics towards technology transition as explained by Geels (2002; Geels & Schot 2007) as well as the process of externalisation are two complementary concepts to explain the shift towards e-mobility in the automobile sector. Based on an extensive literature review the article analyses the drivers for the unjust distribution of benefits and drawbacks and especially the reasons for insufficient political and corporate action to tackle these challenges.

This approach is therefore different to and more profound than previous works of the social and ecological effects of electric mobility: not only the drawbacks are listed and explained by the operating mode of the economic system. However, the importance of the socio-technical regime is highlighted and its inhibiting effect on serious changes, favouring incremental innovation in the mobility sector, while wilfully ignoring the consequent adverse social and environmental effects.

Theoretical background – externalisation and socio-technical dynamics

For many people around the world, the electrification of mobility causes exploitation of labour-power. In addition, it causes the exposure to environmental and ecological risks, marginalisation in terms of social and health conditions and ultimately the destruction of ecosystems.

Prominent theoretical analyses of those dynamics are presented under the headings of 'Externalisation Society' by Lessenich (2016) and 'Imperial Mode of Living' by Brand and Wissen (2017), these will be explained in the first part of this section. The problems analysed by both concepts are very detailed and are based on several kinds of policy sectors and different aspects of everyday practices.

Besides, socio-technical dynamics play a significant role in the genesis of technology. For this reason, the second part presents a brief overview of what Geels has termed the multi-level-perspective of technology transitions.

Externalisation society and imperial mode of living

The analyses of Lessenich and Brand and Wissen shows why electric vehicles are not the silver bullet in mitigating climate change. The habitus of 'externalisation' plays a major role in this regard.

Economic theory describes external effects, also referred to as externalisation, as the phenomenon of transferring costs or socio-ecological adverse effects, that result as consequences of an economic action or decision, to the 'outside'. As a result, affected people or societies do not share the benefits of these decisions but have to bear their social and ecological consequences without getting compensated. With the economic term of external effects, Lessenich offers a sharp sociological analysis of Global North's present state of political, economic and societal acting. He traces the path of externalisation through an analysis of several areas of general life such as travelling, mobility, markets, etc. and uncovers the deep-rooted structures and mechanisms that manifest inequality and dependencies on a global scale (Lessenich 2016: 17). For Lessenich, there is not just one main driver for externalisation or one social actor like powerful economic or political elites. Instead, he describes the source of the externalisation society as a silent agreement and wilful participation of the majority of the population of 'Western' countries. Those Western societies can only stabilise and reproduce themselves on the basis of externalising costs and adverse effects (ibid.: 25).

The origin of externalisation can be found in history and now permeates all parts of society as purported by Lessenich. Brand and Wissen (2017) and their theory of 'Imperial Mode of Living' provides a similar analysis, however, with a stronger focus on how nature and labour become exploited (ibid.: 12), as a result of current capitalistic production and consumptions chains. According to the 'imperial mode of living', the conditions of the westernised way of life that includes a particular way of production can be described as 'imperial'. Imperial means disproportionate and unlimited access of an actor group on the 'outside' of their societal borders. The outside means especially resources in terms of either natural resources for production or human resources (especially labour) as well as the access to natural sinks. In other words, to externalise environmental risks and bads.[2] In this mode, normality is created by masking the destruction (ibid.: 13).

Despite their comprehensive analysis on how externalisation is deep-rooted in everyday life and societal structures, an aspect, which is mainly excluded in the approaches of Lessenich and Brand & Wissen are the socio-technical dynamics. For this reason, the MLP approach is used to add this dimension and to introduce a concept that could integrate the 'habitus of externalisation'.

The multi-level perspective developed by Geels

One macro-perspective understanding regarding the dynamics of socio-technical transitions is offered by Geels (2002). He understands transitions as the result of an interplay of different dimensions on three analytical levels: 'niches (the locus of radical innovations), the socio-technical regimes (the locus of established practices and associated rules that enable and constrain incumbent actors in relation to existing systems), and the exogenous socio-technical landscape' (Geels 2014: 23, see also Geels 2002). In this way, technologies develop within a multi-level system, that is influenced by minor drivers as well as by deep anchored paradigms and paths.

The level for stabilising the system is the regime level (meso-level). On this level, incremental innovations are produced. Stabilising factors of the regime are: 'technology, user practices and application domains (markets), the symbolic meaning of technology, infrastructure, industry structure, policy and techno-scientific knowledge' (Geels 2002: 1262). The regime also includes existing power relations, the influence of institutions, the interest of strong actor groups and different access to resources. Because of that, the 'sociotechnical regime' is the dominant level, where extreme changes are prevented. In contrast, visions or radical and regime challenging innovations arise from niches (micro-level) (see Grießhammer & Brohmann 2015).

On the macro level, the so-called landscape, higher-level processes and events are located. Similar to the niches on the micro-level, the landscape exerts pressure on the regime to change (ibid.: 17). But the landscape can also be constituted in a way that hinders innovation or radical change. Geels describes the external landscape as a layer where 'deep structural trends' (Geels 2002: 1260) are located. Wars and drastic events are part of the landscape, but also environmental problems, norms and values.

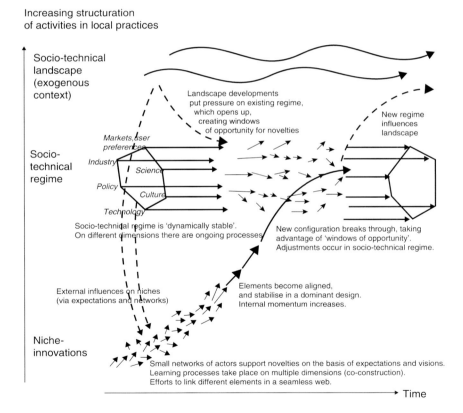

Figure 4.1 Levels which influence technology transitions (see Geels & Schot 2007: 401).

If one views the MLP and the externalisation approach side by side, it becomes apparent that they are not mutually exclusive but have the potential to complement each other. Paraphrasing the term of Jasanoff (2004), it could be that the dynamics of externalisation and the socio-technical dynamics are interdependent in a *co-productive* way, meaning co-producing strong technological regimes.

Drivers for and externalities of electric vehicles

The exploitation and production of resources for electric vehicles and the production chain for electric cars for the Global North fit perfectly to concepts of externalisation or imperial mode of living. This section first provides an overview of international cases where externalisation becomes observable. Second, the dynamics are outlined that stabilise the car regime and influence the technology genesis of the electrification of vehicles.

Externalities of resource exploitation

Increasing demand for resources

The economic profits are predominantly for the benefit of highly developed areas, whereas most of the essential resources are mined in African and South American countries. Thereby the demand for elements central for these technologies is expected to increase significantly mainly as components of (e-vehicle) batteries: the demand for cobalt, of which 60% is mined in the Democratic Republic of Congo, will strongly increase and possibly more than double until 2026 (Al Barazi 2018: 9). A similar development is predicted for lithium, leading to demand two or three times higher than in 2016 by 2026 (Schmidt 2017: 12). Almost half to the lithium originates from Chile, Argentina and Brazil and about 40% from Australia (Schmidt 2017: 43). Other crucial components are rare earth elements, for which China is by far the biggest producer (more than 90%) (USGS 2019: 133).

Environmental hazards

The mining process for rare earth elements, for example, requires vast amounts of water (which leads to lower groundwater levels and desertification) and chemicals. The often chemically and radioactively contaminated residues are stored in insufficiently protected landfills and artificial lakes. Consequently, the toxic residues can be accidentally released to the environment and then pollute land and water (Müller 2018: 28).

The production of lithium located in salt lakes, which is the case in South America, requires significant amounts of water. The massive water consumption states a severe environmental threat to these arid areas because of sinking groundwater levels and drying out of rivers (Öko-Institut 2017: 47f.).

Social and human rights risks

Mining for electric vehicle components gives also rise to a number of social and human rights risks. The contamination of soil and water in the course of rare earth elements mining damages agricultural production of nearby farms and causes severe health problems (Müller 2018: 29). In Argentina, indigenous groups are not adequately informed about the impacts of lithium mining and are not involved in the planning processes for planned mining sites (AI 2019).

Cobalt mining in the Democratic Republic of Congo is especially problematic: particularly in artisanal mines workers lack adequate safety equipment or legal protection. Furthermore, even young children work in many of these mines. One further problem is that about 20% of the cobalt originates from this artisanal mining sector without proper regulations or supervision (AI 2017: 4).

Insufficient monitoring and legislation

Although those problems are widely known and recognised, the supply chains are often not transparent and the sources of the resources unknown. In particular, this is the case for cobalt mining in Congo where a significant part of the cobalt originates in artisanal mining, which is later mixed with cobalt from regular mines. Therefore, human rights groups accuse mining companies, suppliers and car *manufacturers* of inadequate measures to ensure transparency and safe working conditions (AI 2019).

In response to these accusations, several private sector initiatives were founded to enhance the transparency of the supply chain and eliminate the use of cobalt from untrustworthy sources.[3] Additionally, international organisations provide frameworks for responsible mining, which can be adapted by companies. Nevertheless, only a minority of the companies producing and using batteries for electric vehicles use the OECD guidance as standards (AI 2017: 7). Also, the planned measures of the initiatives keep vague and comprehensive tracking of the origins is difficult as long as cobalt from artisanal mining is used and many intermediaries are involved between the mining and battery production (Washington Post 2016). A factor favouring weak monitoring is the lack of legal frameworks in car-producing countries to enforce such regulations. Although strict resource legislation already exists, for example, in the USA for conflict minerals (Dodd-Frank Act, Section 1502) and comes into force in the EU in 2021 (European Commission 2017), both do not include cobalt.

Drivers for the electric automobile regime

The main drivers of the transition of the mobility sector towards electric cars are climate change mitigation, the improvement of air quality as well as maintain or gain competitive advantages.

A major argument for transformation towards electric cars is their potential to lower GHG-emissions. This is supported by a broad range of influential actors, for example by scientific institutions as the IPCC (2014) or the European Environmental Agency (2018), governmental organisations as the European Commission (2019) and the German transport ministry (BMVI 2018) or also companies like the world's leading car-manufacturer Volkswagen (VW 2019b).

While the reduction of global warming can be seen as a global goal,[4] the other drivers benefit only the countries where electric cars are used, which are mainly in Europe and China (WEF 2019a). Another benefit goes to the companies producing electric cars and batteries, which are primarily located in Europe, North America and Asia (Statista 2019a, 2019b). In some mostly Western countries, the automotive industry plays a major role in the domestic industry, employing hundreds of thousand people directly and indirectly and generating significant tax revenues.[5] Accordingly, to gain competitive advantages can be regarded as one of the strongest motives for fostering electric vehicles (Altenburg 2014: 9ff.). Studies predict that in general '[t]he transition from petroleum-based energy to renewably sourced energy will strengthen Europe's economy' (Harrison 2018: 4).

Due to the tax revenues[6] and jobs depending on the car industry, there is a strong political interest to protect this sector. Therefore, the goal is to ensure a car-centric transport sector and maintain the leading role of the current manufacturers. Also, unions support this agenda to safeguard the jobs of the workers (Canzler & Knie 2018: 11f.). It is anticipated that electric mobility and European battery cell production can significantly contribute to growth, employment and competitiveness of the industry of the EU (BMWi 2019).

Alongside economic and political reasons for choosing the electrification of road vehicles, solutions not challenging the car sector, in general, are also favoured due to the decades-long predominance of the automobile regime. Since becoming the predominant mode of transport in the first half of the 20th century it was considerably promoted by political decisions. These led to a higher attractivity of the car, to more users (Canzler & Knie 2018: 31f.) and further consolidated and expanded its dominance (Cowan & Hultén 1994). Today most of the (urban) infrastructure is optimised for road traffic (e.g. streets, parking lots, gas stations) and a shift to other transport modes is difficult due to the built cost-intensive car infrastructure. Although the status of the car as a symbol of independence and a good life is decreasing in the last years, the narrative is still existing and powerful (Canzler & Knie 2018: 58f.). A transformation needs, therefore, not only to change the car-centric infrastructure (in which massive investments were and are made), but also mental path dependencies of the people (Fischedick & Grunwald 2017: 26).

Analysis: externalisation as a stabilising motive of the socio-technical regime

In the following section, the transition in the automobile regime towards electric vehicles will be analysed with the MLP in combination with the theories of Lessenich and Brand and Wissen.

The landscape: wilful ignorance and climate change

Based on the theory of externalisation society and the empirical evidence, it is reasonable to understand the externalisation of social and ecological risks in the course of transition towards electric vehicles as a consequence of in-depth structural trends that are inscribed in societal structures and everyday practices (Brand & Wissen 2017: 48ff.). Externalisation is part of the external landscape as it describes an, in parts, unconscious discourse and mental model of society. Being part of the external landscape, it influences the socio-technical regime and technology transitions.

Including the 'habitus of externalisation', the landscape provides a stabilising effect towards the socio-technical regime of the automobile. Shocking events like the 'diesel-affair' or deep-rooted societal discourses like climate change confront the regime and pressure it to change towards a reduction of fossil fuel use. However, the deep-rooted mentality of externalisation produces a balancing moment regarding this pressuring effects and stabilises the regime in a way that radical changes from niches are not taken up. Demands from the civil society or scientific actors to also reflect socio-ecological problems of the entire value chain are not taken into account. Because of the habitus of externalisation in combination with a perceived urgency caused by current climate change discourses, incremental innovations inside the regime logic seem to be sufficient. The exclusive focus on climate change as the paramount problem cannot overcome the phenomena of social and ecological inequality. The current external landscape facilitates technological strategies that include wilful ignorance and sidetracking.

The discourse about climate change, in this interpretation, creates pressure to react fast, while the need for fast reactions in such dimensions tempts decision-makers and industry to look for answers only in the application of technology and not in the change of societal structures.

The socio-technical regime: externalisation as stabilising mode of living

An 'externalisation society' and the 'imperial mode of living' also fit into the socio-technical regime level. Brand and Wissen describe the imperial mode of living as a habitus or culture that influences decision-making processes and sections policies inside the regime and are part of user practices and markets.

One influencing factor on the regime level, which is rather disregarded in the analyses of Lessenich or Brand and Wissen is the role of techno-scientific knowledge. We observe a robust co-productive relation between science, industry and politics which mutually reinforce one another (Canzler & Knie 2018: 55f.). Accordingly, research funds for the electrification of mobility reach billions of dollars, aiming to optimise the predominant regime instead of changing it (BMBF 2019; BMWI 2019).

Tracing the technical genesis of the automobile reveals that current forms of mobility are not only part and outgrowth of the imperial mode of living (Brand &

50 Fabian Zimmer & Doerte Themann

Wissen 2017: 125ff.), but that vice versa the practice of externalisation also is influencing the technology genesis of the mobility industry today.

Additionally, the development of the automobile is also influenced by path dependencies and lock-ins, based on, for example, 'sunk costs' (lost investments in case of system change), 'scale effects' (cost benefits because of mass production), 'network effects' (high amount of users) (Fischedick & Grunwald 2017: 26) and mental path dependencies. This further stabilises the prevailing automotive regime.

The niches: why do efforts and discourses to overcome externalisation not succeed?

Technical alternatives are not marketable[7] and critical socio-ecological discourses are not strong enough to overcome the externalisation paradigm. The acuteness of climate change screens the regime level from radical niche activities, that would presumably need more time for meeting climate protection requirements. Instead, incremental innovation is sought.

While radical paths and system-questioning discourses from the niche level (for instance degrowth and sufficiency, car-free mobility, and so forth), become more intense, they are also not successful in overcoming the current regime. One reason is that the automobile is a manifest expression of the imperial mode of living (Brand & Wissen 2017: 125ff.).

Conclusions

For a long time, the automobile with an internal combustion engine (ICE) and the interdependent development of analogous areas (e.g. petrochemical industry, specialised professions) dominated the mobility in most countries (Cowan & Hultén 1996). Due to external pressure, the dominance of the ICE is decreasing today and will probably be replaced by the electric motor (BNEF 2019: 1). However as this analysis makes clear, the strong socio-technical regime of the automobile, which is stabilised by different factors like the need for climate protection, political and corporate interests, path dependencies, consumer preferences and overall the habitus of externalisation, prevents a profound change of the transport sector. Thus, only the drive technology is changing while the general auto-centric mobility system remains intact and the subsequent social and ecological externalities are, again, addressed insufficiently.

The further development of this transition is difficult to anticipate because mobility states a complex socio-technical system. Impacts of a path are often visible only at a later point (Fischedick & Grunwald 2017: 12) and are full of 'unknown unknowns' (Eckhardt & Rippe 2016). The probability is high that new path dependencies are created that will make it difficult again to overcome the socio-ecological problems (as resistance against such measures illustrates, e.g. the *gilets jaunes* movement in France). The fading dominance of the established producers and the intensifying competition among old and new

The rise of e-mobility   51

players reduces the probability of a resource policy led by social and ecological considerations, instead low prices and reliable supply, are of tantamount importance.

The actual transition towards electric drives for a still auto-centric mobility, whereby societal structures and the socio-technical regimes remain unaffected, is also caused by a wilful ignorance that is intrinsic in the dynamics of externalisation.

Nevertheless, there are urban areas that already function as learning laboratories and try to show a new practice without the automobile. Also, scientists from different disciplines, as well as NGOs, broaden the discourse beyond the technological focus. However, the question remains, whether such voices will challenge the regime profoundly enough considering the stabilising forces in culture, industry, politics and legislation.[8]

Notes

1 E.g. Volkswagen as the world biggest car manufacturer announced to electrify 'the vehicle portfolio, with investment in this area alone amounting to more than €30 billion by 2023' (VW 2019a).
2 The term of environmental bads is quite common when referring to phenomena of environmental (in-)justice. In environmental justice theory it is used contrary to environmental goods or benefits.
3 Examples are the 'Responsible Cobalt Initiative' to reduce social and environmental risks (CCCMC 2016), the new regulations of the 'London Metal Exchange' to rule out child labour (CNN 2019) or the 'Global Battery Alliance' to ensure a sustainable battery value chain (WEF 2019b).
4 It has to be stated the GHG-reduction potentials of electric cars are still unclear (see for example Hill et al. 2019).
5 In Germany alone more than 800.000 people are directly or indirectly employed in this sector and the manufacturers generate revenues of more than €420 billion (VDA 2018).
6 In the case of VW the state of Lower Saxony is even shareholder of the company (11.8%) (VW 2018).
7 See for example Turcheniuk et al. (2018).
8 E.g. in the German transport legislation priority is given to the needs of individual motorised transport (Bundesregierung 2001; Canzler & Knie 2018: 37).

References

AI. (2017). *Time to recharge: corporate action and inaction to tackle abuses in the cobalt supply chain.* London, England: Amnesty International.
AI. (2019). Amnesty challenges industry leaders to clean up their batteries. Retrieved from www.amnesty.org/en/latest/news/2019/03/amnesty-challenges-industry-leaders-to-clean-up-their-batteries [14.07.2019].
Al Barazi, S. (2018). *Rohstoffrisikobewertung – Kobalt: DERA Rohstoffinformationen 36.* Berlin, Germany: Deutsche Rohstoffagentur.
Ali, S. (2014). Social and environmental impact of the rare earth industries. *Resources* 3(1), 123–134.
Altenburg, T. (2014). *From combustion engines to electric vehicles: a study of technological path creation and disruption in Germany.* Bonn, Germany: Deutsches Institut für Entwicklungspolitik.

Bijker, W. E. (1995). Sociohistorical technology studies. In Sheila J., G. E. Markle, J. C. Petersen & T. Pinch (Eds.): *Handbook of science and technology studies (229–256).* Thousand Oaks, CA: Sage Publ.

BMBF. (2019). Dachkonzept'Forschungsfabrik Batterie'. Retrieved from www.bmbf.de/files/BMBF_Dachkonzept_Forschungsfabrik_Batterie_Handout_Jan2020.pdf [14.07.2019].

BMUB. (2016). *German Resource Efficiency Programme II: programme for the sustainable use and conservation of natural resources.* Berlin, Germany: BMUB.

BMVI. (2018): The future of mobility is electric. Retrieved from www.bmvi.de/SharedDocs/EN/Dossier/Electric-Mobility-Sector/electric-mobility-sector.html [06.09.2019].

BMWi. (2019). Bekanntmachung des Interessensbekundungsverfahrens zur geplanten Förderung im Bereich der industriellen Fertigung für mobile und stationäre Energiespeicher (Batteriezellfertigung). Retrieved from www.bmwi.de/Redaktion/DE/Downloads/B/bekanntmachung-zur-geplanten-foerderung-einer-batteriezellproduktion.pdf?__blob=publicationFile&v=3 [14.07.2019].

BNEF. (2019). Electric vehicle outlook. Retrieved from https://about.bnef.com/electric-vehicle-outlook/#toc-download [14.07.2019].

Brand, U. & Wissen, M. (2017). *Imperiale Lebensweise: Zur Ausbeutung von Mensch und Natur im globalen Kapitalismus.* Munich, Germany: Oekom verlag.

Bundesregierung (2001). Allgemeine Verwaltungsvorschrift zur Straßenverkehrs-Ordnung: Retrieved from www.verwaltungsvorschriften-im-internet.de/bsvwvbund_26012001_S3236420014.htm [19.07.2019].

Canzler, W. & Knie, A. (2018). *Taumelnde Giganten: Gelingt der Autoindustrie die Neuerfindung?.* Munich, Germany: Oekom verlag.

CCCMC. (2016). Responsible Cobalt Initiative (RCI). Retrieved from www.cccmc.org.cn/docs/2016-11/20161121141502674021.pdf [14.07.2019].

CNN. (2018). Carmakers and big tech struggle to keep batteries free from child labor. Retrieved from https://money.cnn.com/2018/05/01/technology/cobalt-congo-child-labor-car-smartphone-batteries/index.html [14.07.2019].

CNN. (2019). The world's biggest metal exchange is getting serious about child labor and conflict minerals. Retrieved from https://edition.cnn.com/2019/04/23/business/london-metal-exchange-child-labor/index.html [14.07.2019].

Cowan, R. & Hultén, S. (1996). Escaping lock-in: the case of the electric vehicle. *Technological Forecasting and Social Change*, 53(1), 61–79.

Dodd–Frank Wall Street Reform and Consumer Protection Act, Pub. L. No. 111–203, § 929-Z, 124 Stat. 1376, 1871 (2010) (codified at 15 U.S.C. § 780).

Eckhardt, A. & Rippe, K. P. (2016). Risiko und Ungewissheit? Bei der Entsorgung hochradioaktiver Abfälle Zurich: Switzerland: vdf.

European Commission (2017). Conflict minerals: the regulation explained. Retrieved from http://ec.europa.eu/trade/policy/in-focus/conflict-minerals-regulation/regulation-explained/#regulation-why [14.07.2019].

European Commission (2019). Clean transport, urban transport: electric vehicles. Retrieved from https://ec.europa.eu/transport/themes/urban/vehicles/road/electric_en [04.09.2019].

European Environmental Agency (2018). Electric vehicles: a smart choice for the environment. Retrieved from www.eea.europa.eu/articles/electric-vehicles-a-smart [04.09.2019].

Fischedick, M. & Grundwald, A. (2017). *Pfadabhängigkeiten in der Energiewende: Das Beispiel Mobilität.* Munich, Germany: acatech.

Geels, F. W. (2002). Technological transitions as evolutionary reconfiguration processes: a multi-level perspective and a case-study. *Research Policy* 31(8–9), 1257–1274.

Geels, F. W. (2014). Regime resistance against low-carbon transitions: introducing politics and power into the multi-level perspective. *Theory, Culture & Society* 31(5), 21–40.

Geels, F.W. & Schot, J.W. (2007). Typology of sociotechnical transition pathways. *Research Policy*, 36(3), 399–417.

Grießhammer, R. & Brohmann, B. (2015). *Wie Transformationen und gesellschaftliche Innovationen gelingen können: Transformationsstrategien und Models of Change für nachhaltigen gesellschaftlichen Wandel*. Baden-Baden, Germany: Nomos.

Harrison, P. (2018). *Fuelling Europe's future: how the transition from oil strengthens the economy*. Brussels, Belgium: European Climate Foundation.

Hill, G., Heidrich, O., Creutzig, F. & Blythe, P. (2019). The role of electric vehicles in near-term mitigation pathways and achieving the UK's carbon budget. *Applied Energy* 251, 1–8.

IPCC (2014). *Climate Change 2014: Mitigation of climate change*. Cambridge, England & New York, NY: Cambridge University Press.

Jasanoff, S. (2004). *States of knowledge. the co-production of science and the social order*. London, England: Routledge (International library of sociology).

Köllner, C. (2018). Seltener Seltene Erden verwenden. Retrieved from www.springerprofessional.de/elektromotor/werkstoffe/seltener-seltene-erden-verwenden/16105028 [14.07.2019].

Lessenich, S. (2016). *Neben uns die Sintflut: Die Externalisierungsgesellschaft und ihr Preis*. Munich, Germany: Hanser Berlin.

Müller, A. (2018). *Rohstoffe für die Energiewende: Menschenrechtliche und ökologische Verantwortung in einem Zukunftsmarkt*. Aachen, Germany: Bischöfliches Hilfswerk MISEREOR.

Öko-Institut (2017). *Strategien für die nachhaltige Rohstoffversorgung der Elektromobilität: Synthesepapier zum Rohstoffbedarf für Batterien und Brennstoffzellen*. Berlin, Germany: Agora Verkehrswende.

Öko-Institut (2019). Gigafactories für Lithium-Ionen-Zellen: Rohstoffbedarfe für die globale Elektromobilität bis 2050. Retrieved from www.oeko.de/fileadmin/oekodoc/Fab4Lib-Rohstoffe-Elektromobilitaet.pdf [14.07.2019].

Schmidt, M. (2017). *Rohstoffrisikobewertung – Lithium: DERA Rohstoffinformationen 33*. Berlin, Germany: Deutsche Rohstoffagentur.

Statista. (2019a). Prognose der Zellproduktion von Batterien für Elektroautos in ausgewählten Ländern weltweit im Zeitraum der Jahre 2016 bis 2021. Retrieved from https://de.statista.com/statistik/daten/studie/896546/umfrage/prognose-der-produktionskapazitaet-von-batteriezellen-fuer-elektroautos-weltweit/ [14.07.2019].

Statista. (2019b). Anzahl der produzierten Elektroautos im Jahr 2016 nach ausgewählten Ländern. Retrieved from https://de.statista.com/statistik/daten/studie/168065/umfrage/anzahl-der-produzierten-elektroautos-nach-laendern/ [14.07.2019].

Turcheniuk, K., Bondarev, D., Singhal, V. & Yushin, G. (2018). Ten years left to redesign lithium–ion batteries. *Nature*, 559(7715), 467–470.

USGS. (2019). Mineral commodity summaries: rare earths. Retrieved from https://prd-wret.s3-us-west-2.amazonaws.com/assets/palladium/production/atoms/files/mcs-2019-raree.pdf [14.07.2019].

VDA. (2018). Zahlen und Daten. Retrieved from www.vda.de/de/services/zahlen-und-daten/zahlen-und-daten-uebersicht.html [14.07.2019].

VW. (2018). Aktionärsstruktur. Retrieved from www.volkswagenag.com/de/InvestorRelations/shares/shareholder-structure.html [14.07.2019].

VW. (2019a). Volkswagen plans 22 million electric vehicles in ten years. Retrieved from www.volkswagen-newsroom.com/en/press-releases/volkswagen-plans-22-million-electric-vehicles-in-ten-years-4750 [14.07.2019].

VW. (2019b). 'Volkswagen accepts climate responsibility'. Retrieved from www.volkswagenag.com/en/news/stories/2018/12/volkswagen-accepts-climate-responsibility.html [06.09.2019].

Washington Post (2016). The cobalt pipeline. Tracing the path from deadly hand-dug mines in Congo to consumers' phones and laptops. Retrieved from www.washingtonpost.com/graphics/business/batteries/congo-cobalt-mining-for-lithium-ion-battery/??noredirect=on [14.07.2019].

WEF. (2019a). These countries have the highest share of electric vehicles. Retrieved from www.weforum.org/agenda/2019/03/chart-of-the-day-half-of-new-cars-sold-in-norway-are-electric-or-hybrid/ [14.07.2019].

WEF. (2019b). Global Battery Alliance. Retrieved from www.weforum.org/global-battery-alliance [14.07.2019].

5 The quest for the holy grail

Can smart cities lead us to sustainability?

Ira Shefer

Introduction

Cities around the world increasingly adopt advanced technologies to solve complexities in urban development and resources use and management. These technologies include information technology (IT) and information and communication technology (ICT), big-data and Artificial Intelligence (AI), among others (de Jong, Joss, Schraven, Zhan & Weijnen 2015). Often, these initiatives are framed as 'smart cities'.[1] 'Smart' can be interpreted as providing, acquiring and managing data to tackle problems and their solutions while addressing resources use and management and sustainability in the urban context (Batty et al. 2012; New, Castro & Beckwith 2017).

However, the endorsement of smart cities raises serious issues. For example, Ahvenniemi, Huovila, Pinto-Seppä and Airaksinen (2017) show how the focus on smart cities can neglect the environmental dimensions of sustainability. Yigitcanlar and Kamruzzaman (2018) revealed that becoming 'smart' did not translate to a reduction in the carbon footprint of cities. Moreover, Kitchin (2014) pointed to problematic aspects of cities' race for big-data; namely, political interventions in data management, emerging technocratic solutions to deal with urban problems, commercialisation of governance and weakening of privacy rights.

This chapter adds a modest contribution to these perspectives. It examines (1) advocating advanced technologies as favourable solutions to urban resource-related problems, in (2) social, economic and political constellations that highly encourage these solutions, while (3) considering urban developmental challenges that cities are faced with, and the challenges that these solutions pose to cities. The chapter claims that given urban development projections in national and global arenas that encourage the use of IT/ICT, building smart cities might not make cities sufficiently (resources) efficient to reach urban sustainability. Instead, it may even bring additional challenges for cities to address. The examination could be useful when considering cities' crucial role in the sustainable use of resources (van der Heijden 2018), and the global pursuit for advanced technologies. For that purpose, the chapter examines Israel, a country in a state of 'hyper-technologisation' undergoing

56 *Ira Shefer*

intensive development while faced with acute environmental problems and climate challenges.[2]

Methodology

The chapter reviewed the literature of smart cities and urban sustainability together with data sets and indices concerning sustainability, innovation and advanced technologies in national and local levels in Israel. One index is the Smart and Sustainable Cities Index developed by the Interdisciplinary Center (IDC) Herzlia, Israel (IDC 2018). The IDC index identifies and assesses urban 'smartness' through several components such as using and sharing data among residents and municipal officials, information-based policy and govern-mentality, community-based services and resources and the application of innovation to tackle local challenges. Another index is the (Israeli) Start-Up Nation Finder (Start-Up Nation Finder 2019). In addition, the chapter applied data, reports and online information from governmental authorities such as Israel Innovation Authority (IIA),[3] from Israeli cities and environmental non-governmental organisations (ENGOs), and from publications in major Israeli newspapers.

The Israeli race for development and technology

A developed economy, Israel nevertheless presents growth of developing/in-transition economies: with a 2% annual population growth, the country is expected to grow from 9 million in 2019 to 15.6 million in 2065 (Central Bureau of Statistics 2018), in an area not bigger than 22,000 km[2]. Israel's population growth and high consumption patterns threaten sustained resources management and future well-being (Brachia 2019; Tal 2016). By 2040 Israel will need 1.5 million new residential units (52,000-67,000 units per year; Raz-Dror & Kost 2017), and many will be built in existing or new urban areas (the majority of Israelis already live in urban areas). Israel's growth patterns affect Israeli cities directly; they will need to continue and provide services and adequate urban environments. These kinds of growth patterns are, therefore, very challenging in terms of the need to reduce the use and enhance the efficiency of resources (Latouche 2018; Lehmann 2018).

However, Israeli decision-makers continuously prioritise private mobility over public transportation and provide insufficient housing planning that considers the sound use of resources. The use of renewable energies increases at a much slower rate than Israel's energy demands. Pollution of air, water and natural areas continues, and so are waste management problems and loss of green areas (Adam Teva V'Din 2019: 6–9). Urban development patterns ei-ther contribute to these problems or are directly affected by them.

In parallel, Israel is known as an entrepreneurial 'Start-up Nation'. Much of this reputation derives from the high rate of tech companies that work or have grown in Israel and broke into global markets (Noy & Givoni 2018).

Perceived as the engine that pushes the Israeli economy forward into the 21st century, the IT/ICT sector enjoys political and economic support as well as social legitimacy. The central government invests about 1.6 Billion NIS (approx. 400 million euros) in supporting this industry (Israel Innovation Authority 2017), and recently announced the establishment of a sustainability-focused innovation lab of approx. 3.5 million Euro (Israel Innovation Authority 2019). Much emphasis from governmental and private stakeholders is put on the transportation sector.

Cities in Israel: the race to get 'smart'

About 40% of Israel's population resides in 15 fiscally-independent cities (known as Forum 15, which now includes three additional cities). Most of them provide a high standard of living and address sustainability to some extent. Other cities often lack capacities and resources to invest in profound sustainability measures.

Entangled in the national enthusiasm to develop and adopt advanced technologies, Israeli cities of all types seem to have what is known as 'fear of missing out' when it comes to innovation. Cities see advanced technologies as economic gain, opportunity to increase national and international reputation, and a way to draw educated wealthy resident profile.[4]

Smart mobility draws special interest. To reduce transportation load and increase the efficient use of infrastructure, various cities experiment with car and bicycle sharing schemes (IDC 2018), intelligent, data-driven management of urban public and private transportation (Toch 2018), and autonomous and electric vehicles (e-vehicles) (Schmil 2019). Concerning energy, the focus is, by large, on managing and informing users (be it residents or officials) of energy demands and distribution; and on providing accurate information to enhance climate adaptation efforts (Toch 2018). Moreover, IT/ICT is increasingly used to inform the public over urban development plans and to improve accessibility to- and of- municipal services (IDC 2018; Toch 2018).

One example is Tel Aviv-Yafo, globally known for its innovation-focused sustainability efforts and Israel's economic centre (EU n.d.; IDC 2018). Formally, the city aims to improve the urban environment and urban services all the while addressing climate adaptation (Tel Aviv-Yafo 2017). Using IT/ICT plays a crucial role in Tel Aviv-Yafo, especially in improving urban transportation and providing information to residents (see also Hatuka & Zur 2019).

Eilat, a city in the southern-most periphery with 52,000 inhabitants, also positions itself as a smart and sustainable city. About 70% of Eilat's day-time electricity comes from renewable energies provided by a public-benefit corporation – the highest and almost single among Israeli cities. Equipped with the European Union (EU) grant, the city recently completed an energy efficiency demonstration in one neighbourhood using ICT. The city runs a pilot project with a private corporation that informs residents of the physical and financial

Figure 5.1 Tel Aviv-Yafo.
Source: photo by Shai Pal on Unsplash.

feasibility of photo-voltaic (PV) instalments on rooftops through an App, to encourage the use of renewable energies (City of Eilat 2018; IDC 2018).

The city of Kfar Saba positioned itself as a city committed to sustainability thanks to the novel waste management system and using natural solutions to urban wastewater and preserving green areas, among others. The political leadership aims now to reduce cars' emissions by engaging with a private corporation to increase the use of e-vehicles and related infrastructure in the city (City of Kfar Saba 2019). Taking part in an EU project, the city was also among the first in Israel to use smart energy meters in public buildings in the mid-2010s.

Other examples are of Israel's capital, Jerusalem, and the city of Netanya which use ICT to track water leaks in municipal infrastructure (New et al. 2017); an issue with high value to the arid Israeli climate. Netanya also experiments with car-sharing and smart solutions to parking.

Can smart solutions lead to more sustainable cities in Israel?

Feasibility of smart solutions in Israel

The examples above indicate how municipalities incorporate IT/ICT to better use resources in the urban sphere. However, this strategy does not necessarily equip them to tackle core problems attributed to resources in urban areas. Moreover, leaning on IT/ICT may even turn Israeli cities more vulnerable.

There seems to be no concrete evidence that Israeli cities managed to reduce their greenhouse gas (GHG) emissions, let alone through IT/ICT (see related studies such as Dor & Kissinger 2017; Goldrath, Ayalon & Shechter 2015; Stossel, Kissinger & Meir 2014). Forum 15 cities have voluntarily agreed to reduce their emissions as early as 2008 (Forum 15 n.d.) and in 2013 committed to gradually adopt the innovative Israeli green building standard in new projects. However, most cities did not pass beyond the initial stage of GHG emissions registry, and by 2018 only 10,500 residential units were built according to the Israeli green building standard, with 900 buildings under construction (MoEP 2018). Compared to the stocks of (non-green) private and governmental building prospects, building initiatives in cities and the resources they require are far from being sustainable.[5]

This reality also reflects Toch's (2018) review that, by large, Israeli cities tend to find solutions to narrow, specific problems rather than looking beyond their borders for broader perspectives and other potential solutions. Israeli cities' 'smart' actions miss the bigger picture necessary to deal with *core* features of sustainable resource use in – and by – cities: dramatic reduction of GHG emissions from the built environment and transportation, circulating or reducing – rather than increasing – resources, increasing renewable energy instalments and speeding-up energy efficiency, among others.

On the contrary, investing in pilots for urban IT/ICT mobility management does not address the acute need to reduce the use of cars (Koren 2019). Similarly, while some Israeli cities paved bicycle lanes to encourage low-carbon mobility, they are often used by e-bicycles and e-scooters (usually operated via apps), which demand energy and are used mostly by those which do not own a car. This kind of smart solutions seems not to have a significant impact on reducing carbon-intensive mobility in municipalities.

More concretely, Tel Aviv-Yafo is indeed a leading city in terms of experimentation in mobility, urban data use and even local energy generation, but at the same time, it does too little use of its political and economic power to make comprehensive demands for greener buildings and infrastructures (see discussions in Shefer 2019). Eilat provides residents with information on renewable energy feasibility, but it might not be a practical investment for a mid-income, peripheral city of its kind. Netanya promotes natural areas in the city and experiments with smart mobility, but as one of the fastest-growing cities in Israel, its new neighbourhoods, like many others in the country, will likely to continue to be car-dependent and with a small share of green buildings.

Further implications of technological solutions

Fast adoption of IT/ICT leads to new challenges which cities need to consider (Israeli cities included). An increasing share of studies claims that

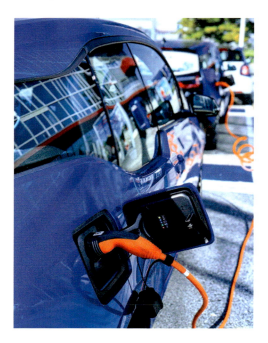

Figure 5.2 E-vehicle.
　　　　Source: photo by John Cameron by Unsplash.

relying on IT/ICT for social interactions may de-construct social systems as we know them (e.g. Calzada & Cobo 2015). This is especially intriguing for cities and their residents, who may face the consequences of changes in how people consume and produce goods and services in- and of- the city. Will Israeli cities need to invest more in easing fragmentations caused by these new communication and consumption habits (see also Hatuka & Zur 2019)?

Moreover, cities in and outside Israel may push for quick adoption of far-reaching innovations such as 5G and the *internet of things*. Especially the latter means, in practice, connecting every resident and her devices to larger governmental and corporate networks and data-sets, infrastructures and services. It raises questions on cities' abilities, roles and governmentality over sustainability: what resources should cities invest in engaging in these developments, and at what expense? Do cities gain or lose power against central governments and corporations? Moreover, as large data-sets and smart solutions may demand much energy and space, how will it affect cities' resources use and management (see also WBGU 2019)?

Furthermore, persistent reliance on IT/ICT for urban functions and services presents also risk and security issues from exogenous threats and system-failures (e.g. Coaffee & Wood 2006). These concerns are of special interest to Israel, given its complex national security. Would cities need to invest resources and change priorities against these threats? Would it affect their ability to promote and/or invest in the more sustainable use of resources?

Cities as instigators for change in Israel, and their limitations

Israel has a centralist political system which formally translates to less power for local authorities. Planning and implementing major infrastructures such as energy, transportation and water are by large steered and managed by the central government. In this regard, Israeli cities are not always able to find an independent voice and may not always have the capacity to lead or implement changes. Moreover, unlike many other developed economies, sustainable consumption and production and addressing climate change are at their initial stages in the Israeli public and private spheres (Tal 2017). Often, the extent of awareness of mayors and municipal officials determine the municipality's sustainability efforts. Lastly, as national security plays a prominent role in Israeli public debate, challenging IT/ICT solutions that address security may not be easily conveyed.

Despite these restraints and given that cities can be both sites for- and in-itiators of- change towards low-carbon activities (Bulkeley, Castán Broto & Edwards 2015), several steps may be at hand to Israeli cities, which could prove insightful to cities elsewhere.

Cities can lead to substantial normative and behavioural changes of resource-use through binding and non-binding measures. Despite the con-straints, Israeli cities do have room for autonomous actions in a variety of issue-areas such as planning, regulations and investments (Dery 2002). Herzlia and Eilat are now promoting the banning of disposable plastic utensils in beach areas through a mix of municipal regulations and dialogue with local stake-holders (e.g. Kuriel 2018). These actions may bring more concrete results in terms of sustainable use of resources in the municipality and set an example to residents and other cities, than experimenting with car-sharing and smart parking management. Likewise, Kfar Saba pioneered in using its regulatory power to demand the covering of 50% of new commercial/industrial roofs with greenery or solar/PV instalments (Levi 2014); as well as new initiatives for open roofing spaces with such instalments. Moreover, Israeli cities could take advantage of their political power by providing more stringent, sustainable patterns of commerce (see Tel Aviv-Yafo 2017 for the city's voluntary Green Label initiative). Despite the limitations of these steps, they nevertheless show how legal and political instruments could lead to profound behavioural changes within city boundaries.

Cities can challenge central planning and policies, even in centralised sys-tems as in Israel. Shmueli, Feitelson, Furst and Hann (2015) showed how planning schemes at Israeli local authorities altered and shaped central level initiatives. In 2018, Haifa, the capital of the northern metropolitan area (ap-prox. one million residents), presented a plan to transform the Haifa Bay's petrochemical complex to a mixed-used area of housing and (clean) industries. The plan, drafted in cooperation with central agencies, is novel in two ways: the will to confront influential stakeholders such as the fossil fuels industry and the vision to design a large area according to its ecological (water-based) characteristics rather than override them. The plan embeds balanced development vis-à-vis climate adaptation and dramatic reduction of GHG emissions (Levi 2019).

A similar novelty can be seen in Tel Aviv-Yafo's plan to incorporate Combined Cooling, Heat and Power (CCHP) instalments in new neighbourhoods.[6] Disseminating and amplifying these efforts may have a more significant impact on sustainable use of resources in Israeli cities than small scale initiatives such as smart meters. In addition, cities may benefit from trends in European cities (e.g. in Germany) which prefer density and conversion of existing building stocks to alternative uses to reach more efficient and lean use of resources (Reißmann & Buchert 2018).

Conclusions

This chapter questioned the often-too-rapid adoption of advanced technologies to reach urban sustainability. While more data and research are needed to more comprehensively analyse Israeli cities, the initial analysis in this chapter suggests that smart cities in Israel, at the way they currently operate, are not serving the function of reaching sustainability. Moreover, they may even enhance this outcome. To avoid any doubt, the chapter does not reject IT/ICT integration in urban systems. Instead, it suggests that adopting and experimenting with technology should not be the goal but rather supplementary to broader social and political priorities to reach sustainable patterns of social and economic urban living (also WBGU 2019).

As in Israel, IT/ICT is the holy grail for many global powers such as China, India, Japan and Germany at national and local levels alike (e.g. Höffken & Limmer 2019). Racing into innovation, cities in these and other countries run the risk of ignoring or delaying treatment of main carbon-intensive practices as well as risking vulnerability to exogenous ICT-related shocks. Uncertainty over issues that derive from smart solutions for resources at the urban sphere such as governmentality and legitimacy is growing, as well as concerning changes in dependency and authority. Cities will need to address these complexities vis-à-vis demands for urban well-being. City authorities will benefit from considering the advantages and disadvantages that IT/ICT innovation brings into these complex systems before they hastily adopt innovation for the sake of being progressive or obtaining short-term political and economic gains.

Sustainability requires profound planning and implementation that removes or at least dramatically reduces, carbon-intensive socio-economic activities. Utilising existing regulatory and legal mechanisms, forming coalitions to resist (external) bad planning and lobbying higher political levels may speed-up reaching this goal. This is particularly, but not solely, true for cities that demand fast-paced development and need to deal with large stocks of resource use and management as in Israel.

Transformation towards sustainable patterns of urban living does not require radical changes of rules and values; but instead changes in *how* and *when*, and perhaps with *who*, to use them. It is certainly not an easy task, especially for cities in centralised systems as in Israel; and with growing needs that require fast solutions to the challenges of urban development. Nevertheless, it might be the smarter choice.

Notes

1 'Smart cities' is often mixed with other concepts such as sustainable cities or eco-cities (de Jong et al. 2015).
2 All data related to Israel excludes the Palestinian Authority and Gaza Strip.
3 Previously Israel Chief Scientist, this governmental agency assesses, promotes and finances IT/ICT and innovation related to Israel. The change of title reflects the economic and political significance of this industry in Israeli eyes.
4 See, for example, www.nytimes.com/2013/04/14/education/edlife/inside-the-technion-israels–premier-technological-institute-and-cornells-global-partner.html; and www.haifaup.co.il (accessed 31 July 2019).
5 In March 2020 Israel's National Planning Authority approved a gradual, mandatory implementation of the Israeli green building standards as of mid-2021. However, it is too early at this point to assess the impacts on urban planning and sustainability policies in Israeli cities.
6 See www.tel-aviv.gov.il/About/Pages/energy.aspx (accessed 31 July 2019).

References

Adam Teva V'Din. (2019). Under pressure report: the 2019 elections and challenges for the next government (in Hebrew). Tel Aviv-Yafo.

Ahvenniemi, H., Huovila, A., Pinto-Seppä, I., and Airaksinen, M. (2017). What are the differences between sustainable and smart cities? *Cities*, *60*, 234–245. https://doi.org/10.1016/j.cities.2016.09.009.

Batty, M., Axhausen, K. W., Giannotti, F., Pozdnoukhov, A., Bazzani, A., Wachowicz, M., and Portugali, Y. (2012). Smart cities of the future. *European Physical Journal: Special Topics*, *214*(1), 481–518. https://doi.org/10.1140/epjst/e2012-01703-3.

Brachia, V. (2019). The problem is not population growth in Israel – but over consumption (In Hebrew). *The Marker*. Retrieved from www.themarker.com/dynamo/.premium-1.6940963.

Bulkeley, H., Castán Broto, V. and Edwards, G. (2015). *An urban politics of climate change: experimentation and the governing of socio-technical transitions*. Routledge.

Calzada, I. and Cobo, C. (2015). Unplugging: deconstructing the smart city. *Journal of Urban Technology*, *22*(1), 23–43. https://doi.org/10.1080/10630732.2014.971535.

Central Bureau of Statistics. (2018). Israel's population predictions (in Hebrew). Retrieved 24 May 2019, from www.cbs.gov.il/he/publications/Pages/2019/תחזיות-אוכלוסיית-ישראל.aspx.

City of Eilat. (2018). Eilat on the path to energy independence (in Hebrew). Retrieved 28 May 2019, from www.eilat.muni.il/?CategoryID=0&ArticleID=3680.

City of Kfar Saba. (2019). Kfar Saba opens the electric car era (in Hebrew). Retrieved 31 July 2019, from www.kfar-saba.muni.il/?CategoryID=255&ArticleID=11836.

Coaffee, J. and Wood, D. M. (2006). Security is coming home: rethinking scale and constructing resilience in the global urban response to terrorist risk. *International Relations*, *20*(4), 503–517. https://doi.org/10.1177/0047117806069416.

de Jong, M., Joss, S., Schraven, D., Zhan, C., and Weijnen, M. (2015). Sustainable–smart–resilient–low carbon–eco–knowledge cities; making sense of a multitude of concepts promoting sustainable urbanization. *Journal of Cleaner Production*, *109*, 25–38. https://doi.org/10.1016/j.jclepro.2015.02.004.

Dery, D. (2002). Fuzzy control. *Journal of Public Administration Research and Theory*, *12*(2), 191–216.

Dor, A. and Kissinger, M. (2017). A multi-year, multi-scale analysis of urban sustainability. *Environmental Impact Assessment Review*, *62*, 115–121. https://doi.org/10.1016/j.eiar.2016.05.004.

EU. (n.d.). European Capital of Innovation (iCapital) 2017. Retrieved 4 July 2019, from European Commission website: https://ec.europa.eu/info/research-and-innovation/funding/funding-opportunities/prizes/icapital/icapital2017_en.

Forum 15. (n.d.). Signs for clean air! (in Hebrew). Retrieved 6 July 2019, from www.forum15.org.il/נקי-אוויר-על-חתום-15-ה-ה-פורום.

Goldrath, T., Ayalon, O., and Shechter, M. (2015). A combined sustainability index for electricity efficiency measures. *Energy Policy*, *86*, 574–584. https://doi.org/10.1016/j.enpol.2015.08.013.

Hatuka, T. and Zur, H. (2019). *Who is the 'smart' resident in the digital age? The varied profiles of users and non-users in the contemporary city*. Urban Studies, 004209801983569. https://doi.org/10.1177/0042098019835690.

Höffken, J. I. and Limmer, A. (2019). *Smart and eco-cities in India and China*. Local Environment, 1–16. https://doi.org/10.1080/13549839.2019.1628730.

IDC. (2018). The IDC index for smart and sustainable cities (in Hebrew). Retrieved 24 May 2019, from Interdisciplinary Center Herzliya (IDC) website: https://smartcities.co.il/.

Israel Innovation Authority. (2017). *Innovation in Israel in 2017 (in Hebrew)*. Jerusalem.

Israel Innovation Authority. (2019). New environmental protection and sustainability innovation lab. Retrieved 24 May 2019, from https://innovationisrael.org.il/en/news/new-environmental-protection-and-sustainability-innovation-lab.

Kitchin, R. (2014). The real-time city? Big data and smart urbanism. *GeoJournal*, *79*(1), 1–14. https://doi.org/10.1007/s10708-013-9516-8.

Koren, O. (2019). 'Today's babies will not drive anymore' (in Hebrew). *The Marker*. Retrieved from www.themarker.com/dynamo/cars/.premium-1.7579695.

Kuriel, I. (2018). The first municipality in Israel with no plastic (in Hebrew). *Ynet*. Retrieved from www.ynet.co.il/articles/0,7340,L-5078202,00.html?fbclid=IwAR1vGTWvZC3noY6a_lRcx2eRR1Aj1ZRKGvDv7XrsduU_S-d-vgmA7vsLffg.

Latouche, S. (2018). The path to degrowth for a sustainable society. In H. Lehmann (Ed.), *Factor X: challenges, implementation strategies and examples for a sustainable use of natural resources* (pp. 277–284). Springer International Publishing.

Lehmann, H. (Ed.). (2018). *Factor X: challenges, implementation strategies and examples for a sustainable use of natural resources*. Springer International Publishing. https://doi.org/10.1007/978-3-319-50079-9.

Levi, D. (2014). Do you want a building permit? You will need to grow a garden on the roof (in Hebrew). *Calcalist*. Retrieved from www.calcalist.co.il/real_estate/articles/0,7340,L-3622880,00.html.

Levi, D. (2019). Strategic plan for Haifa Bay: up to 100,000 residential units instead of refinaries (in Hebrew). *Calcalist*. Retrieved from www.calcalist.co.il/real_estate/articles/0,7340,L-3758298,00.html.

MoEP. (2018). Green building reserves in Israel 2018 (in Hebrew). Retrieved from www.sviva.gov.il/subjectsEnv/GreenBuilding/Pages/greenconstructionisrael.aspx#GovXParagraphTitle2.

New, J., Castro, D., and Beckwith, M. (2017). How national governments can help smart cities succeed. *The Information Technology & Innovation Foundation*. Retrieved from https://itif.org/publications/2017/10/30/how-national-governments-can-help-smart-cities-succeed%0Awww2.datainnovation.org/2017-national-governments-smart-cities.pdf.

Noy, K. and Givoni, M. (2018). Is 'smart mobility' sustainable? Examining the views and beliefs of transport's technological entrepreneurs. *Sustainability*, *10*(2), 422. https://doi.org/10.3390/su10020422.

Raz-Dror, O. and Kost, N. (2017). The Strategic Plan for Housing to 2017–2024 (in Hebrew). Retrieved from economy.pmo.gov.il/councilactivity/housing/documents/strategy050717.pdf.

Reißmann, D. and Buchert, M. (2018). Saving natural resources through conversion and constructional densification in urban areas: ecological potentials and limits. In H. Lehmann (Ed.), *Factor X: challenges, implementation strategies and examples for a sustainable use of natural resources* (pp. 263–276). Springer International Publishing.

Schmil, D. (2019). 32 Israeli cities seek gov't support for electric car charging points (in Hebrew). *Globes*. Retrieved from https://en.globes.co.il/en/article-32-cities-seek-govt-support-for-electric-car-charging-points-1001278801.

Shefer, I. (2019). Policy transfer in city-to-city cooperation: implications for urban climate governance learning. *Journal of Environmental Policy & Planning*, *21*(1), 61–75. https://doi.org/10.1080/1523908X.2018.1562668.

Shmueli, D., Feitelson, E., Furst, B., and Hann, I. (2015). Scale and scope of environmental planning transformations: the Israeli case. *Planning Theory and Practice*, *16*(3), 336–362. https://doi.org/10.1080/14649357.2015.1054419.

Start-Up Nation Finder. (2019). Retrieved 21 July 2019 from https://finder.startupnationcentral.org/.

Stossel, Z., Kissinger, M., and Meir, A. (2014). A multi-spatial scale approach to urban sustainability – An illustration of the domestic and global hinterlands of the city of Beer-Sheva. *Land Use Policy*, *41*, 498–505. https://doi.org/10.1016/j.landusepol.2014.03.013.

Tal, A. (2016). *The land is full: addressing overpopulation in Israel*. New Haven, CT: Yale University Press.

Tal, A. (2017). Will we always have Paris? Israel's tepid climate change strategy. *Israel Journal of Foreign Affairs*, *10*(3), 405–421. https://doi.org/10.1080/23739770.2016.1265821.

Tel Aviv-Yafo. (2017). The strategic plan for Tel Aviv-Yafo: the city vision. Retrieved from Tel Aviv-Yafo website: www.tel-aviv.gov.il/Residents/Development/Pages/strategicnew.aspx.

Toch, E. (2018). Smart city technologies in Israel: a review of cutting-edge technologies and innovation hubs (No. IDB-DP-00591). Retrieved from https://publications.iadb.org/en/smart-city-technologies-israel-review-cutting-edge-technologies-and-innovation-hubs.

van der Heijden, J. (2018). City and subnational governance: high ambitions, innovative instruments and polycentric collaborations? In A. Jordan, D. Huitema, H. van Asselt and J. Forster (Eds.), *Governing climate change: polycentricity in action?* (pp. 81–96). Cambridge University Press.

WBGU. (2019). Towards our common digital future (summary). Retrieved from https://issuu.com/wbgu/docs/wbgu_hgd2019_s?e=37591641/69073504.

Yigitcanlar, T. and Kamruzzaman, M. (2018). Does smart city policy lead to sustainability of cities? *Land Use Policy*, *73*, 49–58. https://doi.org/10.1016/j.landusepol.2018.01.034.

6 Sustainable development as the ultimate target of adopting a nexus approach to resources management

Serena Caucci, Lulu Zhang, Karla Locher-Krause, and Stephan Hülsmann

Introduction and aim

Resource productivity and sustainable development: Challenges and limitations

The United Nations' Agenda for Sustainable Development underlines 17 Sustainable Development Goals (SDGs) with 169 targets. The lack of holistic knowledge on the interdependency between the SDGs and an interpretation of cause-and-effect relationships that connect the SDGs enormously challenges national policymakers that must implement that are in charge of implementing the 2030 agenda at the national level and achieving the goals across environmental, economic, and social dimensions (Griggs et al. 2017; Dörgo et al. 2018). The international scientific community started to measure the trade-offs and synergies between SDGs. For this exercise, it proved helpful to make use of the concept of the water–energy–food (WEF) nexus, which showed that when addressing challenges like water, energy and food security, integrated approaches to resources management across these sectors should be used and dependent resources considered equally (Hoff 2011). The WEF nexus concept is now starting to be implemented and is recognised as an essential tool for achieving and monitoring progress towards SDGs (Bleischwitz et al. 2018; Hülsmann & Ardakanian 2018).

Nevertheless, the WEF is still challenged by a few limitations, in particular concerning comprehensive coverage of the interlinkages between sectors and resources (Albrecht et al. 2018). Besides, nexus assessments are only starting to address all dimensions of sustainability, including the environmental aspect, one primary reason being that ecosystem services (WEF-E) are hardly reflected in nexus tools (Hülsmann et al. 2019). This chapter aims to highlight the necessity of including innovative tools in the assessment of the WEF nexus approach to adopt resources management to achieve Sustainable development. To effectively counteract the potential trade-offs across SDGs, holistic ecosystem management and sustainable practices are required to increase resource productivity.

Sector-oriented resource management often neglects the potential impacts (trade-offs and synergies) on other resources or sectors, causing less resource use efficiency and productivity, thus, increasing the risk of unsustainability (Zhang & Schwärzel 2017a). Exemplification result of this management is the food production sector and its supply that became the lead consumer of nearly 30% of the total global energy and 70% of freshwater resources (FAO 2011). A shift from single-sector/resource-focused management to nexus-oriented resource management is thus a more effective way to deal with the complexity of interactions across sectors, resources, and SDGs under a changing global context (Zhang & Schwärzel 2017b; Nilsson et al. 2018).

Food (SDG2) and water (SDG6) are closely interlinked and to achieving higher food production to guarantee food security for an ever-growing world population significantly depends on more water (in sufficient quality), and land or much higher productivity is required. For productions of quality food, fertile soils and clean water are necessary. However, boosting crop yields in food production implies an intensification of agricultural practices which typically goes along with land and water degradation. Contemporarily, the agriculture produce, biomass and agricultural wastes are potentially a source of renewable energy that creates competition between food (SDG2) and energy (SDG7) security over the same land and water resources. Moreover, using agricultural waste for energy instead of implementing composting and mulching may also decrease soil fertility in the long term.

Boosting the production of food and energy crops, even if primarily achieved by increased efficiency (thus without extending agricultural areas at the expense of natural forests and other terrestrial ecosystems) may compromise ecosystem services supply if not achieved sustainably. It may also compromise the social dimension of sustainability, for example, if working conditions and social standards in the agriculture sector are poor. The intrinsic trade-off briefly outlined for the WEF nexus clearly shows that resource productivity/efficiency only partially represents sustainability which should instead be understood in a broader sense.

WEF-E: Mitigating trade-offs between resource productivity and sustainable resource management

Demand for natural resources utilisation has reached dangerous limits threatening ecosystem functions together with the services that they provide to support essential human well-being (Foley et al. 2011). Evidence from natural system modifications shows that farmlands dominate 38% of the global surface and these sectors (energy and agriculture) are likely to remain dominant drivers of change (Zabel et al. 2019). This increased demand and competition for resources together with the current degradation of land and water systems make clear the need for action at different levels to mitigate natural resources depletion. Understanding how the ongoing land-use change and socio-economic transitions can be turned from a challenge into an opportunity is critical to achieve sustainable development. As highlighted by the United Nations during the recent High-Level Policy Forum (HLPF 2018), such a challenge though needs to be tackled if Sustainable development goals (SDGs) have to be implemented. The reason of the disparities between the social demand and the total capacity of ecosystems to provide goods lies in (1) the so far adopted non-holistic natural resource management and in (2) missing measurable involvement of the society both in terms of participation and benefits (Seppelt et al. 2011; Mach et al. 2015; Hülsmann et al. 2019).

The ecosystem services approach addresses the interconnection between ecosystem services supply and societal demands, providing critical information to disentangle the interconnection between sections (nexus assessments). Furthermore, the approach seeks for a better understanding of the components and functions of socioecological systems, by separating the multiple services and benefits from ecosystems taking into consideration trade-offs and synergies within them (Carpenter & Folke 2006; Rockström et al. 2009; Cord et al. 2017). The information contained in the trade-off and synergies put on the value the importance of ecosystem services for human well-being. Such information are obviously essential for integrated resources management and central element in nexus assessments (for example, De Strasser et al. 2016; Liu et al. 2017). The integration of ecosystem service would thus turn the WEF nexus into a WEF-E nexus (Carmona Moreno et al. 2018).

However, thus far, this has hardly been practised or implemented (Hülsmann et al. 2019). In this context, considerations of the spatial and temporal scale are crucial since ecosystem functions and processes are scale-dependent (Grêt-Regamey et al. 2014; Raudsepp-Hearne & Peterson 2016).

The need to integrate ecosystem service modelling

As mentioned above, on a conceptual level, it is well established that ecosystem services need to be included in nexus assessments. One primary reason why this has thus far not and if, only rudimentarily, established, is that ecosystem services are not adequately reflected in nexus tools. In general, considering several interconnected resources and sectors and the respective processes, fluxes, and actors involved requires making use of appropriate nexus tools for their assessments. Currently, a high and increasing number of tools is available and in use. Such tools include newly designed models addressing the WEF nexus (Kaddoura & El Khatib 2017) as well as the water–energy nexus (Dai et al. 2018) or established tools and concepts which are reframed in nexus context (e.g. life cycle assessment tools). Model frameworks coupling multiple sector-oriented models for nexus assessments are also part of nexus tools.

Nevertheless, the ecosystem perspective was primarily ignored (Howells et al. 2013). Likewise, Albrecht et al. (2018) concluded from an in-depth analysis of current nexus models that all of them fail to consider critical interlinkages, ecosystem services being among the neglected aspects. This fact is of relevance because the supply of one or more ecosystem services could underpin the impact on several SDGs and sectors.

70   *Serena Caucci et al.*

However, some recent case studies and assessments do explicitly account for (specific) ecosystem services within nexus assessments (Martinez-Hernandez et al. 2017; Karabulut et al. 2018; Hanes et al. 2018) based on newly developed tools. At least conceptually, potential pathways on how to better integrate ecosystem services into nexus tools have been proposed (Hülsmann et al. 2019). The main argument for doing that is the need to cover all aspects of sustainability (social, economic and environmental) and address the interconnected SDGs in a comprehensive manner. As argued before (Hettiarachchi & Ardakanian 2016; Hülsmann & Ardakanian 2018; Liu et al. 2018), adopting a nexus approach will be instrumental in achieving SDGs. Any effort towards integrative approaches (e.g. WEF nexus) should be appreciated and will facilitate the unlocking of synergies and minimising trade-offs, thus increasing resource productivity. Ultimately, however, as long as environmental aspects are largely ignored, sustainability is not 'complete' and respective SDGs, e.g. SDG 13 (climate action), SDG 14 (life below water) and SDG 15 (life on land) not adequately addressed. Therefore, the WEF nexus should be extended to a WEFE nexus. With regard to nexus tools, this implies making use of a wide range of models, combine and couple them as required, considering the ecosystem perspective. The choice of the most appropriate (suite of) model(s) might be facilitated by respective model platforms providing detailed information about available tools (Mannschatz et al. 2016).

The need to integrate participatory approaches

Another sustainability dimension typically neglected in nexus assessments is the social one. Addressing it requires adopting a participatory approach (Caucci & Hettiarachchi 2017; Benavides et al. 2019). Linking the complexity of participatory processes to their outcomes to the societal impact of resource management is thus fundamental when targeting Sustainable Development.

Implementation of WEF nexus and the ecosystem services approach can also be fostered by governance practices and participation which are used across different scales when resource management is applied. The participatory components toward Nexus oriented solutions base their effectiveness on the tight interaction between societal stakeholders and resource evidence-based decisions. If properly performed, the outcome of this approach is more socially robust management, actionable knowledge, or sustainable actions (Wiek et al. 2012; de Jong et al. 2016).

Unfortunately, while most nexus research-oriented studies call for theoretic stakeholder participation, empirical evidence on co-creation of action-oriented measures are often missing. The lack of action-oriented measures is aften due to little guidance on how to integrate this tool into the nexus assessment when stakeholders and their role has to be defined. Roidt and Avellán (2019) showed how limited resource management has been when stakeholders are not considered fully into the nexus assessment. The mere biophysical scale of resource management (tools) is insufficient to capture interests and social relations of actors that are not directly confined in the physical boundaries defined by the studies, and thus a multi-scalar approach should be used (Benavides et al. 2019). Moreover, natural resources management intrinsically own a high level of 'wickedness' that could slow down the deployment of policies addressing resource management in a Nexus perspective. Governance participatory approaches are thus a valuable instrument to target Sustainable Development (Kirschke et al. 2018). The explicit representation of this approach in nexus tools could reduce the risk of overlooking barriers impacting the definition of nexus oriented-solutions that instead aim at balancing resource productivity and natural resource management.

Reconsidering the WEF nexus approach under other lenses

Exemplification of concepts in case studies often helps in highlighting good practices and supports the identification of shortcomings (UNU-FLORES 2016; Hettiarachchi et al. 2019). As environmental resources such as water, soil, and waste become increasingly exposed to the impacts of climate change and socio-economic pressure, nexus assessment must go beyond outdated resource management approaches that ignore this interdependence. With the below examples, we intend thus to analyse the helpfulness of the nexus approach toward Sustainable Development. At the same time, criticism to the approach as well as a suggestion for its implementation via the integration of newer nexus tools will be provided.

Case study 1

This case study examines water reuse in agriculture and multipurpose sustainable wastewater management as an application of the nexus approach. The content is based on 'Safe Use of Wastewater in Agriculture: Good Practice Examples' (UNU-FLORES 2016).

Water reuse and wastewater management have a direct impact on the availability and quality of resources such as water and soil when reused in agriculture. Wastewater used in irrigation not only addresses the water demand in water-stressed areas but also helps us 'recycle' the nutrients in it. Sustainable solutions that consider interdependencies when water is managed and reused are exemplified in two projects namely SludgeTec (Resource recovery from wastewater in the Americas – Assessing the Water-Soil-Waste Nexus) and SUWA (Safe Use of Wastewater in Agriculture). The two projects employ a Nexus Approach that focus on understanding resource flows across different scales. The Nexus-assessment performed in the project includes a participatory approach for sustainable decision-oriented options aiming at buffering water scarcity and poor wastewater management. Using this methodology, 16 case studies in the Global South were analysed and results revealed the potential benefits and implications for other sectors and resources, and related SDGs such as health (SDG 3) and food production (SDG 2), thus maximising the co-benefits. Among the sixteen cases analysed, the challenges that the countries had to face at the interface of water, soil, and waste were not unique. The problem in most of the case studies was not the lack of knowledge and resource but rather poor data management, incoherent policy definition for sustainable resource management and the lack of holistic governance enforcement.

In detail, two of the case studies (Mexico and Guatemala) were analysed via multi-method research that combines the baseline description of the case, the definition of the desired target state (sustainable use and management of wastewater) and pathways towards their achievement while applying the nexus approach (UNU-FLORES 2016). The assessment had a transdisciplinary profile, and it has integrated sustainability assessment, social network analysis and wickedness analysis. The application of this approach yielded orientations for action much beyond technical implementation and definition of financial models (Hettiarachchi et al. 2018), and it instead, recommended actions toward a better information collection system and improved information sharing among actors for better decision making. The recommendations provided after the study allowed local stakeholders to take up the ownership of their solution paths and contributed to the resolution of technical issues. Innovative solutions to overcome the non-sustainable water uses have been raised by the participatory process and a citizen observatory for the community–based monitoring system was voted as the best solution in Guatemala, while an open neighbourhood discussion forum and digital media campaign were established by the stakeholders in Mexico.

These two cases clearly show the benefits of an integrated approach both in terms of increased resource efficiency and acceptance of changes. However, the impact of wastewater irrigation practices on the groundwater ecosystem or the impact of wastewater management on public health has been not fully considered. This mainly related to the siloed thinking approach used to identify trade-off and synergies or by the lack of integration of participatory approaches when management practices of resources were enforced. In the future, changes toward a more holistic decision making and management strategies for implementation measures should take place considering the ecosystem services involved in such changes. The SUWA initiative and SludgeTec projects, despite the limitation on ecosystem service inclusion, do provide recommendations on the sustainably accepted solution in terms of management. The projects are also highlighting the need of newer cooperation among ministerial sectors that would include more holistic management of resources thus capitalising on the synergies that these resources could provide to the society in the long run (Caucci & Hettiarachchi 2017). SludgeTec project also indicates co-participatory accepted solutions as a node for a sustainable development and resulting from a multi-disciplinary framework assessment. These solutions range between technical accepted solution, social inclusion and data availability improvement that should be addressed via publicly available databases and platforms.

Case study II

This case study examines integrated reservoir management in the Durance-Verdon basin, France, as an application of a WEF nexus approach. The content is based on Hülsmann, Rinke, Paul and Diez Santos (in press).

Reservoirs increasingly serve multiple uses and provide diverse types of ecosystem services: water is needed for irrigation for crop production, for domestic and industrial use, aquaculture, energy production and storage, ecosystem services, recreation and navigation. Also, storage capacity is required for flood control and drought management. All of these concurring and partly competing water uses need to be considered to maximise co-benefits, minimise trade-offs and deliver services in a synergetic way. This balancing needs to take the temporal variability of water demands as well as site-specific priorities into account. Reservoir management, therefore, requires adopting a nexus approach. Considering the multiple uses of multipurpose hydropower reservoirs in a comprehensive way was the aim of an initiative by Électricité de France (EDF) and the World Water Council (WWC). The SHARE concept (Branche 2017) was proposed as a framework to address the issue of competing for water uses in reservoirs where hydropower is one of them. In this context, SHARE stands for Sustainability approach for all users, Higher efficiency and equity among all sectors, Adaptability for all solutions, River basin perspective for all and Engaging all stakeholders, issues which are all considered essential for a nexus approach.

Among the twelve case studies analysed, the Durance-Verdon basin in France was one of the few indeed multifunctional cases covering virtually all possible uses, demonstrating clear co-benefits and synergies. Drinking water provision, irrigation and tourism were important uses creating benefits, including jobs in the region. Via integrated management water demand by irrigation was decreased by 30%, indicating that governance structures and implemented management schemes, including tariff systems and economic incentives, effectively supported resource use efficiency. Overall, it was shown that the non-power benefits were considerably higher than hydropower benefits alone.

The case of a multipurpose reservoir in the Durance-Verdon basin clearly shows the benefits of integrated management in terms of increased resource efficiency. A neglected aspect was, however, the impacts on ecosystems, mainly related to the disruptive effects of dams. The impact on the ecosystem is a major argument against dams in general, and thus the risk of damaging the ecosystem must be addressed during the planning phase. Once established, the barrier effect can only partly be compensated. However, other adverse effects, e.g. alterations in the thermal regime of the river system can be minimised by managing the discharge from several depth horizons if variable outlets are available (Weber et al. 2017). The SHARE initiative, despite showing case-specific decision on how to allocate water between the different uses and users, provides valuable indications on suitable institutional arrangements to improve the sustainability of water resource management, e.g. basin committees. The case studies also indicate suitable management tools, ranging from planning documents and guidelines to tariff systems and data sharing policies and platforms.

The case studies outlined above, albeit targeting quite different systems, clearly demonstrate the benefits of integrated resources management in terms of increased resource use efficiency. They also provide evidence on the importance of stakeholder involvement and a governance dimension of the nexus (Hettiarachchi et al. 2018). Similar to the conclusion drawn by Hülsmann et al. (2019), the ecosystem perspective was, however, neglected in both cases. Concerning wastewater irrigation, environmental impacts, e.g. on groundwater quality (Caucci & Hettiarachchi 2018; Jampani et al. 2018) or health (Caucci & Meyer 2017) were thus far not fully considered. In the case of reservoir management, notwithstanding various benefits for several sectors, the environmental impacts were not considered in the assessment offered by Branche (2017).

Overall, the cases demonstrate that a cross-sectoral or Nexus Approach, such as WEF or the Water-Soil-Waste (WSW), enhances the synergies towards achieving the SDGs by improving the use-efficiency of natural resources, closing carbon and nutrient cycles and recycling waste as well as balancing the supply and demand of ecosystem services (Lal 2015). However, the success of the implementation largely depends on the coordination across sectors and society, in which a unified understanding of the interdependence of SDGs and shared benefits among users, stakeholders, and politicians must be reached (Zhang & Schwärzel 2017b; Benavides et al. 2019).

To this end, we need to focus on integrative approaches of different interlinking sectors which offer sustainable solutions and adaptive strategies to ensure food, energy and water supply for the future, which was the fundamental motivation behind the nexus concept (Hoff 2011). Here, we argue that too often the focus of nexus assessments was on increasing resource use efficiency, neglecting the environmental and social dimensions and the inherent trade-offs. Sustainable Development indeed calls for a nexus approach to resources management that, while certainly aiming at increased productivity, considers all dimensions of sustainability at the level considered suitable (local, regional, and global) for the nexus case.

Conclusions

The need to consider the social and environmental dimensions in the implementation of the nexus approach for sustainable development

A vital component of achieving solutions is to define the roots of the problems and deal with them instead of mitigating their consequences (Husemann et al. 2013). For this, improved monitoring, modelling, and projecting technologies are essential to facilitate a common understanding of the problem and provide decision-makers and stakeholders with more precise and accurate information regarding trade-offs on ecosystem services (Zhang & Schwärzel 2017b; Benavides et al. 2019). The aspect of achieving a common understanding is indeed essential to ensure the success of the implementation of management initiatives. Identifying the appropriate mix of stakeholders is one crucial step which can be aided by social network analysis (Kurian et al. 2018; Avellán et al. 2019).

Co-creation and sharing of knowledge can be achieved using various tools to ensure stakeholders participation, to first to define the nexus problem and later to identify potential sustainable solutions. The first step can, for example, be supported by workshops, round tables and serious thematic games (Johnson & Karlberg 2017; Mochizuki et al. 2018; Benavides et al. 2019), the second step may involve participatory modelling (Smajgl 2018). Tools for both steps should ideally consider all dimensions of sustainability. The use of tools and co-participatory approaches gives confidence that nexus approaches would be a better way for developing adaptive solutions and measures for resource management, ultimately, ensuring sustainable development.

Recommendations

This chapter aims to highlight the necessity of including innovative tools in the assessment of the WEF nexus approach to adopt resources management to achieve Sustainable development. To effectively counteract the potential trade-offs across SDGs, holistic ecosystem management and sustainable practices are required to increase resource productivity. However, the ecosystem perspective, essential for sustainable resources management, has been identified as a missing element within earlier nexus assessments. Integrating the environmental (i.e. ecosystem services) and social dimensions (i.e. participatory approaches) are crucial in WEF assessments and an improvement of Nexus tools implemented. This would guarantee both the impact of resource management in the society and the social and political dimensions of water, energy, and food. Participatory methods to engage researchers, practitioners, local decision-makers, and communities provide knowledge-sharing activities that contribute to the co-production of solutions. Participatory methods are also able to measure socio-political context for resources efficiency management and ultimately when ecosystem services will be fully considered sustainable development.

Abbreviations

EDF	Électricité de France Fluxes and of Resources
SDGs	Sustainable Development Goals
UNU-FLORES	United Nations University Institute for Integrated Management of Material
WEF	water–energy–food
WEF-E	water–energy–food–ecosystem
WWC	World Water Council

References

Albrecht, T. R., Crootof, A., Scott, C. A. (2018). The Water–Energy–Food Nexus: A Systematic Review of Methods for Nexus Assessment. *Environ Res Lett* 13, 43002. doi: 10.1088/1748-9326/aaa9c6.

Avellán, T. A., Hahn, A., Kirschke, S., Müller, A., Benavides, L., Caucci, S. (2019). *Towards Sustainable Wastewater Systems – Applying a Triangular Research Method in a Nexus View in Two Cases in Latin America.* Sustainability.

Benavides, L., Avellán, T., Caucci, S., et al. (2019). Assessing Sustainability of Wastewater Management Systems in a Multi-Scalar, Transdisciplinary Manner in Latin America. *Water* 11.

Bleischwitz, R., Spataru, C., VanDeveer, S. D., et al. (2018). Resource Nexus Perspectives towards the United Nations Sustainable Development Goals. *Nat Sustain* 1, 737–743. doi: 10.1038/s41893-018-0173-2.

Branche, E. (2017). The Multipurpose Water Uses of Hydropower Reservoir: The SHARE Concept. *Comptes Rendus Phys* 18, 469–478. doi: 10.1016/J.CRHY.2017.06.001.

Carmona Moreno, C., Dondeynaz, C., Biedler, M., et al. (2018). *Position Paper on Water, Energy, Food and Ecosystem (WEFE) Nexus and Sustainable Development Goals (SDGs).*

Carpenter, S. R., Folke, C. (2006). Ecology for Transformation. *Trends Ecol Evol* 21, 309–315. doi: 10.1016/J.TREE.2006.02.007.

Caucci, S., Berendonk, T. U. (2014). Environmental and Public Health Implication of Antibiotic Resistance Genes in Municipal Wastewaters. *Prävention und Gesundheitsförderung* 9, 175–179.

Caucci, S., Hettiarachchi, H. (2018). *The Nexus Approach and Safe Use of Wastewater in Agriculture: A Workshop on Policy and Implementation for Tunisia.* United Nations University Institute for Integrated Management of Material Fluxes and of Resources (UNU-FLORES), Dresden.

Caucci, S., Hettiarachchi, H. ed. (2017). Wastewater Irrigation in the Mezquital Valley, Mexico: *Solving a Century-Old Problem with the Nexus Approach 2017/03/15–17 Mezquital Valley.* United Nations University Institute for Integrated Management of Material Fluxes and of Resources (UNU-FLORES), Dresden.

Caucci, S., Meyer, K. (2017). Your Future Food Will be Grown with Waste Water. The Conversation.

Cord, A. F., Bartkowski, B., Beckmann, M., et al. (2017). Towards Systematic Analyses of Ecosystem Service Trade-offs and Synergies: Main Concepts, Methods and the Road Ahead. *Ecosyst Serv* 28, 264–272. doi: 10.1016/J.ECOSER.2017.07.012.

Dai, J., Wu, S., Han, G., et al. (2018). Water–Energy Nexus: A Review of Methods and Tools for Macro-assessment. *Appl Energy* 210, 393–408. doi: 10.1016/J.APENERGY.2017.08.243.

de Jong, M., Yu, C., Joss, S., et al. (2016). Eco City Development in China: Addressing the Policy Implementation Challenge. *J Clean Prod* 134, 31–41. doi: 10.1016/j.jclepro.2016.03.083.

De Strasser, L., Lipponen, A., Howells, M., et al. (2016). A Methodology to Assess the Water Energy Food Ecosystems Nexus in Transboundary River Basins. *Water* 8, doi: 10.3390/w8020059.

Dörgo, G., Sebestyén, V., Abonyi, J. (2018). Evaluating the Interconnectedness of the Sustainable Development Goals Based on the Causality Analysis of Sustainability Indicators. *Sustain* 10, doi: 10.3390/su10103766.

FAO (2011). Energy-Smart Food for People Climate. 66.

Foley, J. A., Ramankutty, N., Brauman, K. A., et al. (2011). Solutions for a Cultivated Planet. *Nature* 478, 337–342. doi: 10.1038/nature10452.

Grêt-Regamey, A., Rabe, S.-E., Crespo, R., et al. (2014). On the Importance of Non-linear Relationships between Landscape Patterns and the Sustainable Provision of Ecosystem Services. *Landsc Ecol* 29, 201–212. doi: 10.1007/s10980-013-9957-y.

Griggs, D., Nilsson, M., Stevance, A., McCollum, D. (2017). A Guide To SDG Interactions: From Science to Implementation. Paris.

Hanes, R. J., Gopalakrishnan, V., Bakshi, B. R. (2018). Including Nature in the Food-Energy-Water Nexus Can Improve Sustainability across Multiple Ecosystem Services. *Resour Conserv Recycl* 137, 214–228. doi: 10.1016/J.RESCONREC.2018.06.003.

Hettiarachchi, H., Ardakanian, R. (2016). Managing Water, Soil, and Waste in the Context of Global Change. In: Hettiarachchi, H., Ardakanian, R. (eds) *Environmental Resource Management and the Nexus Approach: Managing Water, Soil, and Waste in the Context of Global Change*. Springer International Publishing, Cham, pp 1–7.

Hettiarachchi, H., Caucci, S., Ardakanian, R. (2018). Safe Use of Wastewater in Agriculture: The Golden Example of Nexus Approach. In: Hettiarachchi, H., Ardakanian, R. (eds) *Safe Use of Wastewater in Agriculture: From Concept to Implementation*. Springer International Publishing, Cham, pp 1–11.

Hettiarachchi, H., Caucci, S., Schwärzel, K. eds (2019). *Organic Waste Composting through Nexus Thinking. Practices, Policies, and Trends*. Springer International Publishing (in press).

HLPF (2018). Report of the High-Level Political Forum on Sustainable Development Convened under the Auspices of the Economic and Social Council at its 2018 Session. E/HLPF/2018/7.

Hoff, H. (2011). Understanding the Nexus. In: *Understanding the Nexus. Background Paper for the Bonn2011 Conference: The Water, Energy and Food Security Nexus*. Stockholm Environment Institute, Stockholm.

Howells, M., Hermann, S., Welsch, M., et al. (2013). Integrated Analysis of Climate Change, Land-Use, Energy and Water Strategies. *Nat Clim Chang* 3, 621.

Hülsmann, S., Ardakanian, R. (2018). The Nexus Approach as Tool for Achieving SDGs: Trends and Needs. In: Hülsmann, S., Ardakanian, R. (eds) *Managing Water, Soil and Waste Resources to Achieve Sustainable Development Goals: Monitoring and Implementation of Integrated Resources Management*. Springer International Publishing, Cham, pp 1–9.

Hülsmann, S., Rinke, K., Paul, L., Diez Santos, C. In press. 'Storage Reservoir Management and Operation Including Complex Multiunit and Multipurpose Systems'. In *Springer Handbook of Water Management*, Bogardi, Janos (ed). Springer Berlin Heidelberg.

Hülsmann, S., Sušnik, J., Rinke, K., et al. (2019). Integrated Modelling and Management of Water Resources: The Ecosystem Perspective on the Nexus Approach. *Curr Opin Environ Sustain* 40, 14–20. doi: 10.1016/J.COSUST.2019.07.003.

Husemann, J., Espinosa-Gutiérrez, G., Tadesse, Y. B., et al. (2013). Towards Nexus Approach: Case Studies on Integrated Management of Water, Soil and Waste from China, Ethiopia, Iraq, Mexico, Serbia and South Asia. In: Hülsmann, S., Ito, M., Ardakanian, R. (eds) Proceedings of *International Kick-off Workshop 'Advancing a Nexus Approach to the Sustainable Management of Water, Soil and Waste.' United Nations University Institute for Integrated Management of Material Fluxes and of Resources (UNU-FLORES)*, Dresden, pp 120–142.

Jampani, M., Huelsmann, S., Liedl, R., et al. (2018). Spatio-temporal Distribution and Chemical Characterization of Groundwater Quality of a Wastewater Irrigated System: A Case Study. *Sci Total Environ* 636, 1089–1098. doi: 10.1016/J.SCITOTENV.2018.04.347.

Johnson, O. W., Karlberg, L. (2017). Co-exploring the Water–Energy–Food Nexus: Facilitating Dialogue through Participatory Scenario Building. *Front Environ Sci* 5, 24. doi: 10.3389/fenvs.2017.00024.

Kaddoura, S., El Khatib, S. (2017). Review of Water–Energy–Food Nexus Tools to Improve the Nexus Modelling Approach for Integrated Policy Making. *Environ Sci Policy* 77, 114–121. doi: 10.1016/j.envsci.2017.07.

Karabulut, A. A., Crenna, E., Sala, S., Udias, A. (2018). A Proposal for Integration of the Ecosystem–Water–Food–Land–Energy (EWFLE) Nexus Concept into Life Cycle Assessment: A Synthesis Matrix System for Food Security. *J Clean Prod* 172, 3874–3889. doi: 10.1016/J.JCLEPRO.2017.05.092.

Kirschke, S., Zhang, L., Meyer, K. (2018). Decoding the Wickedness of Resource Nexus Problems—Examples from Water-Soil Nexus Problems in China. *Resour.* 7.

Kurian, M., Portney, K. E., Rappold, G., et al. (2018). Governance of Water–energy–Food Nexus: A Social Network Analysis Approach to Understanding Agency *Behaviour*. In: Hülsmann, S., Ardakanian, R. (eds) *Managing Water, Soil and Waste Resources to Achieve Sustainable Development Goals: Monitoring and Implementation of Integrated Resources Management*. Springer International Publishing, Cham, pp 125–147.

Lal, R. (2015). The Nexus Approach to Managing Water, Soil and Waste under Changing Climate and Growing Demands on Natural Resources. In: Kurian, M., Ardakanian, R. (eds) *Governing the Nexus: Water, Soil and Waste Resources Considering Global Change*. Springer International Publishing, Cham, pp 39–60.

Liu, J., Mao, G., Hoekstra, A. Y., et al. (2018). Managing the Energy–Water–Food Nexus for Sustainable Development. *Appl Energy* 210, 377–381. doi: 10.1016/J.APENERGY.2017.10.064.

Liu, J., Yang, H., Cudennec, C., et al. (2017). Challenges in Operationalizing the Water–Energy–Food Nexus. *Hydrol Sci J* 62, 1714–1720. doi: 10.1080/02626667.2017.1353695.

Mach, M. E., Martone, R. G., Chan, K. M. A. (2015). Human Impacts and Ecosystem Services: Insufficient Research for Trade-off Evaluation. *Ecosyst Serv* 16, 112–120. doi: 10.1016/J.ECOSER.2015.10.018.

Mannschatz, T., Wolf, T., Hülsmann, S. (2016). Nexus Tools Platform: Web-Based Comparison of Modelling Tools for Analysis of Water-Soil-Waste Nexus. *Environ Model Softw* 76, 137–153. doi: 10.1016/J.ENVSOFT.2015.10.031.

Martinez-Hernandez, E., Leach, M., Yang, A. (2017). Understanding Water–Energy–Food and Ecosystem Interactions Using the Nexus Simulation Tool NexSym. *Appl Energy* 206, 1009–1021. doi: 10.1016/J.APENERGY.2017.09.022.

Mochizuki, J., Magnuszewski, P., Linnerooth-Bayer, J. (2018). Games for Aiding Stakeholder Deliberation on Nexus Policy Issues. In: Hülsmann, S., Ardakanian, R. (eds) *Managing Water, Soil and Waste Resources to Achieve Sustainable Development Goals: Monitoring and Implementation of Integrated Resources Management*. Springer International Publishing, Cham, pp 93–124.

Nilsson, M., Chisholm, E., Griggs, D., et al. (2018). Mapping Interactions between the Sustainable Development Goals: Lessons Learned and Ways Forward. *Sustain Sci* 13, 1489–1503. doi: 10.1007/s11625-018-0604-z.

Raudsepp-Hearne, C., Peterson, G. D. (2016). Scale and Ecosystem Services: How Do Observation, Management, and Analysis Shift with Scale? Lessons from Quebec. *Ecol Soc* 21, doi: 10.5751/ES-08605-210316.

Rockström, J., Steffen, W., Noone, K., et al. (2009). Planetary Boundaries: Exploring the Safe Operating Space for Humanity. *Ecol Soc* 14, 32. doi: 10.5751/ES-03180-140232.

Roidt, M., Avellán, T. (2019). Learning from Integrated Management Approaches to Implement the Nexus. *J Environ Manage* 237, 609–616. doi: 10.1016/J.JENVMAN.2019.02.106.

Seppelt, R., Dormann, C. F., Eppink, F. V., et al. (2011). A Quantitative Review of Ecosystem Service Studies: Approaches, Shortcomings and the Road Ahead. *J Appl Ecol* 48, 630–636. doi: 10.1111/j.1365-2664.2010.01952.x.

Smajgl, A. (2018). Participatory Processes and Integrated Modelling Supporting Nexus Implementations. In: Hülsmann, S., Ardakanian, R. (eds) *Managing Water, Soil and Waste Resources to Achieve Sustainable Development Goals: Monitoring and Implementation of Integrated Resources Management*. Springer International Publishing, Cham, pp 71–92.

UNU-FLORES, Hettiarachchi, Hiroshan and Ardakanian, Reza. (2016). *Safe Use of Wastewater in Agriculture: Good Practice Examples*. United Nations University Institute for Integrated Management of Material Fluxes and of Resources (UNU-FLORES), Dresden.

Weber, M., Rinke, K., Hipsey, M. R., Boehrer, B. (2017). Optimizing Withdrawal from Drinking Water Reservoirs to Reduce Downstream Temperature Pollution and Reservoir Hypoxia. *J Environ Manage* 197, 96–105. doi: 10.1016/J.JENVMAN.2017.03.020.

Wiek, A., Farioli, F., Fukushi, K., Yarime, M. (2012). Sustainability Science: Bridging the Gap between Science and Society. *Sustain Sci* 7:1–4. doi: 10.1007/s11625-011-0154-0.

Zabel, F., Delzeit, R., Schneider, J. M., et al. (2019). Global Impacts of Future Cropland Expansion and Intensification on Agricultural Markets and Biodiversity. *Nat Commun* 10, 2844. doi: 10.1038/s41467-019-10775-z.

Zhang, L., Schwärzel, K. (2017a) *Multifunctional Land-Use Systems for Managing the Nexus of Environmental Resources*. Springer International Publishing.

Zhang, L., Schwärzel, K. (2017b) Implementation of Multifunctional Land Management: Research Needs. In: Zhang, L., Schwärzel, K. (eds) *Multifunctional Land-Use Systems for Managing the Nexus of Environmental Resources*. Springer International Publishing, Cham, pp 137–148.

7 The water–energy nexus of Brazil's hydropower

Theodoros Semertzidis and Raimund Bleischwitz

Introduction: the heat is on

The water–energy nexus is a glaring example of resource interdependencies among the United Nations' (UN) Sustainable Development Goals (SDGs): water needs energy to reach final consumers, and energy supply needs water for cooling and other purposes. Pursuing the SDGs on water (SDG 6) and energy (SDG 7) in a silo-type of planning could accelerate risks of water stress and power outages. Attempts to increase resource productivity, in line with the overarching aim of this book and SDG 12, will need to take those interdependencies into account. Our contribution assesses the water use of hydropower in Brazil, i.e. the water dimension of the most relevant energy source in a large emerging economy.

Brazil has a track record in sustainability through hosting the two Earth Summits in 1992 and 2012 as well as through its success in generating renewable energy. The 2018 edition of the Yale Environmental Performance Index puts Brazil ahead of China and India, suggesting a remarkable focus on sustainability in previous years. A case in point is Brazil's high share in hydroelectricity. However, hydroelectricity becomes a risky and much-contested source of energy. The severe droughts in the Southeast of the country in 2014–2015, along with the prolonged drought since 2012 in the Northeast, have unveiled water availability issues that affect the electricity sector, among others, and raised concerns. The crucial importance of this relationship between water and energy is increasingly recognised for future development, but there is a lack of integrated methodological approaches and well-defined metrics. This chapter contributes to a more holistic understanding of the nexus and an Integrated Resource Policy by assessing water evaporation for electricity generation in Brazil. The methodology used for evaporation and water footprint estimation was based on work by Semertzidis (2019). In the broader sense, this contributes to understanding the water cycle, climate impacts, and how it will affect the use of both water and energy in the future. Accordingly, we also discuss the results of a novel scenario analysis for the future of Brazil. Finally, our contribution concludes on the usefulness of this case for the broader narrative of sustainable development and resource productivity.

The evidence base: droughts, energy, and the water cycle

In 2014–2015 Brazil (and more specifically, the Southeast and Midwest) faced its worst drought in 40 years, which resulted in decreased reservoir capacities and consequently hydropower consumption decrease. Inhabitants and the agriculture sector suffered due to the lack of water, while blackouts hit cities like Rio de Janeiro and São Paulo due to weak hydroelectricity generation and high demand for services (for example, use of air conditioning due to high temperatures). To partly alleviate the problem, the assistance of burning more fossil fuels were required since they are used as a back-up energy source in Brazil.

Brazil faced several droughts in the past years, and it is anticipated that this trend will continue and increase in intensity and frequency, mainly in the Northeast of Brazil due to climate change (World Bank 2013). Water availability, in general, is recognised as being an issue for Brazil. This alarming for the electricity sector, since the hydroelectric production in Brazil historically accounts for more than 70% of the country's electricity supply matrix, with a capacity of 91.348 GW in 2014. An additional 31.7 GW of capacity was expected to be installed, as of 2014, in the northern region to match with the country's growing economy (Westin et al. 2014). The primary strategy of the Brazilian government so far has been an expansion of energy supply via the construction of the large-scale hydropower plants in Santo Antonio (3,150 MW) and Jirau (3,300 MW) on Madeira River, and Belo Monte (11,233 MW) on Xingu River, all three being in the Amazon Basin (Andrade Guerra et al. 2015). So, would the water be available to fuel the hydroelectricity demand of the future?

The water system and a water budget analysis

This apparent relationship between water and electricity needs to be explored: while research investigates into energy demand, little has been done to understand water availability and the water cycle at the beginning of the delivery chain. Comparing it with the broader resource productivity debate, this gap is comparable to overlooking essential mining conditions. A concept to assess water more comprehensively and the interlinkages with energy is needed. The resource nexus (Bleischwitz et al. 2018) could, in theory, fit the role of such a concept/approach since it attempts to integrate important aspects of sustainable development. Water and energy interconnections, or the water–energy nexus (WEN), are part of the overall resource nexus thinking, and it is important that they are treated together rather than separately and as distinct resources with their ensuing issues. This way of thinking could help to identify critical tensions between the two resources, highlighting possible synergies, and in turn, providing solutions to pressing problems. A more integrated resource policy would, thus, seek to address water availability along the whole life cycle, beginning with withdrawal and supply onto multiple users and potential re-use.

The depletion of water is highly dependent on the regional and global climate conditions, and it is also site-specific. Hence, ideally, analysis of a hydroelectric system should be done on regional scales with some international and global connections. Also, the fact that the generation of electricity is highly time relevant, deems it important to use a maximum daily time step. Finally, each relevant power plant and water reservoir should be analysed individually. Research needs to quantify as accurately as possible the movement of water in, through and out of a specific volume of water, which makes it feasible to gain knowledge about the availability of water for future planning and decision-making. This type of analysis is achieved through a water budget (or balance). To do a water budget analysis and address the operation of a hydroelectric plant, it is essential to treat the process in a dynamic way since the main variables (precipitation, evaporation and river flow) are all dynamic in nature.

A landmark in recognising the impact of hydroelectricity on water resources was the 'Special Report on Renewable Energy Sources and Climate Change Mitigation' by the Intergovernmental Panel on Climate Change (IPCC) in 2012. The reason for the increased attention was the wide range of estimates on water consumption per unit of energy generated by hydropower plants, but also because these values were considerably more significant than those for all other technologies (Semertzidis et al. 2018). Torcellini et al. (2003) estimated it to be from 0 to 18,000 gallons per MWh (68.14 m^3/MWh). This wide range in values indicates the difficulty to estimate water use factors for hydroelectricity that could be universally applicable. The main consumption comes from evaporation from large reservoirs, which though can be multipurpose, storing water for agriculture, industrial or domestic use as well as for power production (Healy et al. 2015). Thus, water losses cannot only be attributed to power generation purposes alone. However, the vast majority of Brazilian hydropower reservoirs are solely used for electricity generation, which simplifies the problem in this particular case.

As of early 2019, the only existing analysis for all hydroelectric plants/reservoirs in Brazil is that by the Operator of the National Electricity System (ONS) in 2004. Since the climate is changing and evaporation is a dynamic process, the importance of estimating it anew was of great importance for our work. The results of the present study showed that the evaporation of some reservoirs estimated in this research was closely related to that by ONS. However, other reservoirs had a significant difference of even 300 mm per year, which shows the importance of having frequent evaporation estimations.

A model calculating evaporation and water consumption of hydropower, as well as performing a water budget analysis for individual reservoirs, states, and regions was created and used for 218 reservoirs. The model and the analysis were designed and delivered in such a way as to overcome spatial and temporal issues that inhibit water models to be meaningfully linked to energy models. The time step for evaporation and water consumption is hourly, and for the water budget analysis daily, while the spatial boundaries used are political, although hydrological boundaries were also used for the purpose of estimating future projections of river flows. The result is a novel assessment of Brazil's water budget for hydroelectricity and a tool for scenario analysis. Detailed future climatic scenarios for the reservoirs were created to perform a future scenario analysis of the main hydropower system of Brazil. The results and their meaning for Brazil, but also generally, are discussed to offer insight regarding policy implications for the future of hydropower.

Results of scenario analysis: high risks in the North and Northeast

The period chosen for the future projections analysis was 2015–2049. The main inputs for the water model are temperature, incoming short-wave radiation, wind speed, precipitation, and river flow.

Based on projections by IPCC and Marengo et al. (2011), the temperature in Brazil will rise within a range of 1 to about 4 °C until 2050. The exact increase is difficult to project, and so are the variations within the country itself and from season to season. Based on these projections, it was decided to create two different scenarios for evaporation estimation, using an increase of 2 °C and another of 3 °C until 2049, which lie in the middle of the projections above. At the same time, specific projections for incoming short-wave radiation and wind speed do not exist in literature. Based on a sensitivity analysis of evaporation, it was decided that the 2 °C scenario will be accompanied by an increase of 0.5 MJ/m^2 for incoming short-wave radiation and an increase of 0.5 m/s for wind speed. Additionally, the 3 °C scenario will be accompanied by an increase of 1 MJ/m^2 for incoming short-wave radiation and an increase of 1 m/s for wind speed. The first scenario will accompany the two different scenarios selected for precipitation.

The projections for precipitation are more complicated than the ones about temperature, since climate models have uncertainties about the direction of change and detailed impacts, especially since the weather patterns in Brazil are so inconsistent due to the meteorological phenomena present in the region. Generally, the IPCC projected reduced precipitation in the North, with a potential increase over other parts of the country. Also, the Northeast will have decreases, according to Marengo et al. (2016). Finally, Reboita et al. (2014) projected trends of negative precipitation in the more northern region of the country of −1.5 to −2.5 mm/day and increases in the Southeast and South of ~1.5 mm/day in the period 2070–2100. These values are in agreement with Marengo et al. (2016). Since precipitation projections are difficult, it was decided to have four different scenarios of precipitation/river flows, of which two will be presented here. The first one is based on the GCM miroc5 (World Bank n.d.), which projects an extreme upward precipitation future of 1858 mm (from 1439 mm in the period 2010–2015) for the period 2016–2039 and 1865 mm for the period 2040–2049. The second one is based on the GCM ipsl_cm5a_mr (World Bank n.d.), which projects an extreme downward precipitation future of 1190 mm (from 1439 mm in the period 2010–2015) for the period 2016–2039 and 1225 mm for the period 2040–2049. The reason these two scenarios were selected is that they present extreme upward and downward precipitation.

The first two parts of Figure 7.1 show the annual progression of evaporation from 2015 through to 2049 for the two scenarios created. There is an increasing trend for evaporation for both scenarios, mainly due to temperature increases, along with incoming short-wave radiation and wind speed. The progression of the lines in both scenarios is similar, but the difference lies in the values themselves. Both scenarios share the same values for 2015, which is the base year, and then there is a 3–4 mm upward difference every year, except for the South that has 2–4 mm, from scenario one to scenario two. In the 35-year period, the increase of evaporation has been most prominent in the North with an overall increase of about 103 mm more for scenario two than scenario one. The least increase was in the South with 77 mm. Overall, for a 1 °C increase in temperature, a 0.5 MJ/m^2 increase in incoming short-wave radiation, and a 0.5 m/s increase in wind speed, the average difference between the two scenarios for the country was just over 90 mm in total.

The second two parts of Figure 7.1 show the monthly evaporation for the period 2015–2049 for scenarios one and two. The graphs for both scenarios are similar, with the difference lying in small increments throughout the year. Evaporation is rising for every month of the year, with September–February seeing the largest rise in both cases. The average rise per month of the year is from 3.38 mm per month in the South to 4.41 mm in the North, with the country's average being 3.9 mm. The North had increases from 3.7 mm in

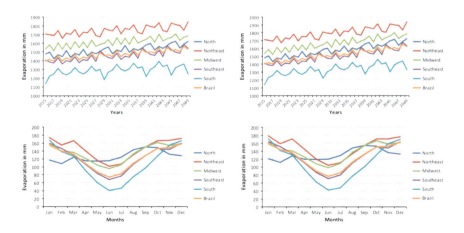

Figure 7.1 Annual evaporation results from scenario one (top left) and scenario two (top right), monthly evaporation results from scenarios one (bottom left) and scenario two (bottom right), for the period 2015–2049.
Source: Semertzidis (2019).

February to 5 mm in August, while the South from 1.75 mm in June to 4.6 mm in February. An interesting observation is that all regions have their minimum evaporation in June, except the North that has it in February. Also, the maximum evaporation occurs in December or January for the Northeast, Southeast and South, October for the Midwest, and September for the North.

More results: increasing water footprints

The first two parts of Figure 7.2 show the water footprint per region for the two different scenarios of precipitation (and river flows) for the period 2015–2049. The general trend in both scenarios is an increase in water footprint values for years with similar conditions. This is due to the steady increase in evaporation, which in turn increases the consumption of water. In the first scenarios, the North has the highest water footprint, whereas in the second scenario the Northeast has a higher one. Also, the Midwest's footprint is comparable to the Southeast's in both scenarios. The reason why this is happening is that these two regions share hydrographic regions and river flow is more important than precipitation above the reservoirs (Semertzidis 2019). The South has, in both scenarios, the lowest footprint.

The second two parts of Figure 7.2 show the monthly water footprint for the two scenarios for the 2015–2049 period. In general, the graphs have similar shaped lines. In both scenarios, water footprint values of all regions are closer in December–February, and the values of all regions are further apart during June–August. As was shown in the first two parts of Figure 7.2 as well, the North and the Northeast have the highest footprint values throughout the

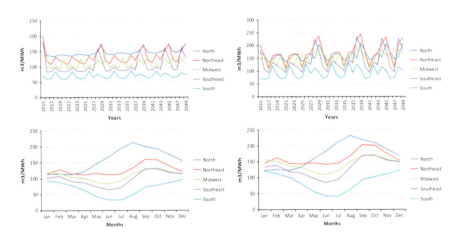

Figure 7.2 Annual water footprint results from scenario one (top left) and scenario two (top right), monthly evaporation results from scenarios one (bottom left) and scenario two (bottom right), for the period 2015–2049.
Source: Semertzidis (2019).

year, with the Midwest and the Southeast following, and the South having the lowest values all year round. The Northeast, the Midwest and the Southeast have their lowest footprint values in June, the South in June and July, and the North in March. On the other hand, the highest values occur in September for the Northeast and the Southeast, in October for the Midwest, in December for the South, and in August for the North.

Decreased water availability in the future could deem electricity production impossible to about 20% of certain months in the North, 30% in the Southeast, and 35% in the Northeast. Such months could potentially occur more frequently in the North and the Northeast. An integrated analysis with the IDA3 energy–water–land model developed by Spataru (2018), showed that Brazil as a whole would not face serious electricity supply issues if investments are targeted towards more regionally adapted hydropower, assisted by wind and solar as well as by better interconnections.

Discussion: regional disparities throughout Brazil

The results show the importance of evaporation for the water cycle when hydropower analyses need to be carried out. Seasonality is an important aspect that research and planning should take into account locations about future plants. We also stress that the evaporation rate is not going to increase uniformly throughout the year, making extremes through the seasons more prominent. As the situation stands, the South and Southeast of Brazil seem to have more sufficient reservoirs. Based on our evaporation assessment, the Northeast seems less suitable for hydropower plants. The North's and the Northeast's evaporation rates will likely increase more than in other regions, a factor that needs to be taken seriously into account for future planning.

The water footprint results showed that there is no 'normal' footprint value that can be used for all reservoirs. On the contrary, each reservoir should be assessed individually, which will allow more accurate comparisons with similar plants and their performance. One important finding was that the inundated area in relation to electricity produced is the key to designing an efficient reservoir/power plant. The South's footprint values are better compared to all other regions in Brazil, and they should be taken as the golden standard and something to strive for. The Southeast also normally performs well, but in times of droughts, water availability causes a large increase in footprint values, which also affects the country as a whole. The North and the Northeast do not have good water footprint values compared to other regions, which means that they suffer during times of reduced water availability, but also that the plants themselves were not built to be particularly efficient.

Future hydroelectricity plans should undergo a more strict water impact assessment. Furthermore, except in an extreme precipitation future, water footprint values for existing plants will most likely rise in all regions, which can magnify problems that some plants already have. From an energy perspective, this underlines the need for grid connections and seasonal back-up supply provisions. Hence it would be useful to assess whether an increase in capacity of some existing plants is possible. Alternatively, the water might be used for other purposes and investments in other electricity sources should be undertaken. Finally, once again, seasonality is important and extremes within the year will become more extreme. New capacity within the country should be sited in order to avoid as much as possible for too many reservoirs being affected at the same time.

An outlook for Brazil

The plans for hydropower have changed numerous times in the past in Brazil; the recent change in the government via the presidency of Jair Bolsonaro indicates less emphasis on environmental policy in general. However, energy security and water stress should be high on the agenda of any government, and hydropower will continue playing an important role. The two most prominent plans have been to either invest further into expansion in the North (Amazon), or more on smaller run-of-the-river plants all over the country. Both options have positives and negatives. Run-of-the-river plants cause significantly fewer environmental problems, but on the other hand, decrease the resilience of the whole system since they cannot withhold any water for times of need. Because of this, run-of-the-river plants are a direct contradiction to energy security. Constructing and operating a hydropower plant/reservoir needs to be done under strict regulations to protect the environment and human settlements. Plans need to be devised with adaptation in mind as well. Continuing with large reservoirs in the North of the country is also in direct contradiction with adaptation principles, because there is an overwhelming reliance on hydropower, with water being highly volatile due to climate change.

Furthermore, although most of the capacity factor values are within reason, what is striking is that the majority of the expansion, located in the North will have an average of 0.476, which is low compared to the rest of the country (Semertzidis 2019), and low compared to South American values. One of the biggest criticisms of the new Belo Monte power plant has faced is its low capacity factor of just over 0.4, meaning that the average capacity factor expected in the North is maintained below 0.5 (Semertzidis 2019). Future policy should thus have a regional angle on the water–energy nexus in the North and Northeast with innovation on the capacity factor.

Our analysis of the water–energy nexus calls for an overhaul of the electricity system of Brazil, with the involvement of experts and stakeholders. The country has a huge wind energy potential in the Northeast and the South, and one could further investigate into solar energy, useful forms of bioenergy and other nature-based solutions. An integrated resource policy with more resilient hydropower, complemented by upscaling wind and solar, could be a sustainable pathway for Brazil. It would need to be assisted by appropriate modelling analysis and participatory integrated resource planning, taking into account adaptation to decreased water availability. A regionally diversified capacity, in combination with better infrastructure, would mitigate risks for the country's future. Beyond electricity, other forms of water use such as agriculture and food, private households and industry will need more research too via advanced nexus assessments. Adapting to climate and social changes, while innovating on the productivity of water and electricity and its distribution are the keys for long-term resilience. We also wish to stress the importance of addressing water in the broader resource productivity debate.

References

Andrade Guerra, J. B. S. O. D., Dutra, L., Schwinden, N. B. C., and Andrade, S. F. D. (2015). Future scenarios and trends in energy generation in brazil: supply and demand and mitigation forecasts. *Journal of Cleaner Production*, 103, 197–210. https://doi.org/10.1016/j.jclepro.2014.09.082.

Bleischwitz, R., Hoff, H., Spataru, C., van der Voet, E., and Van Deveer, S. (eds). (2018). *Routledge handbook of the resource nexus*. London: Routledge. https://doi.org/10.4324/9781315560625.

Healy, R. W., Alley, W. M., Engle, M. A., McMahon, P. B., and Bales, J. D. (2015). The water–energy nexus – an earth science perspective. *U.S. Geological Survey Circular 1407*, 107 p., https://doi.org/10.3133/cir1407.

Edenhofer, O. (2012). *Special report on renewable energy sources and climate change mitigation: summary for policymakers and technical summary*. Geneva: Intergovernmental Panel on Climate change. Retrieved from www.ipcc.ch/site/assets/uploads/2018/03/SRREN_FD_SPM_final-1.pdf.

Marengo, J. A., Tomasella, J., Alves, L. M., Soares, W. R., and Rodriguez, D. A. (2011). The drought of 2010 in the context of historical droughts in the Amazon region. *Geophys. Res. Lett.*, 38, L12703, doi: 10.1029/2011GL047436.

Marengo, J. A., Torres, R. R., and Alves, L. M. (2016). Drought in Northeast Brazil – past, present, and future. *Theoretical and Applied Climatology*, 129(3–4), 1189–1200. doi: 10.1007/s00704-016-1840-8.

Operador Nacional do Sistema Elétrico (2004). *Evaporação Líquida nas Usinas Hidrelétricas*. ONS, Rio de Janeiro.

Reboita, M. S., Rocha, R. P. D., Dias, C. G., and Ynoue, R. Y. (2014). Climate projections for South America: RegCM3 driven by HadCM3 and ECHAM5. *Advances in Meteorology*, *2014*, 1–17. doi: 10.1155/2014/376738.

Semertzidis, T. (2019). *Hydropower in Brazil through the lens of the water–energy nexus*. (Unpublished doctoral dissertation) The Bartlett, UCL, London.

Semertzidis, T., Spataru, C., and Bleischwitz, R. (2018). The nexus: estimation of water consumption for hydropower in Brazil. *Journal of Sustainable Development of Energy, Water and Environment Systems*, 7(1), 122–138. https://doi.org/10.13044/j.sdewes.d6.0229.

Spataru, C. (2018). The five node resource nexus dynamics: an integrated modelling approach. In *Routledge handbook of the resource nexus* (pp. 236–252). London: Routledge. https://doi.org/10.4324/9781315560625.

Torcellini, P., Long, N., and Judkoff, R. (2003). *Consumptive water use for U.S. power production*. National Renewable Energy Laboratory. https://doi.org/10.2172/15005918.

Westin, F. F., Santos, M. A. D., and Martins, I. D. (2014). Hydropower expansion and analysis of the use of strategic and integrated environmental assessment tools in Brazil. *Renewable and Sustainable Energy Reviews*, 37, 750–761. https://doi.org/10.1016/j.rser.2014.04.071.

World Bank (2013). *Annual report*. Retrieved from http://siteresources.worldbank.org/EXTANNREP2013/Resources/9304887-1377201212378/9305896-1377544753431/1_AnnualReport2013_EN.pdf.

World Bank (n.d.). Climate change knowledge portal. Retrieved from https://climateknowledgeportal.worldbank.org (accessed 15 June 2018).

8 Education, sustainable development and resource management

Katrin Kohl and Charles A. Hopkins

Introduction: today's approach to resource management in the economy

The goal of almost every country is to grow its economy and provide better living conditions for its citizens. Many nations have mainly been successful in these attempts. While the global population continues to grow (UNDESA 2019), the combined gross domestic product GDP) is growing even faster, indicating that globally the available total of goods and services per capita is increasing at an astonishing rate (UNDESA/UNCTAD 2019).

The unprecedented development reflected in GDP continues to happen although humankind's growth has long exceeded the Earth's carrying capacity, i.e. the ability of the natural systems to support life without environmental degradation. It is estimated the carrying capacity was exceeded around 1976 (Wackernagel et al. 2002). The Earth's population at that time was a little over 4 billion and the total gross domestic product was USD 6.4 trillion (World Bank 2019a, 2019b). By 2018, the population reached 7.6 billion people. However, the accompanying gross domestic product expanded proportionally at a much faster rate, exceeding USD 80 trillion (World Bank 2019a, 2019b). Is this of concern?

Collectively, our lifestyles are greatly enhanced by the burgeoning services provided but at a considerable cost to the environment and draw-down to the natural resources. With humans becoming the dominating force in impacting the planet, it is accepted that through human impact on the planet we are entering the yet unprecedented era of the *Anthropocene.*

Today's economies, while experiencing this remarkable enhanced pace in their developments, are still highly dependent on the use of natural resources (European Commission 2011). Even with our new-found awareness of global transformations of fundamental life-sustaining natural processes, the removal of non-renewable resources, and the depositing of harmful man-made substances in crucial areas, there is little global discussion or accompanying action initiated to aim at a limit to this exponential economic growth.

The interdependence of accelerated economic growth and fading natural resources

The unfettered growth dilemma has long been known. Reaching international attention in 1962 with her book *Silent Spring*, Rachel Carson drew the connection between economic growth and development with environmental degradation (Carson 1962). When the concept of limits to growth in the context of natural resources was first discussed in the late 1960s by Donella and Dennis Meadows (Meadows et al. 1972), the counter-argument was that scarcity of resources would lead to rising prices. Higher resulting market prices would drive the demand for alternatives to the current (natural) resource and new services, or products would emerge to solve any shortage. But this market theory only works for resources that are replaceable by substitutes.

To date, we are not able to create substitutes for many of the natural resources that are in heavy use or threat by today's economies. Problems abound with substituting breathable air, potable water, oil, natural gas, phosphorus, minerals, etc. If even possible to re-create, the substitute often comes at a higher price and with further – frequently negative – implications. Additionally, in creating the substitute yet another indirectly related resource impact is to be taken into account.

The next recognition of the problem of resource scarcity or depletion and the need for management came in the 1970s and early 1980s during an unprecedented emphasis on environmentalism, mainly in the developed world. While people in the developing world equally treasured their natural resources, they were faced with addressing abject poverty as they struggled with new-found nationhood, being recently emancipated from the status of the colony.

For the first time, in 1987, the United Nations adopted a compromise approach between environmentalism and development. It was the concept of sustainable development:

> Sustainable development is development that meets the needs of the present, without compromising the ability of future generations to meet their own needs.
>
> (Brundtland Report 1987)

According to *Our Common Future*, development is sustainable when it meets the needs of present human development without compromising natural systems and their ability to serve future generations in meeting their own needs (Brundtland Report 1987). Three interconnected areas are thought to be aspects of sustainable development: environment, society, and economy. These three aspects are to be addressed in balanced, interconnected and systemic approaches. The concept of sustainable development is not fighting capitalism or growth but targeting a positive impact from development that sustains the carrying capacity of the planet both now and in the future. The goal is to foster economies and well-being of all life while restoring and enhancing the planet's natural systems.

92   Katrin Kohl & Charles A. Hopkins

Today's economies are still struggling with this paradigm of sustainable development. While aiming at national targets of ambitious economic development, countries are striving to simultaneously meet their international obligations to preserve existing natural resources. Traditionally, these two goals are seen as mutually exclusive initiatives. The current challenge is to prove this understanding to be fundamentally wrong. The international community aims at collaboratively creating a global economic system that enables countries to thrive, serve its citizens equitably and sustain the carrying capacity of the environment for future generations.

Two crucial questions arise:

1   How can the complexity of change be understood to move away from further economic development based on harmfully excavating the planet towards sustainable growth with efficient use of (natural) resources?
2   How can education systems support these initiatives to create a new path to sustainable resource consumption and management worldwide?

The role of education in understanding the need for a sustainable development

When the United Nations adopted the concept of sustainable development in 1987, they subsequently began to negotiate an implementation plan, later called *Agenda 21* (UNCED 1992). Creating this agenda took five (5) years and was facilitated not only by the negotiating governments but with the private sector and civil society forming a global partnership for sustainable development. Each group interpreted sustainable development in its perspectives and objectives. For instance, the private sector understood sustainable development in terms of eco-efficiency and hence profitability while civil society saw the concept more in terms of environmental protection, social justice and equity. Finally, in 1992 at the United Nations Conference on Environment and Development in Rio de Janeiro (Brazil), *Agenda 21* comprised of 40 chapters was adopted. One of the only chapters in *Agenda 21* that passed quickly and with the full support of member states was *Chapter 36 Promoting Education, Public Awareness and Training* (UNCED 1992). The need for these three items as crucial means of implementing not only *Agenda 21* but sustainability itself was largely self-evident to world leaders. Without an educated populace, there would be limited development of any kind let alone sustainable. However, simply more education as in the developed countries would not address sustainability. It was also decided that the purpose of education should be reoriented from development towards sustainable development. Following the 1992 Conference, also known as the 'Earth Summit', the concept of education, public awareness and training with the added focus of reorienting education systems as a unified initiative became known merely as *Education for Sustainable Development* (further: ESD) with its four thrusts.

UNESCO was mandated as the UN agency responsible for the promotion and implementation of ESD on the international level. UNESCO had a history of developing conceptual approaches to education that looked at the outcomes in a humanistic and holistic way, recommending approaches to education beyond the preparation of a workforce to foster national economies.

By 1972, with the *Faure Report* (Faure et al. 1972), UNESCO had already recognised the need to adapt to the enhanced economic growth with the accompanying exhaustion of resources for power and food as a major future challenge. In 1996, a second major education report, the *Delors Report* was published (Delors 1996) that included preliminary concepts of ESD. The document recognised global interconnectedness and promoted learning in partnership while linking education to development policies.

The role of ESD was internationally strengthened with the adoption of the *United Nations Decade of Education for Sustainable Development 2005–2014* (UNESCO 2005). At the Decade's concluding conference, UNESCO member states explicitly agreed upon the need to review the purposes and values underpinning education in their *Aichi-Nagoya Declaration on Education for Sustainable Development* (UNESCO 2014a).

The *Global Action Programme on Education for Sustainable Development 2015–2019* (commonly referred to as *GAP*, UNESCO 2014b) created further momentum in advance of the adoption of the *Transforming our World: the 2030 Agenda for Sustainable Development* with the *Sustainable Development Goals (SDGs)* at its core (United Nations 2015).

Unlike the previous *United Nations Millennium Development Goals (MDGs)* (United Nations 2000), the *17 SDGs* in a historic move now addressed all member states equally and called for fundamental changes to transform our world by 2030. If sustainable development is not achieved globally, climate change, environmental degradation and shifts in human mobility will appear to new extents (United Nations 2015).

SDG 4 on *Quality Education* defines the work program for all levels of formal education within the *2030 Agenda* under the coordination of UNESCO. Abstract concepts, such as ESD and global citizenship, are now explicitly integrated with the seven targets of *SDG 4*. As education was understood as a means of success for the achievement of the *SDGs*, the *Education 2030 Framework For Action* was adopted before at the World Education Forum 2015 in Incheon (South Korea) (UNESCO 2015). Ministers of education and education experts also agreed to monitor their countries' progress on the seven targets in SDG 4 in an independent annual Global Education Monitoring Report (commonly referred to as *GEMR*, see also UNESCO 2016a).

Today, ESD is recognised 'as an integral element of the Sustainable Development Goal on quality education and a key enabler of all the other Sustainable Development Goals' (United Nations 2018), and explicitly stated in *SDG target 4.7*. This statement revealed the role of ESD well beyond *SDG 4* focusing on education and recognised the roles of education, public awareness and training in achieving most other *SDGs* as well. It is evident that ESD would be a crucial means of implementing *SDG 1 No Poverty*, *SDG 2 Zero Hunger* and *SDG 3 Good Health and Well-being*. From a resource management perspective, the implementation of *SDGs 6 Clean Water and Sanitation*, *12 Responsible Consumption and Production*, *14 Life below Water* and *15 Life on Land* would be enhanced by including aspects of ESD.

To further ESD as a crucial concept to be embedded in formal education and training systems, a new stand-alone UNESCO-coordinated work programme following the *GAP* will be launched in 2020 named the *ESD for 2030 Framework* (UNESCO 2019a) broadening the transformative power of ESD for the achievement of all the *SDGs*.

UNESCO also remains a central force in bringing forward contemporary philosophical concepts of education and its purposes. A new report is planned, titled *Futures of Education*, to follow the *Faure Report* and the *Delors Report*, with a focus on the impact of artificial intelligence and technology on humankind. The role of education in the future of sustainability is one of the focus areas in this new undertaking (UNESCO 2019b).

Infusing ESD with its three perspectives recognised at the *Earth Summit* in 1992, i.e. education, public awareness and training, into mainstream education and training systems at all levels requires new thinking. Societies need to rethink the purpose of their education systems in today's world for the generations that will shape a future, yet unknown and impossible to envision. This rethinking is not just a matter of enhanced quantity of education to create the needed changes as currently, the most educated countries are leaving many of the deepest ecological footprints on the planet.

Recognising the need for this reorientation from development to sustainable development will not come easily. Other than many of the developing countries, developed countries do not fully experience major consequences of their lifestyles. They are unlikely to see the injustice and recognise that due to developing countries' inadequate infrastructure and minimal overall resilience, they pay disproportionately for the escalating costs of changing weather phenomena, sea-level rise and forced relocation. Those in the distant developed world likely do not consider that the lifesaving measures, forced on developing nations, divert funds from core services such as healthcare, education and infrastructure. ESD can help address this need for profound human consumptive change to make the planet not only last longer but to create a restorative use of resources and making a sustainable future possible.

Most education systems, still rooted in the age of the industrial revolution, are slow in adapting to change in structures (UNESCO 2019b), and ESD remains a '*Forgotten Priority*'. Issues, such as resource management, sustainable production and consumption, biodiversity depletion, climate change and other global issues are not currently seen as concerns of formal education systems and remain as optional topics at best. Despite calls to prepare teachers to address ESD, only 7% of countries include ESD in teacher education as a mandatory element (McEvoy 2017; UNESCO 2017). The infusion of ESD has not reached its full potential (UNESCO 2016a).

The opportunity for education systems to further sustainable development

Some education systems have recognised the necessary turnaround and are underway educating future generations to assume their role as citizens of a sustainable planet with social, economic and environmental justice. However, getting ministries of education to raise the profile, alter curricula, provide professional development and embed ESD concepts in monitoring and evaluation criteria is still in the distant future in most countries.

Likewise, without public awareness and understanding of the concept of sustainability, lawmakers will not be able to implement the needed legislative and policy changes. Governments are usually concerned with remaining in power and find it challenging to bring in policies without public support, regardless of how necessary they may be. Building a knowledgeable public that will understand and support the profound change to currently accepted and preferred lifestyles, takes concerted planning, effort and resources. Especially, since the impact of the local change will largely benefit those on the other side of the planet, it is crucial to comprehend the world's interdependencies and one's individual impact.

Also, without education and training, the needed shifts in both production and consumption practices will not be forthcoming. This need to address consumptive practices is a complex issue requiring combined input from a wide range of academic disciplines, especially focussing on social sciences and humanities. In sustainable production, the range of disciplines involved is equally great and include but are not limited to natural and applied sciences. Emerging ecological concepts, such as biomimicry, bio-engineering and Nano-technology also have roles to play. While technology and artificial intelligence are holding major promises for the well-being of humankind, they also raise major concerns with their impact on all life forms that share our planet (UNESCO 2019b). Essential considerations, such as the issues of ease, cost and social acceptance add to the complexity.

Understanding the *17 SDGs* as a possible forecaster of the economy of the future may help raise the profile of both sustainable development and ESD. If addressing the major sustainability issues, including the implications for natural resource management, both as aspects of a future overall global economy, as well as the current perception of sustainability as a moral or ethical issue may bring more public concern and eventual action. The perception of the *17 SDGs* as harbingers of the next economy is not unfounded as these issues are already being addressed and will likely only rise in global and local priorities.

In educating the existing workforce for a sustainable future, there is a need to create specialised programming. Understanding new approaches to creating a sustainable economy differs from the normal up-skilling of an experienced professional or the retraining of workers from a disappearing profession to a new emerging green concept. This complexity is further heightened for the new workforce that is about to enter. Training and preparation for employment in larger (green) enterprises or multinational corporations (MNCs) require different sets of technical and interpersonal or soft skills than in small to medium-sized enterprises (SMEs). SMEs are highly dependent on education systems to deliver the workforce immediately needed and usually do not have their in-house training capability. They require the pre-existence of highly trained new employees. MNCs want employees with communications skills, the ability to learn and willingness to move from position to position within the corporation and create their sustainability training approaches. However, both SMEs and MNCs do need the training to be successful in shifting to a sustainable economy. A further layer is added when one considers the need to have workers who can become entrepreneurs as well, creating their own sustainably managed business. These challenges need immediate recognition and addressing by education systems in synergy with the public and private sectors.

Fortunately, there are policy frameworks, programs and innovative pilot projects within both government agencies and the private sector to create or address greening the economy (see also UNEVOC 2017). But again, a concerted synergistic approach by formal education in partnership with other stakeholders in creating a more sustainable future is still too sporadic.

As well as the role of education and training for sustainable production is the role of enterprises of all sizes in shaping the consumer of the future. While too many consumers in the world are limited by poverty or lack of available choice, there remains a large and growing segment of societies who can steer and influence consumption through their purchasing decisions. It is in this wealthier segment of society, where a choice is an option that education and training regarding the best use of the world's resources can be an effective tool.

Having an interest in and understanding of the total lifecycle of the product: its circumstances of origin, including ecological and social implications, transportation footprint, disposal or re-use capability, owned or leased, and overall value to the consumer, are all skills that currently are too often supplanted by consideration of price alone. Further understanding of future issues, such as the circular economy, total cost perspectives and the implications of tax evasion/avoidance are all issues that would be relevant in a meaningful approach to ESD within formal education.

In synergy with ESD, the overarching concept of well-being addresses global and local resource-oriented sustainability issues. An understanding of subjective well-being is needed as it relates to both the individual and includes all life forms with whom we share the planet (UNESCO 2016b). Well-being is more than 'well-off' or wealthy and addresses many aspects, including meaningfulness of one's life, as well as meeting our Maslowian needs. Embedded in sustainability are concepts of individual well-being, societal well-being and well-being for all living entities. Even respect for cultural objects and customs needs consideration. Developing a sense of responsibility for the well-being of future generations, a concept emblazoned in the culture of Indigenous societies, but now lost mainly within our more developed civilisations, needs to be revisited if we are to address sustainable resource management.

Outlook

We know much about developing a sense of respect for our natural resources. It begins with awareness, is enhanced by contact and the respect progresses with ongoing learning and engagement. There are many ways of meaningful involvement with our precious natural resources to create a sense of concern, ownership and responsibility. It is this engagement that is the beginning of a lifelong relationship and concern for our planet and the elements that comprise its delicate, interdependent existence.

The Earth is finite. We can find substitutes for some depletions, but inexperience in both anticipating and facing future resource issues abounds. Profound questions of access, use and disposal/re-use of resources are now before us. Who will discuss, recommend and decide the answers? Hopefully, it will be knowledgeable, unselfish and globally-minded citizens who also have an awareness of intergenerational responsibility that extends beyond humans. We will not have such a cadre of citizens without the structured involvement of our formal education systems. It is time to nourish this engagement.

Abbreviations

ESD   education for sustainable development
SDGs   Sustainable Development Goals
UNCED   United Nations Conference on Environment and Development
UNCTAD   United Nations Conference on Trade and Development
UN DESA   United Nations Department of Economic and Social Affairs
UNESCO   United Nations Educational, Scientific and Cultural Organization

References

Brundtland Report (1987). *Report of the World Commission on Environment and Development. Our Common Future*. Retrieved 26 July 2019 from https://sustainabledevelopment.un. org/content/documents/5987our-common-future.pdf.

Carson, R. (1962). *Silent Spring*. Boston, MA: Houghton Mifflin Harcourt.

Delors, J. (1996). *Learning: The Treasure Within—Report to UNESCO of the International Commission on Education for the Twenty-first Century*. Paris: UNESCO. Retrieved 26 July 2019 from http://unesdoc.unesco.org/images/0010/001095/109590eo.pdf.

European Commission (2011). *Roadmap to a Resource Efficient Europe*. Communication from the Commission to the European Parliament, the Council, the European Economic and Social Committee and the Committee of the Regions. Brussels: European Commission.

Faure, E., Herrera, F., Kaddoura, A., Lopes, H., Petrovsky, A. V., Rahnema, M., and Ward, F. C. Learning to Be. (1972). *The World of Education Today and Tomorrow*. Paris: UNESCO. Retrieved 26 July 2019 from www.unesco.org/education/pdf/15_60.pdf.

McEvoy, C. (2017). Historical Efforts to Implement the UNESCO 1974 Recommendation on Education in Light of 3 SDGs Targets. Retrieved 26 July 2019 from https://unesdoc.unesco.org/ark:/48223/pf0000247275.

Meadows, D. H., Meadows, D. L., Randers, J., and Behrens III, W. (1972). *The Limits to Growth: A Report for the Club of Rome's Project on the Predicament of Mankind*. New York: Universe Books.

UNCED (1992). Earth Summit, Agenda 21, Chapter 36: Promoting Education, Public Awareness and Training. Retrieved 2019, July 26, from www.un-documents.net/agenda21.htm.

UNDESA (2019). United Nations Department of Economic and Social Affairs: World Population Prospects 2019. Retrieved 26 July 2019 from https://population.un.org/wpp/Download/Standard/Population/.

UNDESA/UNCTD (2019). *World Economic Situation and Prospects 2019*. New York: United Nations publication.

UNESCO (2005). *United Nations Decade of Education for Sustainable Development (2005-2014): International Implementation Scheme*. Paris: UNESCO Education Sector. Retrieved 26 July 2019 from http://unesdoc.unesco.org/images/0014/001486/148654e.pdf.

UNESCO (2014a). Aichi-Nagoya Declaration on Education for Sustainable Development. Retrieved 26 July 2019 from http://unesdoc.unesco.org/images/0023/002310/231074e.pdf.

UNESCO (2014b). *Roadmap for Implementing the Global Action Programme on Education for Sustainable Development*. Paris: UNESCO. Retrieved 26 July 2019 from http://unesdoc.unesco.org/images/0023/002305/230514e.pdf.

UNESCO (2015). Education 2030: Incheon Declaration and Framework for Action for the Implementation of Sustainable Development Goal 4. Retrieved 26 July 2019 from https://unesdoc.unesco.org/ark:/48223/pf0000245656.

UNESCO (2016a). *Global Education Monitoring Report 2016: Education for People and Planet: Creating Sustainable Futures for All*. Paris: UNESCO. Retrieved 26 July 2019 from http://unesdoc.unesco.org/images/0024/002457/245752e.pdf.

UNESCO (2016b). *UNESCO Strategy on Education for Health and Well-being: Contributing to the Sustainable Development Goals*. Paris: UNESCO. Retrieved 26 July 2019 from https://unesdoc.unesco.org/ark:/48223/pf0000246453.

UNESCO (2017). *Global Education Monitoring Report 2017/18: Accountability in Education: Meeting Our Commitments*. Paris: UNESCO. Retrieved 26 July 2019 from https://unesdoc.unesco.org/ark:/48223/pf0000259338.

UNESCO (2019a). *Education for Sustainable Development: Towards Achieving the SDGs (ESD for 2030)*. Paris: UNESCO. Retrieved 26 July 2019 from https://unesdoc.unesco.org/ark:/48223/pf0000366797 (draft framework).

UNESCO (2019b). *The Future of Education Report*. Paris: UNESCO. Retrieved 26 July 2019 from https://unesdoc.unesco.org/ark:/48223/pf0000366976.

UNEVOC (2017). *Greening Technical and Vocational Education and Training. A Practical Guide for Institutions*. Bonn: UNESCO-UNEVOC. Retrieved 26 July 2019 from https://unevoc.unesco.org/up/Greening%20technical%20and%20vocational%20education%20and%20training_online.pdf.

United Nations (2000). United Nations Millennium Development Goals. Retrieved 26 July 2019 from www.un.org/millenniumgoals.

United Nations (2015). Transforming Our World: The 2030 Agenda for Sustainable Development. Retrieved 26 July 2019 from www.un.org/ga/search/view_doc.asp?symbol=A/RES/70/1&Lang=E.

United Nations (2018). Decision 72/222. Education for Sustainable Development in the Framework of the 2030 Agenda for Sustainable Development. Retrieved 26 July 2019 from https://undocs.org/en/A/RES/72/222.

Wackernagel, M., Schulz, N. B., Deumling, N., Linares. A., Jenkins, M., Kapos, V., Monfreda, C., Loh, J., Myers, N., Norgaard, R., and Randers, J. (2002). Tracking the Ecological Overshoot of the Human Economy. *Proceedings of the National Academy of Sciences of the United States of America.* Volume *99.* No. 14, pp. 9266.

World Bank (2019a). Population, Total. World Bank Databank. Retrieved 26 July 2019 from https://data.worldbank.org/indicator/SP.POP.TOTL?locations=1W.

World Bank (2019b). GDP (current US$.). World Bank Databank. Retrieved 26 July 2019 from https://data.worldbank.org/indicator/NY.GDP.MKTP.CD?locations=1W.

Part II
Core aspects of an integrated resource policy

9 Systemic analysis of the nexus of greenhouse gas emissions and material use in the energy sector

Ullrich Lorenz

The starting point

The combustion of fossil fuels is one of the major sources of greenhouse gas (GHG) emissions and a primary cause of climate change. One focus of climate policy is to address this issue by demanding the transition from fossil-based energy production towards renewable energy. Such a transition refers to all areas where fossil fuels are currently used, both in industrial production and the private sector, including electricity generation, heating and transportation.

On the other hand, resource efficiency policy seeks to minimise the use of resources by increasing the efficiency of material use (providing the same service with less material), substituting (using substances less harmful to the environment) and simply abstaining from material use (sufficiency).

Material use and energy use are inherently interconnected. All steps in the value chain require energy – the extraction of raw materials, the preparation, transportation, and production of products, and the consumption, use and finally the deposition or recycling of the materials. Additionally, the energy system heavily relies on raw materials, namely fossil fuels like lignite, coal, oil and gas. It makes a huge difference if the material is burned, i.e. chemically and physically altered (with increased entropy), or just transformed into metals which remain metal and can be recycled. Although entropy will also be increased when these metals are distributed in fine particles that cannot be recaptured and recycled and are also lost for further use.

In order to substitute fossil fuels in the energy system, the clear objective should be the replacing of fossil power stations with renewable energy systems. Whatever renewable energy system will is built (e.g. wind power, solar, thermal), materials like concrete, steel, copper, silver, aluminium and other raw earth materials needed for electronics will be used. However, each kilowatt-hour that is delivered by renewable energy systems could theoretically save fossil fuels, assuming the energy demand remains the same and fossil production is reduced at the same rate. Greenhouse gas emissions associated with investments in materials for the renewable energy systems have to be balanced with a reduction in fossil fuel combustion. This way, instead of continuously reducing the stock of fossil fuels, the material is accumulated in power units and builds up an anthropogenic stock of – at least theoretically – reusable materials.

Hence, the area of climate policy that fosters the transition to a renewable energy system has a direct impact on material use and vice versa. On the other hand, a policy that focuses only on the efficiency of raw material use alone has potential to influence GHG emissions for the good and the bad, although currently this potential is not used in a systematic way for the good.

Systemic approaches

System analysis

The word 'system' comes from Greek and means 'a regularly interacting or interdependent group of items forming a unified whole' (Webster's 2019). Systems science is referred to here as the science of systems thinking, systems analysis and systems dynamics. Understanding the connections and relations of the different parts of the system is necessary to understand a certain behaviour of the system (Haraldsson 2004). Understanding a cause and an effect enables the analysis, determination and explanation of how changes come about under certain conditions (Dörner 1996).

This approach also requires one defining the system boundaries. This means the research question defines the extent of the system, which is at first the mental model and collection of connected factors that define and help to explain a certain behaviour. Human thinking tends to be generally linear, not taking into account feedbacks, especially in politics. While in many situations, linear thinking is effective, in complex context linear thinking has its limits (Haraldsson 2004).

There are certain characteristics that appear in the behaviour of systems. Feedback loops can either lead to reinforcing exponential growth (positive or negative) or to a balancing structure (goal-seeking). In complex system ambiguities appear, which means that one factor can affect another factor through different causal pathways – sometimes in opposite that is neutralising directions. Another common effect in systems are delays, where a change in one factor does not immediately change another factor but instead, it takes some time before the effect manifests. A combination of such delays can often lead to a form of oscillatory behaviour in systems. Considering these combined processes, human brains are not able to explain such complex behaviours of a system without the help of tools and a methodology to apply them. Additionally, when a system is a network of multiple variables that are connected to each other through causal relationships and their combination expresses some behaviour, this can only be characterised through observation of the whole system (Sterman 2000). Qualitative modelling is one of the approaches to understand and analyse complex systems.

Qualitative modelling

Qualitative modelling is a form of structural modelling in which gaining an approximate understanding of the (causal) relations and interconnections of factors and concepts is the central aim (Haraldsson 2004). In quantitative modelling, in addition, the objective is to simulate concrete figures for a certain point of time (Lendaris 1980). This article focusses on the result of a purely qualitative exercise. Regardless of the tool used, it is always essential that decisive factors and their relations, are included in the model.

In this chapter, a causal loop diagram (CLD), as known from system dynamics (e.g. Sterman 2000), is presented, analysed and discussed. When connecting two or more factors in a qualitative model, additional information is added in relation to the causal effect. These include the direction of the effect, whether the causal effect is in the same direction (more causes more/less causes less) or opposite direction (more causes less/less causes more), its strength/weighting, and any delay it may involve (e.g. Neumann 2013). Using knowledge of the dominant loops and loop structure, qualitative modelling allows for rough estimates about how a system could behave.

The nexus of greenhouse gas emissions and material use

Understanding the system

The nexus between greenhouse gas emissions and material use in the energy sector can be modelled and displayed using a CLD as shown in Figure 9.1. Both *Production* and *Consumption* require energy in our society. More *Production* leads to more *Consumption* (import/export equals consumption/ production somewhere else) and vice versa. If considered by itself, this reinforcing feedback loop would lead to an exponential growth of *Production* and *Consumption* (and therefore to an exponential growth of energy use and of the use of raw materials). Theoretically, *Production* would be limited by the *Available material,* although under current conditions this limitation is physically not given. Also, either fossil or renewably produced energy that is available for use could be a limitation to the production processes, although this is currently not the case.

Actual consumption has grown over recent years without a limitation of the (geo)physical system manifesting and constraining growth, though this may change. One has to acknowledge that the economic system as a whole is not shown here. Hence, economic factors like price and available money, purchasing power, among others which balance out the production/consumption loop, have been omitted in the model in Figure 9.1. These factors might dump or slow down the dynamics of production and consumption. Nevertheless, for the generic understanding of the nexus these details are not essential at this level of analysis.

Energy (heat, kinetic or electric power) – represented as *Energy demand* in the CLD could either be produced by fossil energy (*Fossil energy production*)

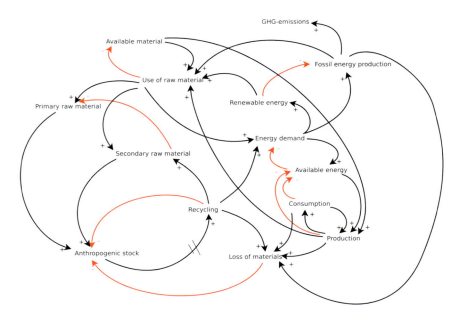

Figure 9.1 Causal loop diagram (CLD) of the nexus of greenhouse gas emissions and material use in the energy sector. Arrows with a '+' (black) represent an equal causal relation (more leads to more or less leads to less), while arrows with a '−' (red) represent an opposing relation (more leads to less or less leads to more). Source: own compilation, first used in UBA (2019).

or renewably (*Renewable energy*). The 'burning' of fossil fuels requires raw materials. The same is true for the construction of infrastructure to produce renewable energy which also requires raw materials (e.g. steel needs iron-ore and fossil fuel for smelting). As mentioned in the introduction, there is a key difference between the *Use of raw material* due to the burning of fossil fuels which are lost after burning (the connection between *Fossil energy production* and *Loss of materials*) and the building of Renewable energy production units. The units there add to the *Anthropogenic stock* and could be recycled later.

The *Use of raw materials* depends on *Available material*. Additionally, the Use of raw materials will be covered either by *Primary raw material*, which includes extraction and transport of raw material, or the demand will be fulfilled by *Secondary raw material* which comes from *Recycling*. In any case, the use of secondary materials and the use of primary materials comprise the *Anthropogenic stock* of materials. The more we use *Secondary raw material,* the less we need *Primary raw material* extraction. While *Recycling* is temporarily taking away material from the *Anthropogenic stock*, it is refilled by *Secondary materials*. The only process truly diminishing the *Anthropogenic stock* is the *Loss of materials*. This could be either dispersion of materials, chemical transformation such as burning and the final deposition of ashes, the contamination of material which might lead to unrecycled and hence deposited materials. Thus, the *Loss of materials* is a result of losses during the production process, during *Consumption*, during *Recycling* – with current recycling rates well below 100% – and during *Fossil energy production*.

Understanding the central loops

The CLD shown in Figure 9.1 contains 32 loops, where 15 loops are balancing and 17 loops are reinforcing. The loops are feedback structures, where a cause becomes an effect and vice versa. Following Senge (1990), no one factor is responsible for changes in the whole system. Therefore it is essential to understand loop interactions and a possible resulting behaviour in order to understand the system and the impacts of action and inaction. This knowledge can help policy analysts identify where the system measures are needed and how to design them leveraging the existing loops. Basically, a reinforcing loop creates either exponential growth while a balancing loop will show goal-seeking behaviour. Certain structures like delays in loop structures (e.g. reinforcing together with balancing loops) normally create some oscillation in the system (Haraldsson 2004). Mostly we find combinations of loops in systems. Certain combinations can create specific patterns which are called systems' archetypes. A very common combination is the connection of a reinforcing and a balancing feedback loop, which in isolation creates a logistic growth function (exponential growth which is slowed down and ends goal-seeking). In combination with a delay an overshot and collapse could be the result (Senge 1990; Lorenz et al. 2017).

The anthropogenic stock and recycling

One loop combination is formed around the anthropogenic stock. The anthropogenic material stock consists of the accumulated materials in buildings, infrastructure and durable goods. This stock constitutes a valuable reservoir of secondary raw materials (Schiller et al. 2017). The anthropogenic stock is contributed to either by primary raw materials or secondary raw materials (Figure 9.2). The process of recycling feeds back across secondary materials, despite a certain loss of material and consideration of energy costs. The linear flow from primary raw material to the anthropogenic stock has led – and is still leading – to the accumulation of material we are experiencing currently. Considering the reinforcing loop from *Anthropogenic stock – Recycling – Secondary raw material,* theoretically the stock would remain stable if not for the delay and the losses due to recycling. This delay and the recycling may lead to oscillations and decay around the anthropogenic stock. The secondary raw materials are not an immediate available.

This has consequences for policy design. Before one could think of using notable amounts of material from the anthropogenic stock, this stock must contain sufficient material to be recycled. If a policy, for example, creates a

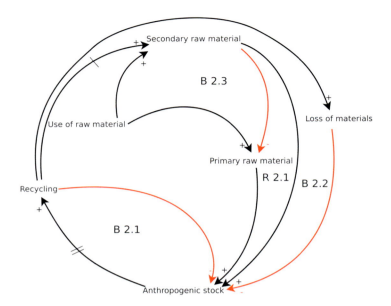

Figure 9.2 Excerpt from the CLD in figure 9.1, showing the central loops around the anthropogenic stock. B 2.1 shows a balancing loop which might reduce the anthropogenic stock; B2.2 marks the balancing loop that through recycling also material is lost. B2.3 shows the balancing of the primary raw material input to the anthropogenic stock. R 2.1 refers to the reinforcing loop filling up the anthropogenic stock.
Source: own compilation.

reduction in the use of primary raw materials (e.g. by the application of taxes or restrictions of exploration/exploitation), it is likely to lead to shortages in production. It will take some time until secondary materials become available and are used. Importantly, this would require installing the necessary additional recycling capacities. Even when recycling processes are fully established, the losses inherent to recycling require a constant inflow of primary raw materials if society wants to keep anthropogenic stock constant. In any case, policy approaches to minimise losses of materials and increase recycling capacities are necessary amendments.

The nexus of energy and resource use

Another crucial combination of loops is centred on the nexus between GHG emissions and the use of raw material (see Figure 9.3). The central 'engine' for the production of GHG emissions is the reinforcing loop R – 3.1 in the figure: more energy demand leads to more fossil power production, which requires fossil raw materials. This flow creates a double adverse effect: next to greenhouse

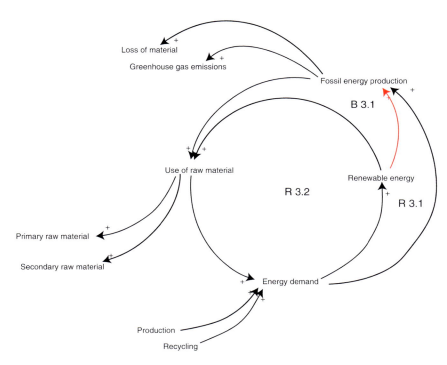

Figure 9.3 Excerpt from the CLD showing the central loops around the nexus of the use of raw material and Greenhouse gas emissions. R3.1 marks the reinforcing loop that more fossil energy production requires more raw material which require more energy. R 3.2 refers to the reinforcing loop that more renewable energy requires more use of raw material. The balancing loop B 3.1 shows the possible reduction of fossil energy production due to increase of renewable energy sources.
Source: own compilation.

gas emissions, the fossil material is lost for further use. The use of raw material includes exploitation and transportation, requiring energy as an investment (see the article of Sverdrup et al.). The same loop is active when accounts for this. At the same time, renewable energy infrastructure may be built (R – 3.2), with the difference that this does not lead to material loss like when burning fossil fuels. The balancing loop B – 3.1 is responsible for the reduction of GHG emissions.

Another pathway to reduce GHG emissions could be the direct reduction of energy demand. However, energy demand (and thus any reduction thereof) is mainly driven by the provision of raw materials, production and consumption. As long as production and consumption rates are high, the only efficiency can reduce the demand for energy. As long as renewable energy infrastructure is built, the use of raw material and energy demand will stay high or even increase, even if demand from fossil fuel use is already on the decline. It must be clear to policy and society that the shift to a renewable energy system itself

110 Ullrich Lorenz

will cost energy, raw materials and time. As long as energy demand is met by an energy mix that contains fossil fuels, the construction of renewable energy infrastructure creates additional emissions of GHG. On the other hand, each renewable energy site contributes to the longer-term reduction of GHG emissions. Additionally, the construction of renewable energy sites and the production of renewable energy create regional welfare and attract (further) investment. One preliminary conclusion for policy is the need to take the amount of time needed for effects to be manifested into consideration and that certain measures require investments, a return on which will take time.

The consumption and production loop

People are consuming things. Some of these fulfil basic needs like nutrition, housing, communication or mobility. All such things (including the required infrastructure) have to be produced. The economy is centred around this loop of supply and demand – the more that is demanded, the more will be produced, and the more that is produced, the more will be consumed, and so on. Both processes, production and consumption, require energy and are leading to loss of materials. The production loop (R – 4.1 in Figure 9.4) is also driving the use of raw material and the balancing loops (B – 4.2 and B – 4.1) are limiting (theoretically) the production. Currently, most raw materials are abundant (although global imbalances and inequities are prevalent). However, the more effort it takes to provide raw materials, the more expensive provision gets and the more critical these raw materials might be from an economic perspective. This economic perspective is not included in this CLD. Nevertheless, the connection of loops shown in Figure 9.4 is a prototype of the limits to growth archetype, showing either a logistic growth curve which eventually stabilises on a high level or more likely leads to some overshot and collapse behaviour (Senge 1990). This prototype is already discussed in Lorenz et al. (2017) with respect to certain megatrends.

Discussion and consequences for policy design

The knowledge of the central feedback loops and causal connections in the nexus–system helps to understand the system's development tendencies and thus to design better policy approaches. It is very likely that sectoral policy will fail since it only addresses certain areas in the system and feedback loops might counteract or partially overcompensate its intention. Another common effect is that a certain measure might act on the central problem but does not resolve it or may in fact cause other problems (shifting the burden). In a good governance system, decisions should be taken on a well-informed basis, finding a systemic solution. In the case of the nexus between GHG emissions and the use of raw materials, it would not be a systemic solution to either only optimise the material use system or to only minimise the GHG at any cost. If the sole focus was given to the renewable energy systems, of course, the use of

The GHG emissions–material use nexus 111

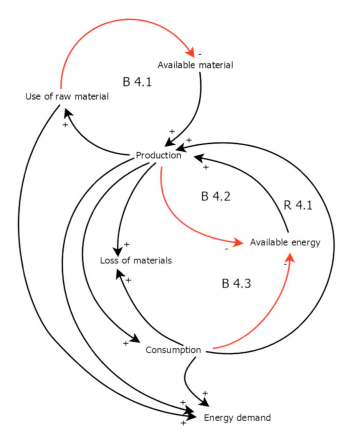

Figure 9.4 Excerpt from the CLD showing the central loops around production and consumption. B 4.1 marks the balancing loop showing the dependence between production of the raw material. B 4.2 shows the limitation of production from the available energy. The loop B 4.3 marks the balancing effect of consumption requiring energy which might (theoretically) limit production. The reinforcing loop R 4.1 shows the production-consumption 'engine'.
Source: own compilation.

fossil fuels (and their GHG emissions) would be reduced. On the other hand, raw materials like copper, aluminium, lithium, and rare earth metals are essential for this, thereby shifting the burden to an extent. The extraction and transport of raw materials cost energy. If other levers in the system are not pulled simultaneously, adverse short-term effects occur. Popular sentiments in German media these days criticise E-mobility or the Energy Transition ('Energiewende') with exactly these 'sectoral' arguments – that more resources and more energy is needed and that this would increase costs and have adverse economic effects and will produce more GHG.

The systemic view, however, suggests a different view: parallel scaling up of recycling capacities, increasing the energy and material efficiency in production, reducing consumption levels (this relates to reduce, reuse, repair, recycle concepts) and closing the secondary loop (minimising material losses at all stages). Of course, most of these concepts and ideas are already known. Interestingly, however, they are promoted by different actors focusing on induvial aspects of the issue and are not brought together into a coherent movement and therefore action is lacking. For example, if focus would only be given to consumption, the effect on GHG emissions could be significant but might be offset by motivations of various actors. The interest of the economy is in this case to produce and to sell. As long as consumers, producers and policy makers are not moving in the same direction they will counteract each other. If policy actors embraced 'consequent' decisions, they (or their affiliates) would be punished at the next election. If a company would decide to produce less and/or only sustainable goods without demand, it would disappear from the market. What motivation does the fossil fuel industry have to stop their business when there are no alternatives? There is no motivation for a consumer who made an expensive investment in a car not use it anymore. The interests of different actors are blocking decisions and progress. This effect is described as a lock-in effect of actors (by Daschkeit et al. 2014).

To overcome this effect, this systemic and a more generalised perspective is helpful. The whole system will only 'move' in the right direction when several levers are pulled at the same time. Public investments are necessary, and revenue will emerge after a certain amount of time. Supporting a common (and well-informed) vision and with this, shifting common value settings will be the result which enables more sustainable consumer decisions. Thus it is the role of (eventually) international policy to change the framework conditions so that industry has incentives to transform and consumers are incentivised to change their consumption patterns based on common values.

List of abbreviations

B   balancing loop
CLD   causal loop diagram
GHG   greenhouse gas
R   reinforcing loop

References

Daschkeit, A., Kristof, K., Lorenz, U., and Veenhoff, S. (2014). *Deutschland 2050. Bausteine für eine nachhaltige Zukunft in Jahrbuch Ökologie.*
Dörner, D. (1996). *The Logic of Failure, Recognizing and Avoiding Error in Complex Situations.* Perseus Books, Reading.
Haraldsson, H. (2004). *Introduction to System Thinking and CLD.* Web version. Department of Chemical Engineering, Lund University.

Lendaris, G. G. (1980). Structural Modeling: A Tutorial Guide. *IEEE Transactions on Systems, Man and Cybernetics 10*(12): 807–840.

Lorenz, U., Sverdrup, H. U., and Ragnarsdottir, K. V. (2017). Global Megatrends and Resource Use – A Systemic Reflection. In H. Lehmann (ed.), *Factor X: Challenges, Implementation Strategies and Examples for a Sustainable Use of Natural Resources*, 67–77. Springer Verlag, Frankfurt.

Neuman, K. (2013). 'Know Why' Thinking as a New Approach to Systems Thinking. *E:CO Issue 15*(3): 81–93.

Schiller, G., Müller, F., and Ortlepp, R. (2017). Mapping the Anthropogenic Stock in Germany: Metabolic Evidence for a Circular Economy. *Resources, Conservation and Recycling 123*: 93–107. 10.1016/j.resconrec.2016.08.007.

Senge, P. (1990). *The Fifth Discipline. The Art and Practice of the Learning Organisation.* Century Business, New York.

Sterman, J. D. (2000). *Business Dynamics, System Thinking and Modelling for a Complex World.* Irwin McGraw-Hill, New York.

UBA (2019). *A Resource Efficient Pathway towards a Greenhouse Gas Neutral Germany.* 2nd edition. Retrieved from www.umweltbundesamt.de/sites/default/files/medien/376/publikationen/190212_uba_fachbrosch_rtd_engl_bf_low2.pdf.

Webster's. (2019). System. Retrieved from www.merriam-webster.com/dictionary/system visited September 2019.

10 Wrong memes
Organic farming and battery electric vehicles

Kai Neumann

Systemic context

The contexts of agriculture and mobility are expansive and include a number of factors to consider. One would be the need to transform into a circular economy based on renewable energy. Another people's fear of change fed by the lobbying of singular interests. Crucial are also potential disruptions from a mixture of effects from climate change, digitisation, demographic change and continued growth of material wealth in developing countries. It is therefore only logical that the nexus between resource efficiency and greenhouse gas emissions needs to be tackled systemically integrating natural, psychological, social, economic, technical and political aspects. People's fear of change and the discomfort that arises from being questioned about our lifestyles and values combined with the lobbying of specific interests foster so-called memes (Dawkins 2016) that hinder the much-needed transformation towards sustainability. This work combines a set of cause and effect models to gain a systemic understanding of the potentials and hinderances of change in these two sectors. In particular, it features a simulation model on Germany's potentials for organic farming and one for a global battery electric mobility. Added to them is the socio-psychological context of change.

Memes and emotional efficacy

Memes are arguments launched and transported via publications, media, social media and through our everyday conversations – planting and manifesting opinions within larger parts of the population. Since they are not necessarily based on facts, they often stem from a normative perspective that some regard as right and others as wrong. The memes, in this case, are the counter-arguments against organic farming and battery-powered electric mobility that people believe despite being debunked by proper science.

These memes are a crucial element of the so-called lock-in effect (Neumann, Grimm & Heinrichs 2014) that is featured in another chapter of this book. Unfortunately, it is not just the need to debunk these memes.

We also need to develop a narrative around emotionally effective (Hamann et al. 2016) alternatives that can pave their way into public discussion. This is based on the insight that human behaviour and the development of civilisations are mostly based not on rational but emotional motives. Therefore our emotions are the crucial drivers for everything, change as well as resistance to change. If actions feel good or if we are criticised for past actions and feel bad we become reluctant to change, and any argument that supports our behaviour is welcomed. If the alternative, however, also feels good, then there is an increased chance for behavioural change. However, in order to be emotionally effective, these alternatives need to be fostered by people around us with effective narratives (Gladwell 2001). After all it is a battle of narratives or memes, for example on one side the argument that we need meat and industrial farming and on the other that organic food and living vegan are better (Wolf 2017). On one hand, that there are not enough resources for battery electric vehicles (BEVs) and the additional electricity is dirty in any case so we should improve our internal combustion engines (ICEs), and on the other side that BEVs are part of a socially appealing large-scale change that we need to start now (Dambeck & Nefzger 2019).

Demographic change, digitisation, climate change and the increase of wealth

The four terms from this subchapter's heading that are crucial for the future of transportation and agriculture are already highly interdependent without mobility and agriculture. More wealth leads to few children and an increase in age. Digitisation can lead to more wealth but also to more inequality. More wealth can lead to more climate change but also help to mitigate the consequences. Climate change, of course, results in most cases to less wealth. Digitisation also could help to mitigate climate change but indirectly also increase it. However, regarding transportation and agriculture we can expect that with the increase of wealth and people there will be a parallel need for more food and more transportation. Both of these demands carry the potential to increase climate change and thus, in turn, threaten the wealth and health of all of us and our future generations. These threats would be the effect of a more or less business as usual (b.a.u.) scenario of more people demanding meat and fish in their diets and more people driving cars and flying as well as more goods being transported around the world.

An alternative would be a change of diet, a change of agriculture, and a different kind of mobility. Digitisation could mean both a more industrialised agriculture, even from things like high tech vertical gardening systems or artificial intelligence-powered robots, or the renaissance of labour-intensive farming, for example, by agroforestry (Armengot et al. 2016) and a wider bioeconomy (Anderson et al. 2019) compensating for the jobs that will be lost from the disruptive developments of digitisation. That change could be accompanied by a change of diet away from industrial meat production and

116 *Kai Neumann*

the domination of corn crops towards healthier vegetables and legumes (Muller et al. 2017; Röös et al. 2018).

The alternatives for business as usual mobility could be both the electrification of public transportation and individual mobility. Integrated systems of public trains, busses and autonomous vehicles including even so-called personal aerial vehicles (PAeVs) may play a role. The transportation of goods and resources could be minimised by shifts towards regional and circular economies with decentralised 3D printed goods (Diamandis & Kotler 2016). Of course, these developments, in general, could be accompanied by either more growth or more self-sufficiency and degrowth depending on the geographic context.

For a change of transportation as well as for that of agriculture and diet we need to take first steps now, starting with debunking two major counter-arguments: organic farming would not work for all the people of this planet, and there would be not enough resources for universally accessible battery-powered e-mobility.

Organic farming

The model shows there are at least three main arguments supporting organic farming: the effects on greenhouse gas emissions from conventional farming from both soil degeneration and the use of artificial fertiliser, the ecological and thus indirectly economic benefits from less contamination of soil, water and wildlife, and the potential shift towards higher quality food and hence less money for meat that causes its own greenhouse gas emissions and contaminations.

The arguments against organic farming are basically that there is not enough demand for organic products and that food would become too expensive and scarce to feed the whole world. The second argument stems from a direct comparison of yields from organic and conventional farming, which clearly shows that conventional acres outperform organic ones in this regard (Seufert et al. 2012). Besides, it is argued that lower productivity would mean the need for more agricultural land, equating to less forests and biodiversity.

To take a closer look at the potential of organic farming, we have developed a quantitative cause and effect model to run simulations on the land use, land-use change and forestry (LULUCF) of Germany. It is a rough model that makes the artificial assumptions that what we eat is what we cultivate and vice versa. This simplification makes sense because we are roughly exporting the same amounts of agricultural products that we import. Also, to evaluate changes we shouldn't assume that a change in agriculture would imply a change in what we eat and vice versa.

The model features numerous aspects from the consumption of different kinds of animal products to the different kinds of forests and the conversion of areas for buildings and infrastructure. The simulation of scenarios reveals some dynamics. For example it shows the shift from less consumption of animal products and hence less manure towards more use of mineral fertiliser. Later comes the shift towards organic farming practices with lower yields. Also there should be the regeneration of wetlands and the conversion of green spaces as well as the minimisation of food waste in order to maximise the reduction of greenhouse gases while potentially feeding the same number of people. All in all, it shows that there are scenarios with a massive reduction in meat consumption and food waste even with increased forestation that nearly allows for feeding the same number of people (Figure 10.1).

What is even more interesting is that the realistic increase of yield from organic farming would potentially lead to a much-improved outcome. This increase could stem from a shift towards different crops, especially legumes, and other farming practices, e.g. agroforestry where applicable. While unrealistic for many industrialised parts of the world, other regions should reconsider an increase of labour productivity in farming and instead try labour-intensive farming practices like permaculture that would increase soil productivity and the conversion of CO_2 from the atmosphere. This argument is bolstered since otherwise for these countries; there seem to be few economic perspectives and job opportunities in an increasingly competitive and automated global economy.

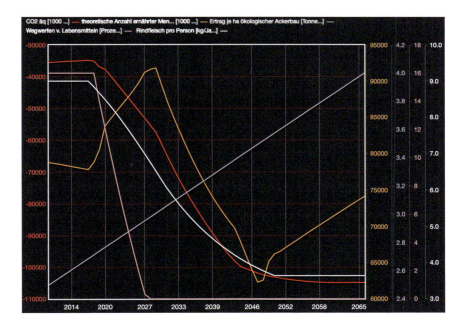

Figure 10.1 Simulation results from a scenario of less food waste (rose), less consumption of animal products (white), 100 per cent organic farming, increased yields from organic farming (light blue) showing less CO_2 (red) and the dynamics of the potentially fed number of people (orange).
Source: Screenshot from model.

118 Kai Neumann

The challenge, however, is that either there needs to be the demand for different farming practice, for example, from a change of values in our societies, or international politics need to pave the way towards a more sustainable future limiting the otherwise destructive forces from the supply side. Such forces will otherwise simply continue overusing soils and converting forests to acres with more and more use of machinery and chemical inputs leading to the slow but inevitable processes of soil degradation, erosion and water contamination. For politics to act there probably needs to be a publicly communicated indicator (Jackson 2016) for the quality of land use.

Battery-powered electric mobility

Mobility needs to change, as well. The model examines three scenarios:

1 one to electrify today's way of transportation that would increase with the growth of material wealth in other parts of the world;
2 one that would include even personal aerial vehicles and other kinds of drones; and
3 one that would bring an interconnected autonomous public transportation system with few if any private vehicles.

No matter which path mobility takes it needs to leave today's internal combustion engines (ICEs) behind. The mere substitution of fossil fuels through synthetic fuels from renewable electric energy is not an option in a broader context because they are needed for long-distance flights, ships and the generation of electricity in times with no wind or sun. This argument stems from the GEE(R) simulation model to examine scenarios for a global transition towards renewable energy and its need for resources. The model shows with all scenarios that it would indeed be possible to end the use of fossil energy, but the peak demand for some vital resources would imply high costs that would increase the need to choose the most efficient paths without losses from unnecessary conversion of renewables to synthetic fuels.

While especially the car manufacturer Tesla has proven that battery-electric mobility would be feasible even for heavy trucks there are still memes in society that perpetuate the claim that there is not enough lithium and that range remains an issue, as do weight and costs.

A continued increase of global transportation is not sustainable, yet with a simulation model for the Federal Environmental Agency of Germany, we examined the potential to switch from ICEs to BEVs, even for commercial vehicles, short distance ships and airplanes. The model uses conservative assumptions from the World Energy Outlook with a considerable increase in worldwide demand for transportation and looking only at lithium as a critical resource. High and low-grade lithium are distinguished based on today's known reserves. The model also considers the increased use of lithium from other sectors, like information and communication technology (ICT). Although there are trials to substitute lithium for the less critical magnesium, today it seems more likely that the energy density of lithium-based batteries will be increased. All other materials will not be as critical, since for example cobalt already can be substituted.

The scenarios looked at both the current technology and what could be expected to change in the future. The results show that passenger cars are the most crucial element as they can opt for smaller battery capacities while commercial vehicles have a predefined capacity because of their more or less constant utilisation. While we will probably run out of high-grade lithium before 2040, we might run out of reserves for low-grade lithium if we continue to oversize the batteries in our cars (>35 kWh) and manage to nearly double today's number of roughly one billion cars within the next 50 years. On the other hand, if we double the efficiency of lithium-based batteries we will run out much later provided that the recycling of lithium starts early and becomes efficient quickly.

While the number of commercial vehicles and their need for battery capacities plays a role, the additional demand for lithium for short distance planes and ships seems to be surprisingly small. Figure 10.2 shows how high-grade lithium would be exhausted by 2039 while from today's known resources of low-grade lithium still quite a lot would be left in 50 years.

The model doesn't feature aspects like grid stabilisation from intelligent charging, the spread of personal aerial vehicles, the benefits (smaller batteries) and trade-offs (for example, marginalisation of railroads) of overhead electric power-lines for trucks, or the potentials for improved utilisation of vehicles from self-driving vehicles (SDVs).

The bottom line is that there is enough lithium and no need to continue using ICEs and less efficient synthetic fuels. Yet the need for capacities to extract lithium, to build batteries, and to recycle them is extreme, and it implies that mining companies in the foreseeable future will face a massive shift from extraction to recycling.

The battle of interests

So yes, we could eat 100 per cent organic and run our vehicles on batteries powered by renewable energy. The actual development, however, will be a battle of interests. The established car industry wants to keep its value creation derived from selling ICEs with support from the oil industry. The agrochemical industry, food industry, and others supported by a strong pro industrial agriculture mindset will oppose any major transition towards organic food production. The consumers, after all, have a demand for inexpensive mobility and food, and they rely on attractive offers. Many of the consumers will 'fight' for their inexpensive meat, dairy products, and fast cars – and they will keep spreading the memes that BEVs and organic food are the wrong way.

120 *Kai Neumann*

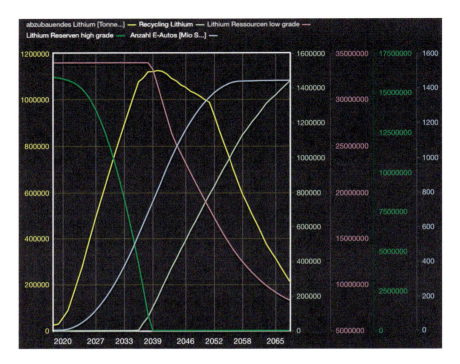

Figure 10.2 Simulation results from a scenario battery electric mobility including commercial vehicles, short-range ships and planes assuming a global increase of mobility, improvement of energy density of lithium batteries, and downsizing of capacity for passenger cars showing the number of cars (blue), the reserves of high-grade lithium (green), low-grade (violet), the needed mining (yellow) and recycling (light green) capacities.
Source: Screenshot from model.

Nevertheless, there is a chance for a subsequent change of values that could foster the demand for alternatives. However, both the food system and the market for mobility solutions are global, as are consumer trends. That means the rest of the world could slow down a transition or fuel the demand for it.

Actually, it would be easy for politics to reward sustainable behaviour by subsidising the right solutions financed by the taxation of unsustainable actions with no adverse effect on either jobs or social justice. However, particular interests spreading wrong memes prevent the political process from achieving this and for now the majority of people are quick to agree that they do not want to pay an extra CO_2 tax on diesel, milk, and flights. This sentiment exists even though low-income individuals would get a refund from 'their' CO_2 budget so that basically only the rich with a bigger ecological footprint would pay more.

Abbreviations

b.a.u.	business as usual
BEV	battery electric vehicles
CO_2	carbon dioxide
GEE(R)	Globale Erneuerbare Energien in Abhängigkeit von Ressourcen (model's name)
ICE	internal combustion engines
ICT	information and communication technologies
kWh	kilowatt hours
LULUCF	land use, land use change and forestry
PAeV	personal aerial vehicle
SDV	self-driving vehicle

References

Anderson, C. C., Denich, M., Neumann, K., Amankwah, K. & Tortoe, C. (2019). Identifying Biomass-Based Value Webs for Food Security in Sub-Saharan Africa: A Systems Modeling Approach. *Sustainability* 11: 2885.

Armengot, L., Barbieri, P., Andres, C. et al., (2016). Cacao Agroforestry Systems Have Higher Return on Labor Compared to Full-Sun Monocultures. *Agronomy for Sustainable Development* 36: article 70.

Dambeck, Holger & Nefzger, Emil (2019). Wie das Elektroauto schlechtgerechnet wird. Retrieved from www.spiegel.de/auto/aktuell/e-auto-schlechtgerechnet-die-ifo-studie-zur-co2-bilanz-a-1263622.html.

Dawkins, Richard (2016). *The Selfish Gene*. New York: Oxford University Press.

Diamandis, Peter & Kotler, Steven (2016). *Bold: How to Go Big, Create Wealth and Impact the World*. New York: Simon & Schuster.

Gladwell, Malcolm (2001). *The Tipping Point: How Little Things Can Make a Big Difference*. New York: Little, Brown and Company.

Hamann, Karen, Baumann, Anna & Löschinger, Daniel (2016). *Psychologie im Umweltschutz: Handbuch zur Förderung nachhaltigen Handelns*. München: Oekom.

Jackson, Tim (2016). *Prosperity without Growth*. London: Routledge.

Muller, Adrian, et al., (2017). Strategies for Feeding the World More Sustainably with Organic Agriculture. *Nature Communications* 8: article 1290.

Neumann, Kai, Grimm, Franc & Heinrichs, Harald (2014). *Entwicklung eines Integrated Assessment Modells: Nachhaltige Entwicklung in Deutschland*. Vol. 2. Dessau: Umweltbundesamt.

Röös, Elin, et al., (2018). Risks and Opportunities of Increasing Yields in Organic Farming. A Review. *Agronomy for Sustainable Development* 38: 14.

Seufert, Verena, Ramankutty, Navin & Foley, Jonathan A. (2012). Comparing the Yields of Organic and Conventional Agriculture. *Nature* 485: 229–232.

Wolf, Nadja (2017). Kann Biolandbau die Menschheit ernähren? Retrieved from www.spiegel.de/wissenschaft/mensch/kann-oekologische-landwirtschaft-die-menschheit-ernaehren-a-1177968.html.

11 What's going on abroad?

Monitoring international resource policies

Monika Dittrich, Andreas Auberger, Christopher Manstein, Detlef Schreiber, and Elisabeth Dürr

Introduction: the relevance of resource efficiency and objective of the research project 'MoniRess'

The current and growing purpose of many countries towards rising prosperity comes along with an increased amount of resources that are needed to facilitate this prosperity. Global raw material extraction has more than tripled since 1970. According to the International Resource Panel of the UN Environment, 85 billion tons of raw materials were extracted worldwide in 2015, on average 11.2 tons per capita, accordingly. Often, intensive resource use is linked to negative social and environmental impacts. The rise in global resource use, thus, has intensified environmental problems such as climate change, soil degradation and the loss of biodiversity. With an increasing world population and continuing economic growth, material use is projected to rise to 180 billion tons in 2050 if current trends continue (UN Environment 2019a, 2019b). Eventually, this would contribute to an even greater increase in global and local environmental impacts.

In this context, policies have been launched at the multinational and national level to promote more efficient and sustainable use of natural resources. Various countries and supranational organisations have formulated policies to promote resource productivity and material efficiency. At the international level, the United Nations International Resource Panel (IRP) released various reports on current state and options of efficient use of resources such as 'Global Resources Outlook 2019' (IRP 2019). The G7 has put resource efficiency on its agenda in 2015, which has since become an established field of activity for the G7. OECD offers policy advice on resource efficiency and conducts several projects to inform countries about resource efficiency potentials (BMU 2015). Moreover, in 2017, the G20 Resource Efficiency Dialogue was launched to share best and good practise examples, to exchange knowledge about policy options and to improve the scientific basis (BMU 2017). Also, the European Commission published the Roadmap to a Resource Efficient Europe (European Commission 2011) and the Circular Economy Action Plan (European Commission 2015). At the national level, Germany ranks among the pioneers in the field of resource efficiency with the adoption of the German Resource Efficiency Programme (BMU 2012, 2016).

In the meantime, many countries worldwide have started to formulate their own policies to foster efficient and sustainable use of natural resources. However, many policies and measures are not known as they are not at the top of the national agendas but parts of strategies or policies.

Against this background, the German Environment Agency (UBA) launched the research project 'Monitoring international resource policies' (MoniRess). MoniRess has been carried out and scientifically elaborated between 2016 and 2019 by the ifeu (Institut für Energie- und Umweltforschung Heidelberg GmbH) in co-operation with GIZ (Deutsche Gesellschaft für Internationale Zusammenarbeit GmbH).

The research project MoniRess aims at bringing to light the variety of measures and policies, which are fostered, abroad to increase the efficient use of resources. MoniRess seeks at providing detailed, regular and up-to-date syntheses of policies and activities of selected countries in the area of resource efficiency. In line with ProgRess, the focus was set on abiotic raw materials in the value chain stages of production, consumption as well as waste management and recycling.

This paper provides an overview of the monitoring approach developed in the project and presents a summary of main results of the MoniRess monitoring. While the monitoring was implemented using a country perspective, this article structures the monitoring results along the value chain. Starting with the overall setting of resource efficiency policies in the countries under study, the article summarises typical approaches and highlights good examples in the area of production, consumption and waste.

Monitoring approach

MoniRess focused on countries, which are not yet analysed regularly, and in detail as e.g. European countries with the series 'More From Less' (EEA 2016). The country selection process was based on a screening of 46 countries outside Europe. Criteria for the selection have been, amongst others, the existence of resource efficiency measures or policies. For this monitoring, the countries Brazil, China, India, Indonesia, Mexico, Russia, South Africa, Republic of Korea and the USA were selected (Dittrich et al. 2020).

As a starting point, individual country profiles were compiled at the beginning of the monitoring in January 2017. Besides, a first survey of the structure of resource use, actors, policies and programs as well as resource efficiency activities, in general, were carried out.

For the quarterly monitoring, a reporting scheme (Figure 11.1) was developed which allows an easy overview of major changes and upcoming issues. The scheme was also used to structure the research during the monitoring phase between 2017 and 2019. The information was gathered based on desktop research, for example, information from ministries and further organisations, as well as based on interviews with local experts.

Figure 11.1 Reporting scheme for monitoring.
Source: © ifeu; Dittrich et al. (2020).

Given that no common understanding of resource efficiency policy exists at the global level, a tight definition of policies was omitted deliberately. On the contrary, the monitoring seeks at comprising a broad collection covering strategic policies, different measures, specific activities, particular threads and good examples that aim at increasing resource efficiency in the countries.

Resource efficiency as part of overarching strategies and actors

Few countries under study have adopted a strategy or law similar to the German Resource Efficiency Program (ProgRess), which explicitly addresses the efficient use of raw materials across the value chain. In this respect, India launched the Indian Resource Efficiency Program (IREP) in 2017. IREP includes a short- and medium-term Action Plan 2018–2020 with action points on material flow indicators, environmental labels, recycling standards, best practices for green mining, industry clusters, sustainable public procurement, information sharing and awareness-raising (NITI Aayog National Institution for Transforming India, EU External Action, 2017).

The majority of the surveyed countries have adopted either an overarching framework or sub-strategies in the areas of sustainable development and green growth. Raw material efficiency is, hereby, often mentioned as an aspect or even designated as a critical component (Renault et al. 2016). South Africa, for example, has developed the National Framework for Sustainable Development (Department of Environmental Affairs South Africa 2011) in which the efficient use of natural resources is a crucial component. Another example is the Republic of Korea where resource efficiency is part of the 2010 Framework Act on Low Carbon Green Growth. Countries such as Mexico,

Brazil and Indonesia promote resource efficiency within the framework of action plans and special programs, which are integrated into overarching strategies for sustainable development.

In other countries, resource efficiency is promoted through so-called partial strategies (Renault et al. 2016). One example is China, a raw material importing country, which has adopted the Circular Economy Development Promotion Law with the objective to integrate secondary materials much stronger to contribute to future raw material supply (Li & Lin 2016). The USA is promoting raw material efficiency as part of the Sustainable Materials Management Program (2009) which supports raw material efficiency in consumption and waste management in the sectors of food, construction and packaging (USEPA 2019b).

In most of all countries under study, the central actors to foster resource efficiency are environmental ministries or administrative agencies and strategic planning institutions within the governments. In the monitored Latin American countries, companies and universities are actively pushing the topic. Civil society and non-governmental initiatives have been found in all countries under study mostly in the field of waste management.

Compared to the other countries under study, the institutional approach in India is outstanding with the Indian Resource Panel established in 2015. The Indian Resource Panel is a group of ten experts who assist the Indian government in advising and promoting resource efficiency. Its members include former environment ministers, NGO representatives, companies and scientists. With its focus on resource efficiency, the panel is the first of its kind at the national level. Its main task is to advise the Indian Ministry of the Environment (MoeFCC) and the National Planning Commission NITI Aayog on the design and implementation of a national resource efficiency strategy (Government of India, NITI Aayog National Institution for Transforming India, 2017).

Approaches in the area of production

All of the countries under study promote raw material efficiency in the production sectors. Mostly, the approaches reflect the level of economic alignment, the sectoral focus of the industries and the strategic field of interest for the development of the countries. In almost all countries, the promotion of raw materials efficiency in production is linked to the promotion of innovation and competitiveness, economic development and the creation or safeguarding of jobs.

The Republic of Korea and China explicitly combine the promotion of raw material efficiency and green technology with the aim of becoming global market leaders in selected industries and technologies. The Republic of Korea addresses a 'green ecosystem of creative industries' focusing on key technologies such as next-generation secondary batteries, LED displays, green PCs, or high-efficiency solar cells (Global Green Growth Institute 2015). China fosters on ten key sectors such as energy-saving vehicles, information and communications technology or aerospace technology in its development plan Made in China 2025 (State Council of the Peoples Republic of China 2015). Based on the Concept of the Long-Term Socio-Economic Development for the Russian Federation for the period up to 2020, Russia aims at the modernisation of traditional industrial sectors such as metallurgy, chemicals and agriculture (Ministry of Economic Development of the Russian Federation 2015). Mexico chose to promote green growth e.g.by supporting the waste and recycling industry and additionally, the government established an additional program for sustainable production and consumption, the Programa Especial de Producción y Consumo Sustentable (Gobierno de Mexico n.d.).

An overall topic is packaging and construction. Both industries were addressed in many of the surveyed countries, regardless of their economic strengths. With respect to packaging, the objective is to reduce the quantity of short-lived packaging and to modify the design to make the recycling as simple as possible. In the material-intensive construction sector, one objective is to reduce the quantity of primary materials by introduction of secondary raw materials as building materials by certification systems and innovative building materials.

The instruments used by governments to promote resource efficiency in production are diverse. Among others, they include economic incentives for resource-efficient production, the definition of 'Best Available Technologies' (BAT) for domestic manufacturing sites, awards from innovative companies and training for companies and fostering cooperation between companies.

In Russia, the modernisation of the production facilities and the domestic industry is realised by the introduction of the best available techniques. The Russian government has created a list of critical areas for which environmental impacts of technologies are assessed and described in specific BAT inventories (Romanov 2016). Addressed sectors are the mining sector, the basic chemicals industry, iron casting and the cement industry. The concept is implemented between 2015 and 2040 by the Bureau of BAT, located in the Chamber of Commerce (Romanov 2016). The implementation comprises economic instruments such as incentives (reduction of environmental taxes) and penalties (fees for environmental pollution) as well as regulative instruments; Production facilities have to comply with best available technology in order to receive an operating license by the Bureau of BAT (GTAI 2018; Romanov 2016).

Awards are widely used, for example, in Indonesia, which credits innovative, and resource-efficient companies with three different awards: The Green Industry Award honours innovative and resource-efficient companies. Besides, there is a Green Company Award, an award by the business magazine SWA in cooperation with the KEHATI Foundation for 'best sustainable performance company'. Indonesia has furthermore PROPER, which includes a particular approach to the corporate procurement system: rating systems and awards for companies (Afsah et al. 2011), creating strong visibility and incentives for companies to build their reputation through actions towards cleaner technologies (Kanungo & Moreno 2003). The United States award the WasteWise Award (USEPA 2019c) and Brazil awards the Fiesp (Federação das Indústrias do Estado de São Paulo) Environmental Merit Award for companies recycling materials and other natural resources (FIESP 2016).

Training and technical advice is an instrument implemented in all countries. In the United State, for example, the Green Suppliers Network provides technical advice how to reduce waste in the supply chain, for example, in automotive industries or health services (USEPA n.d.). For many developing and emerging countries, the promotion of resource efficiency in production and respective training programs is often linked to the UN Program on Sustainable Consumption and Production (SCP). Examples are the SCP networks in Indonesia, South Africa, Brazil and Mexico. Raw material efficiency is often implemented in addition to the approaches to increase energy efficiency. The instruments to promote resource efficiency in production are similar in developing and emerging countries. They include among others training of companies by centres and institutions to analyse and monitor their resource management, as well as online tools and manuals, for example by the National Cleaner Production Center (NCPC) or by the Global Network for Resource Efficiency and Clean Production (RECPnet), both sponsored by UNIDO and UN Environment (UNIDO n.d.).

Fostering cooperation between companies in industrial areas is an instrument, which turns the concentration of pollution and ineffective resource use in industrial zones into opportunities. The spatial proximity between different companies can serve as a breeding ground for cooperation for industrial symbiosis where the residues of one company become the raw material of another. This concept is implemented in China by specifically targeting companies in industrial parks and connecting their material flows (Qi et al. 2016). The USA is promoting the exchange of residual materials and waste streams through regional materials marketplaces (Materials Marketplace n.d.). In South Africa, this approach is implemented managed by the National Cleaner Production Center South-Africa. Three regional programs are operating, in April 2019 the fourth Industrial Symbiosis Program started at the province level. The Western Cape Industrial Symbiosis Program, for example, founded in 2013, consisting of 300 companies sharing their resources. According to their annual report, the program has diverted 4,950 tons of waste from landfill and saved 25,100 tons of greenhouse gas emissions till the end of 2017 (GreenCape 2017).

Approaches in the area of consumption

Raw material efficiency in the area of consumption is a bit more challenging as countries usually avoid the promotion of reduction of consumption but try to govern consumption with the following main approaches being pursued:

a in the context of public procurement, raw material efficiency is one criterion among several sustainability criteria;
b through standards, labelling and certifications;
c through awareness formation and information; and
d through so-called credit or eco-points.

In many countries, public procurement is regulated by environmental standards. In the US, for example, the Environmental Preferable Purchasing Program streamlines environmental performance standards and ecolabels for federal agencies. Another example is the Federal Green Challenge, implemented by the USEPA, which fosters competition between public institutions to reduce the environmental impact (USEPA 2019a). The Republic of Korea has the Act to Promote Green Products and the Mandatory Green Public Procurement, where in particular the second one obligates to prioritise the purchase of environmentally friendly, eco-labelled products.

Voluntary instruments, like standards, eco-labelling or certifications, are established in various countries. The labels cover different aspects, and resource efficiency is included in different ways: for example, by rewarding products (partially) made of recycled material or with low ecological impacts during production and usage. These aspects are addressed, e.g. in the Republic of Korea by the Korean Eco-label and Good-Recycled Mark (Good Recycled n.d.; KEITI n.d.).

Civil society and companies are addressed with educational programmes for sustainable development and programmes to raise awareness. An example of an awareness campaign in the USA is the Waste Recycling Action Program (WRAP) which targets the recycling of plastic film packaging (American Chemistry Council 2019). Another example is the information by the Mississippi Department of Environmental Quality on how to avoid waste of decoration and gift wrap particularly during the holiday season and between Thanksgiving and New Year (ECOS 2017). In Brazil, companies were the target group of guidelines for sustainability in consumption and production (CEBDS 2016).

The Korean government is promoting a sustainable society in its current five-year plan (PCGG 2014). Among others, the Korean Ministry of the Environmental Industry & Technology Institute (KEITI) is pursuing a distinctive approach to provide an incentive for resource-efficient consumption. By using the Green Credit Card, consumers can collect so-called Eco Points when they purchase environmentally friendly products, save energy or use public transport. The points can be used either as cashback at participating companies or for reduced entry into public institutions. As of December 2016, a total of 15 million Green Credit Cards had been issued and 1,957 products from 224 companies were registered (Korea Bizwire 2016).

However, none of the countries under study is pursuing an absolute reduction of consumption or promoting sufficiency approaches.

Approaches in the field of recycling and circular economy

All of the studied countries are promoting the recycling of waste. Yet, the extent of the efforts varies, respectively. Almost all countries have defined recycling rates for individual waste fractions or materials, either centrally or on a local level. Comprehensive approaches on circular economy appear less frequently, although some approaches are widespread in Asian countries.

Within the frame of this monitoring, all countries mention the increase of waste volumes and the growing challenges on disposal of waste as problems. Resource efficiency in general and recycling, in particular, are considered as an approach to reduce the amount of waste. In Russia, for example, still the majority of waste is deposited. With the recent strategy for the Development of Industry of Sorting, Recycling and Treatment of Waste until 2030 and the formation of an integrated system for the treatment of urban solid waste the amount of treated urban solid waste should be raised up to 36% in 2024 compared to currently 4%. Sorting and recycling of waste are important means to reach the goal (Vedomosti, 2019; green evolution n.d.). China as a second example started recently the pilot program Zero-Waste City in order to minimise solid waste for disposal and maximise recycling in urban areas. Until 2020, an index system for waste-free cities, as well as a technical and institutional system for managing waste-free cities, is planned (ChinaDaily 2019).

Beyond minimising the problem of waste, the increase of raw material availability, both in quantity and in the number of raw materials, is an essential driver for the promotion of recycling and closing material loops. Thus, raw material importing countries are more actively implementing comprehensive approaches of the circular economy. For example, China adopted the Circular Economy Development Promotion Law in 2009, and since then, the circular economy is further developed in each of the Five-Year Plans (FYP). For the first time globally, the law explicitly aimed at decoupling as a strategic goal. Thereby, the concept of renewable resources is used to promote the recovery of metals to increase the production of secondary raw materials (Qi et al. 2016). After a period in which eco-design, clean-production strategies in companies and recycling technologies have been developed, the regulative framework for the industrial and national level was set up to implement circular economy at large scale (Qi et al. 2016). In the current 13th FYP, the Economical, intensive, and circular resource use Initiative supports 75% of national industrial parks and 50% of provincial industrial parks, implements 50 industrial centres for re-use and recycling of industrial waste and demonstration centres for raw material recycling in 100 cities (CCCCPC Central Committee of the Communist Party of China 2016).

Among raw material exporting countries, the availability of raw materials has not been mentioned yet as a reason for the promotion of resource efficiency. South Africa is one of the few exceptions promoting the recycling of iron and steel in conjunction with the implementation of export restrictions for metal scrap to compensate for the declining production quotas (ITAC 2019).

The promotion of re-use and recycling comprises a high variety of materials. As the construction sector is one of the most material-intensive sectors the promotion of recycled construction materials is a prominent strategy in many of the monitored countries. South Africa, for example, promotes innovative regional building materials such as blocks of compressed earth with construction waste as part of the Rambrick project (USE-IT 2019). India, as another example, recognises the use of certified paving stones with recycled inputs already as part of the Green Rating for Integrated Habitat Assessment (GRIHA) – the Indian building certification.

Summary of findings, conclusion and outlook

An important finding is that almost all countries are pursuing approaches to promote the efficient use of raw materials. The countries, however, differ in the extent to which they promote raw material efficiency, in the priorities they set and in the application of tools and approaches. By sorting them along the value chain and by considering raw material used in the respective countries, some general observations can be discerned.

The majority of the surveyed countries have adopted either an overarching framework or sub-strategies in the areas of sustainable development and green growth with resource efficiency as an integral part. In other countries, resource efficiency is promoted through so-called partial strategies. Few countries formulated a national resource efficiency strategy.

In almost all countries, approaches concerning waste prevention and recycling are most widespread. Against the backdrop of the environmental pressure resulting from an increasing amount of waste in almost all countries, this stands to reason. Even in countries such as Germany where resource efficiency is a separate policy field, the topic has evolved from the waste sector. Recycling is mainly promoted through quotas and technology funding, in exceptional cases, also by export restrictions. Among the countries under study, China has created one of the most advanced and comprehensive circular economy programs.

Approaches to promote efficient production are found in almost all countries studied. Differences exist between the sectors addressed (for example, basic materials, processing sectors, high technology, services) and the level being aspired (e.g. to reach international production standards, to become a world market leader). Irrespective of the differences in scope, the applied instruments such as consulting tools, incentive schemes (e.g. awards for best practice companies) and the creation of regional/sectoral company networks are very similar.

The approaches addressing consumption are also similar in the countries under study. All approaches focus on informing citizens using educational programs and product labelling or certifications. Specific targets are set exclusively for public procurement. None of the countries has established restrictions or strong governance for private consumption. The approach by the Republic of Korea is the most extensive approach in this context with the nationwide and cross-sectoral Green Credit Card System.

Outlook

The research project MoniRess has successfully implemented a monitoring system of international resource efficiency policies. The results show impressively how complex the topic of resource efficiency and sustainable resource use policies is. Further, the project indicates that the success of policy approaches towards the sustainable use of natural resources can differ strongly among countries. Based on the information gathered in this project, the focus of future research should be channelled towards the analysis of impacts that determine the success of resource efficiency measures in the countries as well as the evaluation of the outcome of respective resource policies. Identifying factors that contribute most effectively to the success of resource efficiency policies will be helpful in order to further develop and conceptualise resource efficiency policies. UBA continues the research project with the start of 'MoniRess II' in autumn 2019.

List of abbreviations

BAT	best available technologies
BMU	German Federal Minister for the Environment, Nature Conservation, and Nuclear Safety
ECOS	United States Environmental Council of the States
FYP	Five-Year Plan
G20	Group of 20
G7	Group of 7
GRIHA	Green Rating for Integrated Habitat Assessment
GTAI	Germany Trade and Invest
IREP	Indian Resource Efficiency Program
IRP	International Resource Panel
MoniRess	Monitoring international resource policies
NCPC	National Cleaner Production Center
NGO	non-governmental organisation
NITI Aayog	Indian National Planning Commission
OECD	Organisation for Economic Co-operation and Development
ProgRess	German Resource Efficiency Program
PROPER	Indonesia's Program for Pollution Control, Evaluation, and Rating
RECPnet	Global Network for Resource Efficiency and Clean Production
SCP	Sustainable Consumption and Production
UBA	German Federal Environmental Agency
UN	United Nations
UNIDO	United Nations Industrial Development Organization
USEPA	United States Environmental Protection Agency

132 *Monika Dittrich et al.*

References

Afsah, S., Sterner, T., and García, J. H. (2011). *The Institutional History of Indonesia's Environmental Rating and Public Disclosure Program (Proper).*

American Chemistry Council (2019). The Wrap Recycling Action Program. www.plasticfilmrecycling.org/recycling-bags-and-wraps/wrap-consumer-content/ (last access 26.07.2019).

BMU (Federal Environment Ministry) (2012). *German Resource Efficiency Programme (ProgRess).* Berlin.

BMU (Federal Environment Ministry) (2015). Resource Efficiency in the G 7. www.bmu.de/en/topics/economy-products-resources-tourism/resource-efficiency/resource-efficiency-in-the-g7/ (last access 26.07.2019).

BMU (Federal Environment Ministry) (2016). *German Resource Efficiency Programme II.* Berlin. Retrieved from Federal Ministry for the Environment, Nature Conservation, Building and Nuclear Safety (BMUB) www.bmu.de/en/topics/economy-products-resources-tourism/resource-efficiency/overview-of-german-resource-efficiency-programme-progress/ (last access 26.07.2019).

BMU (Federal Environment Ministry) (2017). G20 Summit Decision Establishes G20 Resource Efficiency Dialogue. www.bmu.de/en/topics/economy-products-resources-tourism/resource-efficiency/resource-efficiency-in-the-g20/ (last access 26.07.2019).

CCCCPC (Central Committee of the Communist Party of China) (2016). *The 13th Five-Year Plan for Economic and Social Development of the People'S Republic of China.* In: Central Compilation and Translation Press. Bejing. http://en.ndrc.gov.cn/newsrelease/201612/P020161207645765233498.pdf (last access 26.07.2019).

CEBDS (Conselho Empresarial Brasileiro para o Desenvolvimento Sustentável fica no Rio de Janeiro) (2016). Programa de Capacitação em Compras Sustentáveis. https://cebds.org/publicacoes/programa-de-capacitacao-em-compras-sustentaveis/#.XPDbJo_gqMo (last access 26.07.2019).

ChinaDaily (2019). 10 Urban Areas to Pilot China's 'No-Waste City' Plan. www.chinadaily.com.cn/a/201901/28/WS5c4e5aaca3106c65c34e6c17.html (last access 26.07.2019).

Department of Environmental Affairs (South Africa) (2011). *National Strategy for Sustainable Development and Action Plan NSSD 1 (2011–2014).* November 2011, S. 1–48.

Dittrich, M., Auberger, A., Limberger, S., and Ewers, B. (2020): *Monitoring Internationale Ressourceneffizienzpolitik.* UBA-Texte.

ECOS (The Environmental Council of the States) (2017). Mississippi Offers Tips to Promote a Green Holiday Season. www.ecos.org/news-and-updates/mississippi-offers-tips-to-promote-a-green-holiday-season/ (last access 26.07.2019).

EEA (2016). More From Less – Material Resource Efficiency in Europe. www.eea.europa.eu/publications/more-from-less (last access 26.07.2019).

European Commission (2011). *The Roadmap to a Resource Efficient Europe. Communication from the Commission to the European Parliament, the Council, the European Economic and Social Committee and the Committee of the Regions.* Roadmap to a Resource Efficient Europe. COM (2011) 571.

European Commission (2015). *Closing the Loop – An EU Action Plan for the Circular Economy,* COM (2015) 614. Brussels.

FIESP (Federation of Industries of the State of São Paulo) (2016). Semana do Meio Ambiente. http://hotsite.fiesp.com.br/meioambiente/2016/ (last access 26.07.2019).

Global Green Growth Institute (2015). *Korea's Green Growth Experience: Process, Outcomes and Lessons Learned*. Seoul. www.greengrowthknowledge.org/sites/default/files/downloads/resource/Koreas-Green-Growth-Experience_GGGI.pdf (last access 26.07.2019).

Gobierno de Mexico (n.d.). *Plan Nacional de Desarollo 2013–2018 (Programa Sectorial de Medio Ambiente y Recursos Naturales (PROMARNAT))*.

Good Recycled (n.d.). Good Recycled Products Information System. www.buygr.or.kr/ (last access 26.07.2019).

Government of India, NITI Aayog (National Institution for Transforming India) (2017). NITI Aayog and EU delegation to India release the Strategy on Resource Efficiency (RE). http://pib.nic.in/newsite/PrintRelease.aspx?relid=174013 (last access 26.07.2019).

GreenCape (2017). GreenCape Annual Report 2016/17. https://greencape.co.za/assets/Uploads/GreenCape-Annual-Report-LR.pdf (last access 26.07.2019).

green evolution (n.d.). green evolution.ru. http://greenevolution.ru/analytics/pochemu-pererabotka-vtorsyrya-v-rossinizkorentabelna/&xid=17259,15700023,15700105,15700124, 15700149,15700168,15700173,15700201&usg=ALkJrhhplyWaCLyGpINHQeQhj5RY_3xdrw (last access 14.02.2018).

GTAI (Germany Trade and Invest) (2018). *Russlands Maschinenbauer auf Modernisierungskurs*. www.gtai.de/GTAI/Navigation/DE/Trade/Maerkte/suche,t=russlands-maschinenbauer-auf-modernisierungskurs,did=2199158.html (last access 26.07.2019).

IRP (International Resource Panel) (2019). *Global Resources Outlook 2019: Natural Resources for the Future We Want*. United Nations Environment Programme. Nairobi, Kenya.

ITAC (International Trade Administration Commission of South Africa) (2019). ITAC Price Preference System. www.itac.org.za/pages/services/import--export-control/export-control/price-preference-system (last access 26.07.2019).

Kanungo, P. and Moreno, M. (2003). Indonesia's program for pollution control, evaluation, and rating (PROPER). Retrieved from http://siteresources.worldbank.org/INTEMPOWERMENT/Resources/14825_Indonesia_Proper-web.pdf (last access 29.07.2019).

KEITI (Korea Environmental Industry & Technology Institute) (n.d.). Homepage KEITI. http://el.keiti.re.kr/service/index.do (last access 26.07.2019).

Korea Bizwire (2016). *Korean Banks Introduce Credit Card that Accrues 'Eco-Points.'* Seoul.

Li, W. and Lin, W. (2016). Circular Economy Policies in China. In: Anbumozhi,V.; Kim, J. *(2016): Towards a Circular Economy: Corporate Management and Policy Pathways. ERIA Research Project Report 2014-44*, Jakarta: ERIA, pp.95–111.

Materials Marketplace (n.d.). The Materials Market Place. Retrieved from https://pathway21.com (last access 29.07.2019).

Ministry of Economic Development of the Russian Federation (2015). Innovation Policy. http://economy.gov.ru/en/home/activity/sections/innovations/ (last access 26.07.2019)

NITI Aayog (National Institution for Transforming India), EU External Action (2017). *Strategy on Resource Efficiency*. November.

PCGG (Presidential Committee on Green Growth) (2014). *Second Five-Year Plan for Green Growth (2014–2018)*. Seoul, Korea. www.greengrowth.go.kr/menu001/sub002/GRG_001_202.do (last access 26.07.2019).

Qi, J., Zhao, J., Li, W., Peng, X., Wu, B., and Wang, H. (2016). Development of Circular Economy in China. S. 55–83. www.springer.com/de/book/9789811024641 (last access 26.07.2019).

Renault, J-F., Schwietring, T., Schumacher, K., Schumacher, G., Grimm, V., and Konold, D. (2016). *Übergang in eine Green Economy: Notwendige strukturelle Veränderungen und Erfolgsbedingungen für deren tragfähige Umsetzung in Deutschland – Teilvorhaben: Internationale Bestandsaufnahme des Übergangs in eine Green Economy Vorab-Bericht zum Endbericht*. UBA-Texte 03/2016. Dessau-Rosslau.

Romanov, A. (2016). *Implementation of Best Available Techniques in the Russian Federation: Overview*. Presentation during the UNECE Convention on long-range transboundary air pollution working group in strategies and review, 54. Session (13.-14.12.2016), Genoa. www.unece.org/fileadmin/DAM/env/documents/2016/AIR/WGSR/PPT_WGSR54/Item_5/5_Russian_Federation_Implementation_of_BAT.pdf (last access 26.07.2019).

State Council of the Peoples Republic of China (2015). Made in China 2025 plan issued. http://english.www.gov.cn/policies/latest_releases/2015/05/19/content_281475110703534.htm (last access 26.07.2019).

UN Environment (2019a). Global Material Flows Database. www.resourcepanel.org/global-material-flows-database (last access 26.07.2019).

UN Environment (2019b). International Resource Panel. www.resourcepanel.org/ (last access 26.07.2019).

UNIDO (United Nations Industrial Development Organization) (n.d.). National Cleaner Production Centres (NCPCs) & Networks. www.unido.org/our-focus/cross-cutting-services/partnerships-prosperity/networks-centres-forums-and-platforms/national-cleaner-production-centres-ncpcs-networks (last access 26.07.2019).

Unmann (2015). Hausmüllentsorgung ist in Russland ein Zukunftsmarkt. www.russland.news/hausmuellentsorgung-ist-in-russland-ein-zukunftsmarkt/ (last access 26.07.2019)

USE-IT (2019). USE-IT – Our Programs. www.use-it.co.za/our-programs (last access 26.07.2019).

USEPA (United States Environmental Protection Agency) (2019a). Federal Green Challenge (FGC). Retrieved from www.epa.gov/fgc (last access 29.07.2019).

USEPA (2019b). *Sustainable Materials Management*. www.epa.gov/smm (last access 26.07.2019).

USEPA (2019c). 2019 WasteWise Awards. (www.epa.gov/smm/apply-2019-wastewise-awards) (last access 26.07.2019).

USEPA (n.d.). Principles of Green Engineering. www.epa.gov/green-engineering/about-green-engineering#principles (last access 26.07.2019).

Vedomosti (2019). Putin Instructed to Create an All-Russian Operator for Recycling. www.vedomosti.ru/politics/news/2019/01/14/791354-putin-othodov (last access 26.07.2019).

12 Pathways to a resource-efficient and greenhouse-gas-neutral Germany[1]

Jens Günther, Philip Nuss, Katja Purr, Monika Dittrich, and Harry Lehmann

Introduction

Natural resources such as raw materials (biomass, metals, non-metallic minerals, and fossil fuels), water, land, and ecosystems provide the backbone of modern society. Their use enables the provisioning of feed and food, buildings and infrastructure, transportation, communication, and an almost infinite array of products and services. The extraction and processing of raw materials result in more than half of global greenhouse gas (GHG) emissions and over 90% of global biodiversity loss and water stress (IRP 2019). Currently, an estimated average of four out of nine planetary boundaries have been surpassed, irreversibly changing the functioning of major Earth system processes (such as climate change, altered biogeochemical cycles (phosphorus and nitrogen), land-system change, and biosphere integrity) (Rockström et al. 2009; Steffen et al. 2015). Over the last few decades, a combination of changes in land and ocean uses, overexploitation and pollution, climate change, and invasive alien species have led to catastrophic declines in biodiversity as more than 1 million animal and plant species are now threatened with extinction (IPBES 2019). However, raw materials play a central role in renewable energy technologies, sustainable building materials and infrastructure, modern communication systems, and low-carbon mobility (Mancini et al. 2019) and their use are expected to further increases in the coming decades.

Despite an increasing number of measures to mitigate climate change, global GHG-emissions have nevertheless increased from 27 to 49 Gt CO_2-equivalents (CO_2-eq) between 1970 and 2010 (IPCC 2014). Emissions from the burning of fossil fuels and from industrial processes contributed 78% to total GHGs during this time period. As a result, the global average temperature has increased by 0.85 °C between 1880 and 2012. In 2019, the global mean temperature was found at approximately 0.95 °C above the long-term average of the 20th century and 1.1 °C above pre-industrial levels (UBA 2020). The United Nations Framework Convention on Climate Change (UNFCCC) Paris Agreement was adopted in 2015 with the aim to keep the increase in global average temperature to well below 2 °C above pre-industrial levels; and to limit the increase to 1.5 °C (UNFCCC 2015). However, policies

136 *Jens Günther et al.*

presently in place around the world are insufficient and projected to result in about 3.3 °C warming above pre-industrial levels (Climate Action Tracker 2019).

Goal and scope of this project

Against this background, countries need to urgently transition towards GHG-neutrality by phasing out fossil-based energy carriers, significantly increasing energy and material efficiencies across all sectors, and by promoting more sustainable lifestyles. Furthermore, given the foreseen demands for a number of materials and potential supply risks, and environmental and social pressures associated with this, careful examination of the requirements and possibilities to reduce demand for individual materials is necessary.

The RESCUE ('Resource-efficient Pathways towards Greenhouse-Gas-Neutrality') study presented in this chapter explores different trans-formation pathways for Germany towards a raw material-efficient and GHG-neutral society considering all economic sectors. It builds upon the German Environment Agency's study 'Germany in 2050 – A greenhouse gas neutral country' (UBA 2014) which showed that it is technically feasible to reduce national GHG-emissions by 95% until 2050 compared to 1990. The rapid phase-out of fossil fuels via the widespread use of re-newable energy across all sectors of the economy is essential for this transformation. By switching completely to renewable energies and ex-ploiting efficiency potentials, it is possible to reduce territorial GHG-emissions from energy supply and use (electricity, heat, transport) to zero. A central building block is sector coupling with direct electricity use (e.g. the power to heat, electro-mobility) or indirect use via power to gas (PtG) and power to liquid (PtL) for the provisioning of GHG-neutral fuels for transport, feedstocks for the chemical industry, and process heat for in-dustry. However, for certain sectors such as agriculture and LULUCF (land use, land-use change, and forestry), and parts of industry, GHG reductions are limited, so that base emissions remain. However, raw materials use was not considered in previous studies.

Scenario storylines

In this study, ambitious climate protection and materials management are being considered together across all economic sectors. For this, six scenarios are de-veloped which show possible development paths for Germany until 2050. The goal is to (1) quantify the demand for raw materials (i.e. fossil fuels, metals, non-metallic minerals and biomass) associated with a GHG-neutral Germany until 2050, (2) capture the effects of individual measures and assumptions on raw material consumption and GHG-emissions, and (3) highlight possible synergies and obstacles between materials management and climate protection. Land-use changes related to new settlements and transport infrastructure in Germany are partly considered. However, further aspects such as the availability of raw materials or other environmental impacts are only qualitatively discussed and present the basis for future studies.

In all scenarios, Germany continues to be a country with a high population density and competitive industry and is embedded in the European Union (EU) and the world. Today's economic structures are assumed not to change fundamentally until 2050. All scenarios represent target scenarios that meet the GHG reduction targets of −55% in 2030 and −95% in 2050 compared to 1990 levels (BMU 2016). However, the individual development paths to achieve these targets differ by scenario. Furthermore, all scenarios follow population developments from currently 83 million people to about 72 million people in 2050 (option V1 of Destatis 2015). A gradual reduction in infrastructure projects and building activities is assumed which avoids new additional soil sealing by 2050. In all scenarios, the energy system is gradually retrofitted and based entirely on renewable energy by 2050. Improvements in energy efficiency in all sectors (e.g. transport, industry, and buildings) combined with sector coupling and direct electricity use goes hand in hand with the expansion of renewable energy. Nuclear power and carbon capture and storage (CCS) technologies are not considered as they are prone to yet non-manageable environmental risks (UBA 2015) and, therefore, do not represent sustainable future strategies for Germany. The scenarios include those described in the following sections.

GreenEe1 and Ee2 (Germany – resource-efficient and greenhouse gas neutral – energy-efficiency)

The development of GHG-emissions and raw materials demand is modelled on the basis of assumptions made in previous work (UBA 2014). Raw materials demand simulations include materials such as biomass, fossil fuels, metal ores and non-metallic minerals, as well as a number of individual raw materials (e.g. lithium, cobalt, nickel, iron, copper, among others.). The ambitious increase of energy efficiency, including the tapping of yet unrealised energy efficiency potential throughout all economic sectors, is the main characteristic of this scenario. Other countries in the world follow Germany's developments but at a slower pace (~10-year time delay). While in GreenEe1, the domestic production capacities and therefore exports are continuously increasing, in GreenEe2 a more balanced trade situation is assumed (i.e. imports and exports converge and domestic production capacities decrease). Economic growth equals 0.7% per year. Similar to today's situation, energy imports to Germany consists mostly of fuels. By 2050, all fuel imports are fully based on renewables (i.e. PtX facilities built-up abroad). Only applications for which no direct electricity use is possible (e.g. fuels for aviation, heavy-duty vehicles, and certain industrial applications) use fuels produced via PtX routes. In industry, the restructuring towards energy-efficient process technologies based on renewables is complemented by a reduction in process-based emissions to the currently known technically possible level. The transition of the transport sector comprises an increasing share of electric vehicles for personal mobility and public transportation until 2050. Transport avoidance is facilitated by intelligent logistics in freight transport and the 'city of short distances' in personal transport. In addition to technical measures, healthier eating habits of the population lead to reduced livestock in Germany. The development towards mixed forests is continued over time, thus, preserving the forest as a net carbon sink. Biodiversity protection is increasingly integrated into forest management, supported by the expansion of protected land areas for natural forest developments. Increasing use of secondary raw materials and material substitution in particular in the metals industry, chemical industry, and building sector fosters materials efficiency. Following the demographic trends, per capita living space requirement rise until 2030 and total living space is subsequently reduced to the 2010 level. Land-take for transport and settlements is reduced to 20 ha/day by 2030 and moves towards net zero in the subsequent decades until 2050.

GreenLate (late transition)

GHG-emissions are cut by 95% in this scenario as well. However, the transitions process sets in at a later point in time compared to GreenEe. Also, energy efficiencies are raised in a less ambitious manner. Consequently, GHG-emissions have to be reduced more radically and within a shorter time window. As a result, improvements in energy- and materials-efficiency are lower than in the other scenarios. This trend is also visible at the international stage (with a ~10-year delay). In 2050, energy supply is based entirely on renewable sources. However, the energy demand is higher than in the other Green-scenarios as conventional technologies with lower efficiencies are still widely in use due to the late transition. Until 2050, efficient and power-based technologies for sector coupling can only be implemented for applications with short renewal cycles, or in areas for which high investment incentives exist. For example, the transition towards electric mobility for private transport is implemented late. This means that by 2050 a large number of conventional technologies are still in operation, for example., in transport, space heating, and process heat supply. Similarly, measures targeting traffic reduction and relocation are implemented in the last years prior to 2050. The trend towards healthier diets only starts around 2025 and results in a higher share of livestock usage compared to the other scenarios.

GreenMe (material efficiency)

This scenario focuses on raising material efficiency in an ambitious manner and throughout all economic sectors. The restructuring of the energy system and of sectors such as transport, industry, and building and housing develops similar to GreenEe2. However, technologies with a smaller material footprint are favoured. For example, for photovoltaic (PV) systems an increasing number of roof-top thin-film PV modules are installed (smaller material footprint and land requirements than conventional ground-based PV systems). Similarly, foundations and wind towers are designed with durability in mind, so that their service life can be significantly increased. Additional material efficiency measures include, for instance, the light-weighting of vehicles, use of alternative materials (e.g. textile-reinforced concrete for construction), the widespread use of timber buildings, or the use of biotic materials as insulating materials. Assumptions with regard to agriculture and healthy diets follow the GreenEe scenarios.

GreenLife (lifestyle changes)

GreenLife analyses how additional lifestyle/behavioural changes influence GHG-emissions and raw material consumption. Current trends, as well as smaller niche tendencies, are scaled up in this scenario. For example, the demand for durable and repairable products results in innovation in the production- and service sectors. The willingness of each individual to switch to sustainable lifestyles leads to a reduction in the demand for large living space and the retrofitting of larger homes into sub-units. Shared housing options are widely accepted and implemented. The share of multi-family homes in the building inventory increases. As a result, the demand for per-capita living space decreases and land-take is already reduced to 10 ha/day by 2030 and moves towards net-zero until 2050. Resource-efficient construction is widely implemented and the share of wooden buildings increases. Domestic flights are becoming less attractive and by 2050 only ground transportation takes place within Germany (for both private and business trips). Holiday flights to international destinations are increasingly replaced by domestic trips and as a result flight traffic in 2050 is only slightly above 2010 levels. Increasing urbanisation results in the use of fewer cars. Instead, a mix of public transport, walking and biking, and ridesharing are used. Electro-mobility and electrified public transportation outside of urban centres are widely implemented by 2050. As a result, the use of private vehicles in urban areas is negligible by 2050. Increased awareness of environmental and health issues is an essential factor for moving towards more sustainable diets. Food waste is avoided as far as possible and regional and seasonal foods are processed. Animal products are consumed much faster than in the other Green-scenarios so that livestock in Germany decreases faster and more strongly. The technical measures, such as the transformation of the energy system or the integration of new efficient technologies in industry, mobility and buildings, are the same as in GreenEe.

GreenSupreme (minimising future GHG-emissions and raw material consumption)

In this scenario, the most effective measures from the previous scenarios are combined. In summary, this includes a combination of measures from GreenMe on material efficiency together with assumptions from GreenLife on

140 *Jens Günther et al.*

sustainable and healthy lifestyles. In contrast to the other scenarios, which assume an average annual GDP growth of around 0.7%, in GreenSupreme the annual GDP growth is assumed to be net zero after 2030.

Methodology

A combination of five models is used together with various sector-specific data to carry out quantitative assessments of GHG emissions and raw materials requirements in six scenarios between 2010 and 2050. Modelling of the transport sector is based on the Transport Emission Model (TREMOD) which analyses the GHG emissions and energy uses of all means of passenger and freight transportation on a yearly basis (ifeu 2019a; UBA 2019). The energy consumption for space heating and hot water in buildings under the assumption variations in the scenarios is based on the Building Model (GEMOD) (ifeu 2019b). Modelling of the agricultural sector is based on the Agriculture and LULUCF model (ALMOD) (Dittrich et al. 2020a). The cross-sectoral build-up and optimisation of the energy supply is based on the SCOPE model, which complies with the climate targets and ensures supply security and permanent coverage of demands in all applications and sectors (Fraunhofer IEE 2016). We note that only a cost-based optimisation of the energy sector is carried out in SCOPE and other societal and environmental costs are not included in the assessment. The economy-wide use of raw materials including the upstream raw material requirements and GHG-emissions (material and carbon footprints) are derived using the environmental and economic raw materials model (URMOD) (ifeu 2019c).

The material flows into the German economy (i.e. domestic extraction, imports, and secondary material inputs) and exports are determined using economy-wide material flow accounts (EW-MFA). The headline indicator is the RMC (Raw Material Consumption) which represents the primary raw material use for domestic consumption and investments. The RMC is divided into the following raw material categories: biomass, metal ores, non-metallic minerals, and fossil energy materials/carriers. The use of raw materials for internationally traded goods is expressed in raw material equivalents (RME) in order to equally assess raw materials extraction domestically and abroad. RME represents the weight of raw materials used for the manufacture of goods including all raw materials used in the production of these goods both at home and abroad. In addition, a number of single raw materials (for example, metals) are assessed in this project.

Further information on the methodology and detailed results are provided in (Dittrich et al. 2020a, 2020b, 2020c, 2020d, 2020e). A summary of the results is also provided in (Günther et al. 2019).

Results

GHG emissions. In all scenarios, the overall GHG mitigation target for 2030 of the German Climate Action Plan (reduction of 55% compared by

2030 compared to 1990) is reached, in particular, due to the significant progress in the energy sector. With the exception of GreenLate, all other scenarios are able to reach even higher emissions reductions until 2030, namely 60.3% (GreenEe1), 61.4 to 62.6% (GreenEe2/Me/Life), and 69% (GreenSupreme) (all compared to 1990 levels). However, not all individual sector targets are met.

All Green-scenarios have in common that a transformation towards 100% renewable energy (electricity, fuels, and feedstocks) takes place until 2050. By 2050, GHG-reductions of 95% in GreenLate and 97% in GreenSupreme are achieved which considers the GHG-emissions that are also accounted for in the climate targets of the German Federal Government (reduction of 80–95% by 2030 compared with 1990). Through sustainable agriculture and forestry management (i.e. natural sinks), GreenLife and GreenSupreme achieve net-zero emissions and even GreenLate comes close to this goal. The Green scenarios thus show that no carbon capture and storage (CCS) is required for GHG-neutrality in Germany. Because of its even more ambitious measures to limit global warming to 1.5 °C, the GreenSupreme scenario meets the 2050 climate targets already in 2036 with a subsequent reduction of 88% by 2040 compared with 1990 levels.

The development paths of the Green-scenarios are compared with a global average transformation path of the Intergovernmental Panel on Climate Change (IPCC) which should be approximately followed in order to limit global warming to 1.5 °C compared to pre-industrial levels (IPCC global 1.5 °C; IIASA 2019; Figure 12.1). The comparison highlights that in order to develop along the lines of the Paris Agreement, national GHG-emissions should be reduced by around 70% by 2030 compared with 1990 levels as outlined in GreenSupreme. The high level of ambition reflected in GreenEe1, GreenEe2, GreenMe and GreenLife (especially until 2040) does not meet the requirements of the IPCC's average global 1.5 °C emissions pathway. Similarly, the current targets of the German Federal Government and the GreenLate-scenario until 2040 are insufficient to limit global warming well below 2 °C. On the other hand, GreenSupreme, represents a compatible transformation path.

Raw material consumption (RMC). The transformation towards a largely GHG-neutral Germany has considerable effects on the demand for raw materials. The RMC can be reduced through the phase-out of fossil energy carriers when transitioning towards a renewable energy system. Other important leverage points include, e.g. structural policies that reduce the number and size of new settlement areas, increased energy savings, enhanced use of secondary materials, optimisation of manufacturing processes via substitution and increases in material efficiency, and lifestyle changes. In all scenarios, continuous improvements in materials efficiency and in the technological development in Europe and the rest of the world (RoW) are assumed (see scenario details above).

In 2010 (base year), Germany's RMC equals 1.37 Gt and is dominated by non-metallic minerals and fossil fuels (Figure 12.2). Already in GreenLate it is

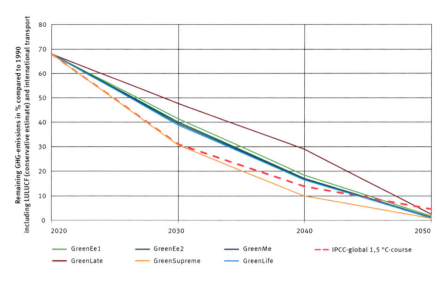

Figure 12.1 Development of the remaining GHG-emissions in the Green scenarios taking into account LULUCF (conservative) and the CO2 emissions of international transport.
Source: Günther et al. (2019).

assumed that energy efficiency potentials across all sectors are unlocked and ambitious sustainable resource policy is implemented (with a time delay compared to the other scenarios). This includes the increased use of secondary materials (see also our companion paper in this book) and material substitution as well as changes towards more sustainable lifestyles (e.g. less meat consumption and changes in transport via avoidance and relocation). As a result, the RMC decreases in GreenLate already by 56% until 2050 compared to 2010 levels. Additional measures to increase both energy and material efficiency (GreenEe2 + material efficiency) supplemented by additional sustainable life-styles changes (e.g. lower per-capita living space or changes in personal mobility) allow for a reduction of RMC by a further 12% (GreenMe). This includes, e.g. tapping the full recycling potentials for materials, additional material substitutions, and the use of innovative materials such as textile-reinforced concrete and timber constructions. In addition, it is assumed that at global-scale efforts towards increased materials efficiency (similar to Germany) also take place and this is reflected in the lower material footprint of imports. Further lifestyle changes (i.e. a reduction of per-capita living space compared to today and consumer preference for more durable goods offered within the framework of a sharing economy) of the GreenLife-scenario combined with a more ambitious transformation of the energy system

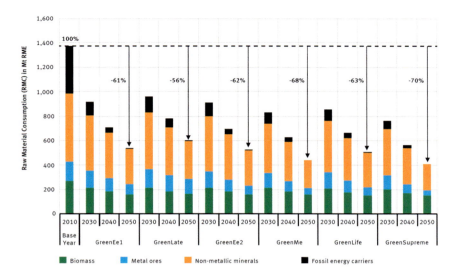

Figure 12.2 Raw material consumption (RMC) by raw materials category for all Green scenarios (2010-2050). RME: raw material equivalents.
Source: Günther et al. (2019).

and the liberation from annual economic growth (GreenSupreme) are capable of reducing RMC by an additional 2% until 2050 (GreenSupreme).

The largest reduction of RMC is associated with the phase-out of fossil energy carriers. Durable products from the chemical industry are produced from 2030 onwards using feedstock obtained through PtX routes using renewable electricity. In 2050, only small amounts of fossil raw materials are still consumed in GreenEe1, GreenLate, GreenEe2 and GreenLife (approx. 5.5 to 8.1 Mt). This is a result of the delayed switch to renewable energies in the rest of the world and imports of products to Germany (footprinting perspective). On the other hand, due to the assumed global phase-out of fossil fuels by 2050 in GreenMe and GreenSupreme, no fossil energy carriers are part of the RMC in 2050 in both scenarios.

Dietary changes such as reduced meat consumption as well as the assumption that no virgin biomass is used for energy purposes after 2030 contribute significantly to the decline in biomass use. In contrast, increasing wood construction in all Green scenarios except GreenLate and the substitution of abiotic materials by wood (e.g. insulating materials) increase the biomass demand (especially in GreenMe and GreenSupreme). Due to the additional demands for metals for restructuring the economy and the energy system, the decrease in the consumption of metal ores equals only –4% to –29% until 2030, whereas a reduction of –16% to –53% can be achieved by 2040. In GreenLate, the transformation of the economy is delayed and does not pick up speed until after 2030.

144   *Jens Günther et al.*

In 2010, RMC per person (RMC/cap) in Germany equalled 16.8 t/cap and is thus above the global average of 11.1 t/cap (IRP 2019). In the Green scenarios, a reduction to 5.7 (GreenSupreme) to 8.4 tons/cap (GreenLate) is achieved in 2050. All scenarios, with the exception of GreenLate, thus reach the corridor of sustainable resource use of 5 to 8 t/cap/year discussed in the literature in 2050 (Bringezu 2015; IRP 2014; Lehmann 2018; UNEP 2011). The comparison shows that reaching a significantly lower RMC per capita in Germany in 2050 might be possible, while at the same time remaining a high standard of the technological and economic level of well-being.

Finally, also the demand for several individual raw materials was examined in this project. Results show that while for a number of materials such as, e.g. iron, copper, aluminium, zinc, and nickel demand decreases over time (due to efficiency gains and lifestyle changes), the demand for a range of speciality metals such as lithium and cobalt is expected to significantly increase in the future, for instance as a result of the widespread implementation of electric vehicles. This is examined in further detail in our companion paper in this book (Dittrich et al. 2020f).

Recommendations

The RESCUE study highlights that GHG-neutrality in Germany together with a significant reduction of primary raw material consumption is possible through bold and ambitious actions. However, the sketched transformation pathways will also increase demands for individual raw materials (see also our companion paper). The six Green-scenarios illustrate that significant progress at all levels is necessary to ensure sustainable climate protection and natural resource conservation. Implementing only technical solutions for lowering GHG-emissions and raw material consumption is not sufficient. Instead, a broad range of strategies and measures targeting substitution, avoidance, and natural carbon sinks to influence GHGs in the atmosphere are needed. Against the background of a globally equitable use of raw materials and to follow the IPCC's average global 1.5 °C emissions pathway, a transformation path analogous to GreenSupreme should, therefore, be pursued.

Abbreviations

ALMOD	agriculture and land use model
CCS	carbon capture and storage
EW–MFA	economy-wide material flow accounts
GDP	gross domestic product
GEMOD	Gebäudeenergiemodell (building energy model)
GHG	greenhouse gas emissions
IPCC	Intergovernmental Panel on Climate Change
LULUCF	land use, land use change and Forestry
PtG	power to gas

PtL	power to liquid
PtX	power to X
RMC	raw material consumption
TREMOD	transport emissions model
URMOD	Umweltökonomisches Rohstoffmodell (environmental–economic raw material model)

Note

1 This chapter is based on a technical report published first by the authors as "Günther J., Lehmann H., Nuss P. and Purr K. "Resource-Efficient Pathways towards Greenhouse-Gas- Neutrality — RESCUE: Summary Report" at https://www.umweltbundesamt.de/en/rescue/summary_report.

References

BMU. (2016). *Klimaschutzplan 2050. Klimaschutzpolitische Grundsätze und Ziele der Bundesregierung.* BMUB.

Bringezu, Stefan. (2015). Possible Target Corridor for Sustainable Use of Global Material. *Resources* 4(1): 25–54. doi:10.3390/resources4010025.

Climate Action Tracker. (2019). Addressing Global Warming. https://climateactiontracker.org/global/temperatures/.

Destatis. (2015). *Bevölkerung Deutschlands bis 2060. 13. Koordinierte Bevölkerungsvorausberechnung.* www.destatis.de/DE/Themen/Gesellschaft-Umwelt/Bevoelkerung/Bevoelkerungsvoraus berechnung/_inhalt.html.

Dittrich, M., N. Gerhardt, K. Schoer, F. Dünnebeil, S. Becker, A. v. Oehsen, S. Koeppen, et al., (2020a). *Transformationsprozess zum Treibhausgasneutralem und Ressourcenschonendem Deutschland – GreenEe.* Climate Change 01/2020. Dessau-Roßlau.

Dittrich, M., N. Gerhardt, K. Schoer, F. Dünnebeil, S. Becker, A. v. Oehsen, S. Koeppen, et al., (2020b). *Transformationsprozess zum Treibhausgasneutralem und Ressourcenschonendem Deutschland – GreenLate.* Climate Change 01/2020. Dessau-Roßlau.

Dittrich, M., N. Gerhardt, K. Schoer, F. Dünnebeil, S. Becker, A. v. Oehsen, S. Koeppen, et al., (2020c). *Transformationsprozess zum Treibhausgasneutralem und Ressourcenschonendem Deutschland – GreenMe.* Climate Change 01/2020. Dessau-Roßlau.

Dittrich, M., N. Gerhardt, K. Schoer, F. Dünnebeil, S. Becker, A. v. Oehsen, S. Koeppen, et al., (2020d). *Transformationsprozess zum Treibhausgasneutralem und Ressourcenschonendem Deutschland – GreenSupreme.* Climate Change 01/2020. Dessau-Roßlau.

Dittrich, M., N. Gerhardt, K. Schoer, F. Dünnebeil, S. Becker, A. v. Oehsen, S. Koeppen, et al., (2020e). *Transformationsprozess zum Treibhausgasneutralem und Ressourcenschonendem Deutschland – GreenLife.* Climate Change 01/2020. Dessau-Roßlau.

Dittrich, M., K. Schoer, J. Günther, Philip Nuss, and H. Lehmann. (2020f). 'Resource Use in a Post-Fossil Germany.' In H. Lehmann (ed.), *Factor X. Challenges, Implementation Strategies and Examples for a Sustainable Use of Natural Resources.* Cham: Springer.

Fraunhofer IEE. (2016). *SCOPE. Sektorenübergreifende Einsatz- und Ausbauoptimierung für Analysen des zukünftigen Energieversorgungssystems.* Kassel.

Günther, J., H. Lehmann, Philip Nuss, and K. Purr. (2019). *Resource-Efficient Pathways towards Greenhouse-Gas-Neutrality.* Dessau-Roßlau, Germany: German Environment Agency (UBA).

ifeu. (2019a). Transport Emission Model (TREMOD). www.ifeu.de/en/methods/models/tremod/.

ifeu. (2019b). Buidlings Model (GEMOD). www.ifeu.de/en/methods/models/gemod/.

ifeu. (2019c). Environmental and Economic Raw Materials Model (URMOD). www.ifeu.de/en/methods/models/urmod/.

IIASA. (2019). *IAMC 1.5 °C Scenario Explorer*. International Institute for Applied Systems Analysis. https://data.ene.iiasa.ac.at/iamc-1.5c-explorer/.

IPBES. (2019). *Summary for Policymakers of the Global Assessment Report on Biodiversity and Ecosystem Services of the Intergovernmental Science-Policy Platform on Biodiversity and Ecosystem Services*. Bonn: IPBES.

IPCC. (2014). *Climate Change 2014: Synthesis Report. Contribution of Working Groups I, II and III to the Fifth Assessment Report of the Intergovernmental Panel on Climate Change*. Geneva: IPCC.

IRP. (2014). *Managing and Conserving the Natural Resource Base for Sustained Economic and Social Development – A Reflection from the International Resource Panel on the Establishment of Sustainable Development Goals Aimed at Decoupling Economic Growth from Escalating*. IRP.

IRP. (2019). *Global Resources Outlook 2019: Natural Resources for the Future We Want*. Nairobi, Kenya: UNEP.

Lehmann, Harry, ed. (2018). *Factor X. Challenges, Implementation Strategies and Examples for a Sustainable Use of Natural Resources*. Cham: Springer.

Mancini, Lucia, Beatriz Vidal Legaz, Matteo Vizzarri, Dominic Wittmer, Giacomo Grassi, and David Pennington. (2019). *Mapping the Role of Raw Materials in Sustainable Development Goals. A Preliminary Analysis of Links, Monitoring Indicators, and Related Policy Initiatives*. Luxemburg: Publications Office of the European Union.

Rockström, Johan, Will Steffen, Kevin Noone, Åsa Persson, F. Stuart Chapin, Eric F. Lambin, Timothy M. Lenton, et al., (2009). A Safe Operating Space for Humanity. *Nature* 461(7263): 472–475. doi:10.1038/461472a.

Steffen, Will, Katherine Richardson, Johan Rockström, Sarah E. Cornell, Ingo Fetzer, Elena M. Bennett, Reinette Biggs, et al., (2015). Planetary Boundaries: Guiding Human Development on a Changing Planet. *Science* 347(6223): 1259855. doi:10.1126/science.1259855.

UBA. (2014). *Treibhausgasneutrales Deutschland Im Jahr 2050. Im Auftrag des Umweltbundesamtes*. Climate Change 07/2014. Dessau-Roßlau: UBA.

UBA. (2015). *Landesgesetz zum Kohlendioxid-Speicherungsgesetz erarbeiten. Stellungnahme vom 28. Februar 2013 zum Antrag der Fraktionen DIE LINKE sowie BÜNDNIS 90/DIE RÜNEN im Landtag von Sachsen-Anhalt*. Dokumentationen. Dessau-Roßlau: UBA.

UBA. (2019). *Emissionsdaten*. TREMOD. www.umweltbundesamt.de/themen/verkehr-laerm/emissionsdaten.

UBA. (2020). Weltweite Temperaturen und Extremwetterereignisse seit 2010. www.umweltbundesamt.de/themen/klima-energie/klimawandel/weltweite-temperaturen-extremwetterereignisse-seit#Chronik.

UNEP. (2011). *Decoupling Natural Resource Use and Environmental Impacts from Economic Growth, A Report of the Working Group on Decoupling to the International Resource Panel*. United Nations Environment Programme. Nairobi, Kenya.

UNFCCC. (2015). Paris Agreement. http://unfccc.int/resource/docs/2015/cop21/eng/l09r01.pdf.

13 Resource use in a post-fossil green Germany

Monika Dittrich, Karl Schoer, Jens Günther, Philip Nuss, and Harry Lehmann

Introduction

Human life requires materials. Our current human experience is that the amount of used materials increases with the level of wealth. According to IRP (2017a) estimates, there could be a doubling of the materials that would be extracted globally by 2050, if significant changes in our way of production and consumption. The extraction and processing of materials are linked to environmental harnessing and damage, such as climate change, loss of soil fertility and biodiversity, water stress, among others. Therefore, it can also be expected that the environmental impact will at least double as well. To mitigate climate change, the fossil-based economies have to change towards a post-fossil, circular, sustainable economy. This raises the question of how many materials are required in a post-fossil world? Likewise, it is of interest to know how many and what kind of materials are necessary for such an economic transformation?

Chapter 12 of this volume has presented different transformation pathways towards a 95% Greenhouse gas emission saving in 2050:

- GreenEe as an energy-efficient pathway.
- GreenLate with a less ambitious and late transformation.
- GreenMe with high efforts in material efficiency.
- GreenLife with high lifestyle changes.
- GreenSupreme, which combines the best of material efficiency and lifestyle changes.

For all of the five pathways, primary resource consumption is declining as demonstrated in Chapter 12. By analysing the material used in more detail, this chapter goes a step further and ponders important questions: What are the relevant strategies and measures that lead to a reduction of primary material demand? How many secondary materials are used? What is the future demand for raw materials? Will there be enough raw materials available for Germany? This chapter answers these questions by partly using selected raw materials as examples.

148   *Monika Dittrich et al.*

Strategies and measures to reduce resource use in green Germany

All green scenarios include strategies with respect to material efficiency, substitution and recycling. However, the pathways differ with respect to their level of ambition. Given the limited scope of the article, we will summarize the most important strategies and differences between the pathways and explain relevant general assumptions as well as specific assumptions with regard to substitution and recycling. For more details, see UBA (2019) and Dittrich et al. (2020a, 2020b, 2020c, 2020d, 2020e).

Overall and structural changes with effects on resource demand

All Green-Scenario assume a declining population in Germany by −12% in 2050 compared to 2010, based on official population projection by Destatis (2015). A declining population affects the whole economy, including the demand for food, energy, products and services as well as the demand for housing and overall infrastructure.

The demand for infrastructure furthermore depends on urban policies. In all Green scenarios, land sealing decreases, and thus the demand for new communal streets, water infrastructure as well as communal electricity and communication infrastructure declines. However, in GreenSupreme and GreenLife far less urban space is developed as people demand less living space (41 m^2 per person) while in contrast, the built-up area is largest in GreenLate with high average living space demand (53 m^2 per person) (Dittrich et al. 2020a, 2020b, 2020c, 2020d, 2020e, forthcoming).

Except for GreenSupreme, all scenarios assume a low overall economic growth of 0.7% p.a. In GreenSupreme, zero growth is assumed which implies that activity rates in several economic sectors are declining while at the same time other sectors are still innovative and expanding (Dittrich et al. 2020a, 2020b, 2020c, 2020d, 2020e, forthcoming). As a result of declining demand for infrastructure, housing, industrial and commercial buildings, the demand for construction services and construction materials declines in all scenarios, most distinctively in GreenSupreme. Likewise, the transformation of the energy system requires innovation and implies growth in the electricity, electronics and machinery sectors. In all scenarios, there is a shift towards services that are less resource-intensive compared to the extraction and industry.

Besides the population development, urban policies and economic growth, a fourth very important factor refer to the transition outside Germany. All pathways described by the green scenarios imply that European countries are transforming their economies towards a resource-efficient and greenhouse gas neutral Europe in the same way as Germany. Thus, all changes regarding substitution, recycling and efficiency described below are relevant in European countries as well. Hence, upstream flows of imports from European countries decline, accordingly. For example, if the energy system changes towards renewables in European countries, respective exports do not carry fossil backpacks anymore. Outside Europe, the world is changing as well. In the majority of Green pathways, the rest of the world is changing its energy system and its production processes with a lag of ten years and thus, reaching the full transformation in 2060. In GreenMe and GreenSupreme the rest of the world has already fully transformed its energy system by 2050 and produces its products and services as resource-efficient as it is assumed in Germany.

Substitution

In all green scenarios there are significant redirections of material flows. The dominant one, of course, is the substitution of fossil fuels by renewable energies: coal, currently used for electricity, is substituted by wind and solar power; petroleum and gas used for heat generation or mobility are substituted by renewably produced electricity and heat or by synthetic fuels. In all green scenarios, no fossil fuels are used in Germany in 2050 anymore – neither fossil fuels for energetic use nor fossil fuels as raw materials for plastics or paints. However, the scenarios differ in the speed and extent at which the substitution is implemented: while in GreenSupreme, both coal and petroleum are already substituted by renewables to a high degree in 2030, in GreenLate the changes start about ten years later.

In all green scenarios the building materials are changing: minerals are replaced by biotic materials. In Germany, there is a slight tendency toward wooden houses. This trend is perpetuated in GreenLate while it is intensified in GreenEe and GreenLife, following the sustainable pathway for building construction in Germany as explained in Deilmann et al. (2017). In GreenMe and GreenSupreme the substitution of minerals used in the housing sector by wooden materials is further strengthened: In 2050, the majority of new houses are built with wooden materials including insulation wherever feasible.

Further substitutions, particularly in GreenMe and GreenSupreme, include for example the use of aluminium instead of copper in electricity wires.

Recycling

In Germany, several materials such as paper, glass, plastics, construction minerals and metals are already being recycled. However, there is still potential to increase the amount of secondary materials used in the German economy. In all transformation pathways, the use of secondary materials increases. The increase in the recycling rate is only small in GreenLate but higher in GreenEe and GreenLife. Wherever feasible, further recycling efforts are implemented in GreenMe and GreenSupreme. In this context, the following paragraphs give some examples.

In 2010, iron scrap held a share of around 47% of input in steel production (UBA 2014). The share of secondary iron can be increased if steel production changes from blast furnace processes towards electric arc furnace processes. In

150 *Monika Dittrich et al.*

GreenLate only 50% of iron scrap is used in steel production in 2050. All other transformation pathways assume a full change of steel production with a share of 67% of iron scrap in 2050. In GreenSupreme the scenario with the fastest overall transformation, steel production technology change starts already in 2025 and is accomplished in 2040.

Similar to iron, copper, aluminium, lead and zinc are recycled. In Germany copper scrap formed about 56% of copper production in 2010. With respect to aluminium, lead and zinc, the secondary materials held an input share of 54%, 73% and 39% in the respective metal production (UBA 2014). In the green scenarios, the shares of secondary materials increase due to improved collection, urban mining and technological changes. In GreenLate the share of secondary copper, aluminium, zinc and lead in metal production increase only up to 70% in 2050. In the other green scenarios, however, the secondary metals hold a share of 90% in the respective non-iron metal production.

Likewise, recycling can further be improved with regard to other metals such as zinc, tin, silver or nickel. However, the data on the rates of secondary inputs in the respective metal production is less reliable due to a lack of data. Therefore, a general approach was used. In GreenEe and GreenLife the share of secondary metals increased by 10% until 2050 compared to the share in 2010. In GreenLate the increase is only 5% while in GreenMe and Supreme the secondary share rises up by 25%.

Further improvements in recycling comprise paper, plastics, wood, glasses and different construction minerals. With regard to some materials, the potential for improvement is low, for example, secondary paper already holds a high share of paper production. The paper industry produced around 23 million ton of paper in 2010, with an input of almost 16 million tons of secondary paper (UBA 2014). Thus, the potential for further increase is small and accounts only for 10% increase in 2050 compared to 2010 in all green scenarios. Recycling of other materials can be improved largely, for example for plastics. In GreenMe and GreenSupreme, 75% of post-consumer plastics are recycled in 2050, compared to 47% in 2017.

Further resource efficiency

All pathways in the green scenarios include further efficiency measures with respect to energy and materials. Again, efforts differ between the pathways. The material efficient design of products, for example, lightweight electric cars, and material-efficient production technology, such as bifacial and thin cells, are used mostly in GreenMe and GreenSupreme. Material efficiency also increases due to improved processes and waste reduction in production and services. In the past, average material efficiency increased by 1% p.a. in Germany excluding structural effects of reunification (Dittrich et al. 2018). With regard to all sectors where no specific change was described, an average increase in material efficiency was assumed. In GreenLate it slows down to 0.9% p.a. which is in line with the European average while in GreenEe and

GreenLife material efficiency increases to 1.1% p.a. and in GreenMe and GreenSupreme the rate raises to 1.2% p.a.

The entire primary and secondary material consumption in the Green pathways

All changes explained above, and further changes described in UBA (2019) and Dittrich et al. (2020a, 2020b, 2020c, 2020d, 2020e, forthcoming) result in a significant reduction of the consumption of primary raw materials (RMC; see Chapter 12, this volume). However, the entire material demand is higher due to secondary materials which are used as well. If the used secondary materials are expressed in raw material equivalents just like the used primary materials, the result reflects the amount of substituted primary materials. Furthermore, the share of secondary materials of in the entire material demand can be interpreted as the degree of circularity of an economy: 100% would be a fully circular economy without dissipative losses and no more demand of primary materials at all; 0% characterizes an economy that only uses primary materials without any recycling or reuse.

In addition to the raw material consumption, Figure 13.1 also shows the secondary materials expressed in tons of raw material equivalents. Secondary metals include iron, copper and aluminium. The other secondary materials comprise paper, wood, plastics and construction minerals such as recycled concrete, sand or gypsum. Secondary construction minerals are conservatively estimated without closed-loop recycling. Thus, the overall amount of used secondary material is a minimum estimation. While RMC decreases in all scenarios by at least −56% (GreenLate) or even by −70% (GreenSupreme) the volume of secondary materials in consumption increases in all scenarios. When following a conservative estimation, at least around 152 million tons (RME) of secondary materials were used in Germany in 2010. In 2050, at least 218 million tons of secondary materials are used in GreenLate and 260 million tons are used in GreenEe. GreenMe shows the highest amount of secondary materials with 270 million tons in 2050. In contrast, the amount is lowest in GreenSupreme with 206 million tons. The difference between GreenMe and GreenSupreme is interesting as in both pathways the shares of recycling materials are equal. Thus, the difference of 65 million tons is a consequence of the decrease in demand and particularly a decrease in the demand for construction minerals. With respect to construction minerals, transportation distances limit the use of secondary construction minerals although they are theoretically available.

The share of secondary materials in the entire material consumption increases in all Green pathways. While in GreenEe the degree of circularity is 10% in 2010, it rises up to 32% in 2050. The degree of circularity is highest in GreenMe (38%) and lowest in GreenLate (27%) with GreenSupreme (33%) and GreenLife (31%) in between.

Figure 13.1 also shows the substitutional effect of renewable energies expressing their contribution in tons of oil equivalents (RME). With growing

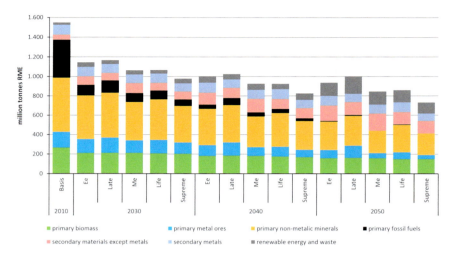

Figure 13.1 Primary and secondary raw material consumption in green scenarios.
Source: own calculation in URMOD (2019).

energy efficiency and energy savings, the overall energy demand (provided by fossil fuels and renewables) decreases in all scenarios. However, the substitutional effect of renewables is highest in GreenLate in 2050 as overall energy demand is highest. In contrast, the effect is lowest in GreenSupreme due to the lowest energy demand in that pathway.

Consumption of selected metals in the green pathways

As explained in Chapter 12 of this volume, and presented in Figure 13.1, primary metal consumption declines at least by 24% in GreenLate and up to 74% in Supreme in 2050 compared to 2010. Including the secondary basic metals, there is still a decline of the entire metal consumption. Thereby, the decrease of primary and secondary metals in GreenLate is lowest with −20% and highest in GreenSupreme with −5 4% (GreenEe (−29%), GreenLife (−35%) and GreenMe (−45%)).

The use of iron is a suitable example to illustrate this trend. In GreenLate only small efforts are made in order to reduce overall iron demand and improve recycling. In 2010, 23 million tons of primary iron (here and in the following: iron content) and further 23 million tons of secondary iron have been consumed in Germany for products and investments. In GreenLate, the consumption of primary and secondary iron decreases to 33 million ton; thereof 16 million tons are primary iron and further 17 million tons are secondary iron. In GreenSupreme the pathway with the highest reduction of overall demand and high improvements of recycling, the consumption of iron is reduced to 24 million tons in 2050; 8 million tons primary and 16 million tons secondary iron, respectively.

The transformation of the energy system implies not only a decreasing use of fossil fuels but also an increasing demand for metals for renewable energy installations. Generators of wind power plants, transformers in solar power, and batteries in electric cars are not operating without a considerable high amount and variety of metals. This trend was described already more than 10 years ago, e.g. by Elshkaki and van der Voet (2006) and further researched during the past decade, e.g. by Marscheider-Weidemann et al. (2016), IRP (2017b) or Rietveld et al. (2018). In the Green pathways the same trend can be observed: against the trend of declining metal consumption, technology and precious metals do not decrease but increase in 2030. In this respect, lithium can be adduced as a good example. Lithium is used in batteries in cars, lorries and busses. In GreenLate only few electric vehicles enter the market in 2030. Thus, demand for lithium for vehicle batteries is only 1,360 tons in 2030 while it is 2,500 in GreenLife where electric vehicles have a fast and wide market entry in upcoming and extensive car-sharing systems. In 2050, demand for lithium is highest in GreenLate with more than 26 thousand ton due to high numbers of vehicles. In contrast, demand is lowest in GreenSupreme with 9.6 thousand tons reflecting a smaller vehicle fleet combined with more efficient battery technology. However, compared to the (estimated) lithium production of 85 thousand tons in 2018 (USGS 2019), even a demand of 9.6 thousand tons would 'occupy" more than 11% of current global production. Thus, meeting the demand not only for Germany but also worldwide requires a significant increase in lithium extraction and the development of recycling structures for lithium batteries.

Besides lithium, demand for graphite, cobalt, silicon metal and further metals for new energy system technologies increase temporarily or continuously during the pathways. However, the demand for basic metals and for the majority of further metals decreases. If demand for steel decreases, demand for steel stabilisers such as chromium, nickel or manganese follows the same downward trend. Thus, the question arises whether the resulting primary metal consumption is still high or moderate. Therefore, the consumption of these raw materials was measured as a share of global production and compared to the share of the German population in world population. Figure 13.2 shows the metal consumption of Germany in 2030 and 2050 with respect to five different metals and differentiates all five transformation pathways as a share of current global production according to USGS.

With respect to iron in the GreenEe pathway, the consumption is 1.20% and 0.690% of current (2018) global production in 2030 and 2050, respectively. At the same time, in the ambitious pathway GreenSupreme the share is only 0.94% and 0.50% in the same years, respectively. Compared to the share of the German population in global population in 2050 (0.78%, assuming medium global population development according to United Nations 2019) the consumption in GreenEe equals the share of population; it exceeds the 'adequate" German share in GreenLate while it is clearly below in GreenMe, GreenLife and GreenSupreme.

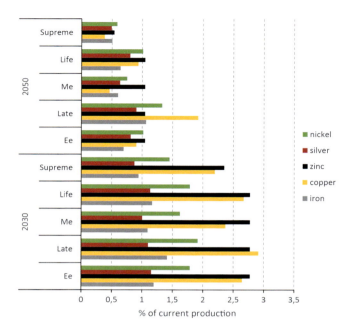

Figure 13.2 Metal consumption in Germany as a share of current global production.
Source: own calculation in URMOD and USGS (2019).

The other four selected metals copper, zinc, silver and nickel show a similar picture: consumption is still high in 2030, exceeding the population share in 2030 in nearly all pathways with respect to almost all metals. Thereby, demand for primary metals is highest in GreenLate and lowest in GreenSupreme. In 2050, in GreenEe and partly in GreenLife the 'adequate" share is met, yet, exceeded in GreenLate and undercut in GreenMe and GreenSupreme. Particularly the copper demand is still high in GreenLate, reflecting the comparatively low ambition in recycling in this pathway in Germany as well as abroad. On the other hand, the low share in GreenMe and GreenSupreme is, among others, a result of efficient use within Germany but at the same time also a consequence of increasing global efficient use of primary copper incorporated in upstream flows of imports.

Discussion and conclusion

Currently, material consumption in Germany accounts for around 1.3 billion tons of primary raw materials. As extraction, procession, use, re-use and disposal is coercively linked to environmental impacts, a pathway towards to sustainable use of materials has to decrease material consumption significantly, in addition to a sustainable extraction, processing, use and recycling of materials. The closed link between material consumption and greenhouse gas emission has been shown and discussed in Chapter 12. In this contribution, we analysed the decrease of material demand and particularly metal demand in more detail.

Recycling, substitution and increasing efficiency are valuable measures in order to minimise material consumption. It is obvious that there is not only one strategy or measure; the combination of all measures and efforts leads as a result to a significant reduction of primary material consumption. However, the different ambitious levels of substitution, recycling and efficiency measures in the varying Green pathways result in different material consumption levels. The consequence of the comparatively low ambitious level in GreenLate is a relatively low decrease in material consumption and a low degree of circularity of the economy. Consequently, we have demonstrated that the resulting share of primary metal consumption of Germany in global production is still high. The fact that other countries also demand metals for their transformation or their economic development implies that global metal production has to increase to meet future global demand. This is linked to serious and increasing environmental consequences and impacts due to extraction, processing, use and disposal as described e.g. by van de Voet et al. (2018).

In contrast, ambitious technological changes, as shown in the GreenMe pathway, resulting in a significant decrease in overall material demand. Combining technological changes and life style changes – without loss of prosperity – make it possible to achieve a strong decline of primary material demand as illustrated in the GreenSupreme pathway. The resulting values of 5.7 tons per person (RMC) in GreenSupreme are clearly below the current global average of 11.98 tons (2015 according to IRP 2016) and already in the line with material consumption targets which were discussed for example, by Bringezu (2015). The degree of circularity was estimated conservatively in the presented approach. A degree of 30% and more is feasible with currently existing technologies. Thus, recycling efforts are significantly contributing to the reduction of primary material demand. This implies that logistics for collecting and separating have to be improved and technical facilities have to be (re)constructed. With respect to selected metals, this chapter has shown that the very ambitious pathways result in a significant decreasing demand for metals.

High ambitious levels lead to a decrease of demand for metals resulting in a low global share of demand. This is important as a fair global distribution is essential for global sustainability. A post-fossil, green Germany can be reached with a significant decrease in material consumption contributing to the mitigation of environmental impacts linked to extraction, processing, use and disposal of raw materials.

List of abbreviations

IRP   International Resource Panel
RMC   raw material consumption
RME   raw material equivalent

156 *Monika Dittrich et al.*

UBA   German Federal Environmental Agency
URMOD   Umweltökonomisches Rohstoffmodell (economic-environmental raw material model)
USGS   United States Geological Survey

References

Bringezu, Stefan. (2015). Possible Target Corridor for Sustainable Use of Global Material. *Resources* 4(1), 25–54. doi:10.3390/resources4010025.

Deilmann, C., Reichenbach, J., Krauß, N., Gruhler, K. (2017). *Materialströme im Hochbau – Potenziale für eine Kreislaufwirtschaft*. Bonn/Dresden.

Destatis (2015). *Bevölkerung Deutschlands bis 2060 – 13. koordinierte Bevölkerungsvorausbere chnung*. Wiesbaden. www.destatis.de/DE/Publikationen/Thematisch/Bevoelkerung/VorausberechnungBevoelkerung/BevoelkerungDeutschland2060Presse5124204099004. pdf?__blob=publicationFile.

Dittrich, M., Schoer, K., Kämper, C., Ludmann, S., Ewers, B., Giegrich, J., Sartorius, C., Hummen, T., Marscheider-Weidemann, F. (2018). *Strukturelle und produktionstechnische Determinanten der Ressourceneffizienz: Untersuchung von Pfadabhängigkeiten, strukturellen Effekten und technischen Potenzialen auf die zukünftige Entwicklung der Rohstoffproduktivität (DeteRess)*. UBA-Texte, 29/2018. Dessau-Roßlau www.umweltbundesamt.de/sites/default/files/medien/1410/publikationen/2018-04-11_texte_29-2018_deteress.pdf.

Dittrich, M., N. Gerhardt, K. Schoer, F. Dünnebeil, S. Becker, A. v. Oehsen, S. Koeppen, et al. (2020a). *Transformationsprozess zum Treibhausgasneutralem und Ressourcenschonendem Deutschland – GreenEe*. Climate Change 01/2020. Dessau-Roßlau.

Dittrich, M., N. Gerhardt, K. Schoer, F. Dünnebeil, S Becker, A. v. Oehsen, S. Koeppen, et al. (2020b). *Transformationsprozess zum Treibhausgasneutralem und Ressourcenschonendem Deutschland – GreenLate*. Climate Change 01/2020. Dessau-Roßlau.

Dittrich, M., N. Gerhardt, K. Schoer, F. Dünnebeil, S. Becker, A. v. Oehsen, S. Koeppen, et al. (2020c). *Transformationsprozess zum Treibhausgasneutralem und Ressourcenschonendem Deutschland – GreenMe*. Climate Change 01/2020. Dessau-Roßlau.

Dittrich, M., N. Gerhardt, K. Schoer, F. Dünnebeil, S. Becker, A. v. Oehsen, S. Koeppen, et al. (2020d). *Transformationsprozess zum Treibhausgasneutralem und Ressourcenschonendem Deutschland – GreenSupreme*. Climate Change 01/2020. Dessau-Roßlau.

Dittrich, M., N. Gerhardt, K. Schoer, F. Dünnebeil, S. Becker, A. v. Oehsen, S. Koeppen, et al. (2020e). *Transformationsprozess zum Treibhausgasneutralem und Ressourcenschonendem Deutschland – GreenLife*. Climate Change 01/2020. Dessau-Roßlau.

Elshkaki, A. and van der Voet, E. (2006). The consequences of the use of platinum in new technologies on its availability and on other metals cycles. In: Loeffe C. V. (ed.): *Conservation and Recycling of Resources: A New Research*. USA: Nova Publisher. 61–92.

IRP (2016). *Global Material Flows and Resource Productivity. An Assessment Study of the UNEP International Resource Panel*. Paris, United Nations Environment Programme.

IRP (2017a). *Assessing Global Resource Use: A Systems Approach to Resource Efficiency and Pollution Reduction*. A Report of the International Resource Panel. United Nations Environment Programme. Nairobi, Kenya.

IRP (2017b). *Green Technology Choices: The Environmental and Resource Implications of Low-Carbon Technologies*. A report of the International Resource Panel. United Nations Environment Programme, Nairobi, Kenya. www.resourcepanel.org/reports/green-technology-choices.

IRP (2019). *Global Resources Outlook 2019: Natural Resources for the Future We Want*. A Report of the International Resource Panel. United Nations Environment Programme. Nairobi, Kenya. www.resourcepanel.org/reports/global-resources-outlook.

Marscheider-Weidemann, F., Langkau, S., Hummen, T., Erdmann, L., Tercero Espinoza, L. (2016). *Rohstoffe für Zukunftstechnologien*. DERA Rohstoffinformationen 28, Berlin. www.isi.fraunhofer.de/content/dam/isi/dokumente/ccn/2016/Studie_Zukunftstechnologien-2016.pdf.

Rietveld, E., Boonman, H., van Harmelen, T., Hauck, M., Bastein, T. (2018). *Global Energy Transition and Metal Demand – an Introduction and Circular Economy Perspectives*. TNO.

UBA (2014). Treibhausgasneutrales Deutschland im Jahr 2050. www.umweltbundesamt.de/sites/default/files/medien/378/publikationen/07_2014_climate_change_dt.pdf.

UBA (2019). *Transformationsprozess zum Treibhausgasneutralen und Ressourcenschonendem Deutschland*. Climate Change 36/2019. Dessau-Rosslau. www.umweltbundesamt.de/rescue

United Nations (2019). World Population Prospects 2019. Total Population – Both Sexes. https://population.un.org/wpp/Download/Standard/Population/.

USGS (2019). National Minerals Information Centre. www.usgs.gov/centers/nmic/.

Van de Voet, E., Van Oers, L., Verboon, M., Kupers, K. (2018). Environmental Implications of Future Demand Scenarios for Metals. Methodology and Application to the Case of Seven Major Metals. *Journal of Industrial Ecology*, 23(1), 141–154.

14 Vertical integration in a multi-level governance system using the example of the German Resource Efficiency Programme

Maic Verbücheln and Bettina Bahn-Walkowiak

Introduction

Global resource use trends show clear evidence of the challenges that have to be addressed urgently if society is to be prepared for the future. One of the most critical tasks is to preserve natural resources, especially in connection with climate protection. This is, inter alia, reflected in the 17 Sustainable Development Goals (SDGs). For example, target 8.4 requires to 'improve progressively, through 2030, global resource efficiency in consumption and production and endeavour to decouple economic growth from environmental degradation' (United Nations 2019). Furthermore, several other subtasks also indirectly refer to the use of natural resources.

A considerably more efficient if not markedly reduced use of resources and its negative environmental impacts are major challenges of our modern western societies which have to be tackled by policy immediately (Bringezu 2014). Germany is among the few countries that have achieved an absolute decoupling of economic growth of raw material consumption during the period 1995 to 2014. However, the per-capita resource use in Germany in 2014 (measured as raw material consumption) was 15.8 tonnes. Therefore, Germany is still a stable resource-intensive nation with an above-average per capita use compared to Europe (13.4 tonnes) and is also well above the global average, which has been growing to about 12.3 tonnes in 2017 (Eurostat 2019).

Against this background, the German Resource Efficiency Programme (ProgRess) was launched in 2012 and advanced in 2016 and 2020 (BMU 2012; BMUB 2016; BMU 2020). The ultimate goal of ProgRess is to make the extraction and use of natural resources more sustainable and reduce associated environmental pollution as much as possible. By doing this – also with responsibility towards future generations – the programme should create a prerequisite for securing a long-term high quality of life. To bring the policy approaches formulated in ProgRess to reality, efforts to implement resource efficiency measures have to be increased at all levels – from international to regional to local.

The chapter intends to provide an impetus for the current debate on ProgRess policy development. The chapter identifies, analyses and describes deficits and possibilities of vertical integration of the German programme in particular and derives recommendations for action which may also serve as indications for other strategies. The following sections are based on results of the advisory report 'Vertical integration of the national resource efficiency programme ProgRess (VertRess)' (Verbücheln & Bahn-Walkowiak unpublished), conducted by the German Institute of Urban Affairs (Difu) and the Wuppertal Institute for Climate, Environment and Energy on behalf of the German Environmental Agency (UBA) and the Federal Ministry of the Environment, Nature Conservation and Nuclear Safety (BMU).

The German federal system and the present structure of ProgRess

Within the debate on policy coherence and policy integration, a distinction is usually made between horizontal and vertical integration (Howlett, Vince & del Rio 2017; Bahn-Walkowiak & Wilts 2017; Candel & Biesbroek 2016; Jordan & Lenschow 2010). Horizontal integration strives for better networking and connection between the various policy areas such as the economy, finance, social affairs, or in environmental policy areas such as climate protection, mobility, energy. Vertical integration seeks better coordination and cooperation between the levels of action and actors in a specific topical field. Both aspects are eminently important, but this chapter will focus on the vertical dimension, which is often neglected. Based on the theoretical policy integration approach, a thorough analysis of the relevant documents, the legal responsibilities and subsequent influences of the governance levels is conducted and the architecture of the governance elements of the programme studied to identify deficits and potentials in the current structure.

Germany is considered to be a pioneer in developing a national resource efficiency agenda (EEA 2016; EEA 2020). With the publication of the 'Programme for the sustainable use and conservation of natural resources' (ProgRess I) in 2012, the German Federal Government has set a milestone for the development of a dedicated policy mix in this field. ProgRess was updated in 2016 (ProgRess II) and recently in 2020 (ProgRess III). The implementation process is challenging, and aspirations differ from reality, thus calling for new action and approaches.

Construction of the federal system in Germany

The German Federal system is complex. In addition to the Federation, the German Federal Republic consists of 16 partly sovereign Federal States (Länder), which – according to the German constitution – have to fulfil their state tasks. The concurrent legislation assigns different legislative tasks to the federal government and the federal states.

In practice, various areas with a high resource relevance are regulated at Länder level (e.g. the innovation policy, public support programmes, public procurement, sustainability agreements with individual companies or voluntary commitments in specific sectors or industries, construction and regional planning and the expansion and optimisation of waste management and recycling (infra-)structures as well as waste prevention and re-use strategies and measures). At the same time, important resource-relevant policy areas in which the federal states have outstanding competencies are not (yet) part of ProgRess or are addressed in other strategies (e.g. mobility/traffic, land management, water balance).

Following the federalism reform in 2006, nature and landscape conservation, soil distribution, spatial planning, and water management are jointly regulated areas by government and federal states, which, of course, also have great municipal relevance (see below). Accordingly, the resource efficiency programme assigns tasks to the respective levels and the 2016 update reports on the specific level activities.

Structure of the German Resource Efficiency Programme (ProgRess)

ProgRess II consists of ten action areas with over 120 individual policy approaches. Unlike the broad European concept of resources (Eurostat n.d.), ProgRess focuses on the material use of resources, including the related environmental impacts. The programme addresses a large number of different activity levels (as shown in Figure 14.1) but bases mainly on voluntary activities and instruments.

ProgRess implementation mechanisms

The governance of ProgRess is shared by the Federal Environment Ministry and Federal Environment Agency (here: BMU and UBA). Main elements in the implementation process of ProgRess are:

- A National Platform for Resource Efficiency (NaRess), established in 2013. Initially comprising the Federal Government and industry associations, the membership was extended to further groups such as environmental organisations, unions and local authority associations. NaRess serves as a platform for sharing information on members' resource efficiency activities and supports the implementation and onward development of ProgRess (BMUB 2016).
- The Centre for Resource Efficiency (VDI ZRE), established in 2011. It develops products notably comprising sector-specific support, methodologies, and information. They include, for example, resource efficiency checks and process systematisation tools to assist manufacturing enterprises with internal resource efficiency improvement projects (BMUB 2016).

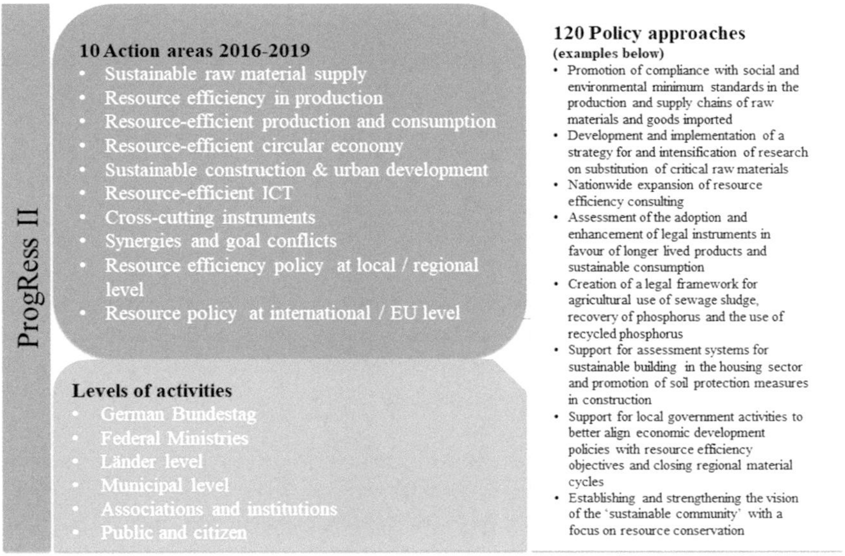
ProgRess II
10 Action areas 2016-2019
• Sustainable raw material supply
• Resource efficiency in production
• Resource-efficient production and consumption
• Resource-efficient circular economy
• Sustainable construction & urban development
• Resource-efficient ICT
• Cross-cutting instruments
• Synergies and goal conflicts
• Resource efficiency policy at local / regional level
• Resource policy at international / EU level
Levels of activities
• German Bundestag
• Federal Ministries
• Länder level
• Municipal level
• Associations and institutions
• Public and citizen
120 Policy approaches
(examples below)
• Promotion of compliance with social and environmental minimum standards in the production and supply chains of raw materials and goods imported
• Development and implementation of a strategy for and intensification of research on substitution of critical raw materials
• Nationwide expansion of resource efficiency consulting
• Assessment of the adoption and enhancement of legal instruments in favour of longer lived products and sustainable consumption
• Creation of a legal framework for agricultural use of sewage sludge, recovery of phosphorus and the use of recycled phosphorus
• Support for assessment systems for sustainable building in the housing sector and promotion of soil protection measures in construction
• Support for local government activities to better align economic development policies with resource efficiency objectives and closing regional material cycles
• Establishing and strengthening the vision of the 'sustainable community' with a focus on resource conservation

Figure 14.1 Elements of the German Resource Efficiency Programme (ProgRess 2016–2020).
Source: own illustration; modified from Bahn-Walkowiak et al. (2019: 44).

- The Resource Efficiency Network (NeRess), established in 2007. The network combines inter-disciplinary expertise and experience in resource efficient production, products, and management (BMUB 2016).

The implementation of ProgRess has been transparently communicated from a range of different thematic perspectives in biannual public Resource Efficiency Network (NeRess) meetings, biannual meetings of the Länder, and conferences of the European Resources Forum (ERF) and the National Resources Forum (NRF).

ProgRess evaluation

A recent evaluation assessed ProgRess to be a successful strategy with important network components and an elaborated updating process. However, the impact on resource use clearly needs to be improved, and material flows need to be optimised (Bahn-Walkowiak et al. 2019; Verbücheln & Wagner-Endres 2018). The leading research question is why ProgRess does not have a greater penetration on all levels and how can this be improved. The objective of this chapter is therefore to highlight options for better integration of Länder and municipalities in the further development and implementation of ProgRess.

Länder: responsibilities and influence on action areas of ProgRess

To date, all 16 Länder have a sustainability strategy, but only 3 of them have a specific strategy for resource efficiency (i.e. Baden-Wuerttemberg, Hessen, Saxony). The Länder that have integrated relevant resource policy activities into their environmental policy are Bavaria (Bavarian Raw Materials Strategy), Saarland (Saar Environmental Pact) and North-Rhine-Westphalia (Sustainability Strategy).

Federal states have various legal and other possibilities to, directly and indirectly, influence the consumption of raw materials. To mention is the field of land management, construction policy, waste and circular flow policies, public procurement, mining laws, regulation of environmental impact assessments. However, some of the resource relevant intervention points of the Länder are not within the defined scope of action of ProgRess, but go beyond it.

The scope for action of the Länder in the areas of raw material extraction and supply, production, consumption, circular economy and sustainable urban development (which represent five of ProgRess' total ten areas of action) is consequently vast and diverse. The authors identified several hundred intervention points in the form of different economic, legal, informational, or sectoral instruments. Multiplied with the individual countries an impressive number of options occurs.

ProgRess areas, which are in the exclusive responsibility of the Länder, are not found in the 120 policy approaches. On the other hand, about 60 of the policy approaches are at least partly under the responsibility of the Länder. That means that competencies/responsibilities are to be shared with the other governance levels and coordination is required. Multi-actor responsibilities are always at risk to lead to no actor feeling responsible, sometimes resulting in inaction.

Municipalities: responsibilities and influence on action areas of ProgRess

Besides the sovereignty of the Länder, it is important to mention that the local self-government of German municipalities includes the right to implement most of the public responsibility independently. However, the municipalities implement obligatory as well as optional tasks on the local level in general. Concerning the constitutional law, it is not possible to allocate duties directly to the municipalities by the Federal State – only the Länder have this option by using their legislation. Therefore, the Federal Government has to go via the Länder level or use other means such as programmes or incentives to address municipalities.

On the municipal level, large quantities of resources are required, such as building materials, water and energy. Resource efficiency is a cross-sectional local and regional issue. Hence, the local politicians, administration and

The German Resource Efficiency Programme 163

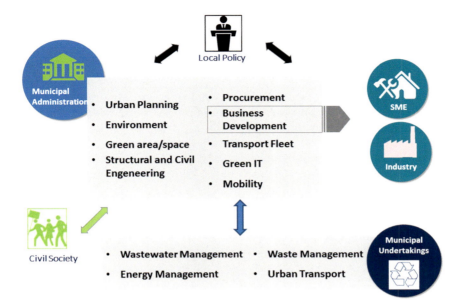

Figure 14.2 Actors and action areas in resource efficiency on the local level.
Source: own illustration; modified from Verbücheln and Wagner-Endres (2018).

municipal undertakings play an important role in resource efficiency, along with actors of civil society and private enterprises (Verbücheln & Wagner-Endres 2018). Figure 14.2 shows the actors and municipal actions fields which have a direct or indirect effect on the use of natural resources.

The local politics (e.g. mayor, council, a county office) sets the agenda on the local level, produces statutes and has a monitoring and controlling function, for example, vis-à-vis the local administration (CEMR 2013). The municipal administration has competencies in different resource relevant action areas (e.g. urban planning, environment; see Figure 14.2). The daily work of the administration comprises planning and implementation. The municipal business development units support small and medium enterprises (SME) or industries in business parks (e.g. resource efficiency). Municipal infrastructure undertakings and economic enterprises (private law organised) take duties from the local government. They mostly provide local and regional infrastructures like energy and water supply, public transport, or waste management. The mentioned actors are in Germany part of the so-called 'municipal family'. The civil society (e.g. Transition Town) pushes bottom-up processes and is important for local action.

Figure 14.2 shows how important the role of municipalities is for the implementation of resource relevant activities. In addition, municipalities play further different roles on the local and regional level – they are initiators, networkers, or partners for the implementation of any resource relevant activities. Local actors have the knowledge to identify on-site potentials, develop networks and adopt measures.

However, there are different interfaces between the 120 individual policy approaches which are described in ProgRess II and the action areas of the municipalities. The evaluation has shown that 34 of the policy approaches are optional, and three are obligatory for the municipalities (Verbücheln and Bahn-Walkowiak, unpublished). For example, the following ProgRess policy approaches have a direct link to municipalities: 'Environment-friendly expansion of material use of regenerative resources' or 'resource-efficient neighbourhood and building development, construction, refurbishment, and use' or 'resource-efficient infrastructure' (BMUB, 2016). An effective implementation of such policy approaches is not possible without the municipalities. Furthermore, municipal activities affect resource relevant action fields which are not included in ProgRess, for example, the field of mobility.

There is a multitude of municipal activities which have a direct and indirect effect on natural resources. But on the local and regional level, resources are not a single action field. In the municipalities, there are usually no separate departments, authorities, or single persons who are responsible for resource protection or resource efficiency. Approaches are mostly sectoral. Furthermore, questions concerning resource efficiency play a minor role in most of the municipal action areas (e.g. urban planning). There are still potentials on the local and regional level which have to be realised in an efficient and consistent way.

Deficits and potentials of the vertical structure of ProgRess

Institutional transmission belts of multi-level systems have to mesh to ensure percipience, responsibility, and also legitimisation. It is important to support activities for the implementation of resource efficiency measures on Länder and municipal level. However, the description above sheds a first light on the weakness of ProgRess: the decentralised design of the resource policy with rather guiding than obliging instruments entails a patchwork of effective and ineffective interventions and (all too often) non-interventions. Without an at least mandatory and specific resource policy addressing the most resource-intensive sectors, the tiger may remain toothless.

The following sections will highlight some deficits concerning the vertical structure of ProgRess as well as the content in more detail.

Policy development process

Firstly, we have to point out the vertical structure for the development of ProgRess (see Figure 14.1). This structure is based on an inter-ministerial exchange between the Federal Ministry for the Environment and the

Federal Ministry for Economic Affairs and Energy, which is, among others, supported by the 'National Platform Resource Efficiency' (NaRess). In NaRess, stakeholders from business and economy as well as the federal states are, for instance, directly addressed by the format. It is a structural deficit that stakeholders from the municipalities are addressed less. This means one of the major actors is only slightly considered in the follow-up development process of ProgRess III. The Länder are involved in the vertical process. It needs to be mentioned, however, that better horizontal exchange and cooperation between the Länder in the context of resource policy would also be reasonable.

In contrast to the ProgRess approach, the German Waste Prevention Programme is a joint programme of the Federal Government and the Länder to which both governance levels are committed. It is thus an example of vertical integration. The Länder either adopt the guidelines or have to develop independent waste prevention programmes. In addition, dialogue takes place for the development of the programme/strategy to involve stakeholders such as representatives of public institutions, industry players, NGOs, scientists, etc. For ProgRess, however, there are considerably more process elements established for the coordination of the actors (NaRess, NeRess, etc.), but there is no reciprocal commitment for participation.

Furthermore, the integration of waste and resource policy is challenging from horizontal and vertical perspective due to the largely separate responsibilities, activities and actors, which can be found in almost all competent authorities from the national to the municipal level.

Content and representation

Secondly, there are deficits in the content of ProgRess. It is important to take into account the partial overlapping, but not congruent actors and institutions targeted by ProgRess – for example, in the context of resource efficiency and circular economy.

The integration of spatial planning, land management, and resource conservation is insufficiently addressed by ProgRess. The Länder-specific possibilities for action in this context are, therefore, insufficiently guided by aspects of resource protection. Sustainable urban development does not cover urban sprawl or the continuing increase in traffic areas and parking spaces.

This has partly led to the countries concentrating on micro-economic resource efficiency and non-regulative instruments to nudge activities, albeit very successfully. More than 70 activities were newly created since the update of ProgRess II in 2016 and identified in the study. 15 Länder offer public financial programmes in order to support enterprises in their efforts to strive for more resource efficiency. However, it has become increasingly clear that the focus on industrial win-win solutions is only successful to a limited extent and the resistance is high, not only in Germany (Tukker & Ekins 2019).

Also, critical sectoral fields of action like the mobility are furthermore not part of ProgRess. The areas construction, housing, and mobility however traditionally play a major role in both state and local policy, especially from an economic point of view. ProgRess' tension between a very broad and comprehensive design of 120 approaches in ten action areas and a narrow focus on abiotic raw materials leads to partly unclear responsibilities and possibly to the problem that actors not feel authorised at all. Moreover, some examples show that the used headings for the action areas in ProgRess are partly vast and not concrete, whereas the subheadings are very concrete. The wording has to be optimised with a focus on the target groups – including a direct designation.

ProgRess implementation

Thirdly, we have to look at the implementation processes. ProgRess is a policy mix acting in a multi-level system, but because of the large number of stakeholders and high amount of levels and legal spheres that are touched, the implementation of the programme is highly complex and confronted with several barriers. This is, inter alia, complicated by changing actors (political configurations) and long-term institutional arrangements.

At Länder level, responsibilities for energy and resource efficiency are usually not split (no state has a resource efficiency ministry). The targeted use of synergies, however, is an exception, for example, for building renovation. As a consequence, the main activities of the Länder to foster resource efficiency have a focus on the industry and small and medium-sized enterprises. An example is the promotion of the information platform Centre for Resource Efficiency (VDI ZRE) which is closely connected to the Association of German Engineers (VDI).

ProgRess is almost unknown on the municipal level, and integrated incentives to engage in resource efficiency do not exist. Moreover, there is no direct contact person on the local level concerning the issue of resource efficiency, despite several intersections. This is a main deficit because the implementation of resource efficiency measures is often driven and implemented on the local level by actors from the municipalities. Better information, as well as incentives for the municipalities, are missing so far.

To foster the protection of natural resources, all potentials in all fields of actions in the different governance levels have to be addressed in the right way. Not all possibilities and potentials, however, have been exhausted on a local and regional level, which is why the issue of resource efficiency needs has to be expanded with the spotlight on actors such as municipalities and their activities. Local management systems aiming for cross-sectoral optimisation of material flows are not firmly entrenched, particularly in cities. On this background, the objective is to optimise the vertical integration of the Länder as well as the municipalities within the further development and implementation of ProgRess.

Recommendations for better vertical integration of the resource efficiency policy in Germany

Better structural integration of the Länder and municipalities

In the past, ProgRess has focused on the optimisation of resource efficiency in small and medium-sized enterprises on two levels. First, through the involvement of association representatives during the development of ProgRess and second, concerning the implementation of measures (e.g. information and incentives for the enterprises). The attention should also, overall, be expanded to other target groups which are relevant for resource efficiency, in particular, the federal states and the municipalities. The involvement of federal states and municipal organisations should be optimised because they are not yet fully integrated in the information and participation formats of ProgRess. A better dialogue between Federal State, Länder and municipalities has also to be put on the agenda.

Therefore, an adaptation or optimisation of the structure of the National Platform Resource Efficiency (NaRess) as part of the ProgRess vertical structure is recommended. A modified structure of the NaRess organisation for a better exchange of information and participation between Federal Ministries, Länder, and municipalities are reasonable. Following levels are recommended:

a   Optimisation of the cooperation between Federal Ministries, also with a view on legislation framework, for example by the establishment of an inter-ministerial committee (including the Ministry of Transport and the Ministry of Food and Agriculture).
b   Optimised integration and exchange with a view on Länder and municipalities (including associations like the Association of German Cities, German Association of Towns and Municipalities, German County Council or German Association of Local Utilities).
c   Use and development of new working groups and cross-sector roundtables with municipal representatives – also with representatives from the administration of bigger cities for examples. For this purpose, existing groups can be used or extended.

All three levels mentioned above have to be connected for an exchange. However, not only the structure but also the format and the content of the NaRess meetings have to be amended.

The governance levels and groups of interests have to be better integrated into the follow-up process to ProgRess III (so far, the focus is on enterprises).

Advancement of the content of ProgRess III

Resource efficiency is a cross-sectional task, and better integration of the different sectors/policy fields should be designed to enable synergies.

Moreover, a stronger focus on activities like urban planning, building and construction, and mobility – all inducing highly resource-intensive material streams and land use – is required. It thus also touches on horizontal integration issues, because integrated approaches are needed.

Increase the awareness level of ProgRess

The awareness level in the municipalities to resource management issues has to be improved clearly. Therefore, the strategic approaches which are already formulated in ProgRess II have to be filled with life. Those approaches are:

1   consolidation of the concept 'sustainable municipalities' – focus: resource efficiency;
2   establishment of specific information – and consultation offers for municipalities; and
3   support of municipal activities which foster the regional economic development regarding resource efficiency.

Against this background, the development of an information platform – similar to the VDI ZRE – for municipalities as a target group is an effective way for the optimisation of the awareness on the local level. The information has to address the local level in general which includes the local policy, the administration, the local business development as well as the civil society. For the implementation of integrated approaches, all these stakeholders play an important role.

Incentives for relevant local stakeholders

The programme is largely based on voluntary activities and instruments. This, however, also touches on the outreach to the target groups: regulatory and economic instruments are naturally perceived much more strongly by all sections of the society.

Incentives are also of integral importance for the cross-sectional topic of resource efficiency to be promoted on the municipal level. A subsidy programme and/or competition and/or the financing of staff (e.g. resource efficiency manager) should be taken into account. This is important also for the awareness rising among actors on the local level but not at least for consumers who are all directly affected by local decision-making in the context of waste, mobility and floor-space management if they are done under resource-efficient aspects.

General conclusions and outlook

A shift in resource use patterns is inevitable when we want to take the climate crisis seriously. Although this chapter has focused primarily on institutional vertical integration in a particular programme in a single country, it is clear that resource conservation is an essential part of any other resource-dependent environmental policy field such as climate protection and land use. With a view on resource scarcity, however, it is also an issue of economy and peace. Resource relevant activities must be brought closer in a more systematic way at national, European and global levels. The segmentation of federal environmental policy in Germany has so far continued at the state level. Better horizontal cooperation between the states should be an objective too!

With a view to European policy development, it has become apparent in recent years that resource efficiency is increasingly understood as an essential element of a broader circular economy. This means highly complex challenges and research demand, not only in the context of global value chains for resources and waste but also and especially in the regional-municipal area, which is characterised by path-dependent infrastructures and small-scale regulation of waste management at a day-to-day basis. A huge number of extremely different actors and stakeholders has to be brought to the table to discuss common objectives and target conflicts in the first place. This points to a necessary in-depth analysis target and conflict-of-goals.

With a specific view on policy integration and especially vertical policy integration, the question should be investigated in more detail as to how such a complex implementation process can be made more participatory and inclusive without the most powerful industries becoming the main decision-makers in the long run. As the Federal Ministry states: 'Comprehensive public participation is vital for gaining broad acceptance of the programme' (BMU 2019) and has introduced a citizens' dialogue for ProgRess III for the second time (comprising a total of 250 randomly selected members of the public who will bring in their suggestions for improving the programme). This extraordinarily successful process could, for example, also be a viable way for local decision-makers in the municipalities to become better involved.

A concluding remark shall acknowledge that new programme 2020–2023 has taken up some of the aspects suggested in this chapter. For example, the promotion of local public transport and an alignment of the municipal economic development towards resource efficiency and closing regional material cycles have been newly included as two priorities.

References

Bahn-Walkowiak, B. and Wilts, H. (2017). The Institutional Dimension of Resource Efficiency in a Multi-level Governance System – Implications for Policy Mix Design. *Energy Research & Social Science*, Special issue: Policy mixes for energy transitions, edited by K. S. Rogge, F. Kern, M. Howlett. Vol 33, November 2017, 163–172. doi: 10.1016/j.erss.2017.09.021.

Bahn-Walkowiak, B., Koop, C., Meinel, U., Nicolas, J. and Wilts, H. (2019). *Evaluation des deutschen Ressourceneffizienzprogramms ProgRess: Teilbericht*. TEXTE No. 43/2019. Dessau-Roßlau: Umweltbundesamt.

BMU (2012). German Resource Efficiency Programme (ProgRess) – Programme for the Sustainable Use and Conservation of Natural Resources. Decision of the Federal Cabinet of 29 February 2012. Berlin: Federal Ministry for the Environment, Nature Conservation and Nuclear Safety (BMU). Retrieved from www.neress.de/fileadmin/media/files/Progress/120309_Overview_ProgRess_engl_01.pdf (14 May 2019).

BMU (2019). German Resource Efficiency Programme (ProgRess) – an Overview. Retrieved from: www.bmu.de/en/topics/economy-products-resources-tourism/resource-efficiency/overview-of-german-resource-efficiency-programme-progress (30 August 2019).

BMU (2020). *Deutsches Ressourceneffizienzprogramm III 2020–2023 Programm zur nachhaltigen Nutzung und zum Schutz der natürlichen Ressourcen*. Berlin: Federal Ministry for the Environment, Nature Conservation and Nuclear Safety (BMU). Retrieved from www.bmu.de/download/deutsches-ressourceneffizienzprogramm-progress-iii (3 August 2020).

BMUB (2016). *German Resource Efficiency Programme II – Programme for the Sustainable Use and Conservation of Natural Resources*. Berlin: Federal Ministry for the Environment, Nature Conservation, Building and Nuclear Safety (BMUB).

Bringezu, S. (2014). Targets for Global Resource Consumption. In: M. Angrick, A. Burger, and H. Lehmann (Eds.). *Factor X. Eco-Efficiency in Industry and Science*. Vol 29. (pp. 41–64). Dordrecht: Springer.

Candel, J. J. L. and Biesbroek, R. (2016). Toward a Processual Understanding of Policy Integration. In: *Policy Sciences*, 49(3), 211–231. https://doi.org/10.1007/s11077-016-9248-y.

CEMR (2013). *Local and Regional Government in Europe – Structures and Competencies*. Brussels: Council of European Municipalities and Regions (CEMR).

EEA (2016). *More from Less – Material Resource Efficiency in Europe: 2015 Overview of Policies, Instruments and Targets in 32 Countries*. EEA Report No 10/2016. Prepared by Paweł Kaźmierczyk et al. Copenhagen: European Environment Agency.

EEA (2020). *Resource Efficiency and the Circular Economy in Europe 2019: Even More from Less; an Overview of the Policies, Approaches and Targets of 32 European Countries* [authors: Kazmierczyk, P., Geerken, T. Contributors: Montalvo, D., Daniell, J., Manfredi, S., Ullstein, B., Bahn-Walkowiak, B. …]. EEA-Report No. 26/2019. Copenhagen: European Environment Agency, 2019. Retrieved from www.eea.europa.eu/publications/even-more-from-less (3 August 2020).

Eurostat (n.d.). Environmental Data Centre on Natural Resources – Overview – Natural Resource Concepts. Retrieved from https://ec.europa.eu/eurostat/web/environmental-data-centre-on-natural-resources/overview/natural-resource-concepts (28 August 2019).

Eurostat (2019). Material Flow Accounts and Resource Productivity. Retrieved from https://ec.europa.eu/eurostat/statistics-explained/index.php/Material_flow_accounts_and_resource_productivity#Raw_material_equivalents_.E2.80.94_towards_a_global_perspective (30 August 2019).

Howlett, M., Vince, J. and del Rio, P. (2017). Policy Integration and Multi-Level Governance: Dealing with Vertical Dimension of Policy Mix Designs. In: *Politics and Governance*, 5(2), 69–78. https://doi.org/10.17645/pag.v5i2.928.

Jordan, A. and Lenschow, A. (2010). Environmental Policy Integration: a State of the Art Review. In: *Env. Pol. Gov.* 20, 147–158 (2010). DOI: 10.1002/eet.539.

Tukker, A. and Ekins, P. (2019). Concepts Fostering Resource Efficiency: A Trade-off Between Ambitions and Viability. In: *Ecological Economics* 155(2019), 36–45. https://doi.org/10.1016/j.ecolecon.2017.08.020.

United Nations (2019). SDG Indicators – Metadata repository. Retrieved from https://unstats.un.org/sdgs/metadata/?Text=&Goal=8&Target=8.4 (29 August 2019).

Verbücheln, M. and Bahn-Walkowiak, B. (unpublished). Implementierung und Fortschreibung des Deutschen Ressourceneffizienzprogramms auf der Ebene der Bundesländer und Kommunen – Endbericht (VertRess). Im Auftrag des Umweltbundesamtes.

Verbücheln, M. and Wagner-Endres, S. (2018). *Hemmnisse und Potenziale zur Ressourceneffizienzsteigerung durch Optimierung regionaler und lokaler Stoffkreisläufe und Stoffströme – RegioRess – Abschlussbericht*. TEXTE No. 63/2019. Dessau-Roßlau: Umweltbundesamt.

15 A strategy to increase the resource efficiency of renewable energy technologies

Hans-Martin Henning, Shivenes Shammugam, Estelle Gervais, and Thomas Schlegl

Introduction

The Paris Agreement, which was negotiated during the 21st Conference of the Parties (COP 21) in 2015, obliges all involved nations to accelerate and strengthen their activities in combating climate change. The main goal of the Paris Agreement is to maintain the global temperature rise below 2 °C while pursuing efforts to limit the rise to 1.5 °C. Within this context, the involved nations are required to outline their climate goals and actions which will collectively contribute to achieving the agreed climate goals. As an example, the climate goals in Germany aim at reducing the greenhouse gas (GHG) emissions by at least 80% compared to the reference emission values from 1990. By the end of 2017, the total GHG emissions in Germany have reduced by 27%. The realisation of these climate goals clearly requires a shift in the electricity production sector from the GHG-intensive conventional power plants towards GHG-free generators. The renewable energy technologies photovoltaics (PV) and wind turbines are among the most competitive electricity generating technologies, can be installed quickly in both centralised and decentralised manner and offer further declining installation costs. The expected increase in the installation of renewable energy technologies opens up the following question: Are there enough raw materials to cater to the increasing demand for renewable energy technologies in the future? In this chapter, the possibility of a raw material supply risk due to the increased deployment of PV and wind turbines will be presented using the example of a global energy transition scenario. In addition to that, ways to increase the resource efficiency of renewable energy technologies will also be discussed.

Energy transformation process and potential demand for raw materials

Energy scenarios are not predictions of how the future energy system will be, but they assist the energy transformation process by providing guidance and presenting possible risks that can occur while pursuing climate goals. The International Energy Agency (IEA) publishes the World Energy Outlook

(WEO) every year which provides an update on the global energy market and the projections of the energy system based on current trends and data. In the latest version of the WEO, three energy scenarios were presented, among which the Sustainable Development Scenario (SDS) is considered to be the most sustainable scenario (IEA 2018). The SDS scenario considers the broader energy picture taking into account the United Nations Sustainable Development Goals (SDGs) on energy, universal energy access, air pollution, clean water and sanitation. According to this scenario, the global energy-related CO_2 emissions will peak at around 2020 and will continuously decline thereafter. The IEA claims that the scenario is fully in line with the trajectory required to achieve a global temperature rise of between 1.7 to 1.8 °C by 2100.

According to this scenario, the global cumulative installed capacity of PV and wind turbines will reach 4240 GW and 2819 GW respectively by 2040. By the end of 2018, a total of 532 GW (PV) and 590 GW (wind) capacities are available globally (IRENA 2019). The expected massive expansion of PV and wind turbines is however conditioned to the supply of large raw material amounts. As an example, the requirements of selected metals are shown in Table 15.1. The demand includes new capacities that have to be installed to substitute older power plants that have reached their lifespan to achieve the proposed cumulative installed capacity in 2040. Furthermore, an annual reduction of 1% is considered for the specific material demand to take material efficiency measures into accounts, such as improvement in the manufacturing process and power conversion efficiencies.

There are several important points that can be understood from the results. Firstly, increasing demand for renewable energy technologies will eventually exhaust the reserve of relevant metals. If the SDS scenario is realised, approximately 13% of available silver reserves would have been mined and manufactured into PV modules by 2040. Although the use of rare earth elements (REEs) in wind turbines does not seem as critical as silver in PV, it should be mentioned that the installations of these technologies will not be ceased in 2040. Instead, the installations will continue beyond that at an even greater rate to reach the long-term climate goals. Secondly, the expansion of renewable energy technologies will most likely be constraint by the production capacity of raw materials, since the growth in annual demand by far outweighs the current production rate. In terms of dysprosium, the production has to be increased by more than 250% of today's level.

Thirdly, renewable energy technologies can expect tough competition from other sectors in securing raw materials for the future. Regarding silver, for instance, only 8% of the current global silver demand goes into manufacturing crystalline Silicon (c-Si) based PV modules, which dominate the global PV market with a share of over 95% per cent. Therefore, a twofold increase of the silver demand required for PV module can create tough competition among other silver-intensive sectors. With the exception of the financial crisis in 2011, the global GDP growth has been positive other the past 50 years.

Table 15.1 Maximum annual and cumulative material demand of selected metals in PV and wind turbines for the Sustainable Development Scenario in WEO 2018

	Metal	Specific metal demand [kg/MW]	Maximum annual material demand [kt]	Global production in 2018 [kt]	Percentage of demand to production [%]	Cumulative material demand 2020–2040 [kt]	Reserve 2018 [kt]	Percentage of demand to reserve [%]
PV	Ag	23	4.6	27	17	72.6	560	13
Wind	Nd	90	13.6	19	71	170.4	23000	0.7
turbine	Dy	7	1.1	0.42	251	13.3	320	4

Sources: The specific metal demand for Nd and Dy are obtained from Shammugam et al. (2019) whereas the specific demand for Ag is obtained from Fraunhofer internal data. USGS (2018) and Viebahn et al. (2015) provided the reserve and annual production of Ag and REEs respectively.

Assuming that this trend continues in the future, growth in all manufacturing sectors can be expected, which consequently creates competition for raw materials between different sectors. In most cases the outcome is predictable; those who are willing to pay the most can secure the raw materials they need.

Apart from the aforementioned arguments, there are several other risks that can occur due to the increasing deployment of renewable energy technologies. One of the most likely ones will be the hike in raw material prices as the availability becomes scarce. Being already the most expensive metal in c-Si PV modules, a strong increase in silver price will definitely hinder the cost reduction of PV modules, which in turn will impede a large-scale deployment. Furthermore, the increase in price might provide producing countries with useful leverage against other countries to increase their profit. This is possible since most of the metals required by renewable energy technologies are found in large concentrations in only a handful of countries. An example of this was the export restriction on REEs imposed by China in 2012, which eventually led Vestas, a major turbine manufacturer, to use squirrel cage induction generators for their turbines instead of their established high-speed generators with permanent magnets.

Material efficiency measures in solar cells and novel concepts

Based on the arguments presented in the previous chapter, it is clear that further improving resource efficiency in renewable technologies is vital in order to ensure their sustainability and cost-effective wide-scale implementation. Resource efficiency in photovoltaics can be achieved via direct or indirect measures. A direct material efficiency measure can be the improvement in the production process of PV products, like solar cells and modules. An example of this is the reduction of kerf losses which occur from the slicing of silicon ingots into thin wafers. By 2018, almost the entire c-Si PV industry switched from the slurry-based wafer sawing to the diamond wire sawing, which reduces the amount of silicon consumed per wafer by approximately 15% (ITRPV 2017). The further material reduction can be expected by using kerfless wafering technologies, thinner diamond wires as well as increasing the rate of recycling for the silicon residue during the sawing process. In addition to that, efforts are undertaken in order to reduce the use of silver in cell metallisation since it is currently – and will most probably remain – the most expensive metal in a crystalline solar cell. Besides reducing the amount of silver via improved screen printing and cell interconnection, feasible ways of substituting it with a mixture of copper and nickel are already available, which allows for comparable efficiency.

Material efficiency can also be indirectly achieved by improving cell efficiency, which reduces the specific demand for all relevant materials, as well as reduction of cell thickness, which improves the material efficiency of silicon. The most common cell thickness of a silicon-based solar cell is 180 µm.

Nonetheless, efforts are being carried out to reduce this, so that thickness as low as 120 μm can already be expected by 2030 for mono c-Si solar cells. In terms of efficiency, the maximum achievable efficiency for c-Si solar cells is limited at 29.4% (Polman et al. 2016). The current maximum recorded c-Si solar cell efficiency is 26.7%, which shows that there is still slight room for improvement (Green et al. 2019). Furthermore, the module efficiency, which lies currently around 17–20%, can also be improved further. For example, losses in cell interconnections can be reduced by utilising shingles solar cells whereas shading losses can be reduced by using frameless modules.

Improved concepts such as the Silicon heterojunction (SHJ) solar cell can help in further reducing specific material content of solar cells due to their high efficiency. SHJ has very high conversion efficiency due to distinctive surface passivation. Compared to other silicon-based solar cells such as Passivated Emitter and Rear Cell (PERC) or Back Surface Field (BSF), the main advantages of SHJ include the simple and low-temperature manu-facturing processes, which decrease the thermal budget and thus the cost of the cell (Louwen et al. 2016). However, the production facility is not yet available on a large scale as main players in the industry often opt to optimise their current portfolio and respective products rather than adopting a new cell concept and corresponding production line. However, this is most likely to change in the future once the cost advantages increase, driven by significant learning effects.

A further increase in efficiency above 30% can be achieved by the transition from one to two or more p-n-junctions, named tandem or multijunction solar cells. In terms of tandem solar cells, one of the most widely discussed concepts is the perovskite cell in combination with Si-cells. This solar cell has gained much attention in the past few years due to the enormous increase in effi-ciency in a very short period of time, as well as the utilisation of inexpensive materials. Nonetheless, the main challenges faced by perovskite cells is the instability issue and the use of lead which is toxic and faces the uncertainty of being banned in the EU Directive for Hazardous Substances (RoHS). Research efforts are already being undertaken to substitute lead with other metals such as bismuth. Nonetheless, the power conversion efficiency is still low compared to the requirement for large scale commercial application. Another promising multijunction concept is the monolithic application of III-V solar cells onto a Si bottom cell. A triple junction configuration has demonstrated to reach efficiencies beyond 37% for terrestrial applications, which clearly offers an enormous material-saving potential (NREL 2019).

Reducing the demand for rare earth elements in wind turbines

The most critical metals in wind turbines are clearly rare earth elements (REEs), namely, dysprosium and neodymium. Improvements in the pro-duction technique can reduce material losses and decrease the utilisation of

REEs. For example, Viebahn et al. (2015) reported that the specific material demand of neodymium in a middle-speed generator in wind turbines can be reduced from the current 50 kg/MW to around 32 kg/MW by 2050. Pavel et al. (2017), on the other hand, project an even more intensive reduction by stating that 35 kg/MW of neodymium can already be achieved by 2030. Apart from improving the production techniques, material efficiency in REEs can also be achieved via substitution measures. Principally, two different substitution measures can be applied. Firstly, neodymium and dysprosium can be substituted by other less expensive metals such as cerium and cobalt doped alloys (Pathak et al. 2015). The problem with this solution is that cobalt can face a severe bottleneck in the future with expected strong demand for batteries in electric vehicles. Therefore, although the substitution of REEs can reduce the cost of wind turbines in the near future, it might not be sustainable in the long run when the price of cobalt spikes due to substantial demand and stiff competition, especially from the automotive industry.

This leaves us with the second substitution measure, namely the utilisation of complementary wind turbine concepts without permanent magnets (PM). There are numerous other PM-free concepts available on the market, namely electrically excited generators such as the synchronous direct-drive generator by Enercon or the doubly-fed induction generator by Siemens-Gamesa. Despite the availability of such concepts, generators with PM remain the preferred concept for offshore turbines in part due to their high reliability. Since maintenance work can be highly costly especially when the turbines are built further from the shores, developers tend to opt for the turbines that require less maintenance and repair works. Therefore, efforts in improving the reliability of wind turbines are necessary to close the gap between electrically-excited turbines and turbines with PMs and thus suppressing the need for REEs. Nonetheless, this substitution measure should be treated with care as the increased use of electrically excited turbines might lead to supply bottlenecks of copper (Shammugam et al. 2019). Therefore, a balance between both generator concepts is necessary to overcome the overall metal supply risk. Further state-of-the-art concepts such as the high-temperature superconducting and the pseudo-direct-drive generators can also facilitate in reducing metal requirements due to their lesser weight and improved efficiency.

Secondary production of metals via recycling

A substantially different way of reducing material demand is recycling. In the example of the cumulative demand for silver, assuming a 100% recycling rate reduces the total demand by 20%. Besides that, the peak silver demand could also be reduced by half. In terms of the demand for neodymium and dysprosium, the total cumulative demand can be reduced by 25% assuming a 100% recycling rate. One could argue that the effect of recycling in reducing material demand might seem small. However, it is essential to mention that most of the metal demand will still be in use in 2040 and will be available for recycling beyond that. Therefore, the virgin demand for manufacturing the technologies in the future can be much lower assuming that most of the material can be won by recycling. In the long term, recycling is probably the most sustainable way of producing metals in order not to exhaust the available raw material resources.

A major challenge faced by the recycling sector is the current lack of market. In Germany for example, although there are around 40 GW of installed PV capacity, most of them were installed from 2010 onwards and will be available for recycling at the earliest by 2035, assuming a lifespan of 25 years. Therefore, it is understandable that there are few available business models and facilities to recycle them. Within this context, First Solar stands out as one of the very few module manufacturers that collects and recycles their own modules. With a reported recycling rate of 90% including semiconductor materials, First Solar not only ensures that the material can be recovered and reused but also has to make sure that no toxic wastes such as cadmium are disposed inappropriately. Similar challenge is also faced by wind turbines since the market is still small for business models and infrastructure developments. In addition to that, a literature review (Jensen and Skelton 2018; Cousins et al. 2019) shows that most of the research today focuses on the recycling of carbon fibres in the turbine blades and very less on the recycling of the generators which contain REEs.

Towards a sustainable energy system with efficient resource utilisation

The Waste Electrical and Electronic Equipment (WEEE) Directive was first introduced in the EU in 2002 to properly manage waste from electric and electronic products. The main goal of the directive is to prevent and reduce the negative environmental effects resulting from the generation and management of WEEE by introducing sustainable production and consumption by reducing, reusing and recycling. Since 2012, this directive also included PV modules and requires manufacturers to take back and recycle their decommissioned products. However, the biggest drawback of this directive is that the exact metals to be recycled are not defined. As an example, the organisation PV-Cycle, which consists of a group of module manufacturers, aims at recycling more than 80% of the weight of PV modules. However, this goal can already be reached if the glass and aluminium frame are recycled, which contributes to more than 90% of the total module weight. Critical metals are often neglected due to their modest amount, which calls for a more specific regulation to define recycling targets for exact metals.

To fully utilise the potential of recycling, a closed-loop recycling process can be implemented. This process means that the materials won by recycling wind turbines and PV modules are used to manufacture new turbines and modules. Such a system is seen as the most effective risk mitigation measure to fend off competitions from other sectors and ensures that the RE industry can secure its long-term material needs. For example, more than half of the silver demand globally is used as financial commodity and jewellery, which rarely gets recycled. Without a closed-loop recycling process, there is a high possibility that the recycled silver demand from PV modules might end being purchased as a financial asset, especially if the price keeps increasing. On a different note, there is also a possibility that decommissioned RE technologies contain more amount of metals than the amount required to manufacture material-efficient RE technologies at certain time points in the future. This is possible if the market growth remains fairly consistent or existing technology is replaced by a much more efficient technology in the future. For example, the existing wind turbines with PM can provide a surplus of REEs assuming that turbines with electrically excited generators will strongly dominate the market in the future. Ultimately, this provides the industry the opportunity to sell the surplus amount of material which contributes to increasing the financial attractiveness of RE technologies. Besides that, a local closed-loop recycling process also reduces the dependency of the producing countries on foreign markets and makes them more immune towards price fluctuations on the global market.

Furthermore, in order to allow efficient implementations of such a recycling process, the idea of recycling has to be integrated already during the manufacturing process. In doing so, a product will be designed in such a way that it can be easily dismantled and prepared for remanufacturing or recycling during the end-of-life stage. Regarding the issue of lack of a general market for recycling, there is ample time for the industry to prepare for the large-scale decommissioning of the technologies. Research activities should nonetheless already be conducted intensively for recycling so that the industry is fully prepared with appropriate infrastructure. Although the entrepreneurial risk might be very high to start a business where the market is currently very limited, such a strategy might be possible with governmental support. These recycling facilities and business models can already be tested using PV modules or wind turbine components that have been prematurely decommissioned due to failures. For example, Shammugam et al. (2019) estimated that almost 30% of the total material demand in a lifespan of wind turbines is a direct result of maintenance, repair and component exchanges due to failures. The significant amount of failed modules shows that a sufficient supply of components will be available to test the recycling facilities and business models before the large-scale decommissioning of RE technologies actually occurs in the near future.

As of efficiency measures and substitution strategies discussed in this chapter to increase the material efficiency of RE technologies, most of them are still being researched and are not available on a large commercial scale. Therefore increased research works are necessary in these fields in order to accelerate the implementation and market entry of these measures. More governmental support is required for start-ups that are willing to venture into innovative and novel technologies to initiate the activities that will eventually attract more players to be involved and eventually increase the learning rate of these technologies and infrastructure. These efficiency measures are all the more important that renewable technologies have an expected lifespan of at least

180 *Hans-Martin Henning et al.*

25 years, which means that the amount of metals in-use will only be available for reuse upon reaching the lifespan. Therefore it is essential to accelerate the implementation of the material efficiency measures to ensure the long-term sustainability of RE technologies.

Acknowledgement

We thank Lorenz Friedrich for valuable input regarding material efficiency measures in solar cells and novel concepts.

Abbreviations

BSF   back surface field
CO_2 carbon dioxide
COP   Conference of the Parties
c-Si   crystalline silicon
GDP   gross domestic product
GHG   greenhouse gas
IEA   International Energy Agency
PERC   passivated emitter and rear cell
PM   permanent magnet
PV   photovoltaics
REE   rare earth elements
RoHS   directive for hazardous substances
SDS   sustainable development scenario
SHJ   silicon heterojunction
WEEE   waste electrical and electronic equipment
WEO   World Energy Outlook

References

Cousins, D. S., Suzuki, Y., Murray, R. E., Samaniuk, J. R. and Stebner, A. P. (2019). Recycling Glass Fiber Thermoplastic Composites from Wind Turbine Blades. *Journal of Cleaner Production*, 209(1252–1263). doi:10.1016/j.jclepro.2018.10.286.

Green, M. A., Hishikawa, Y., Dunlop, E. D., Levi, D. H., Hohl-Ebinger, J., Yoshita, M., et al. (2019). Solar cell efficiency tables (Version 53). *Progress in Photovoltaics: Research and Applications*, 27(1, 3–12). doi:10.1002/pip.3102.

IEA. (2018). *World Energy Outlook 2018*. IEA.

IRENA. (2019). *Renewable Energy Statistics 2019*. Abu Dhabi: International Renewable Energy Agency.

ITRPV. (2017). *International Technology Roadmap for Photovoltaic*. ITRPV.

Jensen, J. P. and Skelton, K. (2018). Wind Turbine Blade Recycling: Experiences, Challenges and Possibilities in a Circular Economy. *Renewable and Sustainable Energy Reviews*, 97(165–176). doi:10.1016/j.rser.2018.08.041.

Louwen, A., van Sark, W., Schropp, R. and Faaij, A. (2016). A Cost Roadmap for Silicon

Heterojunction Solar Cells. *Solar Energy Materials and Solar Cells*, 147(295–314). doi:10.1016/j.solmat.2015.12.026.

NREL. (2019). Best Research-Cell Efficiency Chart. www.nrel.gov/pv/cell-efficiency.html.

Pathak, A. K., Khan, M., Gschneidner, K. A., McCallum, R. W., Zhou, L., Sun, K., et al. (2015). Cerium. An Unlikely Replacement of Dysprosium in High Performance Nd-Fe-B Permanent Magnets. *Advanced Materials*, 27(16, 2663–2667). doi:10.1002/adma.201404892.

Pavel, C. C., Lacal-Arántegui, R., Marmier, A., Schüler, D., Tzimas, E., Buchert, M., et al. (2017). Substitution Strategies for Reducing the Use of Rare Earths in Wind Turbines. *Resources Policy*, 52(349–357). doi:10.1016/j.resourpol.2017.04.010.

Polman, A., Knight, M., Garnett, E. C., Ehrler, B. and Sinke, W. C. (2016). Photovoltaic Materials. Present Efficiencies and Future Challenges. *Science*, 352, (6283, aad4424). doi:10.1126/science.aad4424.

Shammugam, S., Gervais, E., Schlegl, T. and Rathgeber, A. (2019). Raw Metal Needs and Supply Risks for the Development of Wind Energy in Germany until 2050. *Journal of Cleaner Production*, 221(738–752). doi:10.1016/j.jclepro.2019.02.223.

USGS. (2018). *Mineral Commodity Summaries 2018*. US Geological Survey.

Viebahn, P., soukup, O., Samadi, S., Teubler, J., Wiesen, J. and Ritthoff, M. (2015). Assessing the Need for Critical Minerals to Shift the German Energy System towards a High Proportion of Renewables. *Renewable and Sustainable Energy Reviews*, 49(655–671). www.sciencedirect.com/science/article/pii/S1364032115003408. Accessed: 11.05.17.

16 Governing critical infrastructure in digital futures

Louis Klein

Critical infrastructure

Today, we are only a few days away from civil war, say the critical infrastructure providers. Imagine a blackout, no electricity, nowhere in the entire grid. Moreover, the electricity does not come back. A few backup generators will kick in and sustain an emergency mode, for a few days, especially for hospitals, police and army, and some of the rich. Private households seek for a safety net. People run for food and petrol. But stocks will deplete soon. The cooling chain breaks down. Frozen and fresh food turns bad. After three days the shelves are empty, transportation breaks down, and communications fade out. The civil order starts to crumble as people run out of food with little or no information about what is happening. Rumours spread and anxieties grow into panic. Scuffles grow into fights. While in hospitals, patients who cannot be sustained must die. The first gun is fired.

Modern societies are far more vulnerable as the occasional hacker attacks suggest. If critical infrastructure breaks down, society collapses. An electricity black-out maybe just an example a critical infrastructure breakdown, However, in modern society energy is vital for almost everything. Moreover, the more developed a society, the harder the blow. Hence, critical infrastructure is a major concern of institutional and organisational risk management. Yet, there is a trade-off between criticality and efficiency. The more efficient a system, the lower is its resilience, and the higher is its criticality (Klein 2018a). So, if we want to optimise resource efficiency, we need to keep more than a watchful eye on criticality. However, our appetite for energy is limitless. The growth curves described in the so-called Great Acceleration (Colvile 2016; McNeill & Engelke 2014) are exponential. We may debate if the resources we are consuming are three, six or seven times beyond the regenerative capacity of our planet. This debate is futile. The challenge at hand is far beyond incremental solutions. It is a question of bold systems change.

There is no right life in the wrong one, said the German philosopher and founder of the Critical School, Theodor W. Adorno (1951). In a globalised world, in the age of the Anthropocene, there are no sustainable pockets of

Critical infrastructure in digital futures 183

happiness. The dynamic interdependencies of the living world do not allow for small, isolated solutions. Facing the challenges of the Anthropocene in the 21st century, we need to acknowledge that despite campaigns like the UN Sustainable Development Goals, our current debates are missing the point in so many ways. Neither the resource challenge nor the security and resilience of critical infrastructure can be treated and solved in isolation. These challenges go deep and address the very fabric of our societies and the very thinking that brought about those social systems that characterise western modernity. Everything needs to be challenged. Building on Albert Einstein's famous quote that the thinking that brought about the problems will not be thinking that yields the solutions, we need to start looking for new thinking, for an epistemological turn towards Anthropocene Thinking that puts an end to the paradigms of modernity and take it from there.

First, we need to understand our understanding, understand our thinking and the regimes we use to govern (Foerster 2002). We need to acknowledge the ruling matrix of epistemological propositions that determines our world-view. We will learn that it is us who conceived and created the reality we live in. Moreover, advanced technology is only able to support us as far as our ideas can provide for it. We need to understand that there is more than one future (Poli 2011) and that systems change is not a question of incremental project management, but a matter of mind shift and leverage points (Klein 2019). We need to understand that competition yields perverse incentives and scarcity, and that smart rules govern serious games (Klein 2018b) which can manifest the common good not only respecting the sustainability of our planet but contributing to a thrivable living world.

This kind of systems change will allow for sustainable energy regimes that do not deplete resources but grows them. It will enable us to translate sustainable energy regimes into critical infrastructure that supports this sustainability, that meets the requirements of robustness, resilience, and anti-fragility, and performs as effective as efficient. We may in the age of big data, digital transformation, and artificial intelligence (AI) conceive of distributed autonomous infrastructure systems which reliably harvest and distribute renewable energy serving the common good while sustaining a thrivable planet. Technology, however, comes last. First, we need to understand understanding and allow for another thinking.

Anthropocene thinking

We live in a post-truth society not because our political world is full of lies but because we live in a VUCA, a volatile, uncertain, complex, and ambiguous, world which needs more than truth. We need volatility sciences, uncertainty sciences, complexity sciences, and ambiguity sciences. If we want to meet the challenges of the Anthropocene in the 21st century, we need thinking beyond the reductionist paradigms of modernity. Anthropocene thinking (Klein 2018c) identifies three candidates contributing to the necessary epistemological turn in

184 *Louis Klein*

the current scientific debates. First, systems sciences and cybernetics; second, integral theory; and third, theories of resonance.

Systems sciences and cybernetics are certainly the backbones of Anthropocene thinking. Systems sciences and cybernetics and later chaos and complexity sciences went into the challenge of dependent variables, feedback loops, path dependency, the power of context, the sensitivity to initial conditions and emergence (Boulton, Allen, and Bowman 2015). They can model and simulate system dynamics and explore the future implications of any complex system (Forrester 1968). The Report to the Club of Rome about the limits of growth is, undoubtedly, a hallmark of systems sciences and cybernetics (Meadows et al. 1972). Also, the Operations Room to govern the entire economy based on the Viable Systems Model in Allende's Chile in 1973 led by the cybernetician Stafford Beer made it into the pop culture of digital natives (Medina 2011). The relationship of systems sciences and cybernetics to modern sciences is like the relationship of quantum mechanics and relativity theory to classical mechanics. Modern sciences, as well as classical mechanics, are simple, limited cases of the broader theory.

Integral theory is the most popular of the three candidates. It became so popular for addressing individual cognitive and moral development that a plethora of self-help and self-improvement movements highjacked it for their cause. Seen from the perspective of Anthropocene thinking, it is the research on individual and collective development as well as social integration that makes it remarkable (McIntosh 2007; Loevinger 1987). It fills the blind spot systems sciences and cybernetics have with respect of the *conditio humana*. The inevitability of the living body, the conscious self and the social others need to be addressed to relate to human beings and not only to systems (Klein 2012). Integral theory provides this and opens perspectives of alternative developments and different processes of civilisation.

Theories of resonance are new and ancient at the same time. Theories of resonance are new because only lately, the focus broadened from a specific psychological theory to entire social systems (Rosa 2016). They suggest harmonious resonance as the critical criteria for human wellbeing addressing the three inevitable levels of the *conditio humana*. We can be in tune with your living body, your conscious self, and the social others. Communications, groups, and societies can be resonant and in tune. Yet, resonance reaches far beyond the human scale into nature resonating with the totality of the living world as described in the popular Gaia hypothesis (Margulis 1998; Lovelock 1979).

Resonance is a universal phenomenon that travels from the very elementary processes of quantum mechanics via the self-awareness of the human being to the harmonic relationships that rule the stars and the constellation of the cosmos. Looking for resonance allows us to go back in time, and therefore theories of resonance can be considered to be rather acient, before the Enlightenment, before the Renaissance and even before the Axial Age (8th to the 3rd century BCE). In the Vedic scripts of ancient India (1700 to 1100 BCE), meaning was attributed to sound and colour. In physical terms,

Critical infrastructure in digital futures 185

meaning was attributed to a frequency of soundwaves and light waves. This scientific insight suggests that meaning can be processed in the form of those frequencies. Peculiar as it occurs, we have an intuition for this when we speak and communicate. We process meaning in the basic form of frequencies based on resonance and call it words, sentences, stories, and narratives. With theories of resonance, we look at an entirely different paradigm which may revolutionise even our understanding of quantum computing moving away from digital logic towards the computable resonance.

Theories of resonance specify the quality of integration while integral theory addresses the scale and coherence of integration. This combination of integral theory and theories of resonance bridges a scientific understanding of matter, energy, and life in the form of critical spirituality to Daoist traditions (Ames & Hall 2003) and recent developments of Apithology, the discipline that studies the generative causes of health and wellness in living systems (Varey 2008). Both are approaching health and well-being from the larger picture of the totality of the living world, both arriving at what currently features as One Health regarding the future of medicine and healthcare, which argues that there cannot be individual health on a sick planet (Zinsstag et al. 2015; Atlas & Maloy 2014).

Governing good governance

Anthropocene thinking enlarges our understanding of governance. If we look at the different governments and regimes in the world and even when we look at western democracies only, we see plenty of versions featured under the same headline. We may use the explanation that different cultures and different values yield different regimes and various versions of democracy, however, this remains on the very surface. Western democracies, for example, are all founded on a set of the same three fundamental values. *liberté, égalité, fraternité* is the triad of the French revolution. The Germans' national anthem speaks of *Einigkeit und Recht und Freiheit*. It is personal freedom, equality before the law and societal solidarity which address the foundation of a desirable society or to be more precise, as the foundation of the governance of a desirable society. A theory of civilisation based on integral theory argues that there are three levels of societal maturity combined in this triad of social integration. First, there is the level of law and order which overcomes the earlier level of fight and force. With an accepted rule of law, a society can shield itself against civil war and the law of the jungle. It usually comes with a strong hierarchy and negative sanctions. A mighty ruler owning the monopoly of the use of forces will punish those who violate the rules. Second, there is the level of competition and personal freedom to pursue one's happiness participating in this competition.

Competition allows for personal ambition and fuels the individual motivation to go the legendary extra mile. The social integration mechanism is an investment and return. Those who do more deserve more. This leads to meritocracies which come at the price that those at the bottom are not simply

186 *Louis Klein*

unlucky but deserve to have not. In its extreme form competition challenges the right to exist of those who do not, as we say, earn their living. The level of competition builds on the level of rules and regulations to be distinct to the law of the jungle. Third, there is a level of societal solidarity. A society can overcome competition and share what was achieved collectively with everybody. It is not a matter of redistributing individual crops. It is based on the ancient Greek insight, attributed to Aristotle, that the whole is more than the sum of its parts. Collectively we create value beyond the individual returns. This is more than value-added, it is something that, for the lack of a better word, could be called hypervalue (Klein 2017). A society can agree to tap into this hypervalue to mitigate the downside of competition, allowing for both the individual pursuit of happiness and societal solidarity. Hypervalue, in this sense, is the new commons which operate along the lines of agreement and sharing.

In contemporary western democracies, we see all three levels of social integration in place, the rule of law, competition, and societal solidarity. However, increased competition dominates and seems to be applied to almost all walks of life. It looks like a successful paradigm being overstretched to the extent that it yields the right opposite of what it intended (Kuhn 1962). Overstretched competition produces scarcity where there is none for the sake of profit. Integral theory looking into modes of social integration and levels of civilisation as well as systems sciences and cybernetics understanding the emergence and hypervalue provide an understanding that yields new options for good governance.

Context design and individual care lie at the heart of good governance. Understanding the power of context opens a new perspective on rules and regulations. It is a little bit like nudging individuals to do what is better for them (Thaler & Sunstein 2008). The rules and regulations of social systems can also be seen as rules and regulations of serious games, one may be the economy the other politics and so forth. Games, however, have their own character. In the game Monopoly, for example, one player after the other goes bankrupted and drops out until only one player is left owning all the property and having all the money. Or there is a game like Settlers of Catan where all players stay in the game until the very end, rightfully hoping to win while the game unfolds, and the winner wins by a margin. Settlers of Catan was awarded game of the year in 1995 meeting all the criteria which make a good game. There is a lot to learn from game design for governing societies. Moreover, we can learn from systems sciences and cybernetics how the various serious games of society feed into each other.

Choosing futures

Meaning, said the German sociologist Niklas Luhmann, is the unity of the distinction between actuality and possibilities (1984). Psychic systems and social systems can relate to futures in the form of meaning. They need to do so to survive and sustain themselves. We think about futures routinely. However, we are matrix-bound. We can only see what our epistemological proposition allows us to see. If we want to overcome this, we need to challenge our matrix, and the easiest way to do so is to do this together. Exploring the unknown and conceiving of alternative futures scenarios can follow meaningful conversations and facilitating processes which overcome epistemological silos and embrace diversity (Bennett et al. 2016; Poli 2011). We cannot think what we cannot think, but what we could think is already present in the presence. It is in the various ingredients which makes the various futures distinct and unique.

Anticipation translates futures into practices and approaches feasibility (Poli 2010). The possibility of systems analytics in models and simulations adds to the possibility to explore the unknown and draw new maps which allow navigating a VUCA world. Shifting to Anthropocene Thinking allows to widen the view and to change the criteria of evaluation. If a futures scenario is functionally adequate, resilient, and sustainable if it is integrating into the broader scope of the living world and if it is improving resonance it is undoubtedly amongst the desirable futures to choose from.

In the 21st century, artificial intelligence (AI) is inevitable (Harari 2015; Brynjolfsson & McAfee 2014). All futures of critical infrastructure we can think of will revolve around questions of AI. Nonetheless, technology comes last. Technology is an accelerator and supports to scale up, but technology is never a driver or a creator of momentum (Collins 2001). Someone builds technology and this someone as well as the building process is embedded in paradigms, in a specific tradition of theory and practice. In the end, technology is hardwired and coded thinking with all its propositions and dependencies. In this sense, technology manifests, accelerates, and scales a specific worldview and the according to social, cultural and political regimes (Marcuse 1964). And if we want to see systems change, we need to mind technology as the most conservative agent of the past.

Form follows function, is the modernist's building maxim. In the 21st century, we need to understand understanding first and acknowledge that function is already an embedded concept. Technology is never neutral. It is a manifestation of paradigms in use. So, if we use AI to upgrade what we have already, it will yield just more of the same. If we do not want more of the 3same but systems change, we need to critically rethink what we have and conceive of desirable futures and their paradigmatic propositions. Then we can choose wisely before technology becomes hardwired and coded path dependency. This applies not only for critical infrastructure but also for AI itself (Minsky 2006). If you do not get what you wanted, you need to start all over again, if you still have the time given the challenges of the Anthropocene in the 21st century.

Privatising critical infrastructures like electricity or water was a common practice praised in the late 20th century serving the paradigmatic idea of competition as a desirable mode of societal integration. The market competition was thought to serve the people better than rules and regulations of public administration. However, the nature of technology, for example, in energy production was not prone to competition but lead to oligopolies of a handful of players who could afford large investments in power plants and grids and time horizons of 30 to 40 years for a profitable return on investment. Moreover, moving critical infrastructure into competition produced perverse incentives. If a business model is set up to solve a social problem, it is set-up to benefit and profit from that problem. It needs the problem to exist and the greater the challenge, the more significant the profit. The conventional technology of energy production produces scarcity whenever demand rises. It does not support overcoming the problem.

The energy reaching the earth from the sun is abundant. Energy scarcity is not in the resource but in the infrastructure of producing and distributing energy. Changing the infrastructure of harvesting and allocating energy could create commons where energy is shared rather than sold. If we think of this scenario as a desirable future of critical infrastructure, we are looking at entirely different technological requirements, especially for the supporting AI.

We can think of commons, and we need to meet the criticality of energy infrastructure shielding us from the initial scenario of civil war. Critical infrastructure needs to be robust, resilient, and anti-fragile. The solution we see in organic life is next to optimal redundancy, not maximal effectiveness and efficiency. Redundancy, however, is the foe of profit. It became a word with a negative connotation. Yet, competition yields criticality, redundancy fosters sustainability.

Organic life's solution for safeguarding critical infrastructure is autonomous systems like respiration, blood circulation, the lymph system to name but a few. Hence, moving critical infrastructure away from competition does not mean to subdue to rules and regulations of public administration but to move on to the autonomy of commons. If this sounds like science fiction it meets the requirements of exploring a desirable futures scenario very well. The responsible decision, however, lies in the presence.

Desirable AI

AI is matrix-bound and purpose-driven (Tegmark 2017). AI can be curious and self-learning. It is matrix-bound like any other technology. It depends on its epistemological and paradigmatic propositions. If it is coded in terms of law and order, it does rarely exceed the scope of a diligent expert system. But it can be coded following other modes of social integration supporting competition as well as commons. It depends on the purpose. AI is purpose-driven. The purpose is a normative proposition balancing strategic and op-erative requirements, presence and future. Purpose provides orientation. Do we want to make a profit or overcome criticality? Are we want to benefit from scarcity or integrate sustainably into the realms of the living world? According to the criteria we choose we choose.

AI can be curious and self-learning. However, this is where AI imposes another layer of complexity and adds to the gravity of technological choices. Curious and self-learning AI does not only accelerate and scale, but it also grows. The criteria which guide the technological choices will guide the curiosity and self-learning of the AI. If we choose the AI to support competition, it will consequently grow problems, produce scarcity, and deplete resources. It will not stop in optimising itself to do so. It will pursue effectiveness and efficiency, grow lean, eliminate redundancies, and inevitably foster criticality. It optimises what it was built for. AI can also realise and grow commons if we want. It can support a transition from competition to sharing, engaging in different measures and indicators for social integration and quality of life.

We can use the AI to support those serious games we want to play, the good games, like in the strategy games the games industry features since the early 1990s. The generation we call millennials learnt to view the world in this way and to navigate the complexity of the so-called virtual world with ease. They think of society as something that is or should be governed by smart algorithms like those well-designed computer games. They know that flow leads to epic wins and that this bears the potential to change the world (McGonigal 2012). The voice in the Fridays for Future protests that they do not see desirable futures in the current regimes of petty public administration and cut-throat competition. Any human-made system is only as strong as the supporting narrative is shared (Jorgensen & Largacha-Martinez 2014; Boje 2001). What holds for the acceptance of a currency applies to organisations, institutions, and regimes as well. They start to understand that they can choose a more desirable future.

AI does not understand narratives. It 'thinks' fast, not slow (Kahneman 2011). It is operationally closed in its digital logic. It can evaluate quickly according to its digital coding, yet it does not rationalise. It does not process meaning. This holds for its curiosity as well as for its self-learning, at least as far as we can see today. However, it can be used to realise the design of autonomous systems in reference to the hierarchy of human needs (Maslow 1943) and the sequences of personality development (Loevinger 1987). The more basic the level of human needs and the level of personality development, the more AI can be supportive. The more advanced and sophisticated the level of human needs and the level of personality development, the more comprehensive the realms of personal freedom AI can grant.

Beyond critical infrastructure

Imagine a world where curious and self-learning AI serves to safeguards critical infrastructure. A world where the governance of energy, food and water is integrated into autonomous systems based on the logic of the commons, a world where the governance of health, transportation, security, and telecommunications furthers integration and resonance. The world would be safer

190 Louis Klein

and greener for a start. Physiological needs were met, and a lot of psychological stress was eased. There was more room for family and friends, more time for personality development towards empathy, respect, and appreciation, for creativity, spontaneity, and new goals.

2045 would neither be the year of the singularity nor the year of nightfall (Morris 2013). AI would have learnt to govern critical infrastructure according to criteria of functional adequacy integration and resonance. Truth would still be cherished, but it ceased to be the single, limiting source of legitimisation. Progress would connotate advances in personal development and civilisation rather than technological frenzies. We would relate to critical infrastructure as we relate to respiration and heartbeat. We know it is in place, we know it serves us but more than this we could gratefully forget and trust.

The Anthropocene could be the era where anthropocentrism could be overcome, where integration aimed at the largest relevant level, the level of Gaia, the level of all the life on earth (Latour 2015). It could be an era where resonance would not end with the human scale but explore what Gaia has to say and find our place on a thrivable planet.

A better world starts as an exploration of desirable futures. We can change the world. But understanding our understanding comes first. Challenging our epistemological propositions and worldviews makes sure that we get it right. Anthropocene thinking suggests a way to do so.

References

Adorno, T. (1951). *Minima Moralia: Reflections on a Damaged Life* (ed. 2006; E. F. N. Jephcott, Übers.). London: Verso.

Ames, R., and Hall, D. (2003). *Dao De Jing: A Philosophical Translation* (reprint). New York: Ballantine Books.

Atlas, R. M., and Maloy, S. (2014). *One Health: People, Animals, and the Environment.* Washington, DC: American Society for Microbiology.

Bennett, E. M., Solan, M., Biggs, R., McPhearson, T., Norström, A. V., Olsson, P., … Xu, J. (2016). Bright Spots: Seeds of a Good Anthropocene. *Frontiers in Ecology and the Environment, 14*(8), 441–448. https://doi.org/10.1002/fee.1309.

Boje, D. M. (2001). *Narrative Methods for Organizational & Communication Research.* Thousand Oaks, CA: Sage Publications.

Boulton, J. G., Allen, P. M., and Bowman, C. (2015). *Embracing Complexity: Strategic Perspectives for an Age of Turbulence.* Oxford: Oxford University Press.

Brynjolfsson, E., and McAfee, A. (2014). *The Second Machine Age: Work, Progress, and Prosperity in a Time of Brilliant Technologies* (reprint 2016). New York: W. W. Norton & Company.

Collins, J. (2001). *Good to Great: Why Some Companies Make the Leap … And Others Don't.* New York: HarperBusiness.

Colvile, R. (2016). *The Great Acceleration: How the World is Getting Faster, Faster.* London: Bloomsbury.

Foerster, H. von. (2002). *Understanding Understanding: Essays on Cybernetics and Cognition.* New York: Springer.

Forrester, J. W. (1968). *Principles of Systems* (ed. 1973). Cambridge, MA: Wright-Allen.

Harari, Y. N. (2015). *Homo Deus: A Brief History of Tomorrow* (ed. 2017). London: Vintage.

Jorgensen, K. M., and Largacha-Martinez, C. (2014). *Critical Narrative Inquiry: Storytelling, Sustainability and Power*. New York: Nova Science Publishers.

Kahneman, D. (2011). *Thinking, Fast and Slow*. London: Penguin.

Klein, L. (2012). The Three Inevitabilities of Human Being. A Conceptual Hierarchy Model Approaching Social Complexity. *Kybernetes, 41*(7/8), 977–984.

Klein, L. (2017). *Tapping into Hypervalue – Innovating Economic Policy*. Accessed 9. Jan. 2018, von European School of Governance: A Closer Look website: https://europeanschoolofgovernance.eu/tapping-into-hypervalue-innovating-economic-policy/.

Klein, L. (2018a). *Business Excellence: Die Vielfalt erfolgreich managen*. Wiesbaden: Springer Gabler.

Klein, L. (2018b). *Governing the Serious Games of Society*. Accessed 28. Dec. 2018, von European School of Governance: A Closer Look website: https://europeanschoolofgovernance.eu/governing-the-serious-games-of-society/.

Klein, L. (2018c). *Venturing Anthropocene Thinking*. Accessed 28. Dec. 2018, von European School of Governance: A Closer Look website: https://europeanschoolofgovernance.eu/venturing-anthropocene-thinking/.

Klein, L. (2019). Systems Change Revisited. *Systemic Change Journal, 2*(1).

Kuhn, T. S. (1962). *The Structure of Scientific Revolutions* (2nd ed. 1970). Chicago, IL: The University of Chicago Press.

Latour, B. (2015). *Facing Gaia: Eight Lectures on the New Climatic Regime* (ed. 2017). Cambridge: Polity.

Loevinger, J. (1987). *Paradigms of Personality*. New York: W.H. Freeman and Company.

Lovelock, J. (1979). *Gaia: A New Look at Life on Earth* (reprint 2016). Oxford: Oxford University Press.

Luhmann, N. (1984). *Social Systems* (ed. 1996; J. Bednarz & D. Baecker, Übers.). Stanford, CA: Stanford University Press.

Marcuse, H. (1964). *One-Dimensional Man: Studies in the Ideology of Advanced Industrial Society* (ed. 1991). Boston, MA: Beacon Press.

Margulis, L. (1998). *Symbiotic Planet: A New Look at Evolution*. New York: Basic Books.

Maslow, A. H. (1943). A Theory of Human Motivation. *Psychological Review, 50*(4), 370–396.

McGonigal, J. (2012). *Reality is Broken: Why Games Make Us Better and How They Can Change the World*. London: Vintage.

McIntosh, S. (2007). *Integral Consciousness and the Future of Evolution*. St. Paul, MN: Paragon House.

McNeill, J. R., and Engelke, P. (2016). *The Great Acceleration: An Environmental History of the Anthropocene Since 1945*. Cambridge, MA: Harvard University Press.

Meadows, D. H., Meadows, D. L., Randers, J., and Behrens III, William W. (1972). *The Limits to Growth: A Report for the Club of Rome's Project on the Predicament of Mankind*. New York: New American Library.

Medina, E. (2011). *Cybernetic Revolutionaries. Technology and Politics in Allende's Chile*. Cambridge, MA: MIT University Press.

Minsky, M. (2006). *The Emotion Machine: Commonsense Thinking, Artificial Intelligence, and the Future of the Human Mind* (reprint 2007). New York: Simon & Schuster.

Morris, I. (2013). *The Measure of Civilisation: The Story of Why the West Rules for Now*. London: Profile Books.

Poli, R. (2010). The Many Aspects of Anticipation. *Foresight*, *12*(3), 7–17. https://doi.org/10.1108/14636681011049839.

Poli, R. (2011). Steps Toward an Explicit Ontology of the Future. *Journal of Futures Studies*, *16*(1), 67–78.

Rosa, H. (2016). *Resonance: A Sociology of Our Relationship to the World* (ed. 2019). Cambridge: Polity.

Tegmark, M. (2017). *Life 3.0: Being Human in the Age of Artificial Intelligence* (ed. 2018). London: Penguin.

Thaler, R. H., and Sunstein, C. R. (2008). *Nudge: Improving Decisions About Health, Wealth, and Happiness* (rev. ed. 2009). London: Penguin Books.

Varey, W. (2008). Apithology: An Emergent Continuum. *Journal of Apithological Practice*, *1*(1), 1–7.

Zinsstag, J., Schelling, E., Waltner-Toews, D., Whittaker, M., and Tanner, M. (2015). *One Health: The Theory and Practice of Integrated Health Approaches*. Wallingford: CABI Publishing.

17 The energy transition in Deventer

A Hanseatic approach

Ir. Almar Otten and Ron Sint Nicolaas

Deventer: a culture of cooperation since Hanseatic times

A brief history of co-operation

Deventer belongs to the five oldest cities of the Netherlands. In 768 the Frank missionary Lebuinus crossed the river IJssel to convert the Saxons to Christianity. He built a church at the high grounds at the crossing of the river IJssel and the Schipbeek. Deventer became an important trading place and was one of the first Dutch towns to join the Hanze, the economic cooperation between hundreds of towns surrounding the North and the East Sea.

Between the 11th and the 16th centuries, Deventer developed into a city of science and books. Desiderius Erasmus and Geert Grote, founder of the Modern Devotion, studied at the famous Latin School.

In the 18th century industry became the economic engine of the city. The Deventer company Noury van der Lande was one of the founding companies of the Akzo Nobel concern. The recently split off chemical division was therefor called Nouryon.

Nowadays Deventer, blessed with 100,000 inhabitants, has a mixed economic profile. There still are well-known industrial enterprises such as Auping (beds), Ardagh (tin cans), Byk-Cera (additives), Nefit-Bosch (heating systems) and Nouryon (research). Since 1950 however, knowledge industry became more important. Deventer is the home base of large and worldwide operating consultancy firms like Witteveen+Bos and Tauw. During the last ten years new IT- and New Technology firms emerged and grew rapidly on a fertile soil, formed during ages of innovation and co-operation.

A brief history of sustainability

Since 2007 Deventer has a local strategic plan on sustainable energy. The goal of the first plan was to be energy-neutral in 2030. Now, in 2019, this political goal is unchanged. The city council still aims at a fully sustainable energy system in 2030. There is however a growing awareness that 2030 might be too optimistic.

The financial means of the municipality have always been limited. Due to the lack of budget, we have always been focused on cooperation with other parties, such as industries, housing associations, schools, energy companies. In every partnership, the municipality had to be keen on managing the expectations about the governmental role.

From 2007 to 2015 the municipality basically adopted an opportunistic approach. That led for example to a project in which solar systems were placed on 53 government buildings, such as schools and sports halls. The municipality also took the lead in the spatial procedures to enable the construction of two wind turbines, partly owned by the local energy cooperation, at the entrance of the town.

In 2016 the first contours of the National Climate Agreement became clear. It was obvious that the Dutch municipalities would be assigned to take the lead in the local energy transition. At the same time, the Deventer municipality was approached by the two largest housing associations to talk about the future energy management in districts where they owned houses and where they had to decide about the replacement of the old heating system. Would they install new gas-based systems with a depreciation period of 12 years or was this the right time to choose a sustainable, non-fossil fuel dependent source of heat? They asked the municipality to develop a long-term energy strategy. The municipality, the housing associations and the energy network operator started a joint project, called 'Fossil Free and Affordable Housing'.

Zandweerd became the first district to radically start building a new heating system. In the present situation, all houses have individual gas boilers. These will be replaced a collective heat network. This network has two sources of heat. The first is the nearby sewage treatment plan. That delivers water with a temperature of about 40 degrees Celsius. The temperature of this water can be raised by electrical heat pumps to a maximum of 70 degrees, specifically dependent on the isolation state of the individual house of a block of houses.

Towards a new strategy

Goals

In May 2019 the Senate of the Dutch Parliament agreed upon the National Climate Agreement and the Climate Act. The national goals are formulated as follows:

i   49% reduction of CO_2 emissions in 2030, based on the CO_2 emissions in 1990;
ii 95% CO_2-emission in 2050;
iii A zero-emission production of electricity in 2050;
iv 1.5 million of 7 million houses heated free of fossil fuels in 2030.

The Climate Act clearly appoints the municipality as director of the local energy transition. By law municipalities are assigned to develop the following plans:

a   a regional strategy as to produce a certain amount of sustainable energy (2020);
b   a general plan for the transition of heat supply (2021);
c   specific plans for transition of heat supply in districts, covering the whole town (2022).

From the national goals we can derive the following local goals for Deventer:

i   in 2030 half of the energy we use should originate from sustainable sources;
ii   in 2050 near to all of the energy we use should originate from sustainable sources;
iii in 2030 20% of all houses should be free of fossil fuels, that means 10,000 houses must be taken off the gas network in the next decade.

It is obvious that we need to change our strategy to achieve these goals. We cannot hold on to our basically reactive strategy of stimulating, facilitating, enhancing and connecting initiatives taken by others. The Climate Act tells us to take the lead, despite still having hardly any financial power. Moreover, from now on, major decisions must be made. The city council must take a stand in issues that will doubtlessly lead to major political and social controversies.

Although our role and position have changed, our new strategy will still be based on the co-operative way we worked during the last decade, based on mutual trust and understanding of needs and qualities.

Two tasks

The entire climate task exists of two major challenges of an entirely different order:

a   the transition of heat supply;
b   the production of sustainable (electrical) energy.

In directing the transition of heat supply we must deal with a broad range of questions of a technical, social, juridical or financial nature. What makes it even more complicated is that different parties are involved and that no party has the power, the assets and the authority to fulfil the task alone. Co-operation is a strict requirement;

The production of sustainable (electrical) energy is essentially a spatial issue: where do we want or don't want wind turbines or large solar systems? Apart from regulatory conditions, this task is governed by sentiments and political considerations.

Both tasks demand a different strategy. In the chapters below, we will describe our new strategy in the transition of heat supply and the production of sustainable (electrical) energy.

Strategy on the transition of heat supply

General approach

The transition of heat supply in Deventer concerns 45,000 houses, more than 500,000 m^2 offices and industrial buildings. The general approach is focused on districts, areas with a certain similarity in the type of buildings and energy infrastructure.

In 2017 the municipality and the four Deventer Housing Associations started the project 'Fossil Free and Affordable Homes.' Later also the network operators and the Water Board joined the project. The first focus of the project was to support the housing associations in deciding about the heat supply in the homes that were on the list for general maintenance and re-novation. Now this project is the vehicle for the entire heat supply transition task.

Our strategy is based on answering the following questions:

- Where do we start?
- What source of heat do we choose?
- Who is responsible for the new heat infrastructure?
- Who is financing the transformation?

Where do we start?

Investment regimes of the partners involved determining our transformation planning. Therefore, it is of vital importance that partners are willing to share their financial plans in full transparency. That is only feasible if partners work in confidence.

From the start of the 'Fossil Free and Affordable Homes'-project, we have invested in gaining a mutual understanding of each other's position, motives and targets. When different worlds with different rules and regulations collide, an open mind and willingness to accept that, are crucial.

Investment regimes were combined with information such as the type and age of houses, the energy infrastructure, other development plans and social aspects. That lead to a subdivision of the town into 'logical' energy transfor-mation districts.

There was no doubt that Zandweerd would be the district to start. In that district the following developments and opportunities came together:

a   150 new homes were newly developed by a commercial developer on the former site of a skating stadium. By law, these homes should be sustainably heated;

b   200 new homes were built by a housing association;

c   500 houses were on the list of heavy maintenance by another housing association;

d the district is located close to the main sewage treatment plant and the river IJssel, which could serve as sources of heat;
e a collective heat system could in the future serve more than 5,000 homes in the same district.

What source of heat do we choose?

To select the best source of heat we must make three choices:

i Can we use a direct source of heat, such as geothermal or aquathermal, or is there no other possibility than to use electrical heat supply?
ii Do we use individual heat supply systems, such as small heat pumps, or do we prefer a collective heat supply system?
iii Can we supply a low-temperature heat or is a high-temperature heat required, mostly for older and less isolated homes?

Selecting the best system always asks for tailor-made solutions. In depends on many variables such as, age and construction of the houses, the presence of heat network nearby, the availability of a direct heat source and the risk of noise pollution caused by individual heat pumps.

In the project 'Fossil Free and Affordable Homes', we share knowledge and experience from different points of view. That enables us to make the right choice. In the process of decision making, we always must deal with the unknown future. Scientists and business are constantly working on improving existing techniques and developing new techniques. Together with our partners we keep a close eye on promising new techniques and are even willing to invest in the application of such. However, the possible emergence of new heating techniques, such as heating by means of hydrogen gas, is no excuse for a wait-and-see attitude.

We feel it our duty as local government to go ahead, make decisions and accept the risk of regretting some of our decisions.

Who is responsible for the new heat infrastructure?

In the Netherlands, the gas and electricity market are strictly regulated. The distribution network is semi-publicly owned, the supply of gas and electricity is a private market. At this moment the heat supply is not regulated. In Deventer, we have nine existing heat networks, all privately owned and based on fossil fuels, that serve about 10,000 homes.

It seems low hanging fruit to transform the fossil fuel-based networks into sustainable networks. In the present energy market, however, it is not financially profitable to invest in the sustainability of those networks. Network owners have limited willingness to close the gap between loss and profit.

In the district Zandweerd, we are planning to build a new heat network, based on heat from the sewage treatment plant. Here it must be decided who takes responsibility for the construction and the exploitation of the new network. We cannot to wait for the government to develop new legislation for the heat supply market. Pending this new legislation, the municipality has declared willing to take first responsibility in the realisation of heat networks. Later the municipality will decide about keeping that responsibility themselves or sell it on the market.

Who is financing the transformation?

The financial starting point of the transformation is the energy bill not to rise above trend. The energy transition is not supposed to become a burden on the shoulders of individual households. This financial demand severely limits the willingness of private companies to invest in new infrastructure. The municipality itself also lacks the financial means for significant investments. Therefor money must be found elsewhere.

In the short term, the next 2 or 3 years, we depend on the financial support of the national or provincial authorities for closing the gap between the commercial limits of the market and the limits of financially burdening the house owners.

For the long term, the municipalities of Deventer, Apeldoorn, Zutphen and Zwolle actively develop financial arrangements to accelerate the energy transition. This project called Transform aims at making residents and house owners an irresistibly good offer for an alternative energy and heat supply. Tailor-made, feasible and affordable.

An essential tool for Transform is the 'trex': the transition exploitation. The 'trex' contains all the investments and financial flows that are currently provided in the different districts, including the investments and operating costs required for the new energy and heat supply. Transform is, therefore, working on a financing scheme at the district level. National and European Investment banks and pension funds are interested in this and contribute their ideas. The aim of this scheme is that everyone can participate: owner-occupied and rented homes, shops, businesses, schools. All of them without the monthly energy bills increasing. Local projects of energy cooperatives or residents' initiatives are also included in the total area approach.

We are convinced that Transform or similar arrangements will be the financial vehicle for the realisation of the heat supply transition.

Concise Deventer heat transition strategy

Our goal is to transform the heat supply of 10,000 homes from natural gas to sustainable sources in 2030 and 45,000 homes in 2050. Our strategy can be summarised as follows:

a   we divide the city into districts with similar energy infrastructure and types of houses;

b the order of transformation is determined by the investment regimes of the partners involved;
c house owners are primarily responsible themselves for deciding on the applied techniques;
d information is shared to optimise the process of decision-making;
e the possible emergence of promising new heating techniques is no excuse for a wait-and-see-attitude;
f pending the new legislation regulating the heat supply market, the municipality is willing to take responsibility in the realisation of heat networks in the short term;
g the next two or three years we depend on the financial support of the national or provincial authorities for closing the gap between the willingness of the market and the financial strength of the house owners;
h for the long term we actively develop financial arrangements, based on the energy bill not to rise above trend.

Strategy on the transition of production of electricity

Political debate

Contrary to the heat supply transition, the sustainable production of electricity is not a technical challenge. It is essentially a political issue. It is all about balancing values. In general, the construction of large solar parks or huge wind turbines is regarded as a threat to our valuable and vulnerable landscape. In 2014 the city council had to decide about the construction of two 120-metre wind turbines at the entrance of the town, along the highway A1. It was a close finish. The council voted 18 against and 19 in favour of the wind turbines. The political debate was not limited to the city council. The discussion split parts of society.

For four years the subject of wind turbines and solar parks was banned from the political arena. The only thing that happened was an investigation of the appreciation of the wind turbines before and after the realisation. About 1500, randomly selected, inhabitants of Deventer were involved in the study. The results of the study showed that there was a very low appreciation during the period of preparation and decision making. A large majority would have voted against the wind turbines. One year after the placement of the wind turbines the appreciation appeared to have turned 180 degrees. A majority claimed to be proud of the wind turbines.

Our National Climate Agreement puts our local debate or non-debate in another perspective. Now the Climate Law forces us to explicitly make a statement about the sustainable production of electricity on Deventer territory.

Our strategy consists of the following steps:

- development of different scenarios based on energy numbers;
- show the spatial consequences of the scenarios;
- organise the process of realisation.

Energy numbers

It is easy to formulate the goal that all electricity should originate from sustainable sources. Basic questions asked in a political debate are: how can we do it, how much do we need and what are the consequences? To give an impression of the measures required to reach our goals, we built a model that can be used for calculating different energy scenarios.

The first step is to determine what is the total amount of energy we must produce sustainably in 2030 of 2050. The assumption that 50% of the future heating demand cannot be supplied by direct sources, leads to a total sustainable electricity demand of 3642 Terajoule. The model tells us that covering all roofs in town with solar panels provides only 22% of our total demand. We need to do more. But what? Wind turbines? The model shows that we need 135 large wind turbines to meet our demand. From a rapid appraisal, we know that a maximum of 22 wind turbines is feasible within the spatial regulations. So, what else can we do? Solar parks in rural areas? The model shows that we need over 1000 hectares of solar parks. Is that what we want?

Table 17.1 features a possible energy mix for Deventer. For our strategy, these kinds of numbers are of crucial importance. Without numbers the debate has no firm ground and discussions will end in the mud. Now anyone can use our model, change the underlying assumptions and create our own energy mix. This surely supports a good locale climate debate.

Spatial consequences

Figure 17.1 and Table 17.1 show the land use in the entire Deventer municipality. It also shows the locations where the placement of wind turbines is not obstructed by spatial regulations.

The energy mix described above is based on assuming that three additional wind turbines, possibly along the highway A1, is the maximum feasible. In that scenario, a total surface of nearly 800 hectares of solar parks in rural areas is needed to be fully sustainable. Thus, 800 hectares of agricultural land must be transformed into an ocean of glittering solar panels. It is obvious that not everyone will be enthusiastic.

Table 17.1 Possible energy mix for Deventer

	Amount of energy (Tj)	Surface (ha)
Solar on roofs of homes	254	
Solar on roofs of companies	140	
Solar on roofs of farms	79	
Three wind turbines along highway A1	81	
Solar on ground urban areas	163	48
Solar on ground industrial areas	221	65
Solar on ground protected areas	0	0
Solar on ground other rural areas	2704	791
Total	3642	

The energy transition in Deventer 201

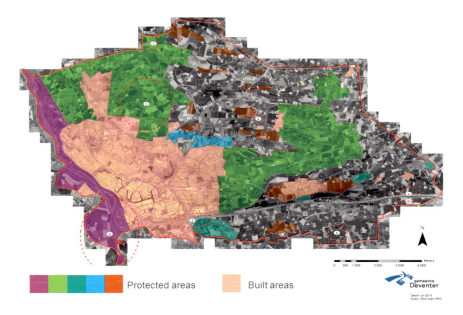

Figure 17.1 Land use in Deventer municipality.

Table 17.2 Land use in Deventer municipality

Usage	Surface in hectares
Town and surrounding villages	2.381
Business and industrial areas	645
Protected rural areas (nature and landscape)	5.074
Other rural areas	5.331
Total	13.432

Ultimately the city council will decide what we are going to do.

The process of realisation

Independently of the local political debate, the Climate Law obliges us to make progress in the production of sustainable electricity. Besides, the exploitation of wind turbines and solar parks is a lucrative business. The municipality is frequently approached by companies that are interested to build wind turbines and solar parks. Pending the outcome of the political debate, we had to take the following temporary measures:

The city council established an action framework for companies that want to build a solar park. One of the most important regulations is that the initiator is primarily responsible for creating broad support in the area surrounding the proposed solar park. This support can be obtained by fitting the plans in the landscape or sharing the financial profit with the people affected by the plan.

For wind turbines, there is no action framework right now. That means that an initiator is fully responsible himself for the development of the plans and creating social and political support. From our experience with the two wind turbines that were built in 2014, we can estimate the total costs of preparation and decision making about several tons. Knowing that the outcome of the political process is highly uncertain, no initiator will start developing plans at his own cost and risk. If the city council agrees on adding three or more wind turbines to the existing two turbines, the municipality will have to take the risk for the preparation costs.

Besides, we have another urgent matter: the actual capacity of our electricity network is insufficient for the transition to locally produced electricity. Especially in rural and industrial areas, the network is already 'full'. Newly built solar systems on farms or factories can simply not be connected to the network. The municipality can only address the problem on a national level and join forces with the network operators.

Conclusion

Due to the lack of financial means, the municipality has always invested in co-operation with companies, housing associations, NGOs, inhabitants and other governmental authorities. We tried to create an atmosphere of transparency and understanding for motives, needs and ambitions of all parties involved. This context always forced the municipality to be clear about role, responsibility and means.

The National Climate Agreement puts our role from a different perspective. The municipality is the appointed director of the local energy transition. We see that our investments in building partnerships immediately pay-off. As in long gone Hanseatic times, we have confidence in the power of co-operation. In high spirit, we step towards a sustainable future.

References

Cooperation of Dutch Network Operators (2019). *Basic Information about the Energy Infrastructure*. The Hague: Cooperation of Dutch Network Operators.

Government of the Netherlands (2019). *The Climate Act and the National Climate Agreement*. The Hague: Government of the Netherlands.

Municipality of Deventer (2009). *A sustainable Deventer: Towards a Climate Neutral Deventer in 2030*. Deventer: Municipality of Deventer.

Municipality of Deventer (2011). *Implementation Plan Sustainability: Towards a Sustainable Balance*. Deventer: Municipality of Deventer.

Rotmans, J. (2017). *Change of an Era: Our World in Transition*. Amsterdam: Boom Publishers.

Vermeij, M. and K. van Koppen (2017). *The Role of the municipality of Deventer in the Local Energy Transition*. Wageningen: Wageningen University and Research.

Part III
Case studies of existing solutions

18 Natural resources as common goods

Alexa K. Lutzenberger, Franziska Lichter, and Sarah Holzgreve

Introduction

Soil, water, air and biodiversity (genetic diversity) are among the most essential sources of life. With the existence of humankind, fierce battles over natural resources started – and continue to exist today. Main drivers of the diverse conflicts are besides climate change, the ongoing economic growth, and the increasing population accompanied by rising consumption patterns. Achieving food-water-energy-security and health, mitigating and adapting to climate change, protecting biodiversity and reduce greenhouse gas emissions, among others, are only a few of the thematic challenges for humanity according to intra- and intergenerational justice and types of ownership. Sustainable resource use and management, which provides a constant everlasting amount of ecosystem services, is only possible if humanity creates a new path away from the existing business as usual capitalism of exploitation and greed (Söllner 2014). Only if politicians, businessmen and civil society learn to treat their resources sustainably according to Brundtland 1987 ('Our Common Future') (Butlin 1989) and inter alia in correlation to the concept of strong sustainability by Ott and Döring (2004) can the survival of humanity can be assumed. The concept of commons might be a vital contribution to overcome unsustainable management and ownership of global resources.

Various approaches are available to derive the topic of resources as common goods. This diversity of approaches comes from various scientific fields and social aspects. From this diversity, however, very different approaches to common goods and justice/distributive justice can be formulated and also approaches to implementation can be found. Discussions and approaches from politics and science are assigned to the following groups, among others:

- Ecological

  - Planetary boundaries
  - Environmental impact

- Ecological-social

  - Health
  - Basic necessities of life

- Social

  - Brundlandt-Kommission – inter- and intragenerational justice
  - Living and working conditions

- Cultural – philosophical

  - Justice as a philosophical approach
  - Social sustainability as a cultural idea

- Socio-economic

  - Living and working conditions
  - Availability of resources
  - Income development, GNP
  - Human resources

- Economical

  - Benefits and costs/benefits etc.
  - Economic growth

- Ecological-economical

  - Green economy, and so on.

Until today no uniform definition of common goods exists, and terminological fuzziness is a scientific reality. Therefore, a key question is: In how far can natural resources be defined as humanity's common goods, and is a concept of common goods and its inherent part of commoning helpful in reducing resource extraction, and preserving existing resources for future generations? The aim is to identify how natural resources can be defined and assorted and, in a second step, how common goods can be derived from that definition and being identified as humanity's common goods.

Definition of natural resources

A resource in the economic sense means to carry out an action and is equated with the term capital. Furthermore, it can be divided into labour capital, physical capital and natural capital, the latter being the only natural resource (Reller et al. 2014). In terms of the geo- and sustainability sciences, natural resources are understood more broadly as all-natural capital used in the past or potentially usable including the environmental compartments water, air, and soil as well as energetic, mineral, and biotic resources as plants and animals (Reller et al. 2014). In the broadest sense, all ecosystem functions of earth and the solar system usable by humans or funding human well-being are included (Schütz & Bringezu 2008; Reid 2005; Bleischwitz et al. 2009). According to this, the *United Nations Environment Programme* (UNEP) International Resources Panel lists water, land, energy, and materials such as minerals,

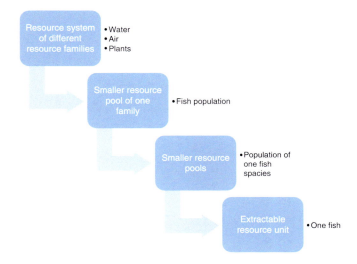

Figure 18.1 Scales of the resource system, pool and unit.
Source: based on Holzgreve (2015).

biomass and fossil fuels as natural resources (UNEP 2012). The German Resource Efficiency Programme (ProGress 2012) adds to the UNEP definition the biodiversity aspect and divides raw materials in abiotic materials like fossil fuels, ores, industrial minerals, and construction material; and material use, food/feedstuff and fuel as biotic material. The use of raw materials is herein closely connected with the use of other resources such as water, land/soil, air, biological diversity and ecosystems (BMUB 2012).

Based on the mentioned definitions, natural resources can be defined broadly as the means for human actions and basis of human livelihoods provided by nature; namely the large-scale resource pools like water, air, soil/land. They are extended by all ecosystem functions of earth and solar system usable by humans or funding human well-being (biodiversity, energy) and the extracted raw materials sub-categorised in biotic and abiotic materials. Their value for humanity – as resource pools embedded in ecosystems or as single resource units – is given by provisioning, supporting, cultural, and regulating ecosystem or resource services (Reid 2005). While local resource extraction reduces services to the provisioning and takes place at the local level, benefits from supporting and regulating services are of global significance.

Definition of commons

The classic economic view on different types of goods (cf. Chapter 1 on capital) is often used as a starting point in commons' discourses (Hardin 1968; de Moor 2011). Thus, goods are grouped normally into public goods, club goods, private goods, and common goods or rather common pool resources. Always depending on the degree of – access to, or exclusion from, as well as on the rivalry of use (scales from low to high) (de Moor 2011; Vanni 2014; Ostrom 1991). This economic classification (private, club, public) is based on forms of ownership, but in case of open access or common pool goods, there is no ownership according to an economic point of view. Furthermore, in classical economics, the Roman res nullius (no one's goods), and res communes (everyone's goods), have been merged into one category and considered to be at free disposal as underlined by Scott Gordon's sentence from 1954: 'Everybody's property is no-ones' property' (Gordon 1954). Differences between the types of collective ownership, public goods, and common goods are often blurred in the discourse on commons and make it necessary to define more clearly between them (Quilligan 2014).

Public goods are characterised by low excludability and a low rivalry of use. They are usually governed by the state to avoid free-riding. Public goods are generally subject to state-imposed regulations and laws on a large scale.

A common or common good in the classic sense refers according to present discourse to resources whose access and use intensity is managed jointly by negotiating rules against the background of traditions, norms, and practices (Quilligan 2014). It is a self-organised social system of assuming responsibility for renewable and finite, tangible (land, rivers) and less to intangible resources (atmosphere, internet) based on shared values and community identity with little link to market and state (Bollier 2014). Unlike a public good, it needs management and protection in order to endure (Hess 2008). Consequently, a common good starts to exist wherever and whenever a community decides to manage a resource collectively with particular attention to equal access, use and sustainability, and this is where the commoning process begins.

By upscaling from a common good unit like a single fish to *common resource pools* (fish species in one lake) to *global commons* (aggregated fish resource pools globally), the intersection with public goods is strongly increasing and raise the question to whom belongs the wind, atmosphere, fish etc. on a global level? As mentioned, a common pool resource consists of many single resource units which are used, mostly owned, and consumed by individuals. Therefore, a common pool resource, as well as a global common, is exploited by a large number of users in a relatively unrestricted and unregulated manner, making it more vulnerable to appropriation (de Moor 2011; Vanni 2014; Ostrom 1996) and due to lower access restrictions and usage regulation in comparison to private goods, prone to overuse and ultimately susceptible to the 'Tragedy of the Commons' mentioned by Hardin (1968). Regulatory forms and commoning are, therefore, regarded as particularly necessary for obtaining common pool resources and global commons (Hess 2008). Furthermore, both are characterised by the fact that they are classified according to economic tradition in the sector of free access and thus in the field of public goods. Therefore more participation rights and greater potential for co-determination are being demanded, as well as stronger regulation for the global commons. Forms of collective administration exist currently only to a small extent for them (de Moor 2011).

Subsequently, a common is here defined as: A system of resource governance consisting of a common pool resource which is compounded by single resource units (common good). The resource is addressed by an identifiable community of users, which initiate an identifiable process of commoning, where a shared aim in resource preservation and regulations for sustainable use, and governance of the relevant resource is discussed, adapted and installed. At least, as Silke Helfrich mentioned, everything can be a common (Helfrich 2012).

From the perspective of the Commons, it is, therefore, necessary to manage all-natural resources, without exception, at the local level according to their global significance as the common heritage of humanity – if we want to preserve them as the essential foundation of life on Earth for future generations.

Development of a common good management concept

Several innovative, regulatory strategies are established through a range of decision-makers, actors, partnerships and networks in a variety of formal and informal ways, including the collective action of common goods. This type of action is often associated with the term governance. According to Mayntz, in relation to the individual nation–state, governance means the totality of all the forms of collective regulation of social situations that exist side by side: 'from institutionalized civil society self-regulation through various forms of interaction between state and private actors, to the sovereign action of state actors' (Mayntz 2010).

In order to evaluate the diversity of ideas on the governance of common goods – concepts and management approach applied in abiotic and biotic common good areas – are filtered out. The underlying question is: What concepts and approaches can be considered successful in maintaining the productive use of common pool resources/common goods?

The identified concepts and approaches were checked for their independent transferability to other resources. The aim was to identify those concepts and approaches that have the potential to successfully manage other resources and to influence their management in a meaningful way. The inventoried concepts do not represent 'blueprints' in themselves. Their essential variables, which have contributed to successful management and collective action, were made visible. In addition, an overview has been given of the areas in which approaches exist and how they are structured. The focus of the study is on the period 1999–2014. This time span is at least necessary to understand the policy change related to sustainability, resource and climate change issues globally and regionally over the last decade. The resource sectors examined show that concrete research on concepts and approaches for the regulation and governance of common goods has been intensified in the last 15 years. The increasing complexity in the field of social interaction with natural resources, intensified by the increasing scarcity of resources, deterioration of living conditions or climatic changes of the last decades, call for new management approaches on all levels of action to be made visible. (1) During the data search, the entire intra-, inter- and transdisciplinary bandwidth was mapped as far as possible. (2) Ecological, economic, social, cultural and political constructs were taken into account in order to do justice to a sustainable understanding. (3) A further main focus was the identification of concepts and approaches in relation to the evaluated CG resources.

In total, 54 usable concepts were identified. All concepts were checked for six attributes. The first attribute, 'located organisational level', checks whether the concept is described at the formal or informal level (distinction at the macro level). The second attribute (collective choice arrangement) refers more precisely to the Community level. Namely, whether the concept is for example determined, regulated and developed by the community, by a social network with, for example, a cultural background (participation, micro-level). The third attribute (clearly defined biophysical boundaries) focuses on whether the biophysical boundaries of the considered common goods are defined. Biophysical properties are decisive: the occurrence, design and preservation of natural capital and influence ecosystem services. The fourth characteristic makes a distinction between common goods unit and common pool resource. It differentiates whether the focus of the concept is to be seen in the large-scale or small-scale perspective. The fifth property (transferability of the concept) assesses the transferability of the concept to other common good units and common pool resource. The last characteristic distinguishes seven categories: ecological, economic, social, cultural-philosophical.

In the category organisation level, most of the concepts (32) are designed at the formal level. This is essential for common goods, as formal management can secure the stability of resources through an organisational structure. Formal structures guarantee the safeguarding of decisions that have been taken or must be taken on the respective planning level (Zell 2011). The efficiency of the organisation of global and regional common goods can be enhanced by formal structures because more decisions can be made or more problems solved within a certain period of time.

Informal organisations include social structures in which interpersonal relationships play a major role (Zell 2011). Nine concepts could be identified with this feature. The aspect of social interaction is a major factor in the design of the commons according to the Institutional Framework for Policy Analysis and Design (IAD) (Polski & Ostrom 1999). Potential for linking the formal and informal level for further developed concepts, which integrate the individual needs and ideas of informal organisation, could be found in 13 of the examined concepts.

In the category Common Good Entity or Common Pool Resource it could be analysed that most concepts (33) focus on common pool resources, nine on common goods units and 11 consider both. Overall, 36 of the 54 concepts analysed, offer a high transfer performance to other resources, with seven being located in the middle of transferability.

It is clear from the document analysis that an interdisciplinary focus seems to be indispensable. Particularly with regard to global commons and common pool resources such as air, water, soil, etc., and especially with respect to the joint management of transboundary natural resources. Many of the biotic and abiotic resources are interrelated and build a common and continuously exchange. These complex contexts are not sufficiently taken into account in the examined approaches so far.

Design principles for the assessment of management approaches

The heuristic study of the management concepts and approaches is intended to address the question: Where and in which sectors are the strengths and weaknesses of the individual common pool resource/common good management concepts if they are reflected by minimum criteria in the design for a sustainable common pool resource/common good management? The referring sub-questions are:

a   What management approaches promote a robust social-ecological system?
b   Where the approaches are different from or similar to each other?
c   Which approaches complement each other sensibly?
d   And which approaches can be combined appropriately depending on the problem?

As a pioneer in the development of principles and criteria that promote sustainable common pool resource/common good management, Elinor Ostrom's work must be mentioned. By 1999, Ostrom had postulated eight principles, which she repeatedly evaluated over the years, and which have been tested, further developed, and supplemented in case studies by various authors (Anderies et al. 2004; Araral 2013; Bunch et al. 2011; Bruns 2008; Cox et al. 2010; Fowler 2003; Gruber 2010; Lindsay 1998; Ostrom 1999, 2008; Pomeroy et al. 1998; Stern 2011).

The aim was to create a matrix consisting of management approaches and evaluated design principles that could be evaluated in the form of a crossing scheme. The methodical procedure was divided into two main steps: First, the management approaches of the previously evaluated case studies were elevated to a meta-management approach for the design analysis. This approach was necessary because it is not about a special resource or a common good in particular, but about an approach that offers the possibility to be applicable for several resources. In order to ensure a better overview, all approaches were grouped together. A distinction was made between (a) a management concept, (b) a governance concept and (c) a more advanced approach. The difficulty in evaluating the individual meta-approaches and concepts was that there were sometimes hardly any uniform definitions, standards or framework conditions for the respective concepts/approaches. Depending on the application, the author's view and the inclusion of different tools and methods or combinations of approaches, the concepts can take more or less social-ecological aspects into account and vary in their design, criteria and principles. Taking into account the divergences, an attempt was made to filter out the generally valid criteria of a concept/approach and to evaluate only these on the basis of the design principles. In addition, approaches are summarised which are to be treated synonymously, such as 'co-management' which is also referred to in the literature as joint-management, collaborative management or cooperative management and so on. In the second step, a literature analysis on the topic of design principles was methodically carried out. In the selection process, only design criteria related to CPR/CG will be considered. In addition, the principles cover as broad an interdisciplinary field as possible. Social, ecological, economic and cultural aspects should be taken into account in as balanced a compilation as possible and take account of the sustainability concept.

In total, the evaluated portfolio – according to in-depth literature analysis – comprises 59 design principles and criteria that promote sustainable and collective use of natural resources. Each principle includes a brief description, which facilitates the subsequent assessment of the respective management approach. In a further step, those principles were extracted which allow an assessment of the management at the macro level. For this purpose, 22 design principles are selected and assigned to a respective major category. The matrix, therefore, includes the following main categories and their design principles:

I Fairness and legitimacy

- Collective choice arrangements.

  - Most individuals affected by the operational rules can participate in modifying the operational rules (Anderies et al. 2004; Bruns 2008; Cox et al. 2010; Ostrom 1990).

- Graduated sanctions.

  - Appropriators who violate operational rules are likely to be assessed graduated sanctions (depending on the seriousness and the context of the offence) by other appropriators, by officials accountable to the appropriators, or by both (Anderies et al. 2004; Bruns 2008; Cox et al. 2010; Ostrom 1990).

- Clear allocation and ownership of rights and obligations (Araral 2013).
- Fairness in the allocation of risks, costs and benefits (Araral 2013).
- Resources and equity (Gruber 2010).

  - Environmental justice is a social imperative that includes recognising local values.
  - Seek to improve (or minimise negative effects upon) the local economy.

Natural resources as common goods 213

- Recognise the need for linkages between conservation and local economy based upon equity, local needs, financial and environmental sustainability.
- Seek equitable and fair distribution of local benefits, potentially including compensation for protecting natural resources.
- Regulated access to natural resources and graduated sanctions can help ensure equity.

II Collaboration

- Networks/collaborative partnerships (Gruber 2010; Pomeroy et al. 1998).

  - Is the bringing together of information and expertise.
  - Networks may take many forms: alliances of support groups, organisations of stakeholders, and federations of resource users.
  - They may be formal or informal.
  - Networking is closely associated with the establishment of four types of linkages: (1) with other communities and projects involved in similar initiatives; (2) with sources of power and influence; (3) with NGOs and business groups, and (4) with donors and government agencies.
  - Networks and partnerships are integral to building social capital and serve as a catalyst synchronise finding innovative strategies and solutions.
  - Collaborative partnerships are vital to leveraging resources and supporting implementation.
  - Stakeholder training, workshops, and other collaborative learning opportunities can build social capital and commitment.
  - Seek agreement among key environmental NGOs, governments, and private sector to work collaboratively and to share resource and responsibilities.
  - Ownership by community members and other stakeholders enhances design, implementation, and operation, support cohesion, and encourages long-term commitment.

- Coordination between government and community (Pomeroy et al. 1998).

  - A coordinating body is established, external to the local group or organisation and with representation from the group or organisation and government, to monitor the local management arrangements, resolve conflicts, and reinforce local rule enforcement.

- Participatory decision making (Gruber 2010).

  - Effective participatory problem solving and decision making is enabled by a well- structured and facilitated dialogue involving scientists, policy makers, resource users, practitioners, and community members.

- Decision making is informed by analysis of key information about environmental and human-environmental systems including life aspirations of local people.
- It is vital to create a shared holistic vision/plan that anticipates probable environmental, social, and economic outcomes.
- The policy creation process should include a wide range of key expert and non-expert constituency/community groups at the table.
- Participatory problem solving should provide opportunities for the sharing of knowledge and collaborative learning about social-ecological systems.

III Information

- Interdisciplinary.

  - Management must be based on the realm of scientific studies and thereby include all disciplines (Fowler 2003).

- Communication and Information Dissemination (Gruber 2010).

  - Well-designed communication systems provide information sharing that support multiple social networks and raises the level of knowledge and awareness.
  - Linkages are provided between different information and knowledge systems to support learning, decision making, and change.
  - Effective communication supports openness and transparency.
  - Promote information sharing between experts and non-experts through multiple approaches including seminars and workshops; printed, electronic, and mass media; and projects.
  - Explicitly state expectations and limits.

- Information based (Fowler 2003).

  - Management must be based upon information, including the products of scientific research, monitoring, and assessment.

- Research and information development (Gruber 2010).

  - There is a common information base that is accessible and useful.
  - Decisions should be based upon a broad but systematic body of information.
  - Integrated information includes technical, scientific, social, quality-of-life, economic, and other forms of local knowledge, including indigenous experiential knowledge.
  - An economic evaluation of environmental assets is a valuable information base.

Natural resources as common goods 215

- On-going research is necessary to improve upon existing solutions including a role for community members in the collection of scientific information.

IV Security

- Risk averse.

  - Management must be precautionary and avoid risk in achieving sustainability.

- Addressing poverty and reducing inequities (Bunch et al. 2011).
- Promoting resilience (health, ecosystem function, biodiversity) (Bunch et al. 2011).

  - 'resilience' as an integrating concept that bridges health and sustainability concerns across scales from individuals to communities and ecosystems.
  - Reduce vulnerability against natural hazards.

- Security of rights (Lindsay 1998).

  - There must be a certainty that the rights cannot be taken away or changed unilaterally and unfairly.
  - The rights must be clear.
  - There must be certainty about the subjects of the rights.
  - The government entity entering into the agreement must have clear authority to do so.

- Conflict management and resolution (Gruber 2010).

  - Difficult realities and conflicts are inherent in community-based social-ecological systems.
  - Plan for and develop capacity and strategies for conflict management and resolution at the time of initiation of a community-based social-ecological initiative.
  - Recognise the central role of institutions outside of the Community-Based organisation in mediation of environment-society conflicts.
  - Work to transcend organisational rivalry and competition between organisations or stakeholder groups.
  - Design participatory decision making processes that promote dialogue and reduce factionalism.

V Adaptiveness

- Adaptive leadership and co-management (Gruber 2010).

  - A robust social-ecological organisation is designed and supported to be a learning organisation that supports adaptive capacity.
  - A learning organisation and an optimum management system are

resilient to perturbation, with an ability to cope with external shocks and rapid change.
- Adaptive co-management and adaptive leadership are dynamic and focused on processes rather than static structures.
- Adaptive co-management approaches include roles for local government, local community members, NGOs, and private institutions and decision making inclusive of people affected by and knowledgeable of the issues.
- An effective co-management approach engages, trains, and mobilises community member in the work of the organisation.

VI Polycentricity

- Devolution and empowerment (Gruber 2010).

  - True sharing of power and responsibility (devolution of authority and responsibility) between government authorities, community groups, and the broader community with enhanced local decision making improve outcomes.
  - Most individuals affected by environmental rules and regulations, including those who are often marginalised, should be included or represented in the group who make or modify the rules.
  - There are nested, multiple layers of governments and enterprises related to role/activities of decision making, appropriation, monitoring, enforcement, conflict resolution, and governance.
  - Devolution of control and decision-making significantly changes the relationship between central governments and rural/regional areas and if done effectively, can engage and build the commitment of local community members.
  - Establishing clear rules, procedures, and regulations can empower the local community.

- Nested enterprises (Anderies et al. 2004; Bruns 2008; Cox et al. 2010; Ostrom 1990).

  - Appropriation, provision, monitoring, enforcement, conflict resolution, and governance activities are organised in multiple layers of nested enterprises.

VII Transparency

- Monitoring the resource (Anderies et al. 2004; Bruns 2008; Cox et al. 2010; Stern 2011; Ostrom 1990).

  - Monitors who are accountable to the users monitor the condition of the resource.
  - Establish independent monitoring of the resource and its use that is accountable to the range of interested and affected parties.

Natural resources as common goods 217

- Public trust and legitimacy/confidence building measures (Gruber 2010).
    - Work must be viewed by the community as legitimate to build community trust.
    - Local leaders are integral to efforts in establishing trust and credibility.
    - Support by local elected officials will build trust and legitimacy.
    - Participatory approaches to problem-solving and decision making are critical to building legitimacy.
    - Transparency in activities, including decision making, supports the building of trust.

Figure 18.2 shows with respect to natural resources as commons the effect of the design principles and management approaches on the one hand and the social cohesion of the community on the other.

Furthermore, the analysis makes it clear that the management approaches available to us create the possibilities to manage a resource collectively from Commons points of view and that it is not necessarily new management concepts required but the existing is able to promote these possibilities. Aspects such as polycentric/decentralisation and co-management, which lie in the broad midfield, show that links on the horizontal as well as vertical scale and level (bridging, linking) do not yet experience sufficient implementation/application in concepts and can be supplemented here by suitable combinations with other management approaches, which have their focus there. Integration potential exists particularly in the implementation on a structural level. The same applies to sanction, poverty or conflict resolution mechanisms in connection with securing rights.

Many of the listed approaches and concepts of the matrix can be freely combined. Some of the possible combinations of individual approaches that can

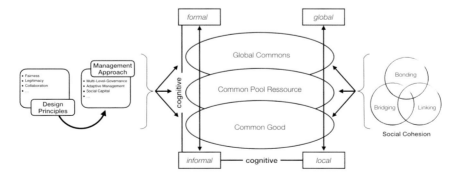

Figure 18.2 The relationship between social cohesion and the management of commons.
Source: Lutzenberger, Lichter and Holzgreve (2015).

very often be found in the Commons-Literature are already pointed out and evaluated in the matrix. For example, Adaptive Collaborative Management, which is made up of the individual approaches of Adaptive and Collaborative Management. Consequently, the matrix focuses on individual approaches, since potential combinations cannot be mapped and evaluated in their entirety in the matrix due to the multitude of possible combinations. However, the matrix can be understood as a tool which enables combinations. On the basis of the matrix it is possible for the observer to read off the evaluation of the individual approach accordingly and to carry out combinations independently. Combinations of individual approaches offer the option to combine and promote different strengths of the respective concepts and to sensibly reduce weaknesses by adding further approaches. This procedure can be carried out theoretically and practically during and before a project phase according to the problem situation and planning.

The listed design principles are thus a guide for the implementation of the commoning process (from weak to strong) as well as for commons research and projects. The design principles are not a methodical checklist per se, and their consideration is not a guarantee for the success of the respective project. However, the inclusion of the design principles can significantly influence the structuring of the process and help to control, inform, and shape the commoning process. Therefore, the design principles are elements of a more effective research process, which supports and applies knowledge generation in order to solve problems or to recognise them in advance. The design principles in the context of the listed management approaches contribute more to the joint management of natural resources, which support the restoration and conservation of ecosystem services and ensure their sustainable use. In addition, synergies and interrelations are created with important international environmental agreements, guidelines and requirements such as Agenda 21, the Millennium Development Goals, or the CBD, to name but a few of them, which, with their principles and framework conditions, also call for the joint and equitable conservation of natural resources.

As already described in the definition chapter, global resources are freely accessible for everyone, can be used without restriction, and thus belong to everyone. There is no direct form of ownership/order which assigns the resource to a person, a state or an organisation, among others, and which regulates it. The difficulty in controlling global resources lies in the lack of property rights. There is still the question who decides about global resources and their legitimateness. These and other questions remain in the scientific discourse by permanent degradation progresses. There is agreement that Antarctica, the oceans, space and the atmosphere are now recognised as global commons. The used definition, however, includes far more resources such as biodiversity, rare earths, genetic resources, etc.

The consequences of the lack of property rights are persistent overexploitation, pollution and lack of responsible use of resources and services, named in literature as the tragedy of the commons. A further difficulty lies in the limits of global commons, which must first be defined by the respective community. This appears more difficult, especially for topics such as biodiversity, seas, and so one. Different interests, risks, finances, property claims, forms of government meet and have to be decided at the highest level in order to be negotiated in the interest of all humanity. Especially the global commons as part of the common pool resources and integrated into an ecological cause-and-effect structure experience severe degradation and waste due to a lack of international regulation and control mechanisms. In this way, seas become no-man's-land and rainforests become bioenergy producers. The consequences of the lack of control and the lack of access to resources as a global common good are directly felt by the world's population. Issues such as the scarcity of drinking water, food security, climate change and energy supply have long been associated with the lack of regulation of global commons. The time scales and the current status of the existing degradation are also problematic. For example, the gases emitted during climate change such as carbon dioxide, methane, and others are globally distributed in the atmosphere for centuries, the extinction of species is irreversible, if a finite resource has been degraded, it will no longer renew itself, etc., which also puts intra- and intergenerational justice even more in the focus. In addition, scientific statements on climate change, biodiversity are subject to rather rough estimates based on scenario analyses, and others, which are partly based on a lack of data and monitoring. The overarching complexity of these systems and their interaction make an accurate analysis and prediction of system changes difficult. The same applies to technologies whose extent and effect cannot be estimated (for example geoengineering) (Stern 2011).

Consequently, there are gaps in communication and information dissemination as well as in the research of global commons as a whole. The consequential and risk costs of the use and overexploitation of global resources have so far been carried by all, e.g. the effects of climate change such as rising sea levels or the increase in periods of drought. The danger of competition for the last global resources, the individual exploitation of economic benefits culminates in collective damage. The individual's concern about the global commons is nevertheless low. One way out of this dilemma would be to convert unrestricted access to a Community ownership regime. The resource would be managed jointly, rights and obligations defined, respected and monitored.

Today, the management challenge for natural resources lies in the fact that resources often do not belong to one state alone but have to be controlled beyond national borders (beyond national jurisdiction and legislation) and remain part of individual nations. This increases the complexity of the process of commoning. The social cohesion of countries must go beyond national boundaries, and all countries must be fundamentally united on management approaches, objectives, and institutions, otherwise the system will return to full access and be exposed to overexploitation. This procedure requires high reciprocity. A reciprocal giving and taking, because interests can collide and a common denominator must be found. Bromley and Cochrane named three possible forms for the control of the international

220 *Alexa K. Lutzenberger et al.*

policy of the commuter (facilitative, inducing, injunctive), whereby injunctive should be the latter option because it determines winners and losers in the process of the convention and leads rather to the exit from the alliance (Bromley & Cochrane 1994).

The goal of international policy agreements should be, that all stakeholders see themselves through a common management in some way as winners and not as losers. Furthermore, the costs and benefits must be fairly shared. For an optimal international policy regime, the costs of leaking from the agreement would have to exceed the costs of accession (Bromley & Cochrane 1994). Dealing with global commons thus implies, to a certain extent, a collaborative political approach (Multilateral political considerations include: (a) several states act jointly cooperatively and, in principle, equally, taking into account all interests; (b) the common interest is formally accredited in the form of contracts and agreed on arrangements that bind all parties involved (Cheneval 2011). Examples of multilateralism would be multilateral federations with common policies such as the European Union, or a multilateral environmental treaty such as the Kyoto Protocol). Opposed to multilateral action, varies states try to promote their own solutions in order to counter climate change and biodiversity loss. For a variety of reasons, states are less multilateral in environmental problems and are leaving risks of global change and cause-effect linkages unrelated. The 22 design principles and the management approaches can, however, provide initial help to analyse the process of control and to optimise it in relation to the design principles, thus positively advancing the commoning process. As a result, control attempts at a global level can be evaluated, compared, and improved, which is not yet the case. The application of the design principles to multilateral instruments thus contributes significantly to the management of global, national, regional, and local commons. The 22 design principles are applicable to all levels, although with growing complexity, increasingly challenging to implement.

Case study: the water framework directive – an instrument for managing global water resources?

The Water Framework Directive (WFD) was adopted by the European Parliament on 23 October 2000 with the aim of establishing a uniform regulatory framework for water policy within the EU. The Water Framework Directive is, therefore, an instrument for managing water pollution at the European level. Implementation takes place through the acceding countries, which results in a multitude of different management approaches for implementation. However, the analysis focus is primarily based on the content and framework of the WFD and less on the later implementation by the acceding countries. For this purpose, the application of the 22 design principles is examined in the establishment of a regulatory framework, namely on the Directive WFD 2000/60/EC.

Theoretical assumption of a commoning process

If one assumes hypothetically that the first part of the commoning process took place, namely to form a community (social union, in this case, a multilateral state alliance), the second step would be to define the resource – in the concrete case of the WFD, it would be water (ground and surface water, river basins, etc.). For the regulation of the resource the European Union (EU) implemented the WFD as an institution. The WFD applies throughout Europe and controls all water bodies with the aim of improving the chemical and ecological condition. Through the multilateral agreement by the member states, one can assume that the EU treat the water bodies as a global common, although it is not named like that in the Directive. Thus the steps in the commoning process would be fulfilled from a theoretical point of view.

Summary of the analysis

The evaluation shows that the WFD has its strengths, especially in the categories of collaboration, information, transparency, and polycentricity. In the categories of fairness and safety, it is clearly below the requirements. The category adaptivity is, however, not included in the regulatory framework at all.

In the cross-section, it can be seen that the Directive has so far failed in its framework to take account of the local level of the accession countries and this is one of the most significant weaknesses in relation to the commoning process. Neither in the Directive nor the Common Implementation Strategy (CIS) – the joint implementation strategy of the WFD – could a reference be found to the local level. Consequently, the related design principles, such as collective choice arrangements or co-management are also negatively affected. Furthermore, it clearly appears, that addressing poverty and inequalities in the distribution of resources, costs, benefits, and risks is given little textual consideration, although poverty problems and conflicts with regard to water use are existent in the EU. Moreover, the issue of conflict management is also not pursued further by the WFD.

The WFD is a supranational institution and requires an implementation to the regional and local level. Due to the heterogeneity of the EU, the choice of management approaches is left to the acceding countries. In this way, they are given the flexibility to take into account their region-specific conditions. Thus the WFD does not exclude any approaches per se. However, exactly for this reason, the directive itself does not create any opportunities for collaborative management approaches. Furthermore, the regulatory framework does not provide an interrelation to the local economy, which is directly dependent on the water resources, and therefore does not create any linkage for the local community to see advantages in protecting the resources. Only in one section is an economic benefit for fisheries emphasised if the waters meet a certain quality standard: 'Protection of water status within river basins will provide economic benefits by contributing towards the protection of fish populations, including coastal fish populations (EC Directive 2000/60/EC 2010). Water users like agriculture, tourism and others more are not addressed. The inclusion of local resources – from a common good unit to resource pools – is addressed mainly from an ecological point of view but only partly from an economic and socio-cultural one. However, the current top-down mechanism of the WFD, that governs the entire water resource across Europe cannot mean the institutional decoupling of the local level in the regulatory framework. There is a strong link between the success of nature conservation and the co-participation of the local communities (Andrade & Rhodes 2012). In the light of the current regulatory framework, the WFD can rather be located in a 'command and control' policy, which has to be modified under an assumed commoning process.

Furthermore, resilience as an approach and equitable distribution of risks, costs, and benefits are not addressed in the WFD. Fairness is also not a concept of the WFD. An adaptive concept approach in the regulatory framework could at least promote the cohesion between resilience and monitoring. Despite everything, when the 22 design principles were applied, the WFD achieved a 68% commoning rate. Assuming hypothetically that the implementation of the 22 design principles corresponds to a 100% commoning process, the consideration of all 22 design principles equates a 'strong commoning'. If, however, no or only a few design principles are taken into consideration, one can speak of a 'weak commoning'. Thus the WFD shows clear tendencies towards a rather strong commoning process.

Overall, the WFD thus achieved a considerable result. With the WFD, the EU as a multilateral alliance confers an approach to global common water on the European level. The trend towards a 'strong commoning' approach can be supported by the addition of complementary management approaches to the WFD framework. The analysed deficits show that a major problem is the lack of integration at the local level.

The optional approaches to improve the commoning process within the framework of the WFD are summarised as follows:

Category: Governance approach

- Adaptive governance

Category: Management approach

- Adaptive governance

Category: Complementary approaches

- Sustainable livelihood approach
- Collective action

- Payments for ecosystem services
- Social capital

The combination of the chosen governance and management approaches covers 86% of the deficit design principles.

References

Anderies, J. M., M. A. Janssen, and E. Ostrom (2004). A Framework to Analyze the Robustness of Social-ecological Systems from an Institutional Perspective. *Ecology and Society*, 9. www.ecologyandsociety.org/vol9/iss1/art18/.

Andrade, G. S. M., and J. R. Rhodes (2012). Protected Areas and Local Communities: An Inevitable Partnership toward Successful Conservation Strategies? *Ecology and Society*, 17.

Araral, E. (2013). A Transaction Cost Approach to Climate Adaptation: Insights from Coase, Ostrom and Williamson and Evidence from the 400-Year-Old zangjeras. *Environmental Science & Policy*, 25, 147. DOI: 10.1016/j.envsci.2012.08.005.

Bleischwitz, R., et al. (2009). *Ressourcenpolitik zur Gestaltung der Rahmenbedingungen: Paper zu Arbeitspaket 3 des Projekts*, Materialeffizienz und Ressourcenschonung' (MaRess) Endversion 2009., Wuppertal.

BMUB (2012). *German Resource Efficiency Programme (ProgRess): Programme for the Sustainable Use and Conservation of Natural Resources*, Berlin.

Bollier, D. (2014). *The Commons as a Template for Transformation*. Retrieved from https://greattransition.org/publication/the-commons-as-a-template-for-transformation.

Bromley, D. W. and J. A. Cochrane (1994). *Understanding the Global Commons*, Madison, US.

Bruns, B. (2008). in *Community-Based Water Law and Water Resource Management Reform in Developing Countries* (Eds.: B. Koppen, M. Giordano, J. Butterworth), CABI.

Bunch, M. J., K. E. Morrison, M. W. Parkes, and H. D. Venema (2011). Promoting Health and Well-Being by Managing for Social–Ecological Resilience: the Potential of Integrating Ecohealth and Water Resources Management Approaches, *Ecology and Society*, 16. www.ecologyandsociety.org/vol16/iss1/art6/.

Butlin, J. (1989). Our Common Future. By World Commission on Environment and Development.' *Journal of International Development* vol.1 no.2 pp. 284–287. Available from: doi:10.1002/jid.3380010208 ISSN 1099-1328.

Cheneval, F. (2011). *The Government of the Peoples: On the Idea and Principles of Multilateral Democracy*, Palgrave Macmillan, New York.

Cox, M., G. Arnold, and S. Villamayor Tomás (2010). A Review of Design Principles for Community-based Natural Resource Management. *Ecology and Society*, 15.

de Moor, T. (2011). From Common Pastures to Global Commons: A Historical Perspective on Interdisciplinary Approaches to Commons, *Nat. Sci. Soc. 19*, 422.

European Community (EC) (2010). Directive 2000/60/EC of the European Parliament and of the Council of 23 October 2000. Establishing a Framework for Community Action in the Field of Water Policy.

Fowler, C. W. (2003). Tenets, Principles, and Criteria for Management:The Basis for Systemic Management. *Marine Fisheries Review*, 65(2).

Gordon, H. S. (1954). The Economic Theory of a Common-Property Resource: The Fishery, *Journal of Political Economy*, 62, 124. DOI: 10.1086/257497.

Gruber, J. S. (2010). Key Principles of Community-Based Natural Resource Management: A Synthesis and Interpretation of Identified Effective Approaches for Managing the Commons, *Environmental Management*, 45, 52. DOI: 10.1007/s00267-008-9235-y.

Hardin, G. (1968). The Tragedy of the Commons, *Science (New York)*, *162*, 1243. DOI: 10.1126/science.162.3859.1243.

Helfrich, S. (Ed.) (2012). *Commons: Für eine neue Politik jenseits von Markt und Staat*, Transcript-Verl., Bielefeld.

Hess, C. (2008). *Mapping the New Commons: Presented at 'Governing Shared Resources: Connecting Local Experience to Global Challenges;' the 12th Biennial Conference of the International Association for the Study of the Commons*, University of Gloucestershire, Cheltenham, England, 14–18 July, Cheltenham.

Holzgreve, S. (2015). *Defining Natural Resources as Common Goods* Bachelorthesis Lüneburg 2015.

Lindsay, J. M. (1998). *Creating a Legal Framework for Community-Based Management: Principles and Dilemmas*, Washington, DC.

Lutzenberger, A., and F. Lichter, S. Holzgreve (2015). *Natürliche Ressourcen als Common Goods IntRess Arbeitspaket 6*. Unpublished.

Mayntz, R. (2010). In *Governance – Regieren in komplexen Regelsystemen: Eine Einführung* (Ed.: A. Benz), VS Verl. für Sozialwiss. Wiesbaden, p. 65.

Ostrom, E. (1990). *Governing the Commons: The Evolution of Institutions for Collective Action. The Political economy of institutions and decisions*. Cambridge University Press, New York.

Ostrom, E. (1991). *Governing the Commons: The Evolution of Institutions for Collective Action*, Cambridge Univ. Press, Cambridge u.a.

Ostrom, E. (1996). Crossing the Great Divide: Coproduction, Synergy, and Development, *World Development*, *24*, 1073.

Ostrom, E. (1999). *Design Principles and Threats to Sustainable Organizations that Manage Commons*. Retrieved from http://dlc.dlib.indiana.edu/dlc/handle/10535/5465. Workshop Working Paper W99-6.

Ostrom, E. (2008). *Design Principles of Robust Property –Rights Institutions: What Have We Learned?*, Lexington Books, Lanham.

Ott, K. and R. Döring (2004). *Theorie und Praxis starker Nachhaltigkeit*, Metropolis-Verl., Marburg.

Polski, M. M., and E. Ostrom (1999). *An Institutional Framework for Policy Analysis and Design*, Lexington Books, Lanham.

Pomeroy, R. S., B. M. Katon, and I. Harkes (1998). *Fisheries Co-management: Key Conditions and Principles Drawn from Asian Experiences.*

Quilligan, J. (2014). In *Commons: Für eine neue Politik jenseits von Markt und Staat* (Ed.: S. Helfrich), Transcript-Verl. Bielefeld, p. 99.

Reid, W. V. (2005). *Ecosystems and Human Well-being: Synthesis: A Report of the Millennium Ecosystem Assessment*, Island Press, Washington, DC.

Reller, A., L. Marschall, S. Meissner, and C. Schmidt (2014). *Ressourcenstrategien: Eine Einführung in den nachhaltigen Umgang mit Ressourcen, WBG – Wissenschaftliche Buchgesellschaft*, Darmstadt.

Schütz, H. and S. Bringezu (2008). *Resource Consumption of Germany – Indicators and Definitions*, Dessau-Roßlau.

Söllner, A. (2014). Globalization, Greed, and Exploitation. How to Break the Baleful Path?, *Journal of Business Economics*, 84, 1211.

Stern, P. C. (2011). Design Principles for Global Commons: Natural Resources and Emerging Technologies, *International Journal of the Commons*, 5, 213.

UNEP (2012). *Responsible Resource Management for a Sustainable World: Findings from the International Resource Panel.*

Vanni, B. (2014). *Understanding the Commons: The Reception of Elinor Ostrom's work in Italian Scholarship, Law, and Jurisprudence.* Bloomington, IN: Paper presented at Colloquium at the Workshop in Political Theory and Policy Analysis. http://hdl.handle.net/10535/9364.

Zell, H. (2011). *Die Grundlagen der Organisation: Lernen und Lehren: Mit Multiple-Choice-Aufgaben,* Books on Demand, Norderstedt.

19 Sustainable resource output

Towards an approach to a multidimensional environmental assessment of biomass production

H. Böttcher, K. Hennenberg, K. Wiegmann, M. Scheffler, and A. Hansen

Introduction

The need for monitoring of the use of biomass resources

The need to use natural resources (e.g. raw materials, air, water, soil, land and ecosystem services through biodiversity) sustainably and efficiently has been identified by science (e.g. Rockström et al. 2009) and generally been recognised by policy (e.g. United Nations 2015). Corresponding initiatives exist at German, European and global level in numerous policy targets and regulations, for example, the German Resource Efficiency Programs (ProgRess, ProgRess II), the Roadmap to a Resource Efficient Europe, and the Resource Panel of the United Nations Environment Program.

The concept of planetary boundaries (Rockström et al. 2009) has established a visual concept for assessing the state of environmental indicators at the global scale. More recent research highlighted the need to consider interactions between indicators and the regional heterogeneity of the processes under-pinning the boundaries (Steffen et al. 2015) but also the need to improve the exchange between science and global policies regarding the definition of these boundaries (Galaz et al. 2012).

Successful implementation of sustainable use of natural resources requires a comprehensive monitoring and assessment system. Such a system uses a range of indicators and metrics and tracks them over time and with relation to specific targets to design and to evaluate the path to sustainable resource use (Pavlovskaia 2014). The bioeconomy, or biobased economy, has not only become a technical term for summarising production systems relying on biomass resources but is also seen as an overarching concept for taking a holistic and systems' perspective on the involved sectors. In fact, O'Brien et al. (2015) proposed a systems dynamics approach that is needed to implement a monitoring system for the bioeconomy.

Limits to the concept of resource efficiency

A common metric to supporting monitoring and assessments on the sustainable use of (natural) resources, in general, is resource efficiency

(Huysman et al. 2015). Focusing on the field of land use and biomass production, this can be defined as the ratio of a specific utility or output of a biomass production system and the associated specific input, consumption or use of natural resources related to biomass production (for instance crop yield/area). Another approach for assessing resource efficiency is the concept of eco-efficiency (WBCSD 2006) defined as the ratio between utility and environmental impacts (for example crop yield/water demand). It is a concept that corresponds to the concept of resource efficiency but is widening the input to environmental impacts.

The utility associated with land use and biomass production is not only provided by the sale of crop products (plant or animal products), but also by the provision of other ecosystem services (TEEB 2010). Following the concept of ecosystem services, the notion of utility can be broadened to include supply services, regulatory services and cultural services. Mere biomass production can be considered a supply service, but it uses other ecosystem services to effectively deliver it, often impacting them negatively. Theoretically, it is desirable to include as many ecosystem services in consideration of utility as possible. However, there is a challenge of identifying, quantifying and integrating appropriate indicators (Albert et al. 2016). The concept of ecosystem services allows a consideration of the multi-dimensional benefits but requires the dimensions to be brought to a common scale of values what can be difficult.

Existing approaches differ regarding the selection of indicators or the environmental aspects covered. These may be very specific, for example, referring to soil erosion, or very general, referring to land as a natural resource. Examples are the framework of human appropriation of net primary production (HANPP; Haberl et al. 2007) or the concept of material input per service unit (MIPS; Schmidt-Bleek 1998). An explicit aggregation of indicators of different dimensions, however, reduces interpretability of the indicator as it reduces the transparency of the approach when a conversion to a common metric has to be done with certain assumptions (Pavlovskaia 2014). The approach of MIPS, for example, cannot be used for assessing specific outputs (e.g. emissions) or specific environmental impacts (e.g. N-balance; Mancini et al. 2012). Indicators must be able to provide quantitative measures that allow an actual assessment and comparison of systems. Therefore, multi-dimensional approaches are used in sustainability assessments that typically present indicators side by side.

A multi-dimensional assessment requires not necessarily a full integration of indicators into common physical units but a standardisation of the dimensions to be considered. Thus, water quality and greenhouse gas emissions as different indicators can hardly be physically combined. However, they can be compared through scaling e.g. regarding the degree of target achievement of a reduction target or the relative exceedance of limits.

Both resource efficiency and eco-efficiency face another critical limitation that must be taken into account when applied as indicators for the evaluation of sustainable production systems. They do not assess the absolute state of resources nor the transgression of sustainability constraints (i.e. leakage effects). Despite increasing resource efficiency, i.e. decreasing input per output produced, the demand for natural resources may increase due to population growth and changing patterns of consumption. Therefore, a relative decoupling of resource use and economic growth by increasing resource efficiency is not sufficient for sustainable resource use and successful resource conservation.

In this paper, we present a new metric for assessing the sustainability of use of natural resources for biomass production by combining existing concepts of resource efficiency and environmental assessment to the sustainable resource output (SRO) and test the metric in two case studies.

Methods

The concept of sustainable resource output

Sustainable resource output can be considered an extension to the classic concept of resource efficiency. In addition to the utility of production and the utilisation of natural resources, it also includes thresholds and limits to natural resource use. These thresholds, if exceeded, cause the metric to be set to zero. The benefits gained through the use of natural resources can also be included. This allows production systems of different productivity to be compared by looking at specific indicators.

There are two elements required for calculating SRO (see Figure 19.1). The absolute utility of biomass production U is normalised in order to assess systems relative productivity U' (0 = low productivity, 1 = high productivity) with $U' \in \{a \in \mathbb{R} \mid 0 \leq a \leq 1\}$. The maximum and minimum values need to be defined, either from literature or from model simulations with alternative scenarios. U can be defined narrowly to include only

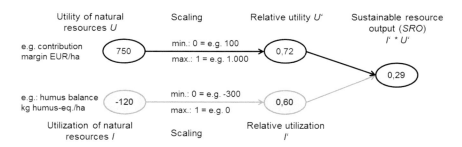

Figure 19.1 Calculation of sustainable resource output SRO from normalised relative utilisation (resource conservation) I' and normalised relative utility U' of natural resources with exemplary figures.

revenues from biomass production but also expanded to include monetised ecosystem services. In any case, assumptions for deriving utility values need to be clearly documented.

Similarly, the absolute value for the use of natural resources I must be normalised into a relational scaling system. This makes different indicators comparable and is used for assessing the degree of resource utilisation or resource conservation I′ (for example, 0 = low resource conservation, 1 = high resource conservation) with $I' \in \{a \in \mathbb{R} \mid 0 \leq a \leq 1\}$. If production reaches an intensity that causes the sustainable use of resources to exceed threshold values, it is set as zero. Such limit and tolerance values can often be taken from literature, from current legislation, as well as from scenario modelling. In the latter case, two guard railing scenarios are established that provide tolerable maximum and minimum values for a certain indicator. SRO then results from the product of scaled relative utility U′ and scaled relative utilisation (resource conservation) I′.

Four steps for assessing the sustainability of biomass production systems should be applied for deriving the two elements needed for the calculation of SRO:

- System definition: It determines the system boundaries of the assessment and the functional unit for the product generating the utility of natural resources U. It is an important prerequisite and often set through the model or assessment tool applied, database, indicators and variables selected. Klöpffer and Grahl (2012) highlight that not only the functional unit needs to be identical, it also needs to be functionally equivalent, e.g. not only the energy unit needs to be the same but also the type of energy.
- Assessment: Depending on the database used, indicators need to be selected that are used to assess resource utilisation I. Indicator selection is an important step of the analysis as it forms the frame for interpretability of results. Indicators should be chosen in a way that considers the aim of the analysis (Albert et al. 2016). Indicators for assessing land use refer typically either to the area or the intensity of land use (Erb 2015).
- Reference: This includes the description of a reference system and variants, e.g. generated by model simulations through a sensitivity analysis or from literature. The choice of the reference system determines the level of indicator performance for a specific system, and is a critical element of the analysis. It needs to be well documented and credible. For production systems of biomass, it is reasonable to establish a reference that presents a scenario without biomass extraction (Koponen et al. 2018).
- Presentation and interpretation: This step determines which type of scaling or standardisation is used to bring indicators into a format that makes them comparable and in which form they are graphically displayed. Interpretation can further introduce prioritisation or weighting of single indicators when aggregating or interpreting results. Both presentation and interpretation of the results must take into account the assumptions made in earlier steps as well as uncertainties of the calculation.

Case study descriptions

System definition

We tested SRO for two production systems, one from agriculture and one from forestry. The systems were designed to reflect different forest management and farm operations:

- Crop and livestock production (different levels of intensity of cash crop production, feed production and grassland management).
- Forestry (spruce forests, alternative scenarios of forest management change and management intensity).

Based on alternative scenarios reflecting different levels of production intensity in the individual systems, it was determined to what extent resource output changed in the scenarios compared to the reference (see detailed system descriptions in Böttcher et al. 2020).

The production systems were set up as artificial management units representing typical situations in agriculture and forestry in Germany, as they can be observed in the field. However, the size of the management units is higher than those of typical private enterprises operating in the field. The aim was to model sufficiently large units to capture landscape effects and to allow for management shifts without disruption. Therefore, the study provides only limited guidance for management decisions at the farm or forest stand level but is rather oriented towards decisions at larger scale level.

Ideally, the utility I associated with land use and biomass production should also include the provision of other ecosystem services. Although the concept of SRO allows such an inclusion, we limited the analysis to the sale of agricultural or forestry products, i.e. the contribution margin (short: margin). The margin is defined as the monetary amount of revenue (product quantity times price) less variable costs of production. Alternative parameters for mapping the benefits could be gross value added, the revenue, dry biomass production, or the energy or protein production.

The utilisation of natural resources U was determined with the help of indicators that describe the impact of the production system on natural resources. The following indicators were considered in the system crop and livestock production:

- Greenhouse gas emissions: given as kg CO_2 eq. per ha and year, and derived from area, crops, nitrogen requirements, yields and application of manure;
- Humus balance: given as humus equivalents in kg C per ha, resulting from the humus balance of crop rotation, catch crops, crop residues and the application of manure;
- Nitrogen balance: given as kg nitrogen surplus per ha and year based on nutrient inputs into and flows out of the system (farm gate balance);

- Nutrient contamination of water: given as a percentage of the area with a nitrogen balance greater than 50 kg/ha, derived from the calculated nitrogen balances.
- Biodiversity: expressed as biotope values, which, for example, take account of the proportion of land used for the cultivation of flowering strips and fallow land, the number of crops in crop rotation, the absence of fertilisers and the proportion of grassland.

Indicators for assessing SRO in forestry were:

a   Growing stock: given as cubic meters of wood per ha, calculated as a single tree volume and aggregated to stand level growing stock, differentiated by tree species groups (beech, oak, other broadleaf species, spruce, fir, Douglas fir, pine, and larch).
b   Growing stock increment: represented as cubic meters of wood increment per ha and year.
c   Harvest amount: given as cubic meters of wood per ha per year, describes the potentially available growing stock separately for logs and other wood (industrial wood).
d   Deadwood stock: given as cubic meters per ha, differentiated by the type of wood (coniferous, oak, other broadleaf).
e   Greenhouse gas removals/emissions: CO_2 removed from the atmosphere through biomass growths and emissions resulting from harvest and biomass decay expressed in tons of CO_2 per ha and year, derived from modelled growing stock and biomass functions for other compartments (roots, branches, leaves).
f   Soil carbon changes: expressed in tons C per ha and year, calculated using a soil carbon model driven by climate parameters and litter composition.
g   Share of old trees: represented by the volume of trees with a diameter of more than 80 cm.

Biomass production in the agricultural and forestry systems was calculated using the simulation model FABio (Forestry and Agriculture Biomass Model), developed at Oeko-Institut (FABio agricultural model: Böttcher et al. 2020; FABio forestry model: Böttcher et al. 2018).

Scenario development

Three alternative management scenarios were designed for crop and livestock production that include a 'cash crop' scenario, a 'moderate extensification' scenario and a 'strong extensification' scenario. The gradient of intensity becomes evident, particularly when looking at crop rotation parameters, which in the cash crop scenario refer to rules of conventional cultivation (for highly productive areas). The moderate extensification scenario uses adapted cultivation rules (as recommended for less productive sites), characterised by longer

232 *H. Böttcher et al.*

crop rotations. In the strong extensification scenario, crop rotation and management rules based on organic farming are applied, including also set-aside areas (for more details on scenario specifications, please refer to Böttcher et al. 2020).

The forestry production system describes a case of forest conversion from pure spruce forest stands to mixed stands dominated by broadleaved trees. This example is based on data from the German National Forest Inventory (Bundeswaldinventur, BWI). A selection of inventory plots with similar conditions (region, tree species composition, and ownership) was selected and treated as one management unit. Four scenarios were simulated over a period of 100 years. As a business as usual scenario, we considered a continuation of production patterns (current target diameters, no species change), derived from publicly available parameters describing the WEHAM base scenario (BMEL 2016). Two alternative scenarios assume a reduction in management intensity (increased target diameters) and a forest conversion of tree species change towards broadleaved trees (introduction of beech trees in regeneration). A fourth scenario combines scenarios of reduced intensity and forest conversion.

Results

The sustainable resource output SRO describes effects of changes in the intensity of management on the individual environmental indicators as the product of relative utilisation I′ (of natural resources measured by environmental indicators) and relative utility U′ (margin). Figure 19.2 shows the results of relative utilisation I′, and utility U′ (Figure 19.2a and 19.2c) compared to SRO (Figure 19.2b and 19.2d) applied to examples in the agriculture and forestry case studies. High values of SRO indicate a high performance, i.e. low impacts on natural resources paired with high output in terms of revenue. Low values show that the management option either impacts environmental indicators negatively and/or leads to a reduced revenue compared to the other options.

In the agriculture case study, the highest margin is achieved when cash crops are produced (see Figure 19.2a). With moderate and strong extensification, the margin is reduced by 50%. However, cash crop production scores low regarding environmental performance. Regarding the carbon balance of soils, the threshold of −300 H-eq/ha is reached, causing the indicator to be set to zero. Also, in terms of all other indicators, the cash crop option results in lower indicator values with largest differences for the biodiversity indicator. Due to the high relative margin that can be achieved with cash crops, the option performs better when looking at SRO, the product of relative margin and relative utilisation (see Figure 19.2b). On indicators that are relatively close for the alternative options on the common scale, such as GHG emissions and Nitrogen balance in the example, large differences in the utility have a larger impact on relative performance.

In the forestry case study, the highest margin can be achieved with a continuation of business as usual management as it achieves the highest harvestable volume.

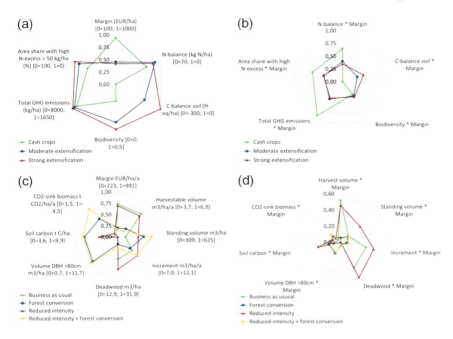

Figure 19.2 Examples for performance of relative utilisation I' (environmental indicators) and utility U' (margin) for case studies on (a) agriculture and (c) forestry, and the resulting sustainable resource output SRO for (b) agriculture and (d) forestry, which allows to assess alternative management options in such biomass production systems (with SRO = I' × U').

Forest conversion to broadleaved trees reduces the margin considerably, whereas for the reduced intensity only a small reduction can be observed. Figure 19.2c) shows that the options perform very differently regarding the different indicators. While reduced intensity seems to be best for the generation of additional deadwood, reduced intensity combined with forest conversion results in the highest CO_2 sink over the simulation period and yields the highest standing volume. Assessing the performance of options using SRO changes the order for a number of indicators, e.g. soil carbon where options including forest conversion result in low values due to relatively low margins that can be achieved (Figure 19.2d). In the case of deadwood, SRO confirms the observation made when ignoring economic performance.

Interpretation and discussion

The SRO concept expands the concept of resource efficiency and allows a consideration of the multi-dimensional use of natural resources by bringing the dimensions to a common scale of values. Compared to resource efficiency, SRO has the advantage that critical boundaries and thresholds are considered, such that increases in efficiency that exceed environmental limits are reflected in the metric. The presented case studies deliver reasonable results and demonstrate the application of the concept. There are, however, a number of challenges that are associated with the approach requiring further assessment and testing.

The selection of indicators should be guided by the purpose of the assessment, directly linking to the environmental concerns to be studied but also needs to reflect system boundaries and data availability. The indicators should be able to adequately reflect the conditions in the production system and its boundaries. Using simulation models, as in this study, allows for a consistent consideration of indicators in one framework but also limits the choice of indicators to model capabilities. A large number of indicators exist, as documented by the SEBI process (EEA 2012) or the MAES initiative (EC 2018). However, particularly with regard to the effects on biodiversity, adequate data is often not available, but also scientific evidence regarding the relationship between management intensity and biodiversity is unclear (Nolet et al. 2018; Sabatini et al. 2019). Combining the approach with a geographical information system would allow detailed spatial representation of indicators.

A major challenge is the selection and implementation of appropriate thresholds and limits as maxima and minima for the scaling of indicators into a common frame. Identifying these values is required to make indicators comparable – similarly to the resource efficiency approach – but also as an input for the calculation of SRO. The choice of maximum and minimum values determines the relative utilisation of natural resources and has therefore strong influence on the value of sustainable resource output in the end. Thresholds might not be easily derived for all indicators, i.e. indicator selection should therefore also consider the availability of such information. We used existing literature values, legal boundary values and also modelled values from sensitivity analyses. We recommend preferably using published literature values for the application of the SRO approach, if that is not possible and values are estimated or generated by models, then a good documentation is crucial.

For plausibility and consistency checks of the values, the following questions should be answered:

i   Do the thresholds and limits reflect tolerable magnitudes or loads regarding policy targets or existing legislation?
ii Are thresholds or limits universally valid for the alternative systems analysed?
iii Are the values sufficiently differentiated to make differences in the production systems visible?

Also, for the scaling of utility U (margin), maximum and minimum values need to be defined. The result of SRO is also very sensitive to the choice of these parameters. They should reflect a realistic range of possible values across alternative management options. As in the definition of resource efficiency, SRO remains with the monetary value of biomass production. Our case studies took into account only revenues from biomass production and costs of biomass extraction. The concept, however, can be extended to include monetised impacts on ecosystem services to fully include external costs (TEEB 2010, 2018). This could be done by including costs for administrative fines or reduced premiums, payments for ecosystem services, CO_2 prices etc. It has to be considered, though, that an inclusion of more aspects into the utility term also requires more efforts to establish adequate and transparent scaling values.

Conclusions

The concept of SRO extends the concept of resource efficiency in a meaningful way and can be used for the multi-dimensional evaluation of the sustainability of biomass production systems. The advantage against the classical concept of resource efficiency is the inclusion of thresholds to reflect the transgression of sustainability limits of production systems. As the major challenge, we identified the selection of threshold values that need to be carefully chosen and well documented. Future work should seek to refine the SRO concept by exploring different indicators and scaling approaches and to test its integration into existing assessment tools.

List of abbreviations

BWI   German National Forest Inventory (Bundeswaldinventur)
FABio   Forestry and Agriculture Biomass Model
GHG   greenhouse gas
HANPP   human appropriation of net primary production
I   utilisation of natural resources
MIPS   material input per service unit
ProgRess German Resource Efficiency Programme
SRO   sustainable resource output
U   utility of natural resources

References

Albert, C., Bonn, A., Burkhard, B., Daube, S., Dietrich, K., Engels, B., Frommer, J., Götzl, M., Grêt-Regamey, A., Job-Hoben, B., Koellner, T., Marzelli, S., Moning, C. et al. (2016). Towards a national set of ecosystem service indicators: insights from Germany. In: *Ecological Indicators* 61, pp. 38–48. DOI: 10.1016/j.ecolind.2015.08.050.

BMEL (2016). *Wald und Rohholzpotenzial der nächsten 40 Jahre, Ausgewählte Ergebnisse der Waldentwicklungs- und Holzaufkommensmodellierung 2013 bis 2052.* Bundesministerium für Ernährung und Landwirtschaft. Berlin, last accessed on 16 Jan 2017.

Böttcher, H., Hennenberg, K. J., and Winger, C. (2018). *FABio-Waldmodell - Modellbeschreibung Version 0.54.* Oeko-Institut e.V. Berlin. Online available at www.oeko.de/fileadmin/oekodoc/FABio-Wald-Modellbeschreibung.pdf.

Böttcher, H., Hennenberg, K., Wiegmann, K., Scheffler, M., Wolff, F., Hansen, A., Meyer-Aurich, A., Grundmann, P., and Vedel, D. (2020). Nexus Ressourceneffizienz und Landnutzung – An-sätze zur mehrdimensionalen umweltpolitischen Bewertung der Ressourceneffizienz bei der Bio-massebereitstellung, *FKZ 3715 31 103 0. Umweltbundesamt,*. Retrieved from www.umweltbundesamt.de/sites/default/files/medien/1410/publikationen/2020-03-04_texte_45-2020_nexus-ressourceneffizienz-landnutzung.pdf.

EC (2018). Mapping and assessment of ecosystems and their services: an analytical framework for mapping and assessment of ecosystem condition in EU, *5th MAES Report*. European Commission, 2018. Online available at http://catalogue.biodiversity.europa.eu/uploads/document/file/1673/5th_MAES_report.pdf.

EEA (2012). *Streamlining European biodiversity indicators 2020: building a future on lessons learnt from the SEBI 2010 process.* European Environmental Agency, 2012.

Erb, K.-H. (2015). Land-use indicators. In: *International Encyclopedia of the Social & Behavioral Sciences*: Elsevier, pp. 238–244.

Galaz, V., Biermann, F., Crona, B., Loorbach, D., Folke, C., Olsson, P., Nilsson, M., Allouche, J., Persson, Å., and Reischl, G. (2012). 'Planetary boundaries' – exploring the challenges for global environmental governance. In: *Current Opinion in Environmental Sustainability* 4(1), pp. 80–87. DOI: 10.1016/j.cosust.2012.01.006.

Haberl, H., Erb, K. H., Krausmann, F., Gaube, V., Bondeau, A., Plutzar, C., Gingrich, S., Lucht, W., and Fischer-Kowalski, M. (2007). Quantifying and mapping the human appropriation of net primary production in earth's terrestrial ecosystems. In: *Proceedings of the National Academy of Sciences of the United States of America* 104(31), pp. 12942–12947. DOI: 10.1073/pnas.0704243104.

Huysman, S., Sala, S., Mancini, L., Ardente, F., Alvarenga, Rodrigo A. F., Meester, S., Mathieux, F., and Dewulf, J. (2015). Toward a systematized framework for resource efficiency indicators. In: *Resources, Conservation and Recycling* 95, pp. 68–76. DOI: 10.1016/j.resconrec.2014.10.014.

Klöpffer, W. and Grahl, B. (2012). *Ökobilanz (LCA), Ein Leitfaden für Ausbildung und Beruf 2. Nachdruck.* Weinheim: Wiley-VCH.

Koponen, K., Soimakallio, S., Kline, K. L., Cowie, A., and Brandão, M. (2018). Quantifying the climate effects of bioenergy – choice of reference system. In: *Renewable and Sustainable Energy Reviews* 81, pp. 2271–2280. DOI: 10.1016/j.rser.2017.05.292.

Mancini, L., Lettenmeier, M., Rohn, H., and Liedtke, C. (2012). Application of the MIPS method for assessing the sustainability of production–consumption systems of food. In: *Journal of Economic Behavior & Organization* 81(3), pp. 779–793. DOI: 10.1016/j.jebo.2010.12.023.

Nolet, P., Kneeshaw, D., Messier, C., and Béland, M. (2018). Comparing the effects of even- and uneven-aged silviculture on ecological diversity and processes: a review. In: *Ecology and Evolution* 8(2), pp. 1217–1226. DOI: 10.1002/ece3.3737.

O'Brien, M., Wechsler, D., Bringezu, S., and Arnold, K. (2015). *Sachstandsbericht über vorhandene Grundlagen und Beiträge für ein Monitoring der Bioökonomie: Systemische Betrachtung und Modellierung der Bioökonomie.* Wuppertal Institut. Wuppertal.

Pavlovskaia, E. (2014). Sustainability criteria: their indicators, control, and monitoring (with examples from the biofuel sector). In: *Environmental Sciences Europe* 26(1), p. 17. DOI: 10.1186/s12302-014-0017-2.

Rockström, J., Steffen, W., Noone, K., Persson, Ã. …, Chapin, F. S., Lambin, E. F., Lenton, T. M., Scheffer, M., Folke, C., Schellnhuber, H. J., Nykvist, B., De Wit, C A, Hughes, T. et al. (2009). A safe operating space for humanity. In: *Nature* 461(7263), pp. 472–475.

Online available at www.scopus.com/inward/record.url?eid=2-s2.0-70349451894&partnerID=40&md5=5db9dbf18fe00b3899ae7b60c2f60f82.

Sabatini, F. M., Andrade, R. B. de, Paillet, Y., Ódor, P., Bouget, C., Campagnaro, T., Gosselin, F., Janssen, P., Mattioli, W., Nascimbene, J., Sitzia, T., Kuemmerle, T., and Burrascano, S. (2019). Trade-offs between carbon stocks and biodiversity in European temperate forests. In: *Global Change Biology* 25(2), pp. 536–548. DOI: 10.1111/gcb.14503.

Schmidt-Bleek, F. (1998). *Das MIPS-Konzept, Weniger Naturverbrauch - mehr Lebensqualität durch Faktor 10*. München: Droemer.

Steffen, W., Richardson, K., Rockström, J., Cornell, S. E., Fetzer, I., Bennett, E. M., Biggs, R., Carpenter, S. R., Vries, W. de, Wit, C. A. de, Folke, C., Gerten, D., Heinke, J. et al. (2015). Sustainability. planetary boundaries, guiding human development on a changing planet. In: *Science (New York, N.Y.)* 347(6223), p. 1259855. DOI: 10.1126/science.1259855.

TEEB (2010). *The Economics of Ecosystems and Biodiversity: Mainstreaming the Economics of Nature: A Synthesis of the Approach, Conclusions and Recommendations of TEEB*. The Economics of Ecosystems and Biodiversity. Online available at www.teebweb.org/our-publications/teeb-study-reports/synthesis-report.

TEEB (2018). *TEEB for Agriculture & Food: Scientific and Economic Foundations*. United Nations Environment Programme. Geneva.

United Nations (2015). *Transforming our World: The 2030 Agenda for Sustainable Development*. Resolution adopted by the General Assembly on 25 September 2015 (A/RES/70/1). United Nations. Online available at https://sustainabledevelopment.un.org/post2015/transformingourworld.

WBCSD (2006). *Eco-efficiency learning module*. World Business Council for Sustainable Development. Geneva. Online available at www.wbcsd.org/Projects/Education/Resources/Eco-efficiency-Learning-Module.

20 More resource efficiency in production and products

Digitalisation supports industry and trades

Peter Jahns

Introduction

In 1992, The Global Earth Summit of the United Nations in Rio advocated for cross-cutting sustainability strategies to meet the unrelenting challenges of sustainable development.

In 2002, Germany adopted a National Sustainability Strategy (Bundesregierung 2016). By 2017, fifteen (15) out of sixteen (16) of the Federal States of Germany, including North Rhine-Westphalia (NRW), had adopted regional strategies to address the challenges of sustainable development (Müller & Reutter 2017).

North Rhine-Westphalia is the most populated federal state in Germany and a central industrial and economic region (Müller & Reutter 2017). Thus, in 1998, the Ministry for the Environment in North Rhine-Westphalia established the Effizienz-Agentur NRW (EFA) with the principal objective of improving the competitiveness of Small and Medium-sized Enterprises (SMEs) by supporting a strategy of sustainable growth (Jahns 2018).

As per the NRW.INVEST GmbH, Knowledgebase NRW (2018), SMEs in North-Rhine Westphalia are the backbone of the economy. Currently, there are 712,100 SMEs in North-Rhine Westphalia and accounting for 78.8 per cent of employment. Out of this total, 12,000 are small and medium-sized manufacturing companies (20 to 500 employees). Furthermore, there are 19,000 craft enterprises with resource efficiency potential. The majority of all training in North-Rhine Westphalia provided by EFA is for these SMEs. The SME sector is, thus, the focus of EFA (Jahns 2018; Bliesner, Liedtke & Rohn 2014).

The Effizienz-Agentur NRW (EFA) has been operating for the past twenty (20) years (Jahns 2018). Jahns indicates that the EFA supports manufacturing companies in North-Rhine Westphalia with advice concerning resource efficiency so that products and processes are made more efficiently to reduce costs and adverse effects on the environment. Jahns further indicates that the company offers support for the financing and implementation of research and development projects and investments in the form of financial advice. Additionally, EFA provides network and knowledge transfer opportunities, information about training courses and workshops, with the aim of increasing resource efficiency and competitiveness in SMEs.

Raw material and material costs represent the most significant proportion of costs for manufacturing companies in Germany. Its share of the total cost of manufacturing is about 42 per cent. Whereas the average Personnel and energy are 18 per cent and two per cent, respectively. It therefore stands to reason to pay careful attention during production and take care when dealing with these natural resources. The focussing on the subject of 'energy' which is unfortunately seen all too often in public discussions in industry and trade does not go far enough. Reducing the cost of raw materials and other materials is the key to separating resource consumption and growth. Efficiency is a decisive factor in this. As far as resource-efficient production is concerned, the focus should be on natural resources. It is, therefore, logical to emphasis the term 'resource efficiency' since the operational goals of EFA are to reduce the use of materials and energy.

EFA is working on concrete projects with small and medium-sized enterprises that allow it (EFA) to create products with less energy and primary resources (Jahns 2018; Kaiser 2018; European Environment Agency 2016). The priority is to avoid waste from the get-go and not wait to start thinking about it in the future. The idea is to prevent waste before it is produced.

The purpose of the chapter is to share some best ways to implement cleaner production and resource efficiency practices that sustainably support industry and trades through digitalisation. The chapter contributes to the conversation on resource efficiency by linking both individual and organisational measures of success with producing more with less energy and primary resources. The remainder of the chapter proceeds as follows. The next section provides a brief description of the Effizienz-Agentur NRW (EFA) Consulting Offer, which is a guide to more resource efficiency. Section two illustrates results from the agency's consultancy practice during a period in which digital networking is becoming the standard. Section three focuses on three cases to illustrate the importance of digitalisation for manufacturing companies, which has been discussed in Germany under the term 'Industry 4.0'. The final section is the conclusion.

The Effizienz-Agentur NRW consulting offer – guide to more resource efficiency

EFA's consulting offer for more resource efficiency goes through a three-pronged process, namely, need for action, initial consultation and solutions (Jahns 2018). Figure 20.1 depicts the three-pronged process.

The three-pronged process, as described by (Jahns 2018) is described in more detail in the following sections.

Need for action

EFA works with clients to systematically determine needs that ought to be addressed. The need for action assesses gaps between current conditions and improved conditions of performance.

EFA CONSULTING
GUIDE TO MORE RESOURCE EFFICIENCY

Figure 20.1 EFA consulting – guide to more resource efficiency.

Initial consultation

The Needs Assessment is a process that helps EFA to understand the clients' needs, motivations, and behaviours – what they do, how they do it, and why. The assessment begins with an initial consultation meeting with the client, which is followed by a company tour. It is an iterative process where common relevance analysis conducted. The common relevance analysis includes compiling and analysing data on trends through interviews, surveys and focus group discussions. After this, EFA discusses a financial framework with the client to set policies, procedures, regulations and standing orders to ensure that public funds are appropriately taken care of. All of these are done at no cost to clients.

Solutions

Immediate recommendations for action, workshops for focusing, in-depth consulting projects and financing advice are then offered.

Conservation of resources and digitalisation = 'Resource Efficiency 4.0'

Industry 4.0 represents the digital networking of industrial processes, starting with the acquisition of raw materials through to the recycling of the products at the end of their service life, i.e. in the sense of a circular economy (Jahns 2018; Müller, Buliga & Voigt 2018). Industry 4.0 solutions can be completely automated and without human influence or partially automated cooperation between man and machine. The automation, which is accompanied by new

Efficiency in production and products 241

manufacturing and working methods, will also fundamentally change our way of living and consuming in a digital society. Classic mass-produced goods are being replaced with products which are more individualised and flexible production processes. Small batches and even the manufacture of individual items are becoming more of the standard. Web-based process control systems and networked sensor systems in the sense of Industry 4.0 are allowing companies to record their processes more accurately and individually control them – even to the extent of autonomous factories. If information is available in real-time, individual production processes and entire value creation chains can be controlled in such a way that optimum use can be made of capacities. The productivity of the German economy could increase by almost twelve per cent by 2025, merely due to additional value creation. At the same time, the chances of avoiding wastage are increasing thanks to requirements-based production.

The 'digital transformation' is therefore associated with significant upheavals, disruptions and new challenges, particularly for manufacturing companies. Existing business models are being questioned, products are disappearing from the market, and services are increasing in importance. While a wide range of new possibilities, offered by digitalisation, is proceeding concurrently with a trend towards the individualisation of production and products, the development of new business areas and business models are also emerging.

The manufacturing companies are operating in this conflict area. Particularly the 12,000 small and medium-sized manufacturing companies (20 to 500 employees) and the approximately 19,000 handicraft businesses with enormous potential for conserving resources have little capacity outside of everyday businesses to fundamentally and continually occupying themselves with this strategically important topic of digitalisation and resource conservation in the sense of 'Resource Efficiency 4.0'. The digitalisation and resource conservation offer Effizienz-Agentur NRW an opportunity to provide advisory support.

Resource Efficiency 4.0 – Digitalisation as a tool

The goal of EFA, i.e. helping companies on the way to more resource-efficient manufacturing, has not changed because of digitalisation. However, that which has changed a great deal for the companies seeking advice are their possibilities about planning and controlling production processes, and adapting products or services to the individual needs of the customer. All action approaches for supporting the companies with a more efficient process design in the digitalisation era have been subsumed into the category of 'Resource Efficiency 4.0' at EFA since 2018. It is crucial to use digitalisation as a useful tool for reducing material and energy consumption and not as an end in itself. Above all, Resource Efficiency 4.0 is an instrument which helps companies with their work. As with all tools, the intention with which you use it is the decisive factor. It is a case of keeping an eye on the 'resource efficiency' indicator.

The digitalisation of a production line is not a cure-all. The experience gained in the initial 'Industry 4.0' projects in foundries and surface refining companies has shown how meaningful it is to create full process transparency through a resource efficiency analysis. The companies obtain the required transparency regarding the respective use of the material and the associated CO_2 emissions. This data forms the basis for introducing or adopting ERP systems. In this way, the decisive success indicators for manufacturing in a more competitive way can first be determined, and resource conservation improved by taking technical measures. On this basis, the competitiveness of the company can be further increased through digitalising production: This approach comes under the expression 'Resource Efficiency 4.0'.

Operational areas of activity

A company is, usually, confronted by four fields of activity within the scope of providing its services, namely: order clarification, order processing, calculation and the future of the company (see Figure 20.2). The first three fields of activity can be regarded as being of equal importance, whereby the latter area, the future of the company, is strategically important and not a part of everyday business. For small and medium-sized companies, in particular, there is a severe risk of this critical area of activity being taken over by day-to-day business and fading into the background.

ORDER CLARIFICATION

The customer's requirements and expectations must first be clarified before manufacturing begins. In this way, the manufacturing of erroneous or defective

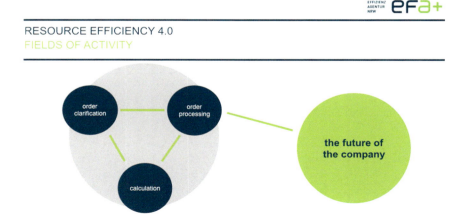

Figure 20.2 Resource Efficiency 4.0 – Fields of activity.

Efficiency in production and products   243

products due to misunderstandings or inaccurate specifications can be avoided right from the start. As banal as this requirement might sound: consultancy practice has shown that following up, often, does not take place with sufficient diligence in this case, or the customer is promised services by the sales department, for example, which cannot be provided.

The order description at least contains the subject, delivery date and price, the quantity and the delivery location, of course. Depending on the type of order, other requirements may be added concerning commissioning, for example. The order description must be stored on the company's central data management system (digital) in such a way that all employees can access the information that is relevant to them if required.

The company procurement department must be involved during order clarification. The reason is that it is impossible to make a meaningful statement about delivery dates without knowledge of part availability (takes place by comparing with company stock levels) and the delivery times of required materials (raw materials, semi-finished products, bought-in parts). The order data cannot be deemed complete until part lists can be generated on the existing data basis.

ORDER PROCESSING

Order clarification is followed by order processing. In particular, it includes planning, optimisation, visualisation and implementation of all orders using a central data management system. The data basis of these sub-steps is identical to that which is used during order clarification, and should ideally be carried out using the same data system (software program) and therefore without media or system disruption, which minimises transmission errors.

The customer order is organised into numerous work and process steps, and the required documents (e.g. company orders or 'routing slips') are generated automatically. A problem-free and complete flow of information is the basis for stable processes. Through automatic analysis of the existing data, it is possible to make the implicitly present process knowledge transparent and therefore usable for improvement processes (process mining), for example.

A smoothly functioning enterprise resource management system is a prerequisite for interruption-free production. As well as incoming and outgoing goods, enterprise resource management also includes the warehouse system and shipping. Central recording of the workflows (booking in and out of deliveries, assignment of defined storage locations) in the data management system provides information about stock levels 'in real-time'. Automated provision of materials is also a part of the scope of work of a contemporary enterprise resource management system and takes the strain off the employees in the production area. Another advantage: Program-controlled material management makes an automatic inventory and stock planning and targeted stock reduction possible to counteract overstocking and the resulting disposals.

244 *Peter Jahns*

Production takes place based on manufacturing plans, which are ideally generated automatically after entering the required data. The definition of the exact system and machine configuration is the task of the production planning and control (PPS) department, which represents the core of a manufacturing company. Here too, digital support from ERP systems, for example, is vital. The production process is monitored and controlled using automatic machine data recording. The efficiency and utilisation of production can be tracked without problems by accurately defining and documenting setup times, the start of orders and the completion of orders.

CALCULATION

The digital connection of machines and systems to the data managing system makes cause-based cost transparency possible concerning orders, products and processes. In this way, it is comparatively easy to check the calculation after processing a request based on actual person-hours, machine run times and material consumption values, and determine whether the assumptions that were made during pre-calculation were correct. In the event of deviations, more accurate assumptions can be used as the basis for a quote when placing future orders.

Costs, particularly material and energy costs, should be assigned in a cause-related way. After all, the material costs are the most significant cost block in the processing industry. To keep the proportion of general costs as low as possible, cost centres should be analysed and redefined if necessary. Personnel costs must be transferred to individual cost centres. The recording of quantity throughput via cost centres is desirable. Write-offs, room costs, maintenance, energy, operating materials and auxiliary materials must be taken into consideration during the determination of hourly machine rates. Overhead charge rates must be updated at regular intervals.

Cause-related cost assignment is made possible by connecting individual machines (machine data recording [MDE]) and also integrating a higher-order data architecture (operational data recording [BDE]), (Management Executive Systems [MES]) in the ERP system. Exact knowledge of the cost structure puts the business operator in a position to reduce manufacturing costs in a targeted way using efficiency measures and to remove products from the product range in good time.

FUTURE OF THE COMPANY

The question of the company's future does not come up every day, but it is essential for the company management to also deal with social changes continue to be able to anticipate the effects on company operations in good time. Against the background of the lack of global resources, it is logical to realise that resource efficiency is a strategic element of company development. Continuous and long-term company development can only be

Efficiency in production and products   245

achieved if the principles of process and resource efficiency are taken into consideration. It is, therefore, advisable to adapt to market changes under resource criteria.

Digital networking is presenting companies with additional challenges. Many processes are easier to comprehend and process because information can be shared quickly. In the same way that trading on the Internet is changing retail structures, production locations that are connected via the Internet will revolutionise manufacturing procedures. Anyone who does not keep a permanent eye on their business environment and researches ways of opening up new business areas is otherwise at risk of losing their market position.

To be able to react to changes quickly, the product development process should have a flexible design. Besides, the topic of resource consumption must always be taken into consideration since 80 per cent of the effects on the environment, and the cost of a product is already defined at the design stage. During product design, it should always be ensured that the product is manufactured in an uncomplicated way, easy to repair or maintain and can be dismantled without problems at the end of its service life. The production of the future has a modular design and is automated to a considerable extent, so that system utilisation is optimal and the wastage quota is minimised. An entrepreneur should orient himself to this vision when he is thinking about the further development of his company.

Competitive advantages are generated in two respects through resource efficiency usage. Firstly, it is generated directly by when the use of materials goes hand in hand with lower material cost. Secondly, and indirectly, when a resource-efficient method of production communicates environmental advantages to the customer.

Illustrative case studies

Effizienz-Agentur NRW carries out about 250 projects per annum for increasing resource efficiency in small and medium-sized industry and trade companies in North Rhine-Westphalia, and also accompanies implementation. In parallel to the rapid increase in the importance of digitalisation for manufacturing companies, which has been discussed in Germany under the term 'Industry 4.0', the consultancy work of the Duisburg agency is also on the increase in this area. Based on the following practical examples, it is easy to understand the significant contribution that elements of digitalisation can make to resource efficiency, i.e. material and energy savings. It is not a case of creating a 'smart factory'. Particularly companies that operate in the value creation chain as suppliers and semi-finished product manufacturers, for example, and are subject to strict customer specifications often only have a limited amount of influence on changes. As far as a consultancy is concerned, here it is a case of finding the correct starting points and making use of digitalisation in locations where it is sensible and useful.

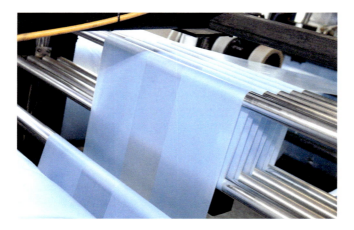

Figure 20.3 mk Plast GmbH & Co KG processes more than 20 tons of plastic per day into plastic films.
Photo: Firma some.oner; Yashar Khosravani.

The three following consultancy cases or practical examples which are described in more detail in the following have been proportionally supported within the scope of the EFRE 'Resource Efficiency' consultancy programme.

Practical example 1 (industry: plastics)

INITIAL SITUATION

The core business of the family-run mk Plast GmbH & Co. KG from the North Rhine-Westphalian town of Monschau is the manufacturing and processing of plastic film which is depicted in Figure 20.3.

Approximately 40 employees work at the location. More than 20 tons of plastic is processed per day with eight production machines (so-called blown film extruders) and production lines. Among other things, the film is used in the form of pouches and sacks in the packing industry and in medical engineering. To increase its process transparency and improve resource efficiency, the company used the resource efficiency consulting of Effizienz-Agentur NRW.

RESULTS AND ADVANTAGES

The process analysis showed that the operational connection of the machine park to the current information systems (Management Executive System MES, Enterprise Resource Planning ERP and Monitoring) and the evaluations thereof did not fulfil the increased demands that were being made concerning order calculation and organisation.

The first step of the consulting, therefore concentrated on the order-specific maintenance systems and their connection to the operational data recording. The data that was collected constituted the prerequisite for providing the existing ERP system with the necessary operational information. The relevant process information such as compressed air flow rate, switch cabinet temperature, flow and return temperatures of the cooling water, total electrical output, melt pressure, cylinder temperature, diverter temperature and melting temperature as well as traction and melt throughput was first recorded on a pilot extruder, stored centrally in the database and then made available to the ERP system for evaluation. A particular challenge was interpreting and technically qualifying the complex variety of data in the sense of making more efficient use of resources.

Another goal of the consulting project was to reduce non-productive setup and downtimes during order changes on the blown film extrusion lines. Setup times and the start and completion of orders can now be accurately defined with the aid of automated machine data recording, and expenditure which is incurred can be documented and evaluated in detail. The setup times at the pilot extruder were able to be reduced by up to approx. 20 hours per year by these measures.

It was accompanied by wastage minimisation of approximately four tons of granules per annum with a throughput of approximately 200 kilograms per hour. At the same time, the productivity of the overall process was improved. Approximately 20 tons of waste production per annum will be saved in future when applied to all eight production lines. The company also expects a further reduction in film wastage of 30 tons per annum by making operative improvements to the cooling section of the blown film extrusion line. In total, mk Plast will save approximately 50 tons of polyethylene thanks to having more efficient process data recording and evaluation. As a result of the measures which have been implemented, including increased value creation and resource productivity, the company is anticipating an annual cost reduction of around 98,000 euros.

Practical example 2 (industry: metal)

BACKGROUND AND GOALS

Putzier Oberflächentechnik GmbH refines sections of steel using the thermal spraying process for mechanical engineering, the paper and electronics industries, and also the food processing industry, among others. Figure 20.4 illustrates how Putzier refines steel parts using thermal spraying processes.

The company from Leichlingen in North-Rhine Westphalia, which has around 40 employees, processes approximately 90 tons of steel and four tons of spray powder per annum. To improve resource efficiency, Putzier used the resource efficiency consulting of Effizienz-Agentur NRW. An initial analysis showed that the operational information systems (Enterprise Resource

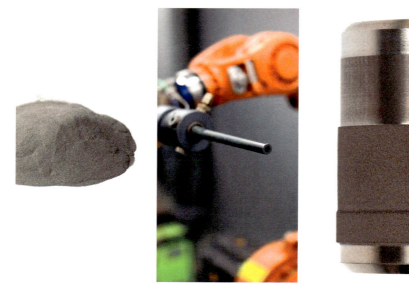

Figure 20.4 Refining of steel parts using thermal spraying processes by Putzier.
Photo: Jens Putzier.

Planning ERP, production planning and control system PPS, operational data recording BDE) and the evaluations from these systems had not been adapted to the increased requirements. To increase potential in this area, the company used one of the Excel tools developed by Effizienz-Agentur NRW for cause-oriented assignment of resource costs (Ressourcenkostenrechnung, RKR, Resource Cost Accounting).

RESULTS AND ADVANTAGES

In the first stage of the consulting, the main focus was on the start-up and auxiliary processing times of the entire value creation and BDE data recording. The analyses were based on structured employee interviews. The results formed the basis for checking the ERP data management system. With the aid of resource cost accounting, the order flow, the handover of the order at the sales side, and also the planning of the orders in the manufacturing system were improved during the next stage. The purchasing processes are now more strongly linked to the order situation. The updating of the cost calculation (pre- and post-calculation) allows Putzier to analyse the cost-effectiveness of the order spectrum continually.

Orders which are uneconomical can now be quickly identified. The time taken for internal organisation, from the technical inquiry to the quotation calculation and the manufacturing order, was reduced by up to 60 per cent after the restructuring. Wastage quotas, internal complaints and stock levels were also reduced, and backlogs were also relieved. The reductions led to annual material savings of 2.4 tons and a three per cent reduction of the material quota within the company.

For Putzier, the process transparency that was gained has opened up an entirely new perspective for the further development of its corporate strategy. Moreover, the first stage of the digital transformation is complete. Other projects for the filling in gaps in the digitalisation are being planned. With the aid of dynamic project management, the company wants to align itself for the future, initiate the generation change and sustainably align its range of products to resource efficiency and Industry 4.0.

Practical example 3 (industry: metal)

BACKGROUND AND GOALS

Stainless steel factory Schmees manufactures high quality cast steel components at its NRW location in Langenfeld for the food and pharmaceutical industries and the mechanical energy engineering. Every year, Edelstahlwerke Schmees processes approximately 2,200 tons of steel into castings (see Figure 20.5).

Approximately 140 employees work at the Langenfeld location. A large number of product variants continuously presents the company with significant organisational challenges. Up until the beginning of 2016, the individual production areas looked after the manufacturing of the orders single-handedly. An initial analysis revealed that redundancies were occurring time and time again in the warehousing area, among others. To organise manufacturing and warehousing more transparently and efficiently, Schmees used Resource Cost Accounting

Figure 20.5 The Edelstahlwerke Schmees processes approximately 2,200 t of steel into castings. Photo: Edelstahlwerke Schmees GmbH.

250 *Peter Jahns*

(Ressourcenkostenrechnung, RKR) from Effizienz-Agentur NRW as part of resource efficiency consulting. A created the data basis for a new module in the ERP system, was, thus created.

RESULTS AND ADVANTAGES

In 2015, with the help of RKR, Schmees recorded materials and energy usage in its cost structures. Based on the data that was collected, a cause-oriented cost accounting system was developed. This made it possible to evaluate individual orders in accordance with specific resource requirements.

The integration of RKR in the new ERP system has now put the company in a position to systematically analyse specific order groups such as rings and housings with regard to their material requirements, compare them and therefore determine the maximum material efficiency potential for each product via time series. Further, the integration of RKR in the new ERP system makes it possible to identify material wasters at an early stage.

This evaluation now constitutes the basis for the central planning and control of the material flow. With the aid of achieved new coordination options, the effectiveness of the manufacturing process was improved in such a way that the timeliness of order processing increased significantly. Also, there was a considerable reduction in the amount of reworking. The entire order process is now controlled centrally via production data acquisition. Schemes also set up a continuous improvement process, meaning that the flow of orders is getting better all the time.

These measures have resulted in a sustainable reduction in the number of unfinished castings and scrap quantities in production. The ERP system which has been supplemented by RKR is an essential step towards further digital networking of its processes for the company. Schmees invested approximately 10,000 euros in the development and implementation of the ERP solution and reduced its material costs by around 400,000 euros per annum.

Summary

Digitalisation fundamentally influences and changes how manufacturing companies produce their products. The bandwidth ranges from simple changes and improvements to operational processes to upheavals which cast doubt upon existing business models and make strategic engagement with the market and the future essential. On the one hand, the market influences products and production samples at increasing speed and in increasingly short cycles by means of digitalisation, and on the other hand the future viability of many manufacturing companies depends on how sensibly they make use of the elements of digitalisation in order to be able to benefit from the advantages thereof.

If you examine the proportion of material costs of about 42 per cent in the manufacturing industry in Germany, it becomes clear how much potential digitalisation has in the material and energy-saving areas, which have a decisive influence on a company's competitiveness. For the purpose of clarification, we can also talk about 'Resource Efficiency 4.0'. The practical examples reveal the concrete savings which can be made in terms of resources and emissions and also costs due to elements of digitalisation, i.e. using Resource Efficiency 4.0. The experience gained during the work of Effizienz-Agentur NRW has shown that dividing up into the elements of order clarification, order processing, calculation and company future in the analysis for evaluating Resource Efficiency 4.0 is useful for identifying weaknesses and initiating improvements accordingly using digitalisation instruments.

The examples also show that the prerequisite for the effective introduction and use of Resource Efficiency 4.0 is exact knowledge of your existing processes. An exact analysis of the relevant processes within the company is needed to do this to provide transparency. Only then can it be seriously decided whether and to what extent elements of digitalisation are to be introduced in the sense of Resource Efficiency 4.0. However, particularly small and medium-sized companies from industry and trade often lack the financial resources, the time and the relevant personnel to carry out appropriate analyses. Neutral and independent external consultancy can help in these cases, such as that which is provided by the Effizienz-Agentur NRW, which works on behalf of the North Rhine-Westphalia Ministry for the Environment.

References

Bliesner, A., Liedtke, C. & Rohn, H. (2014). Resource efficiency and culture – Workplace training for small and medium-sized enterprises. *Science of the Total Environment*, 481, 645–648.

Bundesregierung, D. (2016). *Deutsche Nachhaltigkeitsstrategie: Neuauflage 2016*. Die Bundesregierung: Berlin, Germany.

European Environment Agency. (2016). *More from Less-Material Resource Efficiency in Europe: 2015 Overview of Policies, Instruments and Targets in 32 Countries*. Publications Office of the European Union.

Jahns, P. (2018). Protect Resources, Strengthen the Economy: Good Examples for Resource Efficiency in Industry and Handicraft Businesses. In *Factor X* (pp. 385–393). Springer, Cham.

Kaiser, R. (2018). Germany's Resource Efficiency Agenda: Driving Momentum on the National Level and Beyond. In *Factor X* (pp. 213–232). Springer, Cham.

Müller, J. M., Buliga, O. & Voigt, K. I. (2018). Fortune favors the prepared: How SMEs approach business model innovations in Industry 4.0. *Technological Forecasting and Social Change*, 132, 2–17.

Müller, M. & Reutter, O. (2017). Vision development towards a sustainable North Rhine-Westphalia 2030 in a science-practice-dialogue. *Sustainability*, 9(7), 1111.

21 Eight tons of lifestyle

Monitoring a sustainable material footprint for households in Germany and the world

Jens Teubler, Sebastian Schuster, and Christa Liedtke

Background

The Sustainable Development Goals (SDGs) emphasise the fact that the use of natural resources is directly linked to the household consumption of products and services (Goal 12: Responsible Consumption and Production) (United Nations General Assembly 2015). Its indicator Material Footprint measures the use and extraction of raw materials in an economy and is therefore compatible with similar indicators on the micro-economic level of households.

Lettenmeier and colleagues (Lettenmeier 2018; Lettenmeier, Liedtke & Rohn 2014) based their Material Footprint on the MIPS method, a concept that was developed in the early 1990s at the Wuppertal Institut (Liedtke et al. 2014; Schmidt-Bleek 2000) and has since been further developed and applied in several studies (e.g. recently in Buhl, Liedtke, Teubler, Bienge & Schmidt 2018; Teubler, Buhl, Lettenmeier, Greiff & Liedtke 2018).

It could be shown that 8 tonnes per person and year are consistent with sustainable use of natural resources by households and therefore consistent with the SDG 12 goal for sustainable consumption. This 8-tonne lifestyle is achievable by most, if not all, households at the global level (Greiff, Teubler, Baedeker, Liedtke & Rohn 2017; Lettenmeier, Hirvilammi, Laakso, Lähteenoja & Aalto 2012).

However, sustainable consumption policies affect households differently, in particular when they are confronted with limitations on income, time or freedom of movement (e.g. driving to work). And although it is possible to assess either the average or individual material footprint (per capita or via surveys), we lack methods to describe different types of households, their lifestyles and footprints in a representative manner.

We explore possibilities to do so in this article. Our interest lies in finding an applicable method that allows us to describe the footprint of households regarding their socio-demographic characteristics but also find the causes consumption behaviour. This type of monitoring would enable us to tailor policies for sustainable consumption that respect people's needs and restrictions.

It would enable us to:

a rank such policies by the size of their effect and costs;
b understand and estimate the effects of financial incentives for sustainable products;
c map the effects of digitalisation;
d anticipate social fairness issues regarding additional fees of practices and or bans of products and specific services;
e approach household predominantly that show a high ability and willingness to change their lifestyle: and
f address households with high incomes, high environmental awareness and high footprints.

The authors (and others) conducted several studies regarding average footprints in Germany as well as the footprints of individuals. We use these studies as a starting point to develop a solution.

Previous studies and their limitations

A study in 2017 (Buhl, Teubler, Liedtke & Stadler 2017) used aggregated macroeconomic resource-intensities (resource use per Euro spent) and combined them with microdata on the income and expenditures of households in the German federal State of North-Rhine Westphalia over three (3) periods (survey carried out every 5 years: 2003, 2008, 2013). While the authors found that the overall or average MF did not change that much over ten years (about 31 tons per person in 2013), the data showed a clear shift from resource use in transport, food and housing towards housing, energy and communication[1] in particular. Due to the nature of the method applied (resource intensities based on input-/output modelling), it could not be further investigated to what extent changes in lifestyles or the society itself are responsible for these changes (although the strong link between income and environmental pressure could be ascertained). More importantly, it could not be investigated how individual lifestyle choices (e.g. vegetarian or car-free lifestyles) would affect these results.

Several studies have now been conducted at the household and individual lifestyle levels to methodically differentiate behavioural data and footprints (Buhl 2014; Buhl & Acosta 2015; Greiff et al. 2017; Lähteenoja, Lettenmeier & Kotakorpi 2008; Lettenmeier et al. 2012). The overall consumption fields were considered, as were individual areas such as sport and time use. Following these studies, an online calculator (www.ressourcen-rechner.de) was created, which has been collecting material footprints and socio-economic data since 2015. The researchers combined online surveys or diaries from either small or large random samples with specific characterisation factors. Thus it was possible to match not only socio-economic data, but also socio-demographic data and voluntary information on, for example, willingness to pay or attitudes towards the environment

254 *Jens Teubler et al.*

Table 21.1 Variable importance of predictors and performance of linear and non-linear predictions

Variable Importance	GLM (%)	MARS (%)
Household size (no.)	100	71
Trips local train (km)	88.98	89
Trips car (km)	80.85	100
Dwelling size (m^2)	66.23	57
Car age (a)	49.06	78
Cars in household (no.)	48.44	78
Trips long-distance train (km)	46.34	52
Travel by long-distance train	45.11	40
Conventional electricity (ref. eco)	36.81	28
Gas car (l/100 km)	34.68	
Travels car (km)	29.24	
Holiday long-distance train (h)	26.04	
Holiday flight (h)	24.86	23
Night storage heating (ref. oil)	22.28	
Car drivers (no.)	21.97	
Milk (no. cups 200 ml)	20.62	
Consumption electricity (kWh)	19.27	
Holidays luxury hotel (d)	18.45	
Car passenger > 2 (ref. alone)	18.31	
Electricity source IDK (ref. eco)	18.09	
Holidays car (km)	16.81	
Meat consumption high (ref. vegan)	10.27	
RMSE	0.48	0.60
R^2	0.74	0.61

Source: Buhl et al. (2019)

Note: Variable importance measures the relative decrease in prediction error (MSE & RMSE) with the most important predictor scaled to 100. The importance of categorical items in relation to a reference (ref.). 'Electricity source IDK' is electricity source not known ('I don't know'). RMSE is the rooted mean squared error. R^2 measures the accuracy of the prediction.

to the corresponding resource use from lifestyle choices (see e.g. Buhl, Liedtke & Bienge 2017; Buhl et al. 2018; Buhl, Liedtke, Teubler, Schuster & Bienge 2019).

Table 21.1 shows an example from an online survey with over 60,000 users that investigates the predictors for resource use. While the sample is biased (over-representation of, for example, female vegetarians), the online tool[2] and its set of consumption questions could be used to identify the consumption choices that matter the most. Here, household size, mobility choices and energy use already account for more than 70% of the overall footprints. Reducing the number of questions offers two major advantages. First, it enables the researcher to conduct surveys in a time-efficient manner that allows for integration of additional lifestyle-related questions. Secondly, it highlights the areas where a high level of differentiation of consumption choices is highly relevant for the resulting footprint. As a result, a persons' footprint can be estimated on the basis of less information but still with adequate precision.

Challenges and solution

The two different approaches can be classified as top-down and bottom-up modelling of Material Footprints (or any other environmental impact indicator for that matter). Top-down methods heavily rely on information from macroeconomic tables (usually input-output tables for trade that transform monetary into physical flows). Bottom-up approaches, on the other hand, are often interchangeable with calculations from life cycle assessments (focusing on the function and services of products or products themselves to satisfy needs).

The third possible method for providing relevant and comprehensive environmental data are so-called hybrid approaches, where top-down data is further differentiated with the help of bottom-up modelling. While this solution is promising, in regard to the calculation of a comprehensive average footprint in particular countries, it still does not provide the necessary socio-demographic information to explain which and why households exhibit their individual footprint.

We believe that this gap between footprints per capita (equalising consumption over a large population) and footprints per individuum (with usually highly biased or random samples) can be bridged in other ways. We suggest using a probability based access panel of consumers to achieve both goals: differentiation of consumption and lifestyle choice where it matters the most (especially regarding needs, preferences and restrictions) as well as providing a comprehensive picture of the society and its material footprint.

This type of research design includes a random selection of individuals within a statistical population, observations of the same variables over short or long periods of time and weighting procedures to deal with, for example, non-responses.

This would enable us to corroborate findings from previous studies. It also helps to investigate more deeply how footprints are affected by socio-demographic characteristics like household income, gender or employment status. More importantly, it would allow researchers to link environmental footprints to individual driving forces like needs, parenthood, life satisfaction and opinions or, for example, the willingness to pay for sustainable products (see Figure 21.1 for examples of potential factors that could be investigated).

Advantages of the approach

A panel solution offers several advantages. First, panels exist over a long time with only small changes. The socio-economic and socio-demographic data can, therefore, be used for more than one study. This allows to link data from previous studies with the current Footprint survey to identify additional relevant parameters or to validate results. One example for this would be the impact of so-called critical life events (e.g. unemployment, illness but also marriage and children) on a person's consumption behaviour and one's footprint.

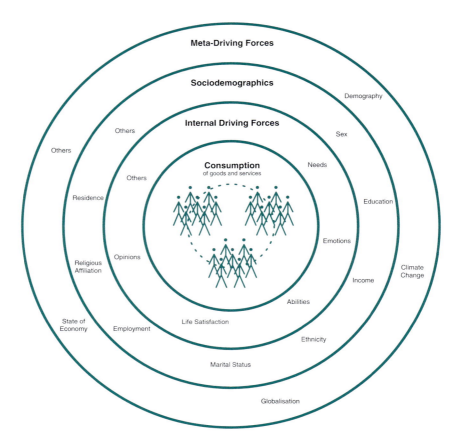

Figure 21.1 Household groups and potential driving forces for sustainable consumption (to be further investigated).
Source: own compilation.

The second advantage stems from the ability of researchers to weight groups in the sample that are over- or underrepresented from either the sampling design itself or from, for example, deviations from non-responses. By using state-of-art methods, the results of the sample can be re-distributed to reflect the society it represents (see Gabler, Kolb, Sand & Zins 2015 for a short overview on approaches and literature). Thus, not only average footprints for the overall society can be calculated but also for parts of the society that fulfil specific characteristics (sex, income, education, age, among others).

A further benefit of using a panel is its usage for trend and foresight analysis. If conducted yearly, trends of consumption can be shown. Therefore, studies over several years could reveal the reactions of households to events or policies in a robust and transparent way.

From the point of view of survey design, such an approach also enables researchers to learn from follow-up surveys. Since it is known whether a household participated the last time and what its responses were, additional questions could investigate more deeply into issues of interest. If, for example, the footprint of car-owners correlates with large footprints, it could be interesting to know if this trend is even more pronounced with the owners of SUVs.

Outside of the traditional survey methods, this approach could also be combined with the increasingly large digital data pools. Big data and App data, if collected with the knowledge and approval of participants, can answer research questions in real-time and mirror them to the actors in politics and society but also the participants themselves. The usage of GPS data, for example, collected by the smartphones of participants, could map movements and mobility choices, giving insights into the cause-effect chains of the environmental footprint of our day-to-day travel.

This integration of digital data also makes it possible to integrate statistics and research on the use of time. Since people use their time to realise their personal goals and needs, it is often more directly linked to the environmental impact of consumption then expenses. Time prosperity is already a relevant topic for many groups in our society, especially for the younger generation (Buhl, Schipperges & Liedtke 2017). Transformation research, in particular for enabling sustainable consumption, can thus generate a higher social and political impact.

Data requirements for environmental data

The matching data on the environmental side of such a panel study can be provided efficiently. Using generic life cycle inventories allows for bottom-up models of consumption choices that are robust enough for overall results (see Teubler et al. 2018; Wiesen, Mathieu Saurat & Michael Lettenmeier 2014; Wiesen & Wirges 2017 for examples). These results can be further differentiated in light of specific research questions. If, for example, watching television is relevant for both time and resource use, it could be beneficial to model characterisation factors for different types of television sets and request information of the participants to that effect.

The limit of this type of modelling lies in its ability to account for all the consumption areas that have a low specific effect, but still, have a relevant share in the overall footprint if combined. These are often also areas where a survey would require many questions (thus time) without affecting the results to a high degree (e.g. ownership of small electrical devices or tools).

One solution for this data gap might be the calculation of a baseline of material footprint. This baseline is attributed to every panel participant regarding basic parameters such as household size or level of income. It could be based on environmental data from macroeconomic studies (e.g. resource intensities) as well as previous bottom-up studies. Although it would not be possible to account for 100% of the overall footprint of an average household,

258 *Jens Teubler et al.*

the authors are confident that this approach would cover most, if not all relevant areas of sustainable consumption.

Outlook (pilot study)

A change in the analytical focus is needed to achieve the objectives of SDG 12 and successfully implement various programmes such as ProgRess and the National Programme on Sustainable Consumption in Germany. Rather than reporting on the average Material Footprint in a country alone, monitoring should include information on modern lifestyles and the specific social situations people find themselves in. The ongoing discussion on CO_2 taxation in Germany is a good example of this requirement. We do not know, as of yet, what groups in our society would benefit from it and which low-income groups would be affected by it without having reasonable options to reduce their overall fossil fuel use.

A more differentiated monitoring could, therefore, help to identify socially inclusive approaches to climate protection (and sustainable resource use overall). It is crucial in our opinion, to devise sustainability policies that distribute the burdens and benefits fairly and ecologically in terms of household budgets and quality of life.

The next step is to plan and conduct a pilot study to test the hypotheses of the authors. Applying the learnings from previous studies (in particular Buhl et al. 2019 and Teubler et al. 2018), a first set of material footprint questions has to be selected that:

- predict most of the material footprint;
- are relevant in regard to current; and
- discuss policies in Germany such as Energiewende (shift towards renewable energies), low-carbon transport or Carbon Tax, can be answered by households without much effort or additional information.

A second group of questions will be then used to match the results with needs, preferences and restrictions of households. They should cover areas like life satisfaction, personality disposition or lifestyles (using, for example, a tool by Gunnar Otte (Otte 2004) that combines several social milieu models with the theory of Pierre Bourdieu).

The calculation of characterisation factors for life-cycle raw material and natural resource use should include both questions and the material footprint of the baseline of 'other and general services'. The survey can then be conducted using an already existing panel (for example the GESIS panel[3]), applying state-of-art methods for sampling and weighting.

Finally, results are investigated with the help of multivariate statistical methods (for example regression models, cluster analysis, factor analysis and latent class analysis), but should also be compared to the results of previous studies. Does the weighted average provide results in the range of macro-economic statistics? Are we able to differentiate between the soft characteristics of households and their footprints? Are there any unambiguous differences between households in urban and rural areas, that have not been taken into account in former studies? Can we replicate, corroborate or falsify findings from smaller random samples? Do we find 'black spots' of household groups that are overwhelmingly underrepresented in the panel? Does the material footprint composition differ significantly between different ethnicities? And are we able to design a similar study that explains the potential effects of a specific policy for sustainable consumption?

Discussion

We have presented a feasible solution for the monitoring of the resource use of households. A solution that, if successful, could be used to test and quantify the effects of explicit measures for lowering the Material Footprint of consumption. Subsequently, it also measures the Material Footprint of the products consumed or the services they provide.

The methodological approach, therefore, addresses central fields for a transformation towards more sustainable consumption: consumption patterns, lifestyles and policies, but also innovative products, processes and business models. It helps to evaluate the sustainability of innovations during the development of product-service systems. The latter is of great importance for sustainability, as many unintended side effects are usually not evaluated during their development (especially innovations based on digital services).

The approach provides numerous applications for sustainability research in the long run. It could, for example, provide insights on the success of nudging policies or on time budgets for households and their relationship with social milieus in a digitalised world. It would certainly facilitate investigations into problem shifts of consumption (indirect rebound effects), because the results are not only differentiated on a socio-economic level. And it could enable producers and software developers with information on how and why households consume the way they are.[4]

This can be achieved using a survey design focused on a panel, and by differentiating along several dimensions. The social dimension allows for the differentiation of societal groups, their preferences, limitations and characteristics. The second dimension, the environmental impacts, is then further differentiated into different areas of consumption (or across those areas to identify potential rebounds). This would provide researchers, policymakers, companies and households alike with the necessary information to steer sustainable consumption fairly and effectively. As such and since it is not restricted to the Material Footprint as a single indicator, a panel approach could also be used to help companies developing sustainable products and services (SDG 12.6). It could raise awareness for sustainable development

(SDG 12.8), identify pressure factors of climate change (SDG 13) or reveal inequalities (SDG 10).

The aim is to achieve a high quality of life for the various lifestyle groups within our ecological boundaries – provided that there is a balance between social and individual development opportunities. The approach described here would be the first step for that.

Abbreviations

GLM   generalised linear regression model
MARS multivariate adaptive regression splines
MIPS   material input per service
MSE   mean squared error
RMSE rooted mean squared error
SDG   Sustainable Development Goals

Notes

1 It is reasonable to assume that this shift towards communication is a direct result of digitalisation.
2 See www.ressourcen-rechner.de.
3 See www.gesis.org/gesis-panel/gesis-panel-home.
4 A current study on the 'Latest initiatives by science and policy to promote sustainable consumption and recommendations to enhance the German Sustainability Strategy'. discusses some of these applications and summarises the scientific discourse on sustainable consumption in Germany. It is expected to be published by the end of 2019.

References

Buhl, J. (2014). Revisiting Rebound Effects from Material Resource Use. Indications for Germany Considering Social Heterogeneity. *Resources*, 3(1), 106–122.

Buhl, J. and Acosta, J. (2015). Work Less, Do Less?: Working Time Reductions and Rebound Effects. *Sustainability Science*. Retrieved 9 November 2015 from http://link.springer.com/10.1007/s11625-015-0322-8.

Buhl, J., Liedtke, C., and Bienge, K. (2017). How Much Environment Do Humans Need? Evidence from an Integrated Online User Application Linking Natural Resource Use and Subjective Well-Being in Germany. *Resources*, 6(4), 67.

Buhl, J., Liedtke, C., Teubler, J., Bienge, K., and Schmidt, N. (2018). Measure or Management? – Resource Use Indicators for Policymakers Based on Microdata by Households. *Sustainability*, 10(12), 4467.

Buhl, J., Liedtke, C., Teubler, J., Schuster, S., and Bienge, K. (2019). A Material Footprint Model for Green Information Systems – Using Statistical Learning to Identify the Predictors of Natural Resource Use. *Cogent Engineering*, 6(1). Retrieved 4 June 2019 from www.cogentoa.com/article/10.1080/23311916.2019.1616655.

Buhl, J., Schipperges, M., and Liedtke, C. (2017). Die Ressourcenintensität der Zeit und ihre Bedeutung für nachhaltige Lebensstile. *Verbraucherwissenschaften* (pp. 295–311). Berlin: Springer.

Buhl, J., Teubler, J., Liedtke, C., and Stadler, K. (2017). Der Ressourcenverbrauch privater Haushalte in NRW. *uwf UmweltWirtschaftsForum | Sustainability Management Forum*, 25, 255–264.

Gabler, S., Kolb, J.-P., Sand, M., and Zins, S. (2015). *Gewichtung. SDM-Survey Guidelines (GESIS Leibniz Institute for the Social Sciences)*. Retrieved 13 September 2019 from www.gesis.org/gesis-survey-guidelines/statistics/gewichtung/.

Greiff, K., Teubler, J., Baedeker, C., Liedtke, C., and Rohn, H. (2017). Material and Carbon Footprint of Household Activities. In D. V. Keyson, O. Guerra-Santin and D. Lockton (Eds.), *Living Labs: Design and Assessment of Sustainable Living* (pp. 259–275). Cham: Springer International Publishing.

Lähteenoja, S., Lettenmeier, M., and Kotakorpi, E. (2008). The Ecological Rucksack of Households: Huge Differences, Huge Potential for Reduction? (pp. 319–337). Retrieved from http://epub.wupperinst.org/frontdoor/index/index/docId/2937.

Lettenmeier, M. (2018). *A Sustainable Level of Material Footprint – Benchmark for Designing One-Planet Lifestyles [Materiaalijalanjäljen kestävä taso –mittapuu yhden planeetan elämäntapojen toteuttamiseen]*. Aalto University. Retrieved from https://aaltodoc.aalto.fi/handle/123456789/31300.

Lettenmeier, M., Hirvilammi, T., Laakso, S., Lähteenoja, S., and Aalto, K. (2012). Material Footprint of Low-Income Households in Finland – Consequences for the Sustainability Debate. *Sustainability*, 4(12), 1426–1447.

Lettenmeier, M., Liedtke, C., and Rohn, H. (2014). Eight Tons of Material Footprint – Suggestion for a Resource Cap for Household Consumption in Finland. *Resources*, 3(3), 488–515.

Liedtke, C., Bienge, K., Wiesen, K., Teubler, J., Greiff, K., Lettenmeier, M., and Rohn, H. (2014). Resource Use in the Production and Consumption System – The MIPS Approach. *Resources*, 3(3), 544–574.

Otte, G. (2004). *Sozialstrukturanalysen mit Lebensstilen*. Wiesbaden: VS Verlag für Sozialwissenschaften. Retrieved 5 August 2019, from http://link.springer.com/10.1007/978-3-322-99335-9.

Schmidt-Bleek, F. (2000). *Das MIPS-Konzept: weniger Naturverbrauch - mehr Lebensqualität durch Faktor 10*. München: Droemer Knaur.

Teubler, J., Buhl, J., Lettenmeier, M., Greiff, K., and Liedtke, C. (2018). A Household's Burden–The Embodied Resource Use of Household Equipment in Germany. *Ecological Economics*, 146, 96–105.

United Nations General Assembly. (2015). Transforming Our World: The 2030 Agenda for Sustainable Development. *United Nations*. Retrieved 30 March 2016 from www.un.org/ga/search/view_doc.asp?symbol=A/RES/70/1&Lang=E.

Wiesen, K., Mathieu Saurat and Michael Lettenmeier. (2014). Calculating the Material Input per Service Unit using the Ecoinvent Database. *International Journal of Performability Engineering*, 10(4), 357–366.

Wiesen, K. and Wirges, M. (2017). From Cumulated Energy Demand to Cumulated Raw Material Demand: The Material Footprint as a Sum Parameter in Life Cycle Assessment. *Energy, Sustainability and Society*, 7(1), 13.

22 C like clever and cycle

Without a smart and systematic conception of the metal industry, product labelling and an indicator system, nothing will happen

Kathrin Greiff, Florian Fiesinger, Christa Liedtke, and Martin Faulstich

Introduction

Metals are essential for a wide range of applications and technologies. These include vehicle construction, information and communication technology, renewable energy production and medical technology (Marscheider-Weidemann et al. 2016). Their availability is of the utmost importance for our society, but this is not guaranteed in the long term. Based on the number of elements in the periodic table, most metals, especially rare earths, are not recovered after use and have recycling rates close to 0% (UNEP 2011). Irrespective of existing static ranges the metal content in the earth is finite. Even if metals such as indium, zinc or zirconium theoretically have static resource ranges of more than 100 years, the limitedness of the earth tells us something different – the elements cannot be multiplied, even if we continuously discover new sources. At present, it is not scarcity that seems to be the problem, but rather the economic availability of primary and secondary sources. This economic availability initially leads to bottlenecks and economic restrictions in the existing growth course. Germany is in a weak position here, as it has no raw material sources. It must, therefore, deal intelligently with its raw materials and budget them if it wants to remain competitive. In the process of the raw material transition, there is no alternative but to meet the long-term demand for metals mostly from secondary raw materials.

In addition to the physical scarcity, the planetary boundaries in the handling of metals must be ensured (Steffen et al. 2015). Specifically, the limit of the remaining CO_2 budget of 420 $GtCO_2$ for the 1.5° target of the IPCC must be fulfilled (IPCC 2018). The global energy consumption of primary metal production is responsible for 7-8% of the global energy expenditure (UNEP 2013). The most effective way to reduce CO_2 emissions and other environmental impacts as land-use change, biodiversity loss or toxic emissions in metallurgy is secondary production. In the case of aluminium, cumulative energy consumption (CED) is reduced by 80 up to 95% and CO_2 emissions by 80% compared to primary production. This balance is similar for other metals (Frischenschlager et al. 2010; Steger et al. 2019).

The earth's capacity to absorb greenhouse gases is ultimately a critical limiting factor in the handling of metals. The fact that the demand for metals far exceeds their secondary production is extremely problematic at this point (Wilts & von Gries 2017). Nevertheless, metals are crucial for climate protection and energy system transformation (Teubler, Kiefer & Liedtke 2018). Examples are the rare earth metal neodymium used in high-performance permanent magnets in wind turbines, the alkali metal lithium as the most important component in batteries, or the metal tellurium used in thin-film solar cells to generate solar power (Marscheider-Weidemann et al. 2016). It is therefore essential to promote the aspects of resource efficiency and to strengthen the critical role of metals in national and European policy programs. Next to a global solution, a European solo effort with predominantly market-based instruments and the effects of committed behaviour by civil society in the European Union (EU), show that the EU can make a considerable contribution to sustainable development on its own (Distelkamp, Meyer & Moghayer 2015). Thus, a comprehensive approach is needed for sustainable metal management in the sense of a circular economy on the European level fostering sustainable production and consumption pathways. But, this need and the special role of metals are not seen in the current debate about resources in society and politics. Due to the fact that in public perception, metallic raw materials are often discussed as less urgent than energy or polymer raw materials, this article aims to highlight the critical role of metals.

Further, the objective of this contribution is to show which prerequisites exist for the development and establishment of a holistic metal management and where political strategies have to start. Challenges needed to be overcome to achieve such a holistic metal strategy and management are highlighted. In particular, the role of the metal industry, circular product design and labelling and corresponding indicator systems is examined. In addition, the special role of digitalisation is being worked out. Finally, conclusions are drawn and shown which aspects have to be considered for a holistic metal strategy and management.

Requirements for circular management

The role of the metal industry

Metallic raw materials are of strategic importance for the highly specialised German economy, especially for the expansion of renewable energies, in the field of (electric) mobility and construction or housing. However, Germany has no economically exploitable metal deposits. Metal ores and concentrates are fully imported. In the criticality study undertaken by the European Commission in 2017, metals used in future technologies such as solar cells, fibre-optic cables and magnets for wind turbines were classified as particularly critical (European Commission 2017). For these metals, suitable recovery processes must be developed which, on the one hand, ensure the necessary purity levels and, on the other hand, are economically viable (Fröhlich et al. 2017). For this purpose, the value-added chains of primary production in Germany and Europe must be maintained, since they are simultaneously used for secondary production. It is a matter of maintaining economic profitability as well as the basic supply of our society with metallic raw materials.

The metal industry is a key industry in Germany. It is divided into the steel and non-ferrous metal sectors. In the steel industry in Germany, 42.1 million tons, steel scrap accounted for 43%, were produced in 2016 by 85,000 employees in 68 companies and generated a turnover of 35.1 billion euros (Wirtschaftsvereinigung Stahl 2018). The products are mainly used in the construction industry, in the automotive industry and for mechanical engineering. Products from the non-ferrous metal industry, on the other hand, are used in high-tech applications in the aerospace, automotive, chemical and electrical industries. In 2017, the non-ferrous metals industry employed 108,000 people in 655 companies and generated a turnover of 51.3 billion euros. Of the 2.634 million tonnes of crude base metal produced in 2017, 52% was made from secondary sources (Wirtschaftsvereinigung Metalle 2018).

This strength in the metal industry is an opportunity to further expand the leading role in the secondary production of metals. The demand for metals will continue to rise in future (Elshkaki et al. 2018). Drivers are countries such as China or India, which want to catch up with the standard of living of industrial countries. Secondary production in Germany and Europe can make a major contribution to meeting the future demand for metals, provided that existing metallurgical structures are maintained or further expanded. Particularly in the case of functional technology elements or materials, new metallurgical structures must be investigated and established for a functioning secondary raw materials economy or preferably circular economy (Reuter et al. 2019). Besides, research activities should also be intensified with regard to accompanying modelling, especially in relation to the modelling of availability and losses.

The role of eco-design

To integrate sustainable development into European environmental legislation, the White Paper on Integrated Product Policy (IPP) was released in 2003. The focus of environmental policy was on the entire life cycle of products and manufacturers were required to assume greater product responsibility for their products placed on the market. Manufacturers know the exact material composition of their products and know best how they can be dismantled in the most efficient way. For this reason, binding take-back and recycling obligations must be introduced for product manufacturers. These represent the optimal way to increase collection and recycling quotas. Various policy instruments exist at European level to implement such objectives. Those instruments protect consumers and the environment from possible negative impacts. Products in the European market should thus become more sustainable. These policy instruments can be divided into 'push and pull' measures. The 'push' instruments set minimum standards that must be met for a product to be approved for the European market at all (exclusion of non-sustainable products from the market). The 'pull' instruments are voluntary requirements that go beyond the minimum standards, for example, product labels (European Commission 2019).

Another way to increase the product responsibility for manufactures is the use of service concepts and business models such as leasing which are already implemented in the product development or design phase. The so-called sharing economy leads to reduced consumption of raw materials by aligning the interests of manufacturers and users (Liedtke, Buhl & Ameli 2013b). A car-sharing vehicle can substitute up to 20 private cars according to a study by the German CarSharing Association (bcs 2016) and saves around 11,440 kg of steel, 190 kg of cast iron and 1,710 kg of aluminium per car-sharing vehicle. However, leasing models must be evaluated more strongly, as otherwise, the design of services could lead to problem shifts and rebound effects (Clausen, Bowry & Bienge 2017). To avoid increased resource usage in production and consumption, such complex value creation models should be tested step by step in real-world laboratories and 'LivingLabs' (Schneidewind 2014, Liedtke et al. 2015). In this way, the effects as mentioned above and objectives can be modelled for implementation in the circular economy and made tangible for policymakers.

80% of all product-related environmental impacts are determined in the design phase (Tischner & Moser 2015). The product design actively influences the criteria longevity, reparability and recyclability of a product and contributes significantly to the conservation of resources of metallic raw materials (Liedtke, Buhl & Ameli 2013a; Liedtke 2018). As the European Environment Agency defines, 'Eco-Design delivers products made with fewer resources, using recycled and renewable resources and avoiding hazardous materials, as well as with components that are longer lasting and easier to maintain, repair, upgrade and recycle' (European Environment Agency 2016: 18). However, the implementation of a design suitable for recycling is associated with certain challenges. The complexity of products in terms of the quantity of raw materials used has increased rapidly over the last 100 years. For example, every technically usable element of the periodic table is used by now. This is symbolised by the increase in the metals required for energy generation technologies as shown by Zepf et al. (2014). For example, modern wind turbines require the entire range of rare earths for high-performance permanent magnets (Marscheider-Weidemann et al. 2016).

With this, the recovery of functional metals becomes very complex or even impossible, due to complex metal interconnections and thus irreversible losses that are 'an inevitable part of industrial circular economy' or rather recycling processes (Reuter et al. 2019: 10.5; Reuter & Van Schaik 2016). These dissipative mechanisms remove metals from the material cycle in a way and on a scale that makes it thermodynamically or economically impossible to recover them. Therefore, it is crucial to understand the functioning of dissipation to prevent it.

A high dissipation rate can be found in particular in the metals classified as critical by the European Commission. These metals are increasingly used in information and communication technology (ICT) or rather for digitalisation (see further below). Losses can be attributed to the use of a variety of metals in complex combinations. Existing recycling schemes are unable to cope with the increasing complexity of these primarily electrical and electronic products and [e-]wastes. Prime examples are smartphones, in which about 56 metals are used (Bookhagen et al. 2018). Most of the metals are not recovered at all and have recycling rates below 1% (UNEP 2011). Accordingly, relevant material research on topics such as corrosion, abrasion or the entropy of metals must be increasingly promoted in order to better understand the mechanisms of dissipative losses. In order to be able to map possible losses due to material composition and interactions, modelling at the product level is necessary, which must be incorporated directly into the design process. For this, Reuter et al. (2019) presented a simulation approach for end of life processes on the product level. With this concept, potentials for a circular economy with high significance can be derived via a bottom-up approach.

However, recycling processes also of basic metals always lead to material loss. European Environment Agency showed for the case of aluminium that 'even in a very circular system only 16% of the aluminium remains in the cycle after 10 years' (European Environment Agency 2017: 25). According to this, recycling should not be the only priority, but the principles of modularity should be given greater consideration and thus the inner loops of circular economy to increase product and material lifetimes (European Environment Agency 2017). Many products contain a large number of different metals which must be used as efficiently as possible. Modularity makes it possible to replace individual defective components in products, thus extending their useful lifetime. A modular design also contributes to better disassembly and separation of the components and higher recovery rates of the metals contained when entering the recycling process (Reuter, Van Schaik & Ballester 2018). Schoch (2019) showed in a case study of mobile phone screens, that design for disassembly could lead to standardisation in the design process. This standardisation enables the exchange and further use of modules so that materials can be kept longer in the economic cycle and thus dissipation of recycling processes is prevented or postponed.

To accelerate the use of recyclable design, it makes sense to introduce binding design guidelines as required in the Eco Design Directive (Directive 2009; Greiff & Liedtke 2019) and incentives for a 'design for recycling' and recovery should be promoted. Furthermore, material databases should be set up, which can be used in the design process. For example, in Switzerland and Germany, networks were formed which want to build up and expand a material database in such a way that construction and design based on key figures of a circular economy are possible (www.materialarchiv.ch).

As described above, the requirements of the Eco Design Directive as a push instrument are representing a minimum standard. To be able to influence products beyond this minimum, a product labelling system should be set up and established with the aim of strengthening the comparability of products among themselves – as already proposed by the Resource Commission at the Federal Environment Agency in Germany (Ressourcenkommission am Umweltbundesamt 2017). This state-installed unit for the supervision of mandatory labelling of products in the area of resource efficiency and re-cyclability has the task of collecting, testing and monitoring certain informa-tion to be supplied by companies for products that are placed on the market in Germany or Europe. It verifies whether the product-related information supplied by the manufacturers or distributors complies with the requirements of the labelling unit (Ressourcenkommission am Umweltbundesamt 2017).

The role of Indicators

For measuring the effectiveness of a circular economy in general and par-ticularly in the metals sector, a set of expressive indicators for monitoring the different CE strategies and also for developing benchmarks is needed. There is no comprehensive approach in place for measuring the circular economy, yet (Potting et al. 2017; Pauliuk 2018; Saidani et al. 2019). Ellen MacArthur Foundation identified the four assessment categories for the circular economy: 'resource productivity, circular activities, waste genera-tion, energy and GHG emissions' (Ellen MacArthur Foundation 2015). Considering resource consumption and raw material productivity, the quantity of resources that remains in the economic cycle through recycling is an essential parameter for assessing resource use in the context of the circular economy. By now, most recycling rates in Europe are based on input streams from recovery plants. With this calculation method, the effectiveness of the circular economy cannot be measured in any way. Even if the calculation method based on output flows is to be standardised in future by an initiative of the European Commission, this indicator reflects the quality of the col-lection and recycling infrastructure, but not how much recycled material is actually returned to the economic cycle. The European Commission has developed an indicator framework to establish monitoring for the circular economy beyond this indicator on macro-level (European Commission 2018). Among others, it is proposed to use this framework to map the proportion of recycled material that is returned to the production process. This framework thus meets the requirement for a substitution rate, as demanded by Resource Commission at the Federal Environment Agency in Germany (Ressourcenkomission am Umweltbundesamt 2019).

At the European level, an attempt is made to map this indicator, called EOL-RIR (End-of-life recycling input rates) at the element level and CMU (Circular Material Use rate) at the European level, on the basis of existing statistics. However, for the CMU the same data basis is used for the calculation of recycling quotas. As a result, the significance is not yet sufficiently valid, but the methodological approach is the right way forward. An improvement in the data situation should nevertheless be sought. Nevertheless, the requirements of the Resource Commission at the Federal Environment Agency go beyond this framework. The returned material should not only be identified on element level and European or national level but also derived at the product level. Especially in the context of metals, it is essential to present and ensure differentiation at the functional level.

This approach to a functional substitution rate can only be part of a comprehensive set of indicators against the background of the diverse CE strategies. As Pauliuk (2018), for example, shows, a large number of indicators are currently being discussed at the product and company level as well as at the macro level, which can be used to measure circularity (see also Bringezu & Bleischwitz 2009; Liedtke et al. 2014). In the case of metals, however, the introduction of a functional substitution rate would be an essential first step. This could also show the actual loss of certain functional materials or the positive effects of circular economy strategies.

Specific role: Digitalisation

In the case of metals, digitalisation plays a special role. On the one hand, digitalisation with the corresponding technological infrastructure generates a high demand for metals, which is also encouraged by rapid innovation cycles. The technologies used are thus an outstanding example of complex products. For example, German data centres contain neodymium with a quantity of about 52 t Nd_2O_3 equivalents (calculations based on data from Stobbe et al. 2015). As already described above, however, the quantities per technical unit are very low, the proportion for a hard disk is about 0.72% neodymium (Stobbe et al. 2015).

On the other hand, the question arises how digitalisation can make a constructive contribution to comprehensive metal management and recycling of metals. Digitalisation is leading to fundamental changes in our society. It enables new forms of economic activity through innovative business models and increased efficiency in processes. These positive effects should be seen as an opportunity for the metal industry to further advance the recyclability of metals.

According to the Wuppertal Institute, a lack of information about the nature, quality, quantity and availability of secondary material is the primary barrier. This lack of information tempts companies to hold on to primary materials instead of using recycled materials (Wilts & Berg 2017). The digital transformation offers a number of possibilities to counteract the lack of information. The development of a digital, automated market and logistics platform between supply and recycling companies could provide a cross-company sales area for secondary metals. Such digital market and platform would reduce search and transaction costs and strengthen the competitiveness of secondary raw materials. The use of the block chain technology could prevent data manipulation and ensure the reliability of the specified product information. Cascade benefits between the companies could also be organised directly in the sense of the above-mentioned material logistics. In addition, eliminating the lack of information, digitalisation offers further opportunities to make the recycling of metals more efficient. By using sensor technology, conclusions can be drawn beforehand about the composition of metal scrap. Based on these results, optimal process routes could be determined in real-time based on data analysis applications. Data availability and processing, e.g. through the use of artificial intelligence, must be used to determine and control material flows more precisely. By modelling and simulating the entire value chain of metallurgy, predictions could be made about recycling rates and qualities (Reuter et al. 2019; Reuter 2016). These predictions would make it possible to detect unintended developments at an early stage and take corrective measures accordingly. However, it should be noted that not all companies have the same possibilities to deal with digitalisation issues. In particular, small and medium-sized enterprises do not have the capacity to make high investments and deal with the associated risks. For these companies, a special support from the state should be considered.

Conclusion

Our high-tech society uses an increasing number of metals. These are used in highly complex products and in very low concentrations in relation to functional metals. A circular use of recycling is further complicated apart from the unavoidable and also dissipative losses of such a process. As part of the overall objective of achieving a sustainable society and economy, the aim must be to reduce these losses to a minimum. The sustainable use of metals is a prerequisite for a sustainable industrial society. For this, comprehensive, resource-efficient metal management which is based on the principles of the circular economy must be developed and established. Due to the fact that in the public perception metallic raw materials are often discussed as less urgent than energy or polymer raw materials, this article highlighted the critical role of metals. As pointed out in this contribution different fields play a crucial role in such systematic metal management: the metal industry, eco-design, comprehensive monitoring via indicators and particularly the role of digitalisation for the support of the previous aspects as well as a driver of metal use. These areas were examined in more detail for the implementation of metal management in the context of a circular economy.

In summary, it was shown that the ferrous and non-ferrous industries are essential pillars of the German economy. They are necessary to supply the German industry with basic materials which are used in many sectors such as the construction sector, the automotive sector or the electronics industry. It is essential that the infrastructure of the primary metal production in Germany and Europe are preserved in order to use them for secondary metal production

270 *Kathrin Greiff et al.*

in the future. In addition, the important role of eco-design in the sustainable use of metals was highlighted. Since 80% of all product-related environmental impacts are determined in the design phase, it is important to integrate topics such as resource efficiency, circularity, reuse, modularity, durability and reparability in this phase already. Only in this way, the impact of dissipation can be counteracted in the best way possible. To monitor the progress of change towards a more sustainable economy, an indicator, such as the substitution rate, is needed. The substitution rate is intended to relate the secondary raw materials employed to the total amount of material used. It can also be used to derive specifications at the product level, which in turn are used in eco-design. Digitalisation can play a decisive role here, especially for the processing of the data required.

As shown in this contribution, there are numerous approaches for the development of functional metal management, but there is still a high research need for a holistic implementation. The main aspects are:

- We need an advanced and flexible metallurgical infrastructure – particularly in the case of functional technology materials, new metallurgical structures and logistics systems must be investigated and established.
- We need eco-design standardisation and labelling on product level regarding circularity aspects as recyclability as well as recycling content.
- We need a strong monitoring system that includes a holistic set of indicators, starting with the implementation of a functional substitution rate.
- We must further develop digital techniques and use them to model circular product systems and, thus, holistic metal management.

In this discussion, the product level is identified as a critical starting point. Thus, these aspects and conclusions can be arranged along with the steps of a general product life cycle as shown in Table 22.1, to demonstrate which measures should be addressed at which life cycle stages (according to Greiff & Faulstich 2018). A bottom-up approach seems to be the best option for metal management at political and industrial level and should be pursued further. Overall, it can be concluded that there will be no circular use of metals without the use of virgin metal. But today we are still a long way from an optimal state and are wasting and, above all, losing a large part of the raw materials that are important to us and which we will never be able to recover in this way. That is why the role of metals at all levels should be given particular importance.

Abbreviations

CE   circular economy
CEC   cumulative energy consumption
CMU   circular material use rate
CO_2 carbon dioxide

Table 22.1 Aspects for a resource-efficient metal management according to products life cycle steps

Life cycle step	Aspects of resource-efficient metal management
Design for circularity and sustainability	Optimisation of product design
	Focus on service design and user needs (target group and benefit specification)
	Integration of indicators for circularity in the design and development process: focus on longevity, reparability and recyclability using modelling or simulation tools
	Focus on product-service systems combined with new business models
	Cooperation with all further life cycle stages
Resource extraction	Concentrations of useful materials will decrease while the environmental impact will increase
	Resource efficiency can be improved by mining fewer raw materials
Production of primary material	Technically optimisation of production process within thermodynamic equilibriums
	Noticeable increases in efficiency by substituting materials
	Closing and decreasing internal material loops along the life cycle or value chain
Production of goods	Optimisation of production processes
	Material efficiency through Remanufacturing or Refurbishment
	Legal requirements for the content of recycled materials
Use of goods	Extension of service life through technical and design aspects or leasing systems
	Use of reparable and recyclable products
	A shift in demand patterns towards consumption of less material-intensive goods or services via product information and labelling
End-of-life (EoL) management	Monitoring of EoL management success by expressive indicators, implementation of standards
	High collection and separation rates by optimisation of infrastructure
	Consideration and cooperation with product development or design phase

EoL	end of life
EOL-RIR	end of life recycling input rate
EU	European Union
GHG	greenhouse gas
Gt	gigatonnes
IPCC	International Panel on Climate Change
IPP	Integrated Product Policy
Nd2O3	neodymium (III) oxide
t	tonnes
UNEP	United Nations Environmental Programme

References

bcs (2016). *Neue bcs-Studie: Mehr Platz zum Leben – wie CarSharing Städte entlastet.* CarSharing fact sheet Nr. 2. Available at: http://carsharing.de/sites/default/files/uploads/bcs_factsheet_nr.2_0.pdf. (Accessed: 5 June 2019).

Bookhagen, B. et al. (2018). '*Rohstoffverbrauch von Smartphones*', In Thiel, S., Thomé-Kozmiensky, E., and Goldmann, D. (eds). Recycling und Rohstoffe – Band 11, pp. 519–532, TK Verlag Karl Thomé-Kozmiensky.

Bringezu, S. and Bleischwitz, R. (2009). *Sustainable Resource Management: Global Trends, Visions and Policies.* Sheffield, UK: Greenleaf.

Clausen, J., Bowry, J. and Bienge, K. (2017). *Five Shades of Sharing Eine Szenariogeschichte Rund Um Die Haken Und Ösen Der Sharing Economy.* Berlin: Borderstep Institut. www.borderstep.de/wp-content/uploads/2017/08/NsB-Ress_5-Shades-7.pdf. (Accessed: 5 June 2019).

Directive (2009). 'Directive 2009/125/EC of the European Parliament and of the Council of 21 October 2009 Establishing a Framework for the Setting of Ecodesign Requirements for Energy-Related Products', *Official Journal of the European Communities.*

Distelkamp, M., Meyer, B. and Moghayer, S. (2015). 'Report about Integrated Scenario Interpretation. Deliverable 3.7a of the POLFREE project'. Available at: www.ucl.ac.uk/polfree/publications/publications-2014/report-d37c.pdf (Accessed: 22 August 2019).

Ellen MacArthur Foundation (2015). *Circularity Indicators: An Approach to Measuring Circularity Project Overview.* Ellen MayArthur Foundation. Available at: www.ellenmacarthurfoundation.org/assets/downloads/insight/Circularity-Indicators_Project-Overview_May2015.pdf (Accessed: 14 February 2019).

Elshkaki, A. et al. (2018). 'Resource Demand Scenarios for the Major Metals', *Environmental Science and Technology*, 52(5), pp. 2491–2497. doi: 10.1021/acs.est.7b05154.

European Commission (2017). *Study on the Review of the List of Critical Raw Materials. Criticality Assessments.* European Commission. Available at: http://hytechcycling.eu/wp-content/uploads/Study-on-the-review-of-the-list-of-Critical-Raw-Materials.pdf (Accessed: 20 March 2019).

European Commission (2018). *Measuring Progress towards Circular Economy in the European Union – Key Indicators for a Monitoring Framework.* European Commission. Available at: http://ec.europa.eu/environment/circular-economy/pdf/monitoring-framework_staff-working-document.pdf (Accessed: 24 January 2019).

European Commission (2019). *Commission Staff Working Document. Sustainable Products in a Circular Economy – Towards an EU Product Policy Framework contributing to the Circular Economy.* European Commission. Available at: http://ec.europa.eu/environment/circular-economy/pdf/sustainable_products_circular_economy.pdf (Accessed: 20 March 2019).

European Environment Agency (2016). *Circular Economy in Europe Developing the Knowledge Base. Luxembourg: Publications Office of the European Union.* Copenhagen: European Environment Agency. Available at: https://doi.org/10.2800/51444.

European Environment Agency (2017). *Circular by Design – Products in the Circular Economy.* EEA Report, No. 6/2017. Copenhagen: European Environment Agency.

Frischenschlager, H. et al. (2010). Klimarelevanz ausgewählter Recycling-Prozesse in Österreich.

Fröhlich, P. et al. (2017). 'Valuable Metals-Recovery Processes, Current Trends, and Recycling Strategies', *Angewandte Chemie*, 56(10), pp. 2544–2580. doi: 10.1002/anie.201605417.

Greiff, K., and Faulstich, M. (2018). 'Resource Efficiency:Trends and Thepotential of Circular Economy'. CEC4Europe. www.cec4europe.eu/wp-content/uploads/2018/11/

Chapter-4.5_Ressource-Efficiency_Factbook-CEC4E_Faulstich_Greiff.pdf (Accessed: 6 February 2019).

Greiff, K. and Liedtke, C. (2019). 'Design für Kreislaufwirtschaft: Ausstieg aus der Wegwerfgesellschaft!', *EntsorgaMagazin* 2–8, 4.

IPCC (2018). *Global Warming of 1.5 °C. An IPCC Special Report on the Impacts of Global Warming of 1.5 °C above Pre-industrial Levels and Related Global Greenhouse Gas Emission Pathways, in the Context of Strengthening the Global Response to the Threat of Climate Change.* Edited by V. Masson-Delmotte et al. doi: 10.1017/CBO9781107415324.

Liedtke, C. (2018). *Design for Sustainability*. A UNA–UK online publication. Available at: www.sustainablegoals.org.uk/design-for-sustainability/ (Accessed: 6 May 2019).

Liedtke, C., Buhl, J. and Ameli, N. (2013a). 'Designing Value through Less by Integrating Sustainability Strategies into Lifestyles', *International Journal of Sustainable Design*, 2(2), p. 167. doi: 10.1504/IJSDES.2013.057124.

Liedtke, C., Buhl, J. and Ameli, N. (2013b). 'Microfoundations for Sustainable Growth with Eco-Intelligent Product Service-Arrangements', *Sustainability*, 5(3), pp. 1141–1160. doi: 10.3390/su5031141.

Liedtke, C. et al. (2014). 'Resource Use in the Production and Consumption System – The MIPS Approach'. *Resources*, 3(3), pp. 544–574.

Liedtke, C., Baedeker, C., Hasselkuß, M., Rohn, H. and Grinewitschus, V. (2015). 'User-Integrated Innovation in Sustainable LivingLabs: An Experimental Infrastructure for Researching and Developing Sustainable Product Service Systems'. *Journal of Cleaner Production*, 97, 106–116. https://doi.org/10.1016/j.jclepro.2014.04.070.

Marscheider-Weidemann, F. et al. (2016). *Rohstoffe für Zukunftstechnologien 2016*, DERA Rohstoffinformationen 28. Deutsche Rohstoffagentur (DERA) in der Bundesanstalt für Geowissenschaften und Rohstoffe (BGR). Berlin.

Pauliuk, S. (2018). 'Critical Appraisal of the Circular Economy Standard BS 8001:2017 and a Dashboard of Quantitative System Indicators for its Implementation in Organizations', *Resources, Conservation and Recycling*, 129, pp. 81–92. https://doi.org/10.1016/j.resconrec.2017.10.019.

Potting, J. et al. (2017). 'Circular Economy: Measuring Innovation in the Product Chain. Policy Report'. PBL Netherlands Environmental Assessment Agency, The Hague. Available at: www.pbl.nl/sites/default/files/cms/publicaties/pbl-2016-circular-economy-measuring-innovation-in-product-chains-2544.pdf (Accessed: 6 February 2019).

Ressourcenkomission am Umweltbundesamt (2017). 'Position der Ressourcenkommission am umweltbundesamt. Produktkennzeichnungsstelle zur Förderung der Ressourceneffizienz und Kreislauffähigkeit von Produkten'. Umweltbundesamt (UBA). Available at: www.umweltbundesamt.de/sites/default/files/medien/1968/publikationen/kru_produktkennzeich-nungsstelle.pdf.

Ressourcenkommission am Umweltbundesamt (2019). 'Position der Ressourcenkommission. Substitutionsquote: Ein realistischer Erfolgsmaßstab für die Kreislaufwirtschaft!' Umweltbundesamt (UBA). Available at: www.umweltbundesamt.de/sites/default/files/medien/421/publikationen/190722_uba_kommp_substitutionsquote_bf.pdf (Accessed: 22 August 2019).

Reuter, M. A. (2016). 'Digitalizing the Circular Economy', *Metallurgical and Materials Transactions B.* Springer US, 47(6), pp. 3194–3220. doi: 10.1007/s11663-016-0735-5.

Reuter, M. A. et al. (2019). 'Challenges of the Circular Economy: A Material, Metallurgical, and Product Design Perspective', *Annual Review of Materials Research*, 49(1), pp. 253–274. doi: 10.1146/annurev-matsci-070218-010057.

Reuter, M. A. and Van Schaik, A. (2016). 'Recycling Indices Visualizing the Performance of the Circular Economy', *World of Metallurgy – Erzmetall*, 69(August), p. 4.

Reuter, M. A., Van Schaik, A. and Ballester, M. (2018). 'Limits of the Circular Economy: Fairphone Modular Design Pushing the Limits', *World Metall. – Erzmetall*, 71(2), pp. 68–79. doi: 10.1016/j.neuron.2008.10.014.Destabilization.

Saidani, M. et al. (2019). 'A Taxonomy of Circular Economy Indicators', *Journal of Cleaner Production*, 207, pp. 542–559. https://doi.org/10.1016/j.jclepro.2018.10.014.

Schneidewind, U. (2014). 'Urbane Reallabore – ein Blick in die aktuelle Forschungswerkstatt', *Pnd Online*, 3, pp. 1–7.

Schoch, K. (2019). 'Normierung für Reuse und Recycling. Masterarbeit'. Burg Giebichenstein Kunsthochschule University of Art and Design.

Steffen, W. et al. (2015). 'Planetary Boundaries: Guiding Human Development on a Changing Planet', *Science*, 347(6223), pp. 1259855–1259855. doi: 10.1126/science.1259855.

Steger, S. et al. (2019). Stoffstromorientierte Ermittlung des Beitrags der Sekundärroh- stoffwirtschaft zur Schonung von Primärrohstoffen und Steigerung der Ressourcenproduktivität, Texte 34/2019. Umweltbundesamt.

Stobbe, L. et al. (2015). *Entwicklung des IKT-bedingten Strombedarfs in Deutschland*. Fraunhofer-Institut für Zuverlässigkeit und Mikrointegration (IZM). Berlin.

Teubler, J., Kiefer, S. and Liedtke, C. (2018). 'Metals for Fuels? The Raw Material Shift by Energy-Efficient Transport Systems in *Europe*'. *Resources*, 7(3), p. 49. doi: 10.3390/resources7030049.

Tischner, U. and Moser, H. (2015). *How to Ecodesign*. Umweltbundesamt.

UNEP (2011). *Recycling Rates of Metals: A Status Report*. A Report of the Working Group on the Global Metal Flows to the International Resource Panel. Nairobi: United Nations Environment Programme.

UNEP (2013). *Environmental Risks and Challenges of Anthropogenic Metals Flows and Cycles*. Nairobi: United Nations Environment Programme.

Wilts, H. and Berg, H. (2017). Digitale Kreislaufwirtschaft – Die Digitale Transformation als Wegbereiter ressourcenschonender Stoffkreisläufe, in brief 04/2017.

Wilts, H. and von Gries, N. (2017). 'Der schwere Weg zur Kreislaufwirtschaft', *GWP – Gesellschaft. Wirtschaft. Politik*, 66(1), pp. 23–28. doi: 10.3224/gwp.v66i1.02.

Wirtschaftsvereinigung Metalle (2018). *Metallstatistik 2017*. Available at: www.wvmetalle.de/fileadmin/uploads/public/Metallstatistik/Metallstatistik_2017.pdf. (Accessed: 22 August 2019).

Wirtschaftsvereinigung Stahl. 'Fakten Zur Stahlindustrie in Deutschland 2017', 2018. Available at: www.stahl-online.de/wp-content/uploads/2017/12/Fakten_Stahlindustrie_2017_rz_web.pdf. (Accessed: 22 August 2019).

Zepf, V., A. Reller, C. Rennie, M. Ashfield, and J. Simmons (2014). *Materials Critical to the Energy Industry. An Introduction*. 2nd Edition. Augsburg: University of Augsburg. Available at: www.mrm.uni-augsburg.de/de/gruppen/reller/downloads/Materials_Handbook_Rev_2012.pdf (Accessed: 22 August 2019).

23 The nexus of procurement and sustainability

Reflection of the limits and opportunities of product labels, using the example of the Forest Stewardship Council

Uwe Sayer and Nina Griesshammer

Introduction

The Forest Stewardship Council (FSC) established a set of rules on how forest management should be done in an ecologically and socially responsible way in the nineties. The idea was (and is) to use market tools such as certification and labels to encourage better forest management practices through demand driven by retailers and consumers. The underlying concerns, at that time, were the constant loss of forests and the maintenance of a relevant renewable source of timber and re fibre. Over the years, FSC has grown to a global system with around 200 Mio. ha of forests FSC certified and more than 38.000 companies associated worldwide. While FSC steadily improved upon its system and is perceived as one of the most trusted brand around responsible forest management worldwide, the nexus of a sustainability label remains. Products carrying a sustainability label (for example on forestry) stand for responsible procurement and wood or fibre product whereas a lot of basic fundamental remain open and unaddressed through the label such as sustainable production in processing or resource efficiency. While this becomes a growing global concern, this chapter reflects this nexus and formulates roles for various groups.

Certification and labels in a changing environment

While markets and consumer recognition of FSC grew steadily over the last years – up to 50% in Germany (prompted, EMNID 2019), expectations and perception on certification and labels also changed.

In the late nineties, certification systems were expected to change the conditions for the production of goods worldwide significantly. Certification contributes to defined requirements for use of resources and/or requirements on production processes worldwide. However new challenges need to be addressed by innovative ways of production and consumption. These challenges are climate change, loss of biodiversity and the pollution of ecosystems, water and soils, use of pesticides and fertilisers through a global intensification of land-use systems.

The growing market relevance and consumer recognition of certification systems and labels led to a reaction from competing market players resulting in various labels used in all sectors. Consumer protection organisations in Germany describe this process as a 'jungle of labels'. They have thus generated tools and platforms to help consumers distinguish between the meanings of the existing labels. Consequently, the media continually evaluates if labels do deliver what they aimed for and if they have a benefit for society. It is remarkable that the evaluation of labels is mostly not based on their own missions and values, but includes more current challenges of production. Some of those aspects may be far beyond current scopes of the related labelling-systems such as climate change and production intensification. As a consequence, the gap between expectations and the reality of systems like FSC acting in a complex, constantly shifting market combined with rapidly changing environmental conditions becomes bigger and bigger. Solutions are not easy to create and are picked up in the following chapter.

The concept of the FSC system

One of the founding ideas of FSC was (and is) a balance between economic, social and environmental aspects in forestry. As a result, FSC developed a 3-chamber-system giving all those aspects equal decision power. Sustainable management needs to integrate social and environmental values in their operational work far beyond what is usually understood as legal or acceptable.

To achieve balance, FSC has its members divided into three chambers: an economic, a social and an environmental chamber. In relevant decisions, all chambers have the same voting rights, and if needed because of the objection of a whole chamber, there is veto power. So according to FSC standard development processes for sustainable forestry need to follow this basic decision principle of considering all three chambers. Examples are international or national board decisions, member decisions or national standard-setting processes.

Primarily, FSC is responsible for forest management. The basis for this is FSC forest standards with national adaptions. After approval by FSC, forest enterprises have to use these standards as a basis for their forest management if they aim for an FSC certification. Independent certification bodies verify the compliance of forest owners with FSC requirements on a yearly basis.

FSC standards ask for:

- compliance with legislation;
- the establishment of consolidated management plans;
- special attention to environmental issues such as the use of pesticides, identification and special treatment of highly valuable and often sensible ecosystems, special treatment of forests along water lines, enhancement of biodiversity through setting aside forest areas;
- safeguards for working conditions in forests;

Limits and opportunities of product labels 277

- compliance with ILO conventions (ILO n.d.); and
- concepts to address unsolved land-use conflicts through FPIC (United Nations 2013).

After a successful audit, forest enterprise can label and sell their products as FSC certified. In the following processing and trading chain, all companies buying and selling certified materials need to be FSC certified if they want to use the FSC claim. As a consequence, they need to be compliant with the technical requirements for processing and trading of FSC certified materials (Chain of custody certification or COC certification). These technical requirements mainly address the physical product such as assembling, reassembling in new packaging formats, mixing with recycling or non-certified materials, among others. The intention of these COC certificates is mainly that FSC claims on products are correct.

New FSC dimensions in processing and trade

A vast variety of environmental and social questions such as recyclability, efficient resources, health questions in production, safe working conditions or fair salaries are not fully covered by COC certification of most environmental and social production labels.

On social issues, FSC in recent years decided to request compliance with minimum social requirements in COC certificates. FSC certified companies in the supply chain must make sure that work is done in compliance with ILO conventions. This global process still has some outstanding and unresolved questions for the implementation and affects around 50.000 FSC certified companies throughout all supply chains worldwide.

On environmental issues, there are also some minimum requirements requested by FSC-companies who want to mix not-certified materials to FSC-certified products. From the very beginning, discussions arose allowing mixing of FSC certified materials with recycling fibres of non-certified materials, particularly in large scale fibre-based industry processes such as pulp, paper or panels. In 1997 first policies have been published (FSC policy for Percentage-Based Claims) in which mixing of wooden materials was allowed under certain conditions. Conditions like continually increasing the FSC certified parts as well as safeguarding minimum environmental and social requirements for the non-certified parts. In the meantime, this concept has evolved into the global concept of Controlled Wood (CW). In this concept, FSC clearly defines unacceptable practices for non-certified wood sources which cannot be mixed with FSC certified materials and need to be avoided by companies (FSC 2017).

These are:

- illegally harvested wood;
- wood harvested in violation of traditional and human rights;

- wood harvested in forests in which high conservation values (HCVs) are threatened by management activities (HCVs are areas particularly worthy of protection);
- wood harvested in forests being converted to plantations or non-forest use; and
- wood from forests in which genetically modified trees are planted.

Besides evaluating the wood streams from FSC certified materials, companies usually need to evaluate their whole wood supply with the controlled wood categories to produce FSC mix-products.

Changes in production and trade through the FSC approach

One fundamental concept used by FSC is the demand or the market-driven approach: The more FSC products are requested in markets, the more forest enterprises have market incentives to certify their forests and sell FSC products.

This has worked pretty well in the last 20 years in Germany based on the fact that relevant partners support FSC publicly and generate credibility. In Germany, FSC is supported by most of the well-recognised environmental organisations such as WWF or NABU (German affiliate of birdlife) as well as the big Labour Unions (IG BAU, IG Metall). Internal global evaluations clearly show that a strong reputation, a trusted brand and credibility are the most relevant aspects for companies to work with FSC followed by global coverage, expertise and efficiency. Based on FSCs balanced 3-chamber approach, social and environmental organisations know that their views are properly reflected in FSCs regulations. As a result, they actively support FSC as a system which helps to implement better social and environmental standards in global forestry and also demonstrates credibility towards society. Utilising FSC in the corporate sector incorporates this credibility into businesses when they sell or produce FSC products. Due to the governance structure, the support from credible partners and then the collaboration with the corporate sector, FSC products are vastly present in German markets covering most of the existing wood and fibre sectors.

Prominent examples of transforming markets through demand

Not only the private corporate sector but also the public procurement sector needs to address concerns around responsible sourcing. With the growing relevance of forest certification schemes, various governments decided to incorporate certification as requirements in the public procurement protocols. In Germany, FSC was mentioned as a possible verification of responsible sourcing for wooden products in public procurements starting in 2007 until today.

In growing markets, the supply situation for FSC material is the limiting factor, but still, companies hesitate to formulate strong procurement policies since they could be publicly denounced. The reasons are that procurement policies are strong tools that demonstrate social and environmentalcommitments. If they are not carefully phrased and properly implemented, they have been interpreted as unambitious and as green-washing. At the same time procurement policies are powerful tools for corporate companies to communicate mid- and long-term goals for specific products.

In the paper and wood sector, there are prominent examples where companies publicly state their expectations towards suppliers for FSC certified wood and paper. Examples are:

- Lidl (Lidl Deutschland 2018): Publication of a position paper requesting all fresh-fibre in food packaging, household and tissue articles changed to Recycling or FSC until the end of 2018. Until 2020 expansion to all textiles, garden articles, furniture, toys, decoration articles, media, stationery, tools and instruction manuals. These sourcing requirements are embedded in a strategic frame of saving resources, the increase of recycled materials and the use of certified fresh fibres.
- Aldi 2018: Aldi North and Aldi South published a timber sourcing policy. Aldi North is explicitly requesting FSC certified wood if products are sourced in risk countries.
- EDEKA (EDEKA 2019): Announcement to shift sourcing of wood, paper and tissue to sustainable sources with Blue Angel or − in case of fresh fibre − to FSC certified sources. On packaging and Edeka owned brands, this was already implemented by the end of 2017.
- OTTO (Otto Group 2019): As part of the CR strategy 2020 FSC certified catalogue paper is planned to be increased to 60% by 2020 and furniture to 100% by 2025.
- IKEA (IKEA 2018): Public policy for 100% FSC certified wood or recycling by 2020.

FSC's impacts on the ground

With growing relevance, there are growing concerns and critical questions on systems like FSC: Are the aims reached and does the system deliver what it promises consumers through its products? Answers are not always easy to give.

Within national standards like the German FSC standard for forest management, it is comparably easy to phrase what the standard requires from forest owners. Relevant examples in Germany are regulations on tree species composition, set aside areas, definition and treatment of high conservation areas, biotope wood, skid trails, safer working conditions, and minimum salaries (including for external subcontractors). Through analysis of corrective actions from the audit, it can be evaluated which issues arise in Germany forest

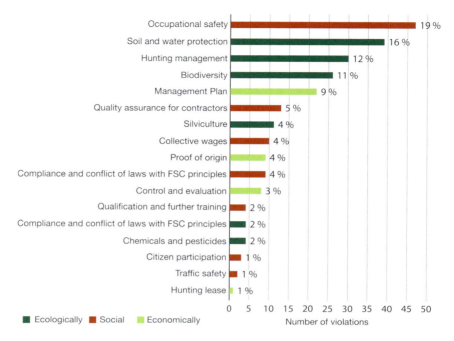

Figure 23.1 Distribution of the analysed corrective action requests divided into different categories, shown as percentages. Issues of corrective action requests through the FSC certification towards German FSC-certified forest enterprises and their relevance/ranking.

enterprises. Most relevant issues are corrections in safety equipment for woodworkers and issues around soil, water, hunting and biodiversity (Strasser & Litschel 2017).

Besides these indirect approaches, there are scientific studies evaluating the impact of FSC. Usually, scientific studies are not easily accessible and are difficult to understand for people outside the scientific world. At the same time, the role of science is to work independently within defined and accepted methods on issues delivering answers to relevant questions of our time. The number of studies evaluating FSC worldwide with scientific approaches is limited but continuously growing. Many studies conclude that FSC has positive impacts on relevant questions, for example, concerning social or environmental issues. Here two relevant examples:

- *Does forest certification really work?* This study (Dasgupta & Burivalova 2017) evaluates the effects of FSC certification in tropical forests separated into environmental, social and economic impacts. An interactive website allows the filtering of specific issues and distinguishes between stronger and weaker evidence regarding the impacts of FSC certification.

Limits and opportunities of product labels 281

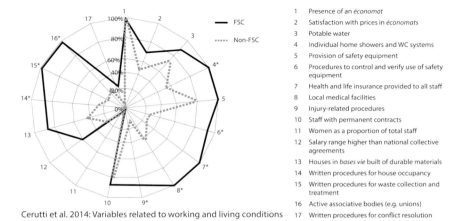

Figure 23.2 Variables related to working and living conditions.

    The study clearly shows a significant positive impact on environmental and social questions through FSC certification.
- *Social impacts of the Forest Stewardship Council certification: An assessment in the Congo basin.* This study (Cerutti et al. 2014) compares FSC-certified with non-FSC-certified operations in central Africa in large areas. The results clearly show positive impacts on many social issues.

The middle of the nexus: perceptions of consumers on sustainable production and labelled products

Current sustainability labels are usually designed to address environmental and social issues around land use and the management of their commodities (i.e. timber from forests, soy/palm oil/cattle breeding from converted farmland, fish from fishery). Besides production aspects, new questions are arising and expected to be covered in environmentally friendly and socially fair labels such as regional sourcing or environmental and social standards in the following processing chain. An example of an existing consumer label already covering various of those aspects including sourcing, processing and health, is the German Blue Angel. The Blue Angel was founded to make environmentally friendly products visible to consumers. Issues touched by the Blue Angel for example with paper products are the use of recycling materials as well as many processing aspects like water pollution, water consumption, energy consumption, use of chemicals and health aspects.

    Beyond those aspects, there are even more questions not addressed at all in current sustainability labels around general resource efficiency such as re-cyclability, efficient use of products, regional sourcing versus far transportation combined with life-cycle-assessments or general questions of the overall ecological/CO_2-footprint of the product. Some of those aspects may qualify for future labelling generations (i.e. recyclability, transport, CO_2-footprint, transparency around life-cycle) while general consumption patterns may by concept not fit with the idea of labelling based on a consumer-driven concept.

NGOs and consumer organisations have over the years touched on some of those questions with conceptional approaches. As early as 2006, a process supported by 48 environmental organisations started phrasing a transformation process for the European paper industry. In 2014 the concept was expanded to a global paper vision formally supported by 108 environmental organisations worldwide (Environmental Paper Network 2014).

The vision phrases seven points for the use and the production of paper in a hierarchical order:

- reduce global paper consumption and promote fair access to paper;
- maximise recycled fibre content;
- ensure social responsibility;
- source fibre responsibly;
- reduce greenhouse gas emissions;
- ensure clean production; and
- ensure transparency and integrity.

The vision includes various opportunities for existing labels like the Blue Angel or FSC certified products. FSC is mentioned as a solution in 'sourcing fibre responsibly'. The vision shows that current expectations from the majority of environmental groups worldwide not only demand responsible sourcing and processing of products but also includes general questions on consumption patterns and personal behaviour beforehand. But even in this vision, a general concept of resource efficiency is not fully covered and addressed.

In the authors' view there is currently no satisfying answer that adequately addresses the responsible use of products including sourcing, processing, use and recycling with the question of consumption as such or an effective or 'wise' use of products in regards to the general challenge of over-consumption of global goods in a world of growing population. Further actions from all involved parties with a high responsibility for public policies and rules are needed.

The certification dilemma

As a demand-driven system, FSC relies to a large extent, and by concept, on the consumption of products. The more FSC products are sold and consumed, the higher the interest for market partners to demand more FSC certified materials with the effect of more certified forest area worldwide where FSC standards are implemented. This dynamic somehow 'releases' consumers from the responsibility to rethink existing consumption patterns. It also 'releases' retailers to reflect very generally the concept of 'selling of more products' or the underlying driving concept of economic growth. There is currently no guiding principles or legal safeguards in selling products with highly negative environmental or social impact. Examples for this is the sale of fresh fibre-based tissue paper, whereas recycling fibre-based tissue paper would be a more appropriate alternative. Similar aspects are concern around the packaging of products, recyclability of goods or effective use of primary products (durable products versus non-durable or throw-away-products).

Following this way of thinking, there is a big bundle of unaddressed questions going beyond the responsible production of goods. Particularly in times of a rapid climate change the following relevant aspects, most of them not touched and covered by sustainability labels like the FSC, include:

- general reduction of consumption;
- increased use of recycled products;
- avoidance of environmentally damaging products (examples for wooden products could be composite products based on wood fibres and plastic);
- transparency on environmental or social impacts on product;
- promoting products with longer life-cycles and reduction of on non-returnable materials;
- considerations of cascading use of products;
- promotion and use of recyclable products; and
- reduction of unnecessary packaging and rethinking or packaging as such (including the replacement of plastic and environmentally unfriendly packaging to sustainable packaging or multiple uses of packaging).

NGOs observe a lack of coordinated approaches and the need for more broadly accepted definitions (i.e. on origin, life-cycle information, social and environmental impacts) and the urgent need for policy harmonisation at all levels of production and trade (i.e. policymakers, researchers, industry).

Within this situation, existing labels remain in the dilemma of delivering positive impacts in some production areas (i.e. FSC delivering products based on environmental and social standards in forestry) while not addressing major questions beyond production and sourcing (see above). As a consequence, the media and major NGOs carefully reflect on their support and their engagement in such systems. Some NGOs balance their work and invest in both (support for responsible primary production and sourcing as well as towards policy work for global consumption aspects) while others focus their engagement more on the broader issue of consumption and the life-cycle of products.

Beyond the dilemma – discussion of possible solutions and recommendations

It is very clear that a general call for less consumption, cascading use of products or alternative products (recycling, recyclability etc.) is at least not simple to touch on with existing tools if these are acting in isolation. It is also very clear that particularly the demand for less consumption is partly in contradiction to the demand-driven approach of labelling schemes. However, some labelling schemes are asking for a change of the management of, for example, land-use and that change could also work and go hand in hand with 'good management' and 'less consumption'.

For sustainability labels like FSC, a good way forward is not trivial. Key questions are if the system should expand its scope to broader sustainability aspects, through increasing complexity or if the systems should focus on its core competences at the risk of working in isolation of broader aspects of responsible consumption.

The authors do not want to give a ready-made answer both on the best way forward, nor on the most likely scenario in which sustainability labels will evolve in the upcoming years rather than contribute to a needed debate about the future role of sustainability labels. Regardless of the development of existing labels, it is very clear, that voluntary demand-driven consumer labels will not be able to touch on the question of consuming as such. Therefore the most likely scenario will be, that systems like FSC remain focussing mainly on the implementation of environmental and social standards in forestry worldwide. As a consequence, the dilemma can only be solved with intelligent combinations of various tools and the embedding of existing labelling systems like FSC in broader concepts. Here are some recommendations of processes to address the dilemma:

Role for all

Most of all modern societies, particularly, in the more developed part of the world, need to rethink their consumption patterns generally. We all need to act more environmentally and socially responsible and need to recognize the limits of the planet. By doing so, this automatically would require less consumption of everything (i.e. change in diet, change in mobility, change in energy consumption). Sustainability labels can only contribute in a positive way if consumption patterns as such are changing. Inhabitants of more developed countries with extremely higher consumption rates are much more in global responsibility than countries with high rates of poverty and low living standards.

This shift will need a fundamental change in personal attitude and behaviour. Parts of this can be done through voluntary and personal changes, the major part of this may require public incentives or legal safeguards.

A part of doing so would be a changed and more honest communication. 'Climate-friendly' has, for example, to be replaced by 'less climate-damaging' in cases where resources are used. Other examples are that 'more consumption of good products' is not necessarily 'better' compared with reduced consumption. Communication needs to be adjusted accordingly at all levels. To name things as they are is a way of taking responsibility and explaining their real picture.

Limits and opportunities of product labels 285

Role of governments

From the authors view the main reason is that a global shift towards less growth and an adjustment and reduction of consumption will have overall positive effects for the society because it can contribute to halting the climate crisis. However, individuals, particularly in more developed countries, could perceive this as adverse effects and would not be supportive pro-actively. As a consequence, individual and corporate behaviour in those areas can only be addressed through administrative actions and related legislations. Possible starting points could be:

- Changes in general frameworks: support of activities and programs need generally be evaluated against positive changes in social and environmental regards and not mainly based on economic considerations. This includes incentives for reduced consumption as well as incentives for more intelligent and efficient resource use (e.g. wood in construction rather than in the energy sector, support for cascading approaches in the use of products etc.).
- Consumption policies including hierarchical views for consumption and production rather than developing sector policies (example: incentives for cascading of products before using forest products directly in the energy sector).
- Tax-systems (i.e. CO_2-taxes) favouring products along the line of responsible consumption.
- Support for sustainability labelling systems. 'Best in class' systems need clear advantages. Evaluations need to be done and published independently of political positions.
- Strict control, consequent and efficient implementation of existing policies already contributing to responsible production and consumption (i.e. EUTR, public procurement policies).
- Establishment of tools to seriously support and implement cascading of product uses.
- Active support of positive examples in responsible sourcing and responsible use of products (i.e. recycling, recyclable, cascading use).
- Public information campaigns about responsible production and responsible consumption at all levels.
- Leading by example to generate spillover effects.
- Shift to an ecological and socially responsible procurement as a legal requirement to operate in all public institutions (e.g. ministries, schools, universities).

Role of the corporate sector

Companies need to adjust products and behaviour to the modern needs of the globe. This goes beyond cost-considerations.

On the product side, need to work on more sustainable products beyond responsible sourcing, including aspects such as recyclability of products, a conceptional shift from non-returnable products to long-living products, reducing packaging, CO_2-considerations, among others.

Beyond products, companies need to rethink and adjust sustainability behaviour at all levels of their footprints, including, procurement, mobility, energy, water, among others.

Role of the media

Much more than in the past, the media needs to shed light on the views of the sectors in the context of the overall picture of responsible production and responsible consumption. A growing role in this regard could be to call out companies not properly delivering on their goals and not behaving accountable. Moreover, to support opinion-building with clear, fact-based honest and frank communication.

Role of NGOs

NGOs could have two roles in this change. On the one hand, there is a consequent need for information on existing labels and on a hierarchical view on consumption (as for example stated in the global paper vision). There is a need for a global 'consumption vision' or 'global product vision' including aspects of reduction, recycling, sourcing, recyclability, cascading, life-cycle etc.. The second role for NGOs is to remain a pressure group towards public authorities, governments and companies to push this change.

Role of existing sustainability labels

Certification systems need to continually evaluate their role in supporting responsible production, processing and trade. At the same time the alliance of sustainability labels needs to continually reflect whether it can contribute in positive ways at the level of overall consumption through mutual communication and strategic exchange with the global retail sector.

Further developments of existing labels should always evaluate if current society (means stakeholder and interest groups) needs are incorporated in technical solutions and if relevant stakeholder groups do support existing solutions and contents of the relevant system.

Abbreviations

COC   chain of custody
CR   Corporate responsibilty
CW   controlled wood
EUTR   European Timber Regulation

FPIC	free prior informed consent
FSC	Forest Stewardship Council
HCV	high conservation value
IG BAU	Industiergewertschaft Bauen Agrar Umwelt
IG Metall	Industriegewerkschaft Metall
ILO	International Labour Organization
NABU	Naturschutzbund Deutschland
NGO	non-governmental organization
WWF	World Wide Fund for Nature

References

Cerutti, P. O., Lescuyer, G., Tsanga, R., Kassa, S. N., Mapangou, P. R., Mendoula, E. E., Missamba-Lola, A. P., Nasi, R., Eckebil, P. P. T., and Yembe, R. Y. (2014). Social impacts of the Forest Stewardship Council certification: An assessment in the Congo basin. *Occasional Paper 103*. CIFOR, Bogor, Indonesia. URL: https://cifor.org/library/4487/ (09.09.2019).

Dasgupta, S. and Burivalova, Z. (2017). URL: https://news.mongabay.com/2017/09/does-forest-certification-really-work/ (09.09.2019).

EDEKA (2019). *Nachhaltige Waldwirtschaft*, EDEKA. URL: www.edeka.de/nachhaltigkeit/unsere-wwf-partnerschaft/holz-paper-tissue/index.jsp (12.09.2019).

Environmental Paper Network (2014). *The Global Paper Vision*. URL: https://environmentalpaper.org/epn-vision/vision/ (12.09.2019).

FSC (2017). *Requirements for Sourcing FSC Controlled Wood FSC-STD-40-005 V3-1 EN*. URL: https://fsc.org/en/document-center/documents/170 (06.09.2019).

IKEA (2018). *Materialien & Rohstoffe bei IKEA*. URL: www.ikea.com/de/de/this-is-ikea/sustainable-everyday/materialien-und-rohstoffe-bei-ikea-pub971c9d11#~Holz%20ist%20der%20Kern%20von%20IKEA (12.09.2019).

ILO (n.d.). *ILO Conventions and Recommendations*. URL: https://ilo.org/global/standards/introduction-to-international-labour-standards/conventions-and-recommendations/lang--en/index.htm (06.09.2019).

Lidl Deutschland (2018). *Positionspapierfür den nachhaltigeren Einkauf von zellulose-haltigen Eigenmarken-produkten und Verpackungen*. URL: www.lidl.de/de/asset/other/16201_FLY_Positionspapier_Zellulose_A4_DE_2_online.pdf (12.9.2019).

Otto Group (2019). Geschäftsbericht 2018/2019 Otto Group. URL: https://ottogroup.com/media/docs/de/geschaeftsbericht/Otto_Group_Geschaeftsbericht_2018_19_DE.pdf (12.09.2019).

Strasser, M. and Litschel, J. (2017). FSC Forstbetriebe unter der Lupe; AFZ-DerWald 2/2017.

United Nations (2013). *Free, Prior and Informed Consent of Indigenous Peoples*. URL: www.ohchr.org/Documents/Issues/ipeoples/freepriorandinformedconsent.pdf (06.09.2019).

24 The role of biomass use in a defossilised and resource-efficient world

Horst Fehrenbach and Nils Rettenmaier

Introduction

There is limited potential on this planet not only for fossil energy resources but also for any kind of renewable energy. Apart from technical restrictions, each source is also reaching its ecological limits. These can always be attached to the available area. However, no energy source is as closely tied to the available area as biomass. No other renewable energy source has such clear use restrictions with regard to planetary boundaries as biomass. On the other hand, the production and use of biomass are essential components of life. The use of biomass by humans is as old as humankind itself and is the source for satisfying a wide range of needs, from nutrition through building and utility material to energy.

Based on the energy demand of the industrialised countries, the almost uncontroversial expansion of the use of biomass for energy purposes ten years ago has now been massively questioned as a sustainable solution. Haberl et al. (2007) calculated that Europe is already using considerably more productive ecosystem services (net primary production) worldwide than it can mobilise on its territory. The German Federal Environment Agency (UBA) acknowledged this conclusion and stated that for covering the high energy consumption in the industrialised countries of the world by the cultivation of biomass disproportionately large proportions of productive arable (Jering et al. 2012). There is undoubtedly a general consensus that food production should be given priority under all circumstances. All the more so as food security in the future will face major challenges, given the further increase in the world population and global food trends (e.g. more animal products that require many times more land than plant-based products).

Particularly with regard to the globalisation of agricultural markets, there are also socio-economic implications which have been intensively discussed in the relevant research on the sustainability assessment of bioenergy in recent years. Increased demand for bioenergy in addition to increasing food markets has been spotted as a driver for an additional increase in land-use change (Laborde 2011). Furthermore, in globalised agricultural markets, such land-use change can appear detached from the actual areas on which the raw materials are produced. This principle is described as indirect land-use change (iLUC). Intensified, yield-only management of forestry land also leads to adverse effects, particularly in the area of biodiversity. Nevertheless, the use of biomass in current energy systems (electricity, heat, fuel) contributes significantly to the share of renewable energies. The current European renewable energy policy enhances the biofuel targets for 2030 (European Parliament & Council of the European Union 2018), but fuels with low risk for land-use change shall be given preference.

In view of the above-mentioned limits, the objective of this article is to critically reflect on which role biomass could play in a defossilised and resource-efficient world and to what extent biomass can be provided with low risk for land-use change.

Biomass with low risk for land-use change

The food versus fuel debate of the past ten years focussed a lot on land-use changes that directly or indirectly might be triggered by increasing demand for crop-based biofuels and bioenergy. It has become clear that land-use changes can only be minimised (or ideally mitigated) by either using biogenic waste and residues or biomass from dedicated crops with low risk for land-use change.

While there is little doubt about the sustainable use of biogenic waste and residues, there is still an ongoing discussion about potential loopholes associated with the use of so-called low iLUC biofuels and bioenergy based on dedicated crops. It is widely held that (indirect) land-use change can be mitigated through (i) yield increases due to improved agricultural practices (beyond levels which would have prevailed in the absence of productivity-promoting schemes for non-food biomass), as well as (ii) the cultivation of crops on land not previously used for the cultivation of crops (e.g. preamble of European Parliament & Council of the European Union 2018). However, this will only lead to a reduced (i) LUC risk if stringent criteria regarding the additionality of such measures are implemented.

Biomass feedstock with low land-use change risk can thus consist of:

- biogenic waste and residues;
- biogenic residues from agriculture, forestry, landscape management (primary residues);
- biogenic residues from industrial processes (secondary residues); and
- true biogenic waste (tertiary residues).

Dedicated crops (energy/industrial crops) cultivated on:

- unused land (land not used for the cultivation of crops for at least a number of years);
- surplus land (becoming available due to yield increases beyond BAU);

- the potentials of these two primary sources of low LUC risk biomass are presented in the following two sections; and
- biomass potentials from dedicated crops with low land-use change risk.

As mentioned in the previous section, there are two options of obtaining biomass from dedicated crops with low land-use change risk: i) biomass cultivated on so-called surplus land and ii) biomass cultivated on unused land. These options are discussed in the following.

Biomass feedstock cultivated on unused land

Unused land is land which was previously not used for the cultivation of crops (cf. definition in European Parliament & Council of the European Union 2018). It is unclear whether the land hasn't been used at all (in this case the definition could even include pristine land) or whether the land is idling for more than a certain number of years (e.g. five years) after ceasing its agricultural use for economic, political or environmental reasons. In the latter case, the term abandoned (agricultural) land would be more appropriate. Apart from unused land and 'abandoned land', there are many other similar terms that are often incorrectly used as synonyms such as degraded land, wasteland or marginal land. Marginal land is often incorrectly used as an umbrella term for all types of land ranging from fallow and abandoned land to degraded land.

However, since the term marginal originates from economics, it is clear that the extent of land defined as marginal could vary subject to the prevailing economic framework conditions. Therefore, a number of completed and ongoing EU-funded projects such as SEEMLA, FORBIO and MAGIC have focussed their research efforts on marginal land, among others trying to come up with a more stable delimitation based on biophysical criteria.

Within the SEEMLA project, marginal lands in Europe have mapped and quantified using the Muencheberg Soil Quality Rating (SQR) system (Mueller, Schindler, Behrendt, Eulenstein & Dannowski 2007). According to Vlachaki et al. (2018), approximately 224 Mha of land in Europe belongs to the poor and very poor classes of the SQR index and is identified as marginal. This area corresponds to 45% of the overall area investigated. Subsequently, the area of marginal land suitable for biomass cultivation was determined (54 Mha) and lastly, the area of marginal land suitable for cultivation of the selected energy crops was quantified (46.5 Mha).

Using a similar GIS-based approach and using biophysical criteria to identify so-called 'areas with natural constraints' (ANC), von Cossel et al. (2018) have mapped and quantified marginal lands in the EU28 within the MAGIC project. Despite a smaller geographical focus (EU28 vs 39 European countries in SEEMLA), the authors identify an area of 64.7 Mha of marginal arable land (53.5 Mha of which influenced by soil constraints according to von Cossel et al. 2019) and report an area of marginal land suitable for cultivation of the selected energy crops of 61.0 Mha.

For Germany, the reported areas are not in line either: according to Vlachaki et al. (2018), the area of marginal land is 3.2 Mha compared to 5.6 Mha underlying the analysis by von Cossel et al. (2018). The observed discrepancies between the two approaches – especially at EU/European level – clearly call for more research and harmonisation.

However, even if the range of results could be narrowed in the future, such analyses based on biophysical criteria still do not tell (i) which share of the land identified as marginal is unused and (ii) whether this land is high carbon stock or highly biodiverse land.

Answering these urgent questions currently is subject to further research since it is clear that only the use of unused, low carbon stock and low biodiversity marginal land avoids indirect land-use changes (iLUC) and negative environmental impacts. Moreover, there are also other alternatives to use marginal land, for example, for other renewable energy sources such as ground-mounted photovoltaic (PV) systems, some of which offer several times greater environmental benefits than biomass production. Last but not least, marginal land is also one of the last retreats for species that already suffer from the intensive use of standard agricultural land (Geffroy 2018; Hallmann et al. 2017), i.e. marginal land plays a vital role in bio-diversity conservation. A broad public discussion is therefore needed as to which proportion of marginal land should be reserved for different competing societal objectives such as bioenergy production, other renewable energies or nature conservation (Rettenmaier, Schmehl, Gärtner & Reinhardt 2018).

Yet, even if the above-mentioned challenge to determine the area of unused, low carbon stock and low biodiversity marginal land was mastered, the result would only represent a static snapshot. In a dynamic world with global popu-lation projected to reach 9.7 billion people by 2050 (United Nations 2015) and changing diets due to economic development, significant cropland expansion is expected, to satisfy the additional demand for food and feed. Thus, using feedstock from unused land areas that would have been converted to cropland anyway (in a business-as-usual counterfactual scenario) would lead to indirect land-use changes. Searle and Giuntoli (2018) suggest using Clean Development Mechanism (CDM) methodology for demonstrating additionality, for example, to demonstrate that the unused land would have remained unused or that conversion of the land would not be profitable without biofuel incentives.

On top of all the above-mentioned issues, further research is also needed to determine potential yields on such land. Only then can the biomass potential of dedicated crops from marginal land be appropriately assessed. Yet, it is clear that marginal lands give marginal yields. The authors therefore conclude that the biomass potential from marginal lands in Europe will only contribute relatively little to meet ambitious targets for biofuels and bioenergy.

Biomass feedstock cultivated on surplus land

Surplus land is land that is not needed any more for food and feeds pro-duction due to yield increases as a result of improved agricultural practices (mainly intensification). Since crop yields tend to increase over time due to technological and agronomical improvements, only additional yield increases beyond a business-as-usual counterfactual scenario would lead to a reduced (i) LUC risk. Again, Searle and Giuntoli (2018) suggest applying CDM methodology to demonstrate additionality by identifying genuinely above-baseline yield increases. To the authors' knowledge, this additionality test has not been used in practice yet. Therefore, it is currently impossible to estimate the biomass potential from surplus land in Europe.

Biomass potentials from biogenic waste and residues

In recent years, numerous studies have been conducted on biomass potentials for energy use, particularly with regard to the available biomass based on biogenic waste and residues (Brosowski et al. 2015; Fritsche et al. 2004; Zeller et al. 2012). Fehrenbach et al. (2019) have examined this work in a comprehensive analysis regarding the comparability of results and approaches. The results revealed the existence of considerable differences even in the definition of biomass potential. The choice of criteria that restrict the physically available potential is critical. The cited meta-study worked out a usable potential for Germany, which includes both the technical limits and demanding ecological restrictions.

Types of biogenic waste and residues

Following material groups can be distinguished:

- wood from forestry;
- residues from agriculture (including straw, other harvest residues, slurry, manure, among others);
- municipal and commercial biogenic waste and residues (biowaste, yard and garden waste, sewage sludge, waste wood, among others);
- material flows from landscape management (cuttings, among others); and
- industrial biogenic waste (saw dust, black liquor, waste from food industry, among others).

The definition of what is to be understood in many studies as the potential of so-called residual forest wood is very inconsistent. It is often understood to mean small pieces of leftover from the harvesting of wood, which is counted as potential. However, the extraction of these material fractions is viewed critically from the point of view of biodiversity protection and the conservation of nutrients.

Fehrenbach et al. (2019) avoid the term residual forest wood for two reasons and refer to forest wood restricting the actual potential for energy use by excluding the small-sized assortment (<7 cm). Therefore, the relevant quantities of forest wood already used for energy purposes are to be counted as solid

Biomass use in a defossilised world   293

wood (>7 cm) or low-value roundwood that is not used in the sawmill industry for economic reasons. Fehrenbach et al. (2019) refer exactly this material applying the term dendromass for the potential determination. A distinction was then made between the material dendromass part and the energetically usable part taking the request of paper and board industry into account. Under consideration of exactly these criteria, Ewald et al. (2017) specify the energy wood potential with 1.8 m^3 per hectare and year.

Quantities of biogenic waste and residues in Germany

The various biomass potential studies show considerable bandwidths for individual residual materials. For forest wood, there is about a factor of 3 between the lower end of 8 million tonnes (Fritsche et al. 2004) and the higher end of 30 million tonnes (Brosowski et al. 2015), adding current energetic use and additional potential. For straw, the bandwidth is even a factor of 4, ranging from 5 million tonnes per year (Fritsche et al. 2004) to 20 million tonnes (Zeller et al. 2012). Fehrenbach et al. (2019) evaluated 50 studies and applied a number of criteria to derive the final quantity according to demanding ecological restrictions, as mentioned above. A selection of the criteria applied is listed in Table 24.1.

In order to determine the total energy potential for energy recovery from all residual and waste materials, the estimated quantities are converted from tonne data into a primary energy potential (petajoule, PJ). The conversion is made either by the lower calorific value or by the specific gas formation rate. The second applies for waste/residues with negative calorific value due to their high water content and which are used energetically by fermentation.

In this way, the average potential of available primary energy based on biogenic waste and residues of 900 PJ per year is determined. If the collection

Table 24.1 Selection of the criteria applied to determine the potential of residual biomass under demanding ecological restrictions

Criteria referring to agricultural residues	Criteria referring to forest wood
No land-use change	Clear cutting ban
Consideration of organic farming with 20% area	10% natural forest development in state-owned forests
Safeguarding nutrient balances and humus balancing	Consideration of nature conservation areas
Consideration of ecological conservation compensation areas	Consideration of forest certifications
Yield increases	Biodiversity goals in used forests
Competition for use	Limit for non-solid wood (<7 cm)
Development of livestock	
Consideration of grazing livestock husbandry	

of solid manure and various industrial substrates is intensified, the amount can be increased to 960 PJ. If the restriction on the extraction of forest wood is tightened, the total potential is reduced to 880 PJ. This amount of energy does not correspond to the final usable energy (electricity, heat, fuel). For this purpose, the conversion losses of the respective conversion techniques must first be included.

Additional bioenergy potential from biogenic waste and residues in Germany

The analysis of Fehrenbach et al. (2019) does not answer the questions to what extent the available biomasses already used in the energy system. Nevertheless, the study provided indications since the literature on the status quo of use has also been considered. Figure 24.1 compares the potential determined by Fehrenbach et al. (2019) with the quantities that are already energetically used.

Three groups can be distinguished here:

1 Those materials that are already used to a greater extent than the sustainably available potential provides for; this group includes the woody biomasses, in particular, forest wood.
2 Those materials that are already used to the extent that they are actually generated; this group includes a number of municipal and industrial waste types.
3 Those materials that still have an untapped potential; this applies primarily to straw group includes but also to solid manure and other agricultural residues.

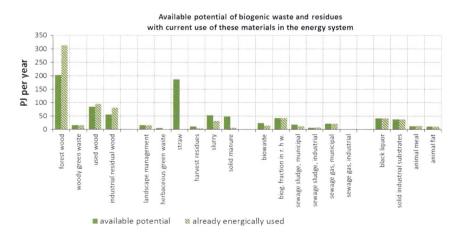

Figure 24.1 Comparing the available potential of biogenic waste and residues with current use of these materials in the energy system.
Source: own illustration based on data from Fehrenbach et al. (2019).

While Fehrenbach et al. (2019) figure out 900 PJ as the available potential of biogenic residues and waste, approximately 770 PJ are already in some form of energetic use. In the case of forest wood, the potential is even clearly overused so that a reduction would be necessary here. Moreover, a large share of the forest wood a large proportion of the forest wood utilised for energy purposes is used as logs for heating buildings. Against this utilisation pathway, however, the production of industrial process heat shall be preferred.

On the other hand, there is a significant additional potential for the energetic use of straw. Of the 190 PJ (equivalent to 13 million tonnes) determined to be available, only less than 1 per cent has so far been used for electricity, heat and fuel production.

All in all, there remains an additionally available net potential of 130 PJ and the recommendation to redirect parts of currently used biomass into priority paths (process heat, fuels for aviation or shipping).

Thrän et al. (2019) come to very similar figures as far as the technical biomass potential for biogenic residues and waste is concerned. They estimate 876 PJ as the sum of already used and still mobilisable materials.

Future avenues for biomass use are:

- bioenergy and biofuels from biogenic waste and residues in Germany; and
- matching biomass types and utilisation paths

To identify preferred utilisation paths in the electricity, heat and fuel markets, the technical and economic boundary conditions of current and future conversion technologies must be analysed. Against this background, available and future technological concepts for the production of secondary and final energy sources for bioenergy sources based on biogenic waste and residues needs to be analysed and evaluated from a process engineering, environmental and economic point of view. To this end Fehrenbach et al. (2019) evaluated a total of 19 technologies according to their suitability of the selected techniques for converting waste or residues into electricity, heat or fuels for transport.

The evaluation was carried out on the basis of the following five criteria, rated after a 3-scale value level:

- Energy efficiency (including exergy as a measure).
- Greenhouse gas balance (saving against fossil reference).
- Production costs (compared to fossil reference).
- Other ecological aspects, such as air pollutants, pollution of water or soils, risk due to further waste streams, the closing of material cycles.
- Compatibility for the transformation of the energy system (relevance regarding substitution of fossil fuels, usefulness for the energy system, storage capability, flexibility).

The pathways for the use in the heat sector achieve the best rating for a total of almost 90% of the energetic potential of waste and residues. In absolute numbers, the output is approximately 600 PJ heat. However, this beneficial result is only valid for direct energetic use in a boiler plant or a combined heat and power plant with the generation of process heat. In the case of residential heat the use of biomass is less favourable, in particular, because of available renewable alternatives (solar, heat pump, insulation) and increased air pollutant emissions. On the other hand, there are mostly no renewable alternatives available for process heat demand in the industrial sector.

For the waste or residues associated with higher moisture contents, the production of biomethane, predominantly for transport fuel production (to which 10% of the input is attributed, resulting in 25 PJ fuel) is the best evaluated option. Here, too, the favourable rating applies under the condition of a special use: The use of fuels in aviation or shipping, since here renewable alternatives are more difficult to implement than in road transport.

The stability of the results the set boundary conditions of the evaluation approach was varied in the sense of a sensitivity analysis. A significant change in the ranking occurs if the criterion production cost is excluded from the evaluation. The energy use to be preferred will then be allocated to only 55% industrial heat (370 PJ), 38% as fuels for transport (190 PJ) and 7% for electricity generation (16 PJ).

Matching bioenergy supply and energy demand in Germany

The analysis of Fehrenbach et al. (2019) follows a bottom–up approach. They do not question whether the potential quantities of the most suitable target uses assigned based on a list of criteria are also in demand there to the same extent. Nor are these prioritised utilisation pathways aligned with the scenarios for a Resource-Efficient and Greenhouse-Gas-Neutral Germany (RTD) or the long-term and climate change scenarios for Germany (Pfluger, Tersteegen & Franke 2017).

After the completion of the study, we now examined how the energy sources allocated to the utilisation pathways correspond to the demand in these sectors. Figure 24.2 shows that both the demand for industrial process heat and aviation fuel is significantly higher than the supply that can be covered by biomass. The metal industry alone requires approximately 550 PJ of process heat at high or medium temperature. The chemical industry has a demand of about 360 PJ (Pfluger et al. 2017). Biomass is an attractive option for industry to avoid greenhouse gases. It allows heat to be transferred to a relatively high temperature level (depending on the calorific value), as well as being available in various aggregate states.

The role of biomass in forward-looking scenario studies

Biomass plays a vital role in most forward-looking scenario studies using energy systems models such as Pfluger et al. (2017), Gerhardt et al. (2015) or

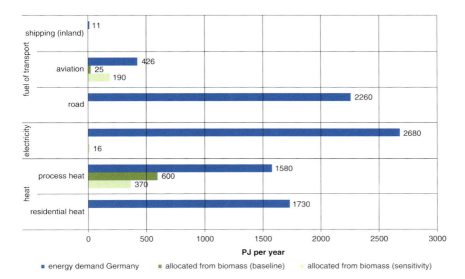

Figure 24.2 Comparing the useful energy from available potential of biogenic waste and residues with the current demand of heat, electricity and transport fuel. Baseline: biomass allocated according to the evaluation by five criteria (see text); sensitivity: evaluation without the criteria production costs.
Source: own illustration based on data from Fehrenbach et al. (2019), Pfluger et al. (2017), AG Energiebilanzen e.V. (2019).

Repenning et al. (2015). These studies differ in terms of underlying biomass potentials (biogenic waste and residues, available land for the cultivation of dedicated crops as well as the amount of biomass imports) and biomass allocation to the various sectors. In Günther et al. (2019), no use at all of the dedicated crops is foreseen in the future (see also Chapters 12 and 13 of this volume). All studies conclude that biomass should primarily be used in those sectors where there are no or few affordable alternatives for decarbonisation, respectively defossilisation. Most often, aviation and shipping, as well as high-temperature heat for industrial processes, are mentioned as the main future applications. But also the chemical industry must not be neglected which needs a renewable carbon source in the future This could either be recycled carbon via PtG/PtL (especially for short chain-length molecules) or biomass, from which longer, more complex molecules synthesised by nature could be obtained.

Conclusions

The role of biomass in a future without fossil CO_2 emissions is complex. On the one hand, biomass is a readily available resource and should also be used within the framework of a resource-efficient economy. On the other hand, biomass potentials are limited by various factors. Biomass production is linked to land area, which – given the growing world population – must be used for food supply first. For this reason, the potential for non-food uses of biomass from dedicated crops will always be sharply limited.

Yet, there is a potential of dedicated crops from marginal land or surplus land with low risk for indirect land-use change (iLUC). As these land categories have not yet been clearly defined, data on potentially available areas are therefore not comparable. In addition, conflicts with biodiversity often arise when these types of land are used. Moreover, the yields from marginal areas are marginal. The realisation of greater potential for the use of these areas is therefore not to be expected.

The question of how much forest wood is available is a particularly complex one: even the distinction between wood as the actual harvested good and what is called residual forest wood is unclear. The decisive factor is the forestry strategy: is the forest rather a production site for maximised wood yield or a near-natural ecosystem with high carbon storage? If priority is given to the second option, the potential for use is also significantly lower here. Besides, there are the imponderables of forest restructuring and climate change, which may result in a high volume of timber in the short term. The long-term potential may continue to decline.

Among the multitude of different biogenic wastes and residues, straw accounts for the largest unused energy potential to date. The more recent studies estimate this at a range of 140 to 200 Petajoules. Manure also offers the possibility of expanding the production of biogas. Otherwise, the majority of substances are already used for energy.

On the way to a climate-neutral world, biomass thus makes a contribution to directly replacing fossil fuels. The results presented here on the potentials of biogenic waste and residues as well as of cultivated biomass on unused and surplus land show that it is difficult to increase the domestic biomass supply compared to today. According to most forward-looking scenario studies, the future biomass demand for energy in the sectors transport (aviation and marine fuels) and industry (high-temperature heat) will remain high or even rise. Besides these, the demand for biomass for material use, e.g. in the chemical industry, could continue to rise. It is clear that biomass demand will exceed domestic biomass supply, so significant biomass imports may be necessary. Alternatively, the demand for hydrocarbons for fuels and chemicals could also be met by PtG/PtL technologies, but at significantly higher costs (also in the future). Biomass should, therefore, be used in particular where there are no, or only a few, very expensive renewable alternatives available. To answer this question, further research activities are needed to determine more precisely the future role of biomass in a defossilised world.

Abbreviations

ANC   Areas with Natural Constraints (Articles 31 & 32 in European Parliament & Council of the European Union 2013)

BAU   business as usual

CDM	Clean Development Mechanism, one of three market-based mechanisms under the Kyoto Protocol
EU	European Union
GIS	Geographical Information System
iLUC	indirect land use change
LUC	land use change
PJ	petajoule
PtG	power-to-gas
PtL	power-to-liquid
PV	photovoltaics
RED II	Renewable Energy Directive II (European Parliament & Council of the European Union 2018)
RTD	Ressourceneffizientes und treibhausgasneutrales Deutschland (Resource-Efficient and Greenhouse-Gas-Neutral Germany) (Günther et al. 2019)
SQR	(Muencheberg) Soil Quality Rating (Mueller et al. 2007)

References

AG Energiebilanzen e.V. (2019). Energiebilanz der Bundesrepublik Deutschland 2017. Retrieved 19 June 2019 from https://ag-energiebilanzen.de/index.php?article_id=29&fileName=bilanz17d.xlsx.

Brosowski, A., Adler, P., Erdmann, G., Stinner, W., Thrän, D., Mantau, U., … Reinholdt, G. (2015). *Biomassepotenziale von Rest- und Abfallstoffen (Status quo in Deutschland). Schriftenreihe Nachwachsende Rohstoffe* (Vol. 36). Gülzow-Prüzen, Germany: Fachagentur Nachwachsende Rohstoffe e.V. (FNR). Retrieved from https://mediathek.fnr.de/downloadable/download/sample/sample_id/1251/.

European Parliament & Council of the European Union. (2013). Regulation 2013/1305/EU on support for rural development by the European Agricultural Fund for Rural Development (EAFRD) and repealing Council Regulation (EC) No 1698/2005. *Official Journal of the European Union*, 56(L 347), 487–548. Retrieved from http://eur-lex.europa.eu/legal-content/EN/TXT/?uri=celex:32013R1305.

European Parliament & Council of the European Union. *Directive (EU) 2018/2001 of the European Parliament and of the Council of 11 December 2018 on the promotion of the use of energy from renewable sources (recast), Official Journal of the European Union*, (L 328), 82–209. Retrieved from https://eur-lex.europa.eu/legal-content/EN/TXT/PDF/?uri=CELEX:32018L2001.

Ewald, J., Rothe, A., Hansbauer, M., Schumann, C., Wilnhammer, M., Schönfeld, F., … Zahner, V. (2017). *Energiewende und Waldbiodiversität. BfN-Skripten* (Vol. 455). Bonn, Germany: Bundesamt für Naturschutz (BfN).

Fehrenbach, H., Giegrich, J., Köppen, S., Wern, B., Pertagnol, J., Baur, F., … Wiegmann, K. (2019). BioRest: Verfügbarkeit und Nutzungsoptionen biogener Abfall- und Reststoffe im Energiesystem (Strom-, Wärme- und Verkehrssektor). *UBA Texte* (Vol. 115/2019). Dessau-Roßlau, Germany: Umweltbundesamt (UBA). Retrieved from www.umweltbundesamt.de/sites/default/files/medien/1410/publikationen/2019-09-24_texte_115-2019_biorest.pdf.

Fritsche, U., Dehoust, G., Jenseit, W., Heinz, A., Thrän, D., Reinhardt, G., ... et al., (2004). *Stoffstromanalyse zur nachhaltigen energetischen Nutzung von Biomasse [Material Flow Analysis of Sustainable Biomass Use for Energy]*. Darmstadt, Germany: Öko-Institut e.V. Retrieved from www.oeko.de/oekodoc/236/2004-025-de.pdf.

Geffroy, L. (2018). Where Have all the Farmland Birds Gone? *CNRS Le Journal*. Retrieved from https://news.cnrs.fr/articles/where-have-all-the-farmland-birds-gone.

Gerhardt, N., Sandau, F., Scholz, A., Hahn, H., Schumacher, P., Sager, C., ... Müller, T. (2015). *Interaktion EE-Strom, Wärme und Verkehr*. Kassel, Germany: Fraunhofer-Institut für Windenergie und Energiesystemtechnik (Fraunhofer IWES). Retrieved from www.iee.fraunhofer.de/content/dam/iee/energiesystemtechnik/de/Dokumente/Veroeffentlichungen/2015/Interaktion_EEStrom_Waerme_Verkehr_Endbericht.pdf.

Günther, J., Lehmann, H., Lorenz, U. & Purr, K. (2019). *A resource efficient pathway towards a greenhouse gas neutral Germany*. Dessau-Roßlau, Germany: Umweltbundesamt (UBA). Retrieved from www.umweltbundesamt.de/sites/default/files/medien/376/publikationen/190212_uba_fachbrosch_rtd_engl_bf_low2.pdf.

Haberl, H., Erb, K. H., Krausmann, F., Gaube, V., Bondeau, A., Plutzar, C., ... Fischer-Kowalski, M. (2007). Quantifying and mapping the human appropriation of net primary production in earth's terrestrial ecosystems. *Proceedings of the National Academy of Sciences of the United States of America*, 104(31), 12942–12947. https://doi.org/10.1073/pnas.0704243104.

Hallmann, C. A., Sorg, M., Jongejans, E., Siepel, H., Hofland, N., Schwan, H., ... de Kroon, H. (2017). More than 75 percent decline over 27 years in total flying insect biomass in protected areas. *PLoS ONE*, 12(10), e0185809. https://doi.org/10.1371/journal.pone.0185809.

Jering, A., Klatt, A., Seven, J., Ehlers, K., Günther, J., Ostermeier, A. & Mönch, L. (2012). Globale Landflächen und Biomasse nachhaltig und ressourcenschonend nutzen. *UBA Positionen*. Dessau-Roßlau, Germany: Umweltbundesamt (UBA). Retrieved from www.umweltbundesamt.de/publikationen/globale-landflaechen-biomasse.

Laborde, D. (2011). *Assessing the Land Use Change Consequences of European Biofuel Policies*. Washington, DC: International Food Policy Research Institute (IFPRI). Retrieved from http://ebrary.ifpri.org/utils/getfile/collection/p15738coll5/id/197/filename/198.pdf.

Mueller, L., Schindler, U., Behrendt, A., Eulenstein, F. & Dannowski, R. (2007). *The Muencheberg Soil Quality Rating (SQR) Field Manual for detecting and assessing properties and limitations of soils for cropping and grazing*. Müncheberg, Germany: Leibniz-Centre for Agricultural Landscape Research (ZALF) e.V. Retrieved from www.zalf.de/de/forschung_lehre/publikationen/Documents/Publikation_Mueller_L/field_mueller.pdf.

Pfluger, B., Tersteegen, B. & Franke, B. (2017). *Langfristszenarien für die Transformation des Energiesystems in Deutschland*. Berlin, Germany: Bundesministeriums für Wirtschaft und Energie (BMWi). Retrieved from www.bmwi.de/Redaktion/DE/Artikel/Energie/langfrist-und-klimazenarien.html.

Repenning, J., Emele, L., Blanck, R., Dehoust, G., Förster, H., Greiner, B., ... Ziesing, H. (2015). *Klimaschutzszenario 2050*. Berlin, Germany: Öko-Institut e.V. Retrieved from www.oeko.de//oekodoc/2441/2015-598-de.pdf.

Rettenmaier, N., Schmehl, M., Gärtner, S. & Reinhardt, G. (2018). Final report on environmental assessment covering LCA & LC-EIA (supported by the EU's Horizon 2020 programme under GA No. 691874). *SEEMLA project reports*. Heidelberg, Germany: IFEU – Institute for Energy and Environmental Research Heidelberg. Retrieved from http://seemla.eu/en/project-deliverables/.

Searle, S. & Giuntoli, J. (2018). *Analysis of high and low indirect land-use change definitions in European Union renewable fuel policy.* Washington, DC: International Council on Clean *Transportation (ICCT).* Retrieved from https://theicct.org/sites/default/files/publications/High_low_ILUC_risk_EU_20181115.pdf.

Thrän, D., Lauer, M., Dotzauer, M., Oehmichen, K., Majer, S., Millinger, M. & Jordan, M. (2019). *Technoökonomische Analyse und Transformationspfade des energetischen Biomassepotentials (TATBIO).* Leipzig, Germany: Deutsches Biomasseforschungszentrum (DBFZ). Retrieved from www.bmwi.de/Redaktion/DE/Publikationen/Studien/technooekonomische-analyse-und-transformationspfade-des-energetischen-biomassepotentials.html.

United Nations. (2015). World Population Prospects. *Key Findings and Advance Tables. 2015 Revision.* New York, NY: United Nations Department of Economic and Social Affairs, Population Division. Retrieved from http://esa.un.org/unpd/wpp/Publications/Files/Key_Findings_WPP_2015.pdf.

Vlachaki, D., Gounaris, N., Dimitriadis, E., Galatsidas, S., Gerwin, W., Repmann, F., … Volkmann, C. (2018). Final guidelines for the sustainable exploitation of MagLs for bioenergy (Deliverable D6.8). *SEEMLA project reports.* Orestiada, Greece: Democritus University of Thrace (DUTH). Retrieved from http://seemla.eu/en/project-deliverables/.

von Cossel, M., Iqbal, Y., Scordia, D., Cosentino, S. L., Elbersen, B., Staritsky, I., … Lewandowski, I. (2018). Low-input agricultural practices for industrial crops on marginal land (Deliverable D4.1). *MAGIC project reports.* Stuttgart (Hohenheim), Germany: University of Hohenheim. Retrieved from http://magic-h2020.eu/documents-reports/.

von Cossel, M., Lewandowski, I., Elbersen, B., Staritsky, I., Van Eupen, M., Iqbal, Y., … Alexopoulou, E. (2019). Marginal Agricultural Land Low-Input Systems for Biomass Production. *Energies*, 12(16), 3123. https://doi.org/10.3390/en12163123.

Zeller, V., Thrän, D., Zeymer, M., Bürzle, B., Adler, P., Ponitka, J., … Wiegmann, K. (2012). *Basisinformationen für eine nachthaltige Nutzung von landwirtschaftlichen Reststoffen zur Bioenergiebereitstellung (DBFZ Report).* Leipzig: Deutsches Biomasseforschungszentrum (DBFZ). Retrieved from www.dbfz.de/fileadmin/user_upload/Referenzen/DBFZ_Reports/DBFZ_Report_13.pdf.

Part IV
Pioneering innovations

25 Big, environmentally friendly events

Sparing resources, respecting nature, setting limits – an attempt by the German Protestant Festival (Deutscher Evangelischer Kirchentag) at organising a big event on a sustainable footing

Oliver Foltin, Christof Hertel, and Jobst Kraus

Introduction and objective of the article

The objective of this chapter is to give an overview over the way the Kirchentag is organised in a sustainable manner. Furthermore, the chapter mentions and discusses measures that are implemented since a long-time or are currently invented.

The German Protestant Festival (hereinafter referred to as 'Kirchentag' (DEKT) or 'Kirchentag' Festival') takes place every two years in a German city. The cities chosen for the Festival over the last few years were Bremen, Dresden, Hamburg, Stuttgart as well as Berlin in 2017, where it was celebrated in conjunction with the anniversary of the Reformation and Dortmund in 2019. The Kirchentag Festival lasts five days, from Wednesday until Sunday. The participants, numbering more than 100,000 and covering all age groups, are predominantly Protestants while some may follow no or other faiths; they come from everywhere, from all parts of Germany and the world; approximately 80 nations are represented, and the visitors are above all young people half of whom are under 30 years of age (Pickel, Jaeckel & Yendell 2015; DEKT n.d.). A Kirchentag Festival opens with a church service on Wednesday and ends with a final church service on Sunday. Kirchentag Festivals offer dedicated groups and initiatives a stage on which to present their concerns and projects. To this end, around 2,500 cultural, spiritual and social-policy events take place over the duration of five days (DEKT n.d.).

There are a variety of formats from workshops, exhibitions, concerts, church services to Bible work. During lectures and podium discussions, the most varied topics, aspects and issues concerning religious and social life, such as the fair organisation of a globalised world, the preservation of Creation and human dignity – are discussed with representatives from the world of politics, science, media, business, church and public life. At the 'Market of Possibilities' (Markt der Möglichkeiten), national as well as local church and social initiatives present themselves and their work to visitors of the Festival as part of a large exhibition. The Kirchentag Festival saw the light of day in 1949 as a movement of Protestant laymen who were brought together by their belief in Jesus Christ and their commitment to the Church and the world (Ueberschär 2017). The objective of the Kirchentag Festival was formulated in 1955 in the preamble of the 'Procedural Rules of the Deutsche Evangelische Kirchentag' and remains valid to this day: 'The Kirchentag Festival wants to bring together people who look for the Christian faith. It wants to gather Protestant Christians and strengthen their faith. It wants people to take on responsibilities within the Church and enable them to bear witness, serve the world and contribute to the community of worldwide Christendom' (DEKT 2015: 1).

The organisation and execution of the Kirchentag Festival would be impossible without the commitment of teams of volunteers, who are involved in planning and structuring the content of the event. The logistics and the on-site organisation too very much depend on the dedication of around 4,000 to 5,000 volunteers with youth ministry or scouts background. Overall, the preparation of each Kirchentag Festival takes around one and a half years with the organisers having access to a well-established organisational structure (DEKT 2019). The so-called 'Central Office' in Fulda acts as the permanent institution whose primary task is the selection of the topics to be covered at the Kirchentag. The actual organisation and direct execution of the event is the responsibility of the Field Office (Geschäftsstelle), which, every two years, sets up its headquarters in the respective host city. The costs for organising and carrying out a Kirchentag Festival amount to around 20 million euros of which 30 per cent are raised through the sale of entrance tickets, donations and sponsoring and which is supplemented by money provided by the respective host cities, federal states and federal-state churches as well as project funds (DEKT 2018a).

Methodology

The authors are partly members of the so-called counselling task force 'environment', one author is employed by the Kirchentag (DEKT) and works for environmental projects in the 'Field Office'. Besides counselling the organisation in questions of environmental management and proposing new projects, all of us were practically involved in some projects voluntarily. Under these circumstances, we took a quite critical look at the current way of organising mobility, procurement, energy consumption, nutrition etc and how the DEKT cope with planetary challenges and the practice of ecological management. In a certain sense, we didn't carry out a scientific study, but we tried to reflect the practice of DEKT critically and also in solidarity. Our aim is to challenge the DEKT to more efforts towards sustainability.

Discussion: an eco-friendly event through environmental management at the Kirchentag Festival

Framework for environmental management

A big event such as the Kirchentag Festival has, due to a large number of people gathering there, always both a direct and indirect impact on the environment. In Germany and Europe, however, the systematic environmental management of big events is still far from being the norm. Nevertheless, the benefits of environmentally conscious event planning are quite obvious: Apart from reducing the impact on the environment, it leads to cost savings due to a reduced and documented use of resources and helps convey a better image of the event among the public. Hence, the organisers of the Kirchentag Festival did, some years ago, set themselves the goal of organising the Kirchentag in a way that is as green and climate-friendly as possible. The aim was to reduce and/or restrict in particular the negative effects of an event of this size. As part of a project funded by the German Ministry of Environment and the Federal Environment Agency (Umweltbundesamt), the first eco-controlling exercise was introduced in 2003 which, apart from systematically recording the environmental effects of the Kirchentag Festival, evaluates the established indicators. The eco-controlling exercise was the basis that led to a further step in 2004 when, as per the EMAS Regulation,[1] a validation of the Central Office in Fulda was undertaken (Cierjacks, Teichert & Diefenbacher 2008). With the Eco-Management and Audit Scheme (EMAS), an environmental management system developed by the European Union, the environmental performance of companies and organisations of any size and from any industry can be continually improved. This ensures that environmental aspects are systematically taken into consideration. The eco-management system based on EMAS sees itself as a comprehensive environmental assessment tool aimed at reducing the usage of substances, materials and resources and at continually improving environmental performance. As the last step involving the 2007 Kirchentag in Cologne, the Field Office and the event itself were included in the EMAS evaluation and were successfully certified. Since then, the Kirchentag Festival has been the first and only big event in Germany that succeeded in permanently enshrining such an eco-management system (Umweltgutachterausschuss beim Bundesministerium für Umwelt, Naturschutz und nukleare Sicherheit 2017).

Principles of environmental management of the Kirchentag Festival

The foundation and basis of the environmental work of the Kirchentag Festival is its environmental policy and the guidelines formulated therein, which were last reviewed and updated in 2018:

> Our environmental programme is a firm part of all fields of organisation. All co-workers receive intensive training and have the opportunity to present their ideas on the topic. The Board assumes commercial responsibility for topics involving the environment.

We consider environmental protection to be an ongoing process. While preparing, carrying out, following up on and administrating the Kirchentag Festival, we are continually striving for sustainability, which, to us, not only

308   *Oliver Foltin et al.*

means complying with the applicable laws and standards but developing our very own standard. By using the EMAS eco-management system set forth in the EU Regulation, we undertake to continually and voluntarily improve our environmental performance. In conjunction with our suppliers and service providers as well as with the authorities, associations and other interested parties, we work out environmentally relevant standards. By doing so we reinforce sustainability within the value creation chain and in the public sector.

By analysing the environmental aspects within the life cycle of the Kirchentag Festival we recognise opportunities and risks within the organisational context. Through our own environmental programme and established environmental controlling, we continually improve our impact.

On account of the size of our event, we attach great importance to reducing resource utilisation and environmental impact with regard to energy and water consumption, transport, material procurement and catering, construction technology, use of land and waste disposal. We furthermore encourage a closed-loop cycle of resources.

The development and fostering of future-proof ecological alternatives constitute another priority of our environmental work. We explicitly want to increase the use of regenerative energy. We furthermore want to develop a sustainable mobility culture and use resources more intelligently by way of digital solutions.

Our material procurement and catering are geared towards being as ecological, fair and regional as possible. By doing so, we want to help producers, suppliers and traders, both regionally and worldwide, adopt an eco-friendlier approach.

Waste is to be avoided if at all possible. Unavoidable waste is preferably recycled or disposed of in an environmentally-friendly manner.

Through our public relations and educational work, we want to convey environmental knowledge to our employees, co-workers, business partners and participants, increase their environmental awareness and make them change their everyday behaviour in a way that has a lesser impact on the environment' (DEKT 2019: 7).

Implementation of measures

Before every Kirchentag Festival, current environmental goals are looked at in detail and further developed where necessary. The general intention is to minimise or, as far as possible, avoid in its entirety the use of natural resources and the emission of climate-warming relevant gases. Specific environmental goals are defined based on a comprehensive evaluation of the relevance of different environmental aspects and the resulting risks and opportunities with regard to the established environmental impact. Below, we refer to the 2017 Kirchentag Festival in Berlin to present the environmental goals as well as the measures that were implemented and discuss possible further developments with regard to the 2019 Kirchentag in Dortmund (DEKT 2019).

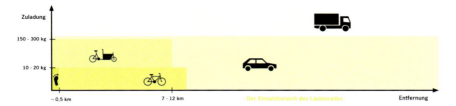

Figure 25.1 Filling the transport gap with cargo bikes since the Kirchentag Hamburg 2013. Source: Hertel & Spott (2014: 12 f).

Catering – consuming organic and fairly traded products

Catering includes the consumption of food during the planning and execution phase of the Kirchentag Festival. During those stages at the 2017 Kirchentag in Berlin, around 170 tonnes of food were consumed. Based on the strategy that the 'Kirchentag isst ökofair' (the Kirchentag is about consuming organic and fairly traded products) and considering the enormous amount of food as well as its impact on production and processing, the 2013 Kirchentag in Hamburg developed and put into practice its own fair, ecological catering concept, which ensures that the catering is continually improved in terms of its environmental effects (DEKT 2019). The objective of the catering concept consists above all in reducing the use of valuable resources through a deliberate selection of food. Hence, the following guidelines apply to the procurement of food (DEKT 2019: 20):

- ecologically grown food;
- food from countries of the global South are fairly traded;
- considering regionality and seasonality of food;
- focussing on vegetarian and vegan options, offering small quantities of organic meat; and
- optimising quantity management.

As far as the catering for participants and helpers at the Kirchentag in Berlin is concerned, the proportion of food produced in line with the EU Eco-Regulation was increased from around 50 per cent to more than 70 per cent. Specialist training sessions and workshops organised prior to the event led to greater awareness among the organisers of the 2019 Kirchentag in Dortmund 2019; the volunteers involved in choosing the (fully vegetarian) food options for gatherings such as the 'Meet and Greet' opening night of the Kirchentag, were given a cookery book titled 'Was für ein Geschmack' (What a taste), which had been specially developed for the event and was meant to assist them in implementing the standards set by the Kirchentag (DEKT 2019). In order to help the canteens develop a sustainable nutrition strategy for the Kirchentag, the transparent 'Gläserne Restaurant' practices seasonal, regional and organic

310   *Oliver Foltin et al.*

dishes.[2] To give hotels and conference venues an idea of how to meet the Kirchentag standards a brochure for chefs and managers was produced.[3]

Mobility – the use of sustainable modes to and at the Festival

One of the goals of the Kirchentag is to boost environmentally-friendly mobility options. Car and air travel are to be reduced through increased use of low-emission or no-emission means of transport such as trains and bicycles. Those who work for the Kirchentag itself are encouraged to do so by the organisers who provide them with a Bahncard 100 for frequent travellers, the option of video-conferencing and the use of cycle couriers during the event. Instead of using cars and vans to transport goods within the 'transport gap' (see Figure 25.1), 12 young volunteers with load bikes completed almost 500 jobs, covering 3.366 km with a corresponding re-duction in CO_2, nitrogen oxides and particulate matter (Hertel & Spott 2014: 39).

At the 2017 Kirchentag in Berlin, for example, the number of the cycle couriers used to transport material between individual event locations was increased. By purchasing a plug-in hybrid car for the Field Office of the Kirchentag in Dortmund, the organisers were able to reduce fuel consumption during the planning stages of the Kirchentag (DEKT 2019). This does, however, only constitute a small part of the mobility concerning the Kirchentag. The mobility options provided to the volunteers and participants of every Kirchentag are much more relevant. What is primarily needed here is a change of awareness through information on environmentally compatible alternative ways of travel and offers available. According to transport statistics, 23 per cent of the visitors of the Kirchentag Festival travels to the event by car while more than 70 per cent use trains and buses/coaches (DEKT 2018b). Since 1981, entrance tickets for the Kirchentag have included a ticket for public transport in the respective host city (HVV 2015: 21). In most cases, people can get from A to B by walking or by hiring bikes, which the Kirchentag makes available in conjunction with the respective suppliers. Participants registering online for the Berlin Kirchentag could furthermore use a link to compensate for their emissions by making a voluntary payment to a respective supplier (DEKT 2019).

Energy-split and remaining emissions

During the 2017 Kirchentag in Berlin, around 85 per cent of the electricity used for preparing and carrying out the event was generated ecologically via regenerative sources of energy. To this end, a cooperation agreement was signed with a respective provider who, for the duration of the event, supplied the open–air stages and exhibition halls with the necessary power and who was independent of the coal and nuclear energy industry. The site in Berlin turned out to be quite vast compared with other host cities. Furthermore, there were fewer participants than expected, which meant that, compared with other Kirchentag Festivals, more fuel was used and too much material was procured,

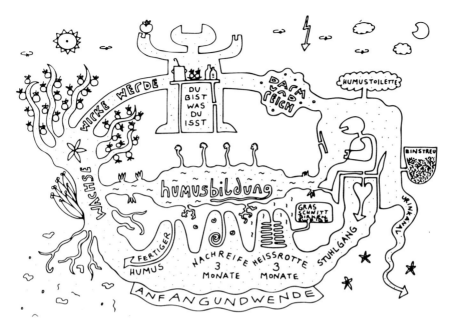

Figure 25.2 Humus Bildung – Humification-Education. Postcard designed for the Kirchentag compost-toilet project 2015.
Source: Bruno Nagel, www.sprachbehausung.de 2015.

which led to an increase in energy and emission values absolute and per head (DEKT 2019).

Sustainable procurement of products and services

The Kirchentag Festival in Berlin succeeded in further enhancing sustainable procurement. The textiles, for example, that were for sale at the Kirchentag shops were exclusively made from organic cotton. Besides, more than 90 per cent of all publications on offer at the Kirchentag was printed on recycled paper. The use of disposable carpets in the exhibition sections of the trade fair area has, for many years, been reduced. Where carpets cannot be dispensed with, carpet tiles are used, which, following the Kirchentag, can be re-used at other trade fairs. In addition, the offices of the Kirchentag are cleaned with predominantly ecological cleaning agents (DEKT 2018b).

Waste reduction and recycling

As soon as the events are being planned and the Kirchentag Festival enters the preparatory phase, a calculation of the necessary as well as the ordered and procured quantities for a multiplicity of products must be undertaken. At the

Kirchentag in Berlin, a specially developed orientation tool for the co-workers was used listing the material and quantities for the many event formats on the basis and experience of previous Kirchentag Festivals. In addition, the procurers are trained to thoroughly review the required quantities as far as their purpose is concerned (DEKT 2018b).

Many of the items on offer at the Kirchentag shop cannot be sold during one Kirchentag Festival. To make products less perishable, general claims without year and city are used, to ensure that these items can be sold at a later date. Left-over textiles such as unsold Kirchentag scarves are, among other things, re-used in small upcycling projects. A workshop for disabled people, for example, turned 2000 scarves from Berlin into bedding that is sold online via kirchentag.de/shop. The Festival set up water stations that form part of so-called information towers where bottles and cups can be refilled. The use of deposit crockery and refillable drinks bottles is the rule at the 'Meet and Greet 'opening night of the Kirchentag Festival and whenever food and drink is provided to the helpers (DEKT 2019).

Responsible water consumption

Due to the water available at public water stations during the event and the frequent use of tap water during meetings, water consumption is somewhat higher than if bottled water were used. The organisers of the Kirchentag Festival are aware of this and accept it because, to them, the frequently superior tap water quality and a reduction of waste are an essential priority. In order to reduce water consumption, the organisers of past Kirchentag Festivals tried to use composting toilets. The advantage of composting toilets is that they do not require water and chemical additives and that, if the composting is performed by experts, the 'muck' left behind by the visitors of the Kirchentag Festival is turned into fertile humus soil (DEKT 2019; see also Figure 25.2 for an artistic view on the process).[4]

Environmental communication and employee trainings

Apart from the external communication of environmental topics and successful case studies, internal communication in the form of employee training sessions is an important factor to ensure the acceptance and implementation of environmental measures. An internal wiki called KiWi is a major base for knowledge transfer for environmental issues from one Kirchentag to the next one (DEKT 2019).

Kirchentag adapting to climate change-related weather extremes

By introducing the project 'Climate Change Adaptation of Big Events based on the 37th Kirchentag Festival in Dortmund in 2019' the Kirchentag Festival has added another dimension to its environmental work. The project, which is funded by the German Ministry of the Environment, consists of an attempt at adapting big events to the consequences of climate change. These climate change adaptations are summarised in a guideline and be made available to other event organisers in the future. The project involved the definition of around 35 measures[5] that refer above all to the adaptation to climate signals such as heat, heavy rains, storms and thunderstorms. They were implemented, and their effectiveness reviewed at the 2019 Kirchentag Festival in Dortmund. Apart from safety issues and questions involving event technology, it is above all about enhancing the awareness of the participants and using available resources such as cool or shady places as preventative measures (DEKT 2019).

Perpetuated environmental standards applied by the Kirchentag Festival

In addition to these measures for the Kirchentag Festival, there is a range of established environmental standards of the Kirchentag that have become a matter of course for many years. The most important are listed below (DEKT 2018b, 2019):

- Office material of past Kirchentag Festivals is re-used.
- The Central Office and, if possible, the Field Office is powered by green electricity.
- The energy-saving default is pre-set on all computers, monitors and printers.
- The default setting when it comes to printing documents on all printers and computers is the 2-sided, black-and-white standard.
- The publications contain references to the quality of the recycled paper.
- Collection points for various special types of waste (CDs, batteries, energy-saving lamps, toner cartridges).
- In the offices and meetings, rooms, boards and table displays contain information about environmental management.
- During tendering, preference is given to regional service providers and companies with a good ecological track record.
- Obligatory Training courses for employees are organised that cover the environment and environmentally friendly behaviour.
- During the event, cycle and cargo-bike couriers are also used for logistics (see youtu.be/fH0-ilgRneQ for the emission-free logistics project in 2013 in Hamburg).
- Each unit within the Field Office is provided with at least one service bicycle.
- 'Paper waste' printed on one side only is used to produce scribbling note pads.

The results of environmental controlling of the Kirchentag Festival

Pursuant to the EMAS Regulation No. 1221/2009, the eco-management system of the Kirchentag must fulfil specific requirements when it comes to the establishment and presentation of key figures. To this end, so-called vital indicators are used to convey environmental achievements. This is meant to ensure a transparent presentation of the environmental successes and a comparison between the different Kirchentag Festivals to make potential changes visible. All EMAS reports could be downloaded on kirchentag.de/umwelt. The key environmental indicators collated by the Kirchentag cover energy sufficiency, water, waste, material use, bio-diversity and emissions. The period covered by environmental controlling at a Kirchentag always includes the entire preparatory and planning stage as well as the time when the actual event takes place. As far as the presentation of the figures that follow the absolute figures for this two-yearly period are halved. This is in line with EMAS Regulation referring to one calendar year and to the number of permanent visitors to a Kirchentag as a reference value. (DEKT 2018b). The figures collated in the field of energy efficiency suggest that the annual use of electricity per permanent participant and based on a reference value of about 105,000 permanent participants per Kirchentag, has been reduced from 6.0 kWh at the 2013 Kirchentag in Hamburg to 3.8 kWh at the 2017 Kirchentag in Berlin. The annual water consumption per participant, however, has risen from 67.1 litres to 74 litres over the same period. The amount of waste was, however, kept at the same level of around 0.5 kg per permanent participant. The same applies to material consumption which, since the 2013 Kirchentag only rose slightly from 0.65 kg to 0.79 kg at the 2017 Kirchentag. The entire annual emissions of greenhouse gases (CO_2 equivalent) have increased slightly and risen from 29.8 kg to 36 kg per permanent participant. Overall, the 105,000 permanent participants of the Berlin Kirchentag including its preparation caused carbon dioxide emissions of around 8,000 tonnes (DEKT 2018b). One must, however, take into consideration that one cannot always compare the figures of one Kirchentag Festival with those of another. Many environmental effects depend on the circumstances on-site. Nevertheless, the environmental indicators help establish a framework of measurable environmental effects within which the execution and organisation of a Kirchentag Festival are to take place and which can be continually improved through the implementation of the measures.

Outlook: conclusion and recommendations

The DEKT has achieved some things that are worth seeing, but on which it is not possible to rest. Like all major events, it continues to be challenged both nationally and internationally in view of the global challenges. In order to further reduce its ecological footprint step by step, it is not enough to be a kind of real laboratory for sustainable development for the respective host city and to strengthen existing transformation approaches by taking up local-regional issues with commitment. Rather, it seems necessary to us that, in addition to the continuation of an ambitious sustainability course, the Kirchentag, as an advance requester on the market, also initiates sustainable innovations vis-à-vis trade fair companies and producers. Ultimately, DEKT must also ask itself what the transition to a post-fossil society means for the organisation of events and what is a tolerable size for such an event. Efficiency cannot and must not then be the sole yardstick. In addition, there is the challenge as a learning organisation to look for concretions of a culture of sufficiency that can be practically lived by visitors, participants and organisations. To pass on these experiences to new employees, but also nationally and internationally to other event organisers with reports on their experiences and in the discourse, also in order to benefit from them, will remain an important and challenging task.

In view of the challenges of not crossing the planetary borders, not exceeding the Paris climate target of 1.5 degrees Celsius, and also as an organiser of major events to take care of the implementation of the Sustainable Development Goals, all major events – party conventions, city or sports festivals, trade fairs, etc. should enter into a cheerful competition with the Kirchentag for the most environmentally friendly and sustainable event. This would have several positive effects. Here are three of them:

- Suppliers and service providers (e.g. caterers) must adapt to new requirements – and if several do so, the pressure to change increases.
- When green events become mainstream, politics is increasingly required to follow suit and create the necessary framework conditions (or abolish them).
- Event visitors are increasingly confronted with a new culture of food, mobility, infrastructure etc. and motivated to change their own behaviour.

List of abbreviations

CD   compact disc
CO_2 carbon dioxide
DEKT   Deutscher Evangelischer Kirchentag (German Protestant Church Festival)
EC   European Commission
EMAS   Eco-Management and Audit Scheme
kg   kilogram
kWh   kilowatt hour
sqm   square metre

Notes

1 See ec.europa.eu/environment/emas/index_en.htm.
2 See youtu.be/UBN2dplKlYY.
3 See dxz7zkp528hul.cloudfront.net/production/htdocs/fileadmin/dateien/zzz_NEUER_ BAUM/Ueber_uns/Umweltengagement/PDF/KleVer/DEKT34_Leitfaden_Klever.pdf.
4 See also youtu.be/k3J1hq3w9zk.
5 See www.klimaangepasst.de.

316 *Oliver Foltin et al.*

References

Cierjacks, A., Teichert, V., and Diefenbacher, H. (2008). *Umweltmanagement von Grossveranstaltungen.* Heidelberg: Forschungsstätte der Evangelischen Studiengemeinschaft e.V.

DEKT (ed.) (2015). Ordnung des Deutschen Evangelischen Kirchentages. Retrieved from https://dxz7zkp528hul.cloudfront.net/production/htdocs/fileadmin/dateien/ zzz_NEUER_BAUM/Ueber_uns/Organisation/DEKT_Ordnung_des_Deutschen_ Evangelischen_Kirchentages.pdf.

DEKT (ed.) (2018a). Finanzen So wirtschaftet der Kirchentag. Retrieved from www. kirchentag.de/ueber_uns/finanzen/.

DEKT (ed.) (2018b). Aktualisierte Umwelterklärung 2017 des 36. Deutschen Evangelischen Kirchentages nach der EMAS-Verordnung Nr. 1221/2009. Retrieved from https://dxz7zkp528hul.cloudfront.net/production/htdocs/fileadmin/dateien/ zzz_NEUER_BAUM/Ueber_uns/Umweltengagement/PDF/Umweltmanagement/ DEKT_aktualisierte_Umwelterklaerung_2017.pdf.

DEKT (ed.) (2019). *Eine Bestandsaufnahme vor dem Deutschen Evangelischen Kirchentag in Dortmund 2019 mit den Standorten Zentrales Büro Fulda und Geschäftsstelle Dortmund sowie den Umweltbilanzzahlen der Jahre 2010 bis 2018 vom Zentralen Büro.* Fulda: Verein zur Förderung des Deutschen Evangelischen Kirchentages e.V. Retrieved from https://dxz7zkp528hul. cloudfront.net/production/htdocs/fileadmin/dateien/zzz_NEUER_BAUM/Ueber_uns/ Umweltengagement/UEberarbeitete_Seiten/Umwelterklaerung_Dortmund.pdf.

DEKT (ed.) (n.d.). Was ist Kirchentag? Wie er ist. Was er will. Woher er kommt. Retrieved from www.kirchentag.de/ueber_uns/was_ist_kirchentag/.

Hertel, C. and Spott, M. (2014). Leitfaden Lastenräder einsetzen. Bei Großveranstaltungen, in Großeinrichtungen. Stuttgart: 34. Deutscher Evangelischer Kirchentag Hamburg 2013 e.V. Retrieved from: https://dxz7zkp528hul.cloudfront.net/production/htdocs/fileadmin/ dateien/zzz_NEUER_BAUM/Ueber_uns/Umweltengagement/PDF/Lastenrad/DEKT34_ Leitfaden_Lastenraeder_einsetzen.pdf.

HVV (ed.) (2015). *50 Jahre HVV. Magazin. Jubiläumsausgabe 2015.* Hamburg. Tempus Corporate GmbH.

Pickel, G., Jaeckel, Y., and Yendell, A. (2015). *Der Deutsche Evangelische Kirchentag – Religiöses Bekenntnis, politische Veranstaltung oder einfach nur ein Event?.* Baden-Baden: Nomos.

Regulation (EC) No 1221/2009 of the European Parliament and of the Council of 25 November 2009 on the voluntary participation by organisations in a Community eco-management and audit scheme (EMAS).

Ueberschär, E. (ed.) (2017). *Deutscher Evangelischer Kirchentag. Wurzeln und Anfänge.* Gütersloh: Gütersloher Verlagshaus.

Umweltgutachterausschuss beim Bundesministerium für Umwelt, Naturschutz und nukleare Sicherheit (ed.) (2017). 36. Deutscher Evangelischer Kirchentag erhält EMAS-Ehrenurkunde. Retrieved from www.emas.de/aktuelles/2017/30-05-17-kirchentag-emas-ehrenurkunde/.

26 The Kwawu resilient entrepreneurial ecosystems

A complex adaptive systems approach to achieving the Sustainable Development Goals

Eben Anuwa-Amarh, Christoph Hinske, Nana Kwabena Bamfo-Debrah, David Sefa, Sheriff Amarh, and Stephen Nassam

Introduction

The relationship between recourse efficiency, entrepreneurial action in business ecosystems and regional economic development is receiving increasing attention from scholars and policymakers (Roundy, Brockman & Bradshaw 2018; Galindo & Méndez 2014; CII–GBC International Conference on Resource Efficiency n.d.). There is the recognition that social constructions and cultural values have the potential of generating entrepreneurial action, which in turn drive economic development and revitalisation at local, regional and state levels (Roundy et al. 2018; Strickling 2016; Arruda, Nogueira & Costa, 2013). Researchers are, therefore, gradually shifting their focus from studies of entrepreneurial action to complex, resilient entrepreneurial ecosystems and systems-level leadership (Dreier, Nabarro & Nelson 2019). Entities such as the World Business Council for Sustainable Development are offering high-level Business Ecosystems Training in cooperation with KPMG a multinational professional services network focusing on financial audit, tax, and management consulting services (World Business Council for Sustainable Development n.d.).

Whereas studies of entrepreneurial ecosystems have focused mainly on identifying the core attributes of the elements in established ecosystems (Spigel 2016), little has been done to seek to understand the extent to which complex systems of interdependencies between the said elements create emergent patterns (Roundy et al. 2018; Mack and Mayer 2016) and social innovation towards sustainability (Mulgan 2019). Nonetheless, it is this focus on the complex interactions among agents, organisations, and socio-cultural forces, that demonstrates how entrepreneurial ecosystems emerge. According to a recent Deloitte Article (Kelly 2015) these business ecosystems are characterised by way of how their interaction dynamics allow individual actors to 'achieve something together that lies beyond the effective scope and capabilities of any individual actor (or even group of broadly similar actors)'.

In their report, the authors highlight examples where business ecosystem strategies were used to tackle complex nexus problems such as'water resource management, […] and food safety' (Kelly, 2015).

The objective of this chapter is to examine the nature of the resilient entrepreneurial ecosystem among the people of Kwawu in Ghana through the lens of complexity science. The study assesses how the Kwawu people have progressed in terms of nurturing a resilient entrepreneurial ecosystem through a complex network of agents, community resources, assets, and support systems that help entrepreneurs to thrive and succeed.

The rest of the chapter is organised as follows. Firstly, a brief description of the Kwawu of Ghana is provided. It is followed by a review of existing literature resilient entrepreneurial ecosystem, and complexity theory. Next, the flexibility of qualitative and interpretive methods is considered as particularly appropriate for studying the complex Kwawu resilient entrepreneurial ecosystems. Finally, findings and propositions of the study are discussed, and the implications for researchers, practitioners and policymakers are suggested.

The Kwahu of Ghana

Kwahu is an area and group of people that live in the Eastern region of Ghana. They are a part of the Twi-speaking Akan group. Their motto is 'Asaase Aban, Yenti Gyae'. 'Asaase Aban' means 'Natural Fortress', given its position as the highest habitable region in Ghana. 'Yenti Gyae' stands for 'We Do Not Quit.' Put together, 'Asaase Aban, Yenti Gyae' means 'Natural Fortress, We Do Not Quit'. Colloquially, it implies 'Natural Fortress, We Do Not Understand Stop'. It shows the tenacity of purpose and the willingness to charge forward in spite of the odds or obstacles in one's way and to cause things to happen.

The paramount king (Omanhene), and the royal lineage of the Kwawu lives at Abene, north of Abetifi on the edges of the highlands. Till date, the road from Abetifi to the enclave of Abene, which houses the Omanhene, is surrounded by some unease, given the stories recounted of the battles fought along the route. The Kwawu people of Ghana, over three centuries, have developed unique but successful, complex, resilient entrepreneurial ecosystems. These emergent ecosystems enable them to find better solutions to business problems than their peers, despite facing similar challenges and having no extra resources than their peers.

Literature review

Entrepreneurial ecosystems

According to Roundy et al. (2018), it was Bahrami and Evans (1995), who were the first to introduce the term 'ecosystem' into the academic entrepreneurship literature. The central notions of entrepreneurship studies, thus, shifted away from individual, personality-based enquiry, towards a broader viewpoint that incorporated the role of social, cultural, and economic forces in the entrepreneurship process (Roundy et al. 2018; Stam & Spigel 2016).

Despite its popularity, there is currently no widely accepted definition of entrepreneurial ecosystems amongst researchers or practitioners. Roundy et al. (2018) attempted an explanation. They split the term, entrepreneurial ecosystem, into two elements. The authors considered the first element, en-trepreneurial, as a process by which opportunities for producing innovative goods and services are examined, appraised and utilised. The second element, the ecosystem, is a biological metaphor, which connotes the interaction of interdependent actors in a geographic community. Thus, entrepreneurial ecosystems focus on the entrepreneurial culture, and supportive policies 'cultures, institutions, and networks that build up within a region over time' (Roundy et al. 2018: 2).

Entrepreneurial ecosystems are, thus, historically produced (Saxenian 1994; Kenney & Patton 2005) with high levels of innovativeness (Acs et al. 2014). Further, entrepreneurial ecosystems create a cohesive social and economic system that supports the creation and growth of new ventures (Spigel 2016). In this chapter, an entrepreneurial ecosystem is defined as 'a set of interdependent actors and factors coordinated in such a way that they enable productive entrepreneurship within a particular territory and community (Stam & Spigel 2016: 2).

Resilience and entrepreneurial ecosystems

Korber and McNaughton (2018) reviewed extant literature at the intersec-tion of resilience and entrepreneurial ecosystems. The authors posited that the resilience construct is essential for entrepreneurial ecosystems for several reasons. Firstly, academics frequently use resilience as synonyms for pre-paredness, hardiness, persistence, or self-efficacy to justify why some en-trepreneurs and their firms perform better than their non-resilient counterparts. Secondly, intellectual and behavioural entrepreneurial qualities and distinct patterns of entrepreneurship are said to nurture the capacity of individuals and firms to adapt to new conditions and to contribute to long-term sustainability through innovation. Thirdly, is the ability of en-trepreneurial ecosystems to foster macro-level (regions, communities, economies) resilience within the context of entrepreneurial failure, recovery and transformation.

An entrepreneurial ecosystem is, thus, resilient when it is able to 'absorb' disturbances and undergo the changes necessary to transform its essential behaviours, structures, and identity into a system that is better able to re-spond to disruptions (Stam & Spigel 2016; Walker, Holling, Carpenter & Kinzig 2004). It can survive disruptions without suffering a significant loss of function and, can be stronger after the disruption (Stam & Spigel 2016; Holling 1986).

320   *Eben Anuwa-Amarh et al.*

Complexity systems and entrepreneurship, and emergence

Typically, complexity systems analyse the interactions between seemingly unpredictable patterns, behaviours, and structures produced at one level to develop from and influenced by processes operating at different levels and by the interactions of the overall system (Roundy et al. 2018; Anderson, Drakopoulou Dodd & Jack 2012; Lissack & Letiche 2002). Systems that exhibit complexity are adaptive and can change based on experience (Schindehutte & Morris 2009). Within such systems, the individual elements continually interact with one another and the environment across levels, altering the system and its response to disruptions and allowing it to adapt to changes (Roundy et al. 2018; Messier & Puettmann 2011).

Fundamentally, both complexity theory and entrepreneurship scholarship are the focus of the concept of emergence and new arrangements, which include structures, processes, and system-wide properties that emerge within and across the system (Lichtenstein 2011). Thus, the complexity lens explores exchanges and emergent phenomena at multiple levels of analysis and stress the significance of nonlinear and unpredictable processes that create new and emergent formations (Roundy et al. 2018; Lichtenstein 2011).

Resilient, Entrepreneurial ecosystems practised with complexity theory enable business people to practice entrepreneurship sustainably. According to Shepherd and Patzelt (2011: 6), sustainable entrepreneurship can be defined as:

- The discovery, creation and exploitation of opportunities to create future goods and services that sustain the natural and communal environment and provide development gain for others.
- These sustainable entrepreneurial activities are generally consistent with sustainable development goals and are, in turn, relevant for tackling fundamental societal challenges such as the development of sustainable production and consumption patterns (Goal 12 of the Sustainable Development Goals).

The thrust of this chapter is that entrepreneurial ecosystems are the sets of actors, institutions, social networks, and cultural values that produce and sustain entrepreneurial activity. They are resilient to the extent that they can respond to disruptions while balancing the seemingly paradoxical tension between the diversity and coherence of its elements. Complexity systems examine the interactions between seemingly unpredictable patterns, behaviours, and structures produced at one level in an entrepreneurial ecosystem to develop from and influenced by activities operating at different levels and by the reactions of the overall system.

Method

The study, which is qualitative, employs an inductive and interpretive approach to data collection. It aimed at gaining insight and a more in-depth understanding of what makes the Kwawu entrepreneurial ecosystem more resilient and sustainable. Studies within the interpretive paradigm aim at giving voice to the various actors to construct their interpretation and meanings (Burrel & Morgan 1979). A primary concern of the researchers was to create an understanding, describe and explain what currently obtains in the complex, resilient Kwawu entrepreneurial ecosystem from the actors themselves. To achieve this objective, the researchers studied the actors within their social contexts. As a result, close contact qualitative methods, such as ethnographic and participant observation, mental model mapping, in-depth interviews, and focus group discussions, were used.

Before starting the study, prior consent was sought from the Omanhene of the Kwawu people. In-depth interviews were conducted with seven elders of the Omanhene and thirty Kwawu entrepreneurs. Three focus group discussions, consisting of a total of twenty-eight participants, were held.

Findings and discussions

The study presents findings on three factors that influence the interactions and interrelations in complex, resilient ecosystems. They are: (a) durable enabling entrepreneurial culture; (b) an interdependent learning cycle, which consists of five inter-related elements – observing, doing, adopting, adapting and replicating; (c) and spiriting (wisdom dispensing and 'grey hair' services) and social inclusion.

Enabling entrepreneurial culture

An enabling entrepreneurial culture, within this context, is the affirmative sense of empowering individuals to become successful entrepreneurs. One principal way by which the Kwawu community bolsters this shared

Figure 26.1 The eight elements of the Kwawu entrepreneurial ecosystem.

entrepreneurship (free enterprise, private enterprise) philosophy to promote prosperity and expand equitable opportunity, is the continuous investment in an enabling entrepreneurial (business, commercial, risk-taking, ground-breaking, empire-building) culture. This nurturing and self-sustaining culture is as vital as the air they breathe and the water they drink.

The community has quality mentors, who are a network of successful entrepreneurs, that are handy, to offer entrepreneurial mentoring. An important asset of the community is the availability of start-up capital, which is usually generated within these trusted networks. The entrepreneurial cultural outcomes they cherish include: created wealth, trusting and faithful relations, imaginative and inspired thinking, less wastefulness and a developed ability to 'sniff' business opportunities. Even though entrepreneurship is driven by the 'self', they also value cooperation and collaboration with business associates through the sharing of business ideas and products.

Proposition 1: *you become what your culture is.*

An interdependent learning cycle

Observing

From childhood, the Kwawu observe the traits, personas, behaviours and mannerisms of their entrepreneurial parents, uncles, aunties and other close associates and attempt to mimic them later on in life. They see close associates start businesses and fail and start again. They then develop the inclination towards having a resilient mindset that business failures can be faced squarely and overcome. Primarily, they learn the basic rules of the game of entrepreneurship and jump in almost effortlessly. Factors that encourage the inclination towards developing by observing include:

- The availability of actors such as parents and close associations who are seen to be warm, nurturing, and who reward entrepreneurial behaviour.
- Successful entrepreneurs who are wealthy and admired and have high social status.
- Community leaders who inspire entrepreneurial confidence.

Proposition 2: intense observation improves your ability to interact with your surroundings and other people to produce the desired outcome.

Doing

'Development by doing' is realised by putting observed behaviour into practice to achieve detectable levels of excellence. Development by doing is complemented by coaching from close associates to accomplish a shared agenda of successful entrepreneurial development. According to the Kwawus, most of these skills cannot be learned in the formal lecture halls of our universities. However, it is this type of universal, time-tested apprenticeship has always been critical in addressing skills shortages globally.

The World Economic Forum echoed this when it noted that there would be no guarantee of success when one when throws intelligent and highly educated persons on a commodities trading floor without any level of apprenticeship (Stefanova Ratcheva & Leopold 2018). However, when intelligent and intuitive individuals on the factory floor or trading floor learn the complex supply chain, then they would not earn a well-paying job with growth potential, but also acquire personalised skillsets to flourish in the role and the industry. This is what the Kwawus call 'Development by Doing'.

Proposition 3: *you become what you do.*

Adopting

Sometimes, transitioning from a non-entrepreneurs to entrepreneurs involve choosing new ways of thinking and doing things. For the Kwawu, it encompasses the informed selection and accepting of other people's tested entrepreneurial ethos as your own. The Kwawus do this by deliberately choosing to embrace the philosophy of self and personal responsibility, without abandoning group interactions. They also embrace the ethos of constant and consistence learning from, and packaging themselves after, successful pace setters and the adopting of new technologies, products and service. This adopted ethos eventually becomes part of them.

Proposition 4: *what you adopt becomes part of you.*

Adapting

Developing by adapting is done in response to changing business circumstances and environment (for examples, changes in social, political and economic conditions; the emergence of new technologies, products and services). The purpose is to ensure relevance, survival and to remain competitive in changing markets. This sort of development is not only done to mitigate undesirable impacts of past decisions and actions about the business and business environment, but also to explore new ways of making better decisions and improving outcomes. The adaptation involves cooperation and collaboration with business associates and at formal and informal gatherings and festivals that encourage individual input and self-achievements.

Proposition 5: *when you adapt, you stay relevant.*

Replication

Replication refers to a situation where tested and established business strategies of the Kwawu are tried elsewhere in a new geographical area or a new market, or for a new set of customers. Replication often leads to the leaners setting up new businesses or trading systems where the ability which has already been acquired is used to set up expanded or new companies. For the Kwawu people, replication is meant to reproduce and multiply business outcomes through themselves or selected individuals.

Proposition 6: *when you replicate, you reproduce.*

Spiriting

Spiriting, in this context, connotes dispensing wisdom and 'grey hair' services to the entire community. It is about incarnating one's self into individuals and the community by descending into the system to give birth to one's entrepreneurial kind. The Kwawu Spiritors are holders and the embodiment of entrepreneurial wisdom. They encourage and stir up the community to entrepreneurial action. The Spiritors are few but noticeable. They are very experienced community leaders who are vision carriers and successful pace-setters who have great wisdom. The role of Spiritors are as follows:

- Empowering and enabling the community to create and preserve entrepreneurial culture.
- Figuring out and shaping how the community creates and maintains the entrepreneurship edge.
- Describing how the community creates an emergent entrepreneurial ecosystem.

They provide:

- Insight, awareness and comprehension about entrepreneurship.
- Influence, encouragement and guidance on entrepreneurship.

The most desired future of the Spiritors includes valuing and exploiting future socio-economic-environmental ideals, grooming of future holders of the vision and collaborating with current vision bearers to build businesses in Ghana.

Proposition 7: *when you 'spirit' out, you multiply and spread over a wide area.*

Social inclusion

It is the character and atmosphere that holds the elements of the entrepreneurship development together. Social inclusion provides the required energy and conditions for mutual sustainability. The Kwawus do this by staying mindful that welcoming, accommodating, nurturing and interacting with many different peoples and cultures (internal and external stakeholders) for mutual benefits and sustainability are vital.

> Proposition 8: *social inclusion leads to improved opportunity and ability of humanity to live in dignity.*

Contributions to sustainable management and development theory and practice

The Kwawu project is an ongoing international effort and intents to make some contributions to sustainable management and entrepreneurial theory and practice. Firstly, it combines entrepreneurship ecosystem, resilience and complexity systems theory to develop an ecosystem-level unit of analysis. By using an ecosystem and complexity lenses, researchers can better observe the competitive, collaborative and cooperative characteristics of business organisations.

Secondly, the findings suggest that increasing the degree of enabling entrepreneurial culture, interdependent learning cycles and spiriting, can enhance levels of interaction and interrelations in ecosystems, resulting in more efficient use of social and material resources for economic development. Consequently, more skills, knowledge, ideas, resources, and different forms of support can be exchanged within complex entrepreneurial ecosystems to make it resilient, robust, enriched and sustainable. These insights are aligned with research done by the United Nations Global Compact and Volans (n.d.), stating that business collaboration in ecosystems drastically increases their resource performance and ability to deliver against the United Nations Sustainable Development Goals.

Thirdly, understanding to create and sustain entrepreneurial business ecosystems is an essential component of the implementation of the circular economy (Valkokari, Tura, Ståhle, Hanski & Ahola 2019). By analysing mental models, our chapter shows how entrepreneurs, over centuries, successfully collaborated in networks to co-create value.

Finally, the insights from this chapter are constantly tested and further developed with a wide range of ecosystem partners from research and practice. Together they are applying the described principles in reality labs, developing policies and systemic actions. These projects are co-hosted by the Institute of Development and Technology Management, Cape Coast, Ghana, The Engagement Company and SAXION University of Applied Sciences, Academy of Finance, Economics and Management (Engagement Company 2019).

Acknowledgements

This project was a pre-study of the early version of ARISE before it (ARISE) was funded. ARISE is an acronym for 'Africa Renaissance, Integration and Sustainable Entrepreneurship', which is a think tank registered in Ghana. The vision of ARISE is to be the pivotal facilitator in driving Africa's prosperity through sustained entrepreneurial development.

References

Acs, Z. J., Estrin, S., Mickiewicz, T., and Szerb, L. (2014). *The continued search for the Solow residual: The role of national entrepreneurial ecosystem.* IZA Discussion Papers, No. 8652.

Anderson, A. R., Drakopoulou Dodd, S., and Jack, S. L. (2012). Entrepreneurship as connecting: some implications for theorising and practice. *Management Decision*, 50(5), 958–971.

Arruda, C., Nogueira, V. S., and Costa, V. (2013). The Brazilian entrepreneurial ecosystem of startups: An analysis of entrepreneurship determinants in Brazil as seen from the OECD pillars. *Journal of Entrepreneurship and Innovation Management*, 2(3), 17–57.

Bahrami, H. and Evans, S. (1995). Flexible re-cycling and high-technology entrepreneurship. *California Management Review*, 37(3), 62–89.

Burrell, G. and Morgan, G. (1979). *Two dimensions: four paradigms. Sociological Paradigms and Organizational Analysis*, 21–37.

CII-GBC International Conference on Resource Efficiency. (n.d.). Retrieved 26 October 2019, from http://globalbusinesscoalition.org/gbc-initiatives/cii-gbc-international-conference-resource-efficiency/.

Dreier, L., Nabarro, D., and Nelson, J. (2019). Systems leadership can change the world – but what exactly is it? [Blog post]. Retrieved 26 September 2019, from www.weforum.org/agenda/2019/09/systems-leadership-can-change-the-world-but-what-does-it-mean.

Engagement Company. (2018). Activating high value business ecosystems to achieve the U.N. SDGs together! Retrieved 12 August 2019, from www.theengagementcompany.co/saxion-event-testimonial-page.

Engagement Company. (2019). What if … we hacked the 'social code' that permits all Dutch organizations by 2021 to recruit (and keep) young, high-educated talents, thus, enabling them to shape the 4th Industrial Revolution? Retrieved 3 October 2019, from www.theengagementcompany.co/saxion-leadership-journey-2019-landing-page.

Galindo, M. Á. and Méndez, M. T. (2014). Entrepreneurship, economic growth, and innovation: Are feedback effects at work? *Journal of Business Research*, 67(5), 825–829.

Holling, C. S. (1986). The resilience of terrestrial ecosystems: local surprise and global change. *Sustainable Development of the Biosphere*, 14, 292–317.

Kelly, E. (2015). Introduction: business ecosystems come of age. Retrieved 18 September 2019, from www2.deloitte.com/us/en/insights/focus/business-trends/2015/business-ecosystems-come-of-age-business-trends.html?id=us:2el:3lk:4di_gl:5eng:6di&range=0/45/3/1/3/57/86/0:0,1/1/45/3/1/3/57/86/0:1.

Kenney, M. and Patton, D. (2005). Entrepreneurial geographies: support networks in three high-technology industries. *Economic Geography*, 81(2) 201–228.

Korber, S. and McNaughton, R. B. (2018). Resilience and entrepreneurship: a systematic literature review. *International Journal of Entrepreneurial Behavior & Research*, 24(7), 1129–1154.

Lichtenstein, B. B. (2011). Complexity science contributions to the field of entrepreneurship. *The Sage Handbook of Complexity and Management*, 471–493. Thousand Oaks, CA: Sage.

Lissack, M. R. and Letiche, H. (2002). Complexity, emergence, resilience, and coherence: gaining perspective on organizations and their study. *Emergence, A Journal of Complexity Issues in Organizations and Management*, 4(3), 72–94.

Mack, E. and Mayer, H. (2016). The evolutionary dynamics of entrepreneurial ecosystems. *Urban Studies*, 53(10), 2118–2133.

Messier, C. and Puettmann, K. J. (2011). Forests as complex adaptive systems: implications for forest management and modelling. *Italian Journal of Forest and Mountain Environments*, 66(3), 249–258.

Mulgan, G. (2019). Social innovation comes of age: the idea that societies need innovation is becoming more mainstream, but there's still a long way to go. [Blog post]. Retrieved 8 November 2019, from www.nesta.org.uk/blog/social-innovation-comes-age/?utm_source=Nesta+Weekly+Newsletter&utm_campaign=ae2ed14096-EMAIL_CAMPAIGN_2019_11_12_09_39&utm_medium=email&utm_term=0_d17364114d-ae2ed14096-182109293.

Roundy, P. T., Bradshaw, M., and Brockman, B. K. (2018). The emergence of entrepreneurial ecosystems: a complex adaptive systems approach. *Journal of Business Research*, 86, 1–10.

Saxenian, A. (1994). Regional networks: industrial adaptation in Silicon Valley and route 128.

Schindehutte, M. and Morris, M. H. (2009). Advancing strategic entrepreneurship research: the role of complexity science in shifting the paradigm. *Entrepreneurship Theory and Practice*, 33(1), 241–276.

Shepherd, D. A. and Patzelt, H. (2011). The new field of sustainable entrepreneurship: studying entrepreneurial action linking 'what is to be sustained' with 'what is to be developed'. *Entrepreneurship Theory and Practice*, 35(1), 137–163.

Spigel, B. (2016). Developing and governing entrepreneurial ecosystems: the structure of entrepreneurial support programs in Edinburgh, Scotland. *International Journal of Innovation and Regional Development*, 7(2), 141–160.

Stam, F. C. and Spigel, B. (2016). Entrepreneurial ecosystems. *USE Discussion Paper Series*, 16(13).

Stefanova Ratcheva, V. and Leopold, T. (2018, September 17). 5 things to know about the future of jobs. Retrieved 12 October 2019, from www.weforum.org/agenda/2018/09/future-of-jobs-2018-things-to-know/.

Strickling, J. A. (2016). Developing entrepreneurial ecosystems: integrating social evolutionary theory and signalling theory to explain the role of media in entrepreneurial ecosystems.

United Nations Global Compact and Volans. (n.d.). Collaborative ecosystem in a nutshell. Retrieved 23 October 2019, from http://breakthrough.unglobalcompact.org/breakthrough-business-models/collaborative-ecosystem/.

Valkokari, P., Tura, N., Ståhle, M., Hanski, J., and Ahola, T. (2019). Advancing circular business. Retrieved from www.vtt.fi/sites/datatowisdom/PublishingImages/publications/FINAL%20Advancing%20circular%20business.pdf.

Walker, B., Holling, C. S., Carpenter, S., and Kinzig, A. (2004). Resilience, adaptability and transformability in social-ecological systems. *Ecology and Society*, 9(2).

World Business Council for Sustainable Development. (n.d.). www.wbcsd.org/Programs/Redefining-Value/Business-Decision-Making/Measurement-Valuation/BET/Business-Ecosystems-Training-BET-Program-Overview. Retrieved 23 September 2019, from www.wbcsd.org/Programs/Redefining-Value/Business-Decision-Making/Measurement-Valuation/BET/Business-Ecosystems-Training-BET-Program-Overview.

27 Exploring the possibility of a meat tax

Floris de Graad

Significant changes start small. With a new starting point. Paying the actual price of a product is such a starting point. It can lead to change on all levels. In this case we explore the effects of paying the actual price of meat.

The significant challenges of our era come together in our meat consumption. It's like a magnifying glass that projects the issues at the focal point on our plates. But because we all eat every day, this is also the field in which we're not powerless. We are all part of it. And the hopeful thing is: if we can create changes regarding this complicated issue, it can be done for many other areas, too.

Of course, good intentions and conscious consumption are commendable. But it won't be enough. To paraphrase Adam Smith's famous words, an invisible hand is intervening. Also as long as this invisible hand intervenes root causes of today's food-related problems can only poorly be addressed. This invisible hand consists of the principle that many of the costs related to the production and consumption of meat are not included in the price. Food products from systems that cause the most damage appear to be the most affordable, while more sustainably produced food seems expensive. Biojournaal (2018), Benveniste (2018), Schravesande (2009). In short, we do not pay the actual price for meat.

To be sustainable, all social costs which come with the production and consumption of meat should be included in the price. Although these costs are still invisible in most cases today, they're no less real because of that. Sooner or later, they have to be paid by someone. Choosing for a realistic price – in this case of meat – is a matter of moral consciousness. It's not about left or right. It is just that consumers can't organise this themselves. But it can be done with the introduction of a meat tax.

This meat tax should at least cover the social costs of production and consumption of meat. Think about deforestation, climate change, soil erosion, antibiotic resistance, water consumption, ammonia emissions, health, among others. Social costs are being made and left unpaid for in all these areas.

The problem

The demand for food is ever increasing. World population is projected to grow to 9 billion people by 2050. To meet the growing demand, the

United Nations Convention to Combat Desertification expects global food production would need to increase by 50%. Others, like the FAO project a 60% increase or even a doubling.

Apart from the growing population, the demand for animal protein is increasing due to changing consumption patterns. Booming economies like China are increasing their consumption of meat while diary is becoming more popular in India. In general, these countries follow the same route Western Europe did half a century ago.

On the other hand, a reverse transition away from animal products is about to breakthrough in Europe and the United States. This reverse transition is an important trend, since animal protein has disproportionate environmental impacts, particularly, when produced in intensive production systems employing massive use of feed crops.

For food sustainability, climate change is often considered paramount. However, about a dozen of the most critical issues were listed by Rockström et al. (2009), who identified and quantified several boundary values that should not be transgressed. Subsequently, these were ranked by Aiking (2014, 2018), showing that food production is an essential driver of all of them, without exception. The rate of biodiversity loss, the nitrogen cycle disruption and climate change did already cross the boundary of non-reversible impact, with biodiversity loss being most dramatic.

The production of animal proteins (meat, dairy and eggs) is, in many cases highly inefficient. Animals need to be fed to 'produce' proteins. Conversion losses from plant to animal protein by livestock are 85% on average (both nitrogen and energy). As a consequence, 77% of all agricultural land is dedicated to livestock and livestock feed production.

This land claim means a big share of the problems associated with food production, in general, has, after all, to be assigned to the production of animal proteins.

Poore and Nemecek (2018) claim moving from current diets to a diet that excludes animal products has transformative potential, reducing food's land use by 3.1 (2.8 to 3.3) billion ha (a 76% reduction), including a 19% reduction in arable land. Food's greenhouse gas emissions would be reduced by 6.6 (5.5 to 7.4) billion metric tons of CO_2eq (a 49% reduction).

The transformative potential of a diet without animal products also include acidification by 50% (45 to 54%); eutrophication by 49% (37 to 56%); and scarcity-weighted freshwater withdrawals by 19% (−5 to 32%) for a 2010 reference year.

In short: an area as large as Africa could be withdrawn from agriculture when the world would shift to a plant-based diet. However, the optimum from the land use-perspective is probably a diet with little use of dairy, since some pasture lands can only be used for livestock, while grazing on pasture lands is possible with little harm to environment and biodiversity.

But for now, over the past 50 years, increased demand for animal products has accounted for 65% of agricultural land-use change.

Meanwhile, the conditions for increased food production are worsening, mainly due to land degradation. The causes of land degradation are many and often intertwined with the problems mentioned above, but land degradation poses a problem in its own right. Land degradation is the most severe threat to food production, food security, and natural resource conservation in Africa, particularly for the poor and vulnerable population of the drylands. About 73% of the African drylands are degraded, and 51% are severely degraded. At least 485 million Africans are affected by land degradation which is a widespread problem that affects soils, landscapes, and human welfare (Bado & Bationo 2018). Some scholars call land degradation even 'the single most pressing current global problem'. However, reliable data on land degradation is still scarce.

Furthermore, intensive animal protein production requires 10–1000 times more water than plant protein.

Antibiotic resistance is becoming an increasingly severe threat to human health through the progressive loss of effective therapeutic treatment options for many diseases and infections. While a large part of this problem stems from over-use of antibiotics in medical care, another part comes from their use in agriculture. Apart from costs related to the production of animal proteins, there are also many costs associated with the consumption of (mainly red) meat:

> The consumption of red and processed meat exceeds recommended levels in most high and middle-income countries and has been associated with a range of adverse health impacts. In 2015, the cancer agency of the World Health Organization, the International Agency for Research on Cancer (IARC), classified the consumption of red meat, which includes beef, lamb, and pork, as carcinogenic to humans if eaten in processed form, and as probably carcinogenic if eaten unprocessed. In addition to being linked with cancer, the consumption of red and processed meat has also been associated with increased rates of coronary heart disease, stroke, type 2 diabetes mellitus and overall mortality.
>
> (Springmann et al. 2018)

According to Springmann et al., the consumption of red meat was associated with 860,000 deaths globally in the year 2020, and that of processed meat with 1,530,000 deaths. When assessed together, those represented 4.4% of all projected deaths in the analysis in that year.

About two-thirds of attributable deaths (64%) occurred in middle-income countries, one third (32%) in high-income countries, and a small portion (4%) in low-income countries: 'Those impacts and the IARC's classification raise the question whether the consumption of red and processed meat should be regulated similar to other carcinogens or to other foods of public health concern, such as sugary drinks' (Springmann et al. 2018). Much of the cost that comes with the above has already been calculated; some subjects need further research. But they have never been added up.

What can be calculated and monetised

It sounds unusual; we are buying something of which we don't know the price. However, everything points to the price being high. Research into the actual cost of meat is therefore necessary. The good news is that modern techniques and extensive mathematical models make it easier to calculate the actual price. Due to health regulations the food chain is becoming more and more transparent. In the EU for example, meat companies are obligated to trace down and give insight into the origins of their meat within four hours after request. With an identification number for GlobalGAP number (a farm assurance programme, guaranteeing good agricultural practice) printed on labelled food, a registration system is already in place that can be used to trace down to the farm level.

Anyone who thinks of the principle of a real price as flights of fancy does not take into account that large companies, insurers and consultancy firms have been working to calculate the financial consequences of applying a real price to their industry for some years now. These calculations are made only because they expect that society will desire the use of an actual cost in the near future. A leading think tank of investors from the banking and insurance world expects the time for the introduction of a meat tax to be ready within five years.

No academic studies have yet attempted to estimate the total costs of agricultural externalities throughout the European Union as a whole, but the campaign organisation Compassion in World Farming (2016) estimated total negative externalities of agriculture in the EU to be just under €170 billion per year. Still this estimate appears incomplete since not from all countries necessary data was available.

It is clear, however, that the hidden costs of nitrogen compounds release alone already outweighs the profits made in the continent's agricultural sector. Intensive livestock production releases nitrogen compounds such as ammonia into the atmosphere, contributing markedly to climate change. According to the European Nitrogen Assessment in 2011, this damage amounted to some 70 to 320 billion dollars in Europe. The study concluded that this sum could exceed all the profits made in the agricultural sector.

For the UK, The Sustainable Food Trust calculated the total hidden costs of food £120.14 billion. Not all costs in this study can be solely related to animal protein (like the costs of unhealthy diets in general), but the breakdown of some costs is still instructive. The hidden water-related costs are estimated at around £1.49 billion, including water pollution and flooding due to poor soil maintenance. The report also cites a study by Eswaran, Hall and Reich, in which it is estimated that the cost of worldwide soil degradation have increased from $400 billion per year ($70 per person per year) to between $6.3 trillion and $10.6 trillion annually. This estimate includes erosion, degradation, and the loss of ecosystem services. It is worrying that the United Nations Convention to Combat Desertification estimated this year the annual costs of land degradation range between $18 billion and a 20 trillion.

Table 27.1 The 'real' price of meat for the Netherlands

	Pork	Beef	Chicken
Retail price	€7.75	€12.17	€7.00
Climate damage	€1.06	€1.29	€0.62
Environmental damage	€2.81	€2.73	€1.10
Land use (biodiversity)	€0.09	€0.12	€0.05
subsidies	€0.02	€0.42	€0.01
Animal diseases	€0.10	€0.53	€0.03
'external benefits'	€0.00	−€0.20	€0.00
'Real price'	€11.83	€17.06	€8.80
Additional costs as percentage of retail price	53%	40%	26%

Source: CE Delft, de echte prijs van vlees.

Climate change is maybe the hardest aspect to calculate. Valuing a tonne of carbon based on the full social impact on human society and the environment is a complex task and estimates for the social cost of carbon range widely, from $21 to $900 per tonne. Also, the impact loses (and benefits) of climate change seem hard to predict and can mostly only be determined afterwards.

One of the most accurate studies into the 'real' price of meat has been carried out in the Netherlands by CE Delft. CE Delft calculated the 'real' price of meat for the Netherlands (Table 27.1).

As CE Delft indicates in the report, conservative estimates are used to define the costs, and liberal estimates are used to define the external profits (additional profits, actually not calculated in the retail price). CE Delft created a manual for pricing environmental costs (*Handboek Milieuprijzen*) with indicative prices for a wide range of environmental costs, both for production in the Netherlands as the EU as a whole. The study finds that retail prices would increase significantly when a real price is adapted for pork (+53%), beef (+40%) and chicken (+26%). Though this study seems quite elaborate, it does not yet cover health-related costs.

In the UK, around 45% of antibiotics are used for animals, and in the EU as a whole, the figure is about 66%. Antibiotic resistance is becoming an increasingly severe threat to human health through the progressive loss of effective therapeutic treatment options for many diseases and infections. While a large part of this problem stems from the over-use of antibiotics in medical care, another part comes from their use in agriculture. Many of these are not used to treat sick animals but are added to feed and water used for preventative purposes. Livestock is increasingly developing drug-resistant bacteria in their intestines and sometimes on their skin that can remain on meat and pass to humans. The Sustainable Food Trust report cites a UK study on the economic burden of antimicrobial resistance, indicating that the cost to society could be as high as £10 billion per year.

On the consumption side, also estimates of hidden health-related costs circulate. Springmann et al. (2018) attribute $285 billion to the consumption of red and processed red meat worldwide, three-quarters of which were due to processed meat consumption. According to Koorenman (2013) a rough calculation shows that the annual costs in the Netherlands for the curative treatment of cardiovascular diseases alone amounts at around 7 billion euros.

Taxation

Interestingly, both Springmann et al. and Koorenman estimate the effect of taxation. Koorenman (2013) suggests raising taxation for meat to a level effectively halving the consumption of meat. The €7 billion associated with the curative treatment of cardiovascular diseases would fall by €1 billion. The assumption is that a halving of meat consumption leads to a decrease in health care costs for cardiovascular diseases by 16%. This numbers relate to that part of the population that is currently not a vegetarian (around 95%). Besides the costs of treating cancer, diabetes, cancer and arthrosis will fall.

The extra tax revenue would be around three billion euros. Current spending on meat in the Netherlands is approximately six billion euros a year. With a doubling of the retail price and halving of the consumption, total spending will remain the same, with half of the amount being tax revenues. This can be used for low-income compensations masseurs, the promotion of sustainable agriculture and the compensation for job losses in the meat sector.

Springmann et al. (2018) describe an 'optimal taxation', which prevents the danger of malnutrition in low-income countries due to higher meat prices. He forecasts that under 'optimal taxation', prices for processed meat will on average increase by 25%. (ranging from 1% in low-income countries to over 100% in high-income countries). Prices for red meat will increase by 4%, ranging from 0.2% to over 20%.

This will lead to a fall of consumption by 16% on average, ranging from 1% to 25%, while red meat consumption remained stable as substitution for processed meat.

As a result, the number of deaths attributable to red and processed meat consumption decreased by 9 and attributable health costs decreased by 14% ($41 billion) globally. In both cases the highest reduction is to be foreseen in high and middle-income countries.

In the Netherlands, the True Animal Protein Price Coalition and the Dutch Vegetarian Society asked CE Delft to calculate the possibilities and impact of a meat tax. This report (Vergeer et al. 2019) builds upon the report mentioned above (and therefore does not include hidden health costs) and will be released in September 2019. Based on the concept, CE Delft concludes the introduction of a meat tax will be feasible within two years when adopted in phases and reaching full implementation and impact by 2030. By this year per kg meat, the consumer price will be raised with €5.70 for beef, €4.50 for pork and €2.04 for chicken.

The most simple methodology suggested in the report levies taxes at the point of selling (retailers and butcher's shops), based on the kind and weight of the meat purchased. This will stimulate producers to use less meat in their products. As a result, meat consumption is expected to fall by 50% when fully implemented. The monetised positive impact amounts of 1.5 billion euros. Tax revenues will be 2390 billion euros annually.

A more comprehensive variant includes an emission registration system (fine dust, NH_3, NOx, greenhouse gasses) for farmers, which will allow for immediate reflection in the tax level at the point of sale. The benefit of this variant is the incentive for farmers to implement sustainability measures and innovations. The impact on consumer behaviour is expected to be the same in both variants.

The suggested taxation systems do also cover imported meat, whilst meat production destined for export is excluded. This way, legally no obstacles are to be expected, since no producer category either national or abroad, is favoured or disfavoured by the system. Apart from VAT taxes, which are defined by basis and limited by scope, EU member states are free to levy new kinds of taxes.

The report corrects the environmental impact of the tax on changing consumer patterns. Consumers will substitute meat by other products, like cheese or meat-replacers, also harming the environment.

Conclusion

Naturally, the income from a meat tax must be spent on measures that mitigate or compensate for the impact of meat production and consumption. How this happens will always depend to a large extent on the political leanings of the government. But in this context, measures are also conceivable that compensate the initial loss of purchasing power through the meat tax. CE Delft proposes to return half of the tax revenues to taxpayers, so in the end a majority of taxpayers benefit. This kind of measures can make a meat tax more acceptable to politics but are not part of the ethics of a true price as such.

In a later phase, it would be logic to broaden the scope of a meat tax to a tax on animal proteins in general. Many of the mentioned negative aspects of meat also apply to milk and eggs. For the beginning, however, it seems recommendable to start with a meat tax.

Abbreviations

CO_2eq carbon dioxide equivalent
FAO   Food and Agricultural Organization of the United Nations
IARC   International Agency for Research on Cancer, the cancer agency of the World Health Organization
NH_3 ammonia
NOx   nitric oxide

References

Aiking, H. (2014). Protein Production: Planet, Profit, Plus People? *The American Journal of Clinical Nutrition* 100(suppl. 1), 483S–489S.

Aiking, H. (2018). *The Next Protein Transition.* Amsterdam: Netherlands Institute for Environmental Studies, VU University.

Bado, V. and Bationo, A. (2018). *Advances in Agronomy* 150, 1–33.

Benveniste, A. (2018). Average Americans Can't Afford to buy Green. Retrieved from www.bloomberg.com/news/articles/2019-03-07/it-s-not-cheap-being-a-green-consumer.

Biojournaal (2018). Waarom is biologische voiding duur(der)? Retrieved from https://allesoverbio.be/artikels/waarom-is-biologische-voeding-duur-der.

Compassion in World Farming (2016). *Cheap Food Costs Dear.* Godalming: Compassion in World Farming. Retrieved from http://tinyurl.com/zpy3y8t.

Koorenman, P. (2013). *Belastend vlees en vleesbelasting. ESB Economisch Statische Berichten, jaargang* 98, 19 April.

Poore, J. and Nemecek, T. (2018). Reducing Food's Environmental Impacts through Producers and Consumers. *Science* 360, 987–992.

Rockström, J. et al., (2009). A Safe Operating Space for Humanity. *Nature* 461, 472–475.

Schravesande, F. (2009). Biologisch voedsel is zo duur, maar hoe komt dat? Retrieved from www.nrc.nl/nieuws/2009/09/16/biologisch-voedsel-is-zo-duur-maar-hoe-komt-dat-11782972-a457899.

Springmann, M., Mason-D'Croz, D., Robinson, S., Wiebe K., Godfray, H. C. J., et al., (2018). Health-Motivated Taxes on Red and Processed Meat: A Modelling Study on Optimal Tax Levels and Associated Health Impacts. *PLOS ONE* 13(11). Retrieved from https://doi.org/10.1371/journal.pone.0204139.

Vergeer, R. et al., (2019). *Duurzaamheidsbijdrage vlees.* Delft: CE Delft.

28 Facilitating sustainable dietary choices for positive nutritional and environmental outcomes

Maysoun A. Mustafa, Ayman Salama, and Sayed Azam-Ali

Introduction

Egyptian mythology immortalises a deity – Suchos – with a mission to protect its subjects from natural threats, such as annual flooding of the river Nile which drastically affected food production and human populations (Naether 2019). Millenia later, despite humanity's mastery of shaping its environment, the struggle with balancing food production and environmental protection continues across the world.

Food systems fall within a nexus of agriculture, environment and health (Figure 28.1). To ensure access to sustainable food systems, the spheres of agriculture, environment and health need to operate in harmony with each other. The challenge we face is to manage the current needs of human populations against the capacity of our planet to provide these services for future generations (Foley et al. 2005). The role of Suchos as a protector of humanity is far from over, but now the power lies in the decisions that individuals make daily, and their capacities to make **su**stainable **cho**ices.

This chapter addresses the nexus between agriculture, environment and health. It introduces an artificial intelligence (AI) based platform – SuChos – designed to facilitate sustainable dietary choices. Section A of the chapter provides an overview of barriers and opportunities for sustainability in food systems. Section B outlines the intervention that was developed by the team to deliver data-driven solutions to pressing global challenges. It outlines the AI-based platform that is designed to link communities to demonstrated solutions with measurable outcomes. Finally, section C describes the pathways towards adoption of the technology and its anticipated impact.

Defining sustainable diets

Sustainability is built on the delicate balance of three key elements: social inclusion, economic development and environmental sustainability (Mustafa et al. 2019). Within the context of food systems, this balance

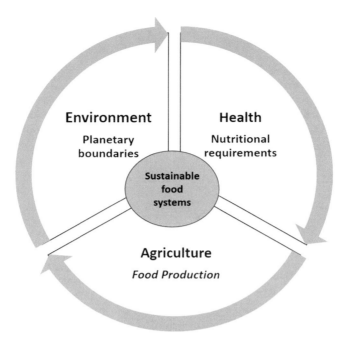

Figure 28.1 Nexus of agriculture, environment and health.
Source: adapted from Mabhaudhi et al. (2019).

presents as an attempt to ensure equitable access to healthy and safe food that is not at the expense of future generations. As we expect to see a 36% increase in global populations by 2050 (Tilman & Clark 2014), food demands will naturally increase as well. The increase in food demands could have a drastic impact on depleting natural resources beyond planetary boundaries. The term 'planetary boundaries' implies the safe operating space within Earth's system based on nine dimensions: greenhouse gas emissions, nitrogen and phosphorus loading, ozone depletion, chemical pollution, freshwater use, ocean acidification, land-use change, aerosol loading and loss in biodiversity (Rockström et al. 2009).

More than ever, there is a need to define sustainable diets. Recently, the EAT Lancet report (Willet et al. 2019) was developed to establish a consensus on what constitutes a sustainable diet. In addition to the nutritional value of diets, the report also acknowledged the environmental impact of global foods and their production systems (Willet et al. 2019). Building on this consensus on nutritional value and environmental impact as important determinants of sustainable diets, this chapter includes societal demands as the third aspect to fulfil the requirements for a sustainable diet.

Nutritional demands

Our modern food system is deeply challenged. For the third year in a row, hunger is on the rise (FSIN 2019). The proportion of the global population facing chronic food deprivation has increased from 804 million in 2016 to 821 million in 2017 (FSIN 2019). While an estimated 500 million people in Asia and 250 million in Africa face chronic undernourishment, an estimated 2 billion adults globally are overweight or obese and face threats of diet-related non-communicable diseases (FSIN 2019; Willet et al. 2019). Paradoxically, undernourishment and obesity can at times occur within the same country, community and even same household (NamZ 2018). Known as the 'nutritional paradox' or 'double burden of malnutrition', this has severe economic and health burdens as quantified using the comprehensive metric disability-adjusted life years (DALYs) (Godecke et al. 2018; NamZ 2018).

The consumption of nutrient-poor diets through inadequate quantities of fruit, vegetables and dietary fibres (Herforth et al. 2019) is now a major cause of non-communicable diseases. High-calorie nutrient-poor foods are increasingly found in urban settings and upper-middle and high-income countries (Baker & Friel 2016). As unique and ethnic food habits are lost, consumption of processed and ready-to-eat food has increased the global consumption of free-sugars, fats and animal products (Herforth et al. 2019). While such consumers would have access to their minimum caloric requirements, alas they would be deficient in one or more essential micronutrient. As a result of these inadequacies in today's food system, an estimated 2 billion people globally suffer from 'hidden hunger' (Godecke et al. 2018).

To address the challenge of poor diets, we need to move from merely quantifying food security in terms of caloric intake, towards a more holistic discussion of nutritional security. This means addressing aspects of micronutrient deficiencies and related dietary deficiencies. Diets that comprise a diverse range of nutrient-dense foods are generally recommended as optimal for positive nutritional outcomes (Mustafa et al. 2019; Willet et al. 2019).

Environmental demands

A broader understanding of the environmental impacts of food production is emerging. While most people drink an average of two litres of water per day, per capita use of water is a staggering 3000 litres when the water used to produce their daily quota of food is considered (Economist 2008). Food production utilises approximately 70% of freshwater withdrawals as well as an estimated 85% of ground and surface water (FAO 2011). Thus, anticipated increases in food demand as populations grow and increase in affluence, will undeniably increase global pressures on our limited water resources (Rockström et al. 2009). Freshwater withdrawals are expected to increase by almost 55% between 2000 and 2050 (Sokolow et al. 2019), while earlier estimates from the International Water Management Institute foresee an additional 2000 more cubic kilometres will be needed to feed a growing population by 2030 (Economist 2008). This is already a reality in a world that struggles with issues of water scarcity and climate challenges that exacerbate water accessibility.

Metrics to measure the water footprint of crops were developed by Mekonnen and Hoekstra (2014). They identified that most fruits and vegetables have lower water footprint and higher nutrient density than staple crops (Mekonnen & Hoekstra 2014). Similarly, Nyathi and colleagues (2019) found traditional vegetables to possess higher nutritional yield and lower water footprint compared with non-native vegetables. Such indicators that account for both nutrition and environmental considerations are essential in our bid towards a more sustainable and resilient food system.

Evidence is increasingly becoming available on the carbon footprint of agricultural activities, thus allowing a better interpretation of the environmental costs of food production (Clune et al. 2016; Tilman & Clark 2014). The Intergovernmental Panel on Climate Change (IPCC) special report on climate change and land describes a reality where food production is explicitly involved in the climate challenges that the world faces today and will likely be exacerbated (IPCC 2019). Emphasising the critical role of land use in combatting climate change, the report outlines that 23% of greenhouse gas emissions are derived from agriculture related activities (IPCC 2019). It outlines future scenarios with optimistic outcomes, which require changes in food systems towards healthier plant-based diets.

Societal demands

Access to information is key in influencing choices. Public awareness and education campaigns can impact dietary habits and food choices and effectively encourage informed decision-making by the public (Herforth et al. 2019). A strong interplay exists between individual decision-making and the accessibility of services. In addition, increasing digital literacy has seen the increase in development of and uptake of applications and the potential to use digital tools for sustainable food choices. Digitisation is profoundly changing our society, changing the way we work, produce, communicate or even how we consume. This is key in the integration of technologies for the development of SuChos.

A big question lies in the influence of food chains on consumer choices. Do big corporation or communities control markets? For example, in Asian markets, which are characterised by young populations and open markets, there is a clear increase in the presence of transnational food and beverage markets, specifically in ultra-processed food (Baker & Friel 2016). More work is underway to explore the influence of price, accessibility, taste, convenience, nutrition on consumption and markets (Herforth & Ahmed 2015), as well as empowering communities as drivers of changes in the food system (Nisbett et al. 2017).

Integration of technologies

Our team developed a mobile-based application, SuChos, to facilitate sustainable dietary choices for individual consumers with potential to expand to communal actions. The platform integrates available data on sustainability aspects of food using state-of-the-art digital technologies. SuChos' backend computational systems (database, data engine, AI algorithm, data storage, data manager, visualisation) are hosted on the Google Cloud Platform. The mobile application is available on both Google and iOS store and integrates the following technologies.

Global Food Database

SuChos aims to build the largest food structured and unstructured database in the world. To date, the database at the core of SuChos contains data from five countries in three continents with more than one million food products and 70 million data points. SuChos integrates unstructured text data about food from 179 languages from the Wikipedia project. Data and text mining techniques are used to extract knowledge for semi or non-structured knowledge systems. One of SuChos' approaches is to integrate existing global efforts in collecting and curating food data, as well as incorporating food data that is not widely accessible.

Food behaviour is non-static and changes over time, occupying different meanings for different communities. SuChos recognises this need for agility and does not rely on conventional methods of applying rigid definitions and documentation of food. Thus, providing a constant flow of emerging knowledge around food culture and habits.

Scientific tools to measure impact

Based on the available data from the Global Food Database, nutritional values and environmental impact for each food item are calculated. A 'Health Index' is developed to visually assess and represent the nutritional value of specific foods using a 5-star ranking system (1 being least positive, and 5 being most positive). This ranking is based on the Food Standards Agency Nutrient Profiling System (FSA-NPS) that assesses the content of nutrients that are associated with health outcomes (Julia & Hercberg 2017). It is combined with the Nutrient Balance Score, a novel approach that evaluates the content of nutrients in composite meals and daily diets (Fern et al. 2015).

Earth Index

An 'Earth Index' is developed as an approximate measure of the greenhouse gas emissions of the food item consumed (Clune et al. 2016; Tilman & Clark 2014), as well as the water footprint of the food item (Mekonnen

& Hoekstra 2014). Both water and carbon footprint are allotted equal weighting and represented using a 5-star ranking system that is comprehensible for a diverse audience.

Intelligence Recommendation, Identification and Categorisation Engine (IRICE)

At the core of SuChos is an Intelligence Recommendation, Identification and Categorisation Engine (IRICE); an AI engine designed to recommend the most suitable food to consumers. In a world of expanding knowledge, businesses have increasingly adopted recommendation engines to assist customers in the selection of content that is relevant and related to their habits. The nudge algorithm is a key component of IRICE, designed to recommend food choices that are better, both nutritionally and environmentally (Arno & Thomas 2016). This allows consumers to choose foods that match their personal preferences and have a better environmental and nutritional impact.

As an example of the use of SuChos, we can imagine a customer walking into a restaurant or grocery shop and wishing to rapidly access the health and environmental information on a particular food item in a readable and visually appealing form. SuChos uses state-of-the-art technologies to provide such information within seconds. For this, the customer simply snaps a picture of the food product using the SuChos application. The image travels to the nearest cloud data centre of the SuChos network and is analysed using the best image classification (Russakovsky et al. 2015), using a deep neural network model to identify the food from millions of food products in less than a second (You et al. 2018). The IRICE engine compiles the relevant nutritional and environmental information and sends it back to the customer's phone in a visualisation form.

The SuChos recommendation engine is based on the most extensive food knowledge system in the world (Lops et al. 2011). Manual and automatic data collection are ongoing processes to mine and integrate all possible existing knowledge about food. The unstructured data is used for Natural Language Processing Machine Learning to compute a vector space of food knowledge. It is the base operational stage for the IRICE search and approximation engine for food identification and recommendation. Combining food knowledge with users' explicit preferences is used to build the turning-key knowledge-based recommendation engine that will serve SuChos users.

As the number of SuChos users and data generation expand, the IRICE recommendation engine will be ready to implement a 'Collaborative Filter' recommendation engine which enriches users' choices using their implicit and explicit interactions. The SuChos' approach is to implement a hybrid IRICE collaborative filter and content-based model to increase the accuracy of the SuChos recommendation engine to provide the best user experience in their food journey (He et al. 2017).

Pathway to sustainable impact

Globally, communities increasingly wish to celebrate and embrace healthier and more sustainable foods. This is particularly evident in the growing number of food-based dietary guidelines that are adopted by national and international bodies (Herforth et al. 2019). Such guidelines identify links between dietary habits and health outcomes, translating existing evidence on food and health into recommendations to influence policies and consumer behaviour. SuChos is designed as a platform building on an expanding database of global foods and eating habits to actively advise consumers on their dietary habits.

SuChos integrates a global food database comprising of ingredients and photos with scientific tools to measure nutritional and environmental data, along with stories from communities (Figure 28.2). Using AI-assisted solutions, this platform aims to support communities in making informed choices on the food they consume and plan for balanced and healthy diets. It aims to build a culture of transparency on the food that is produced and marketed globally by engaging commercial food producers in the process and encouraging communities to measure the impact of the food they consume using user-friendly scientific tools. Badges and digital prizes are designed to match rewards to global targets for the United Nations Sustainable Development Goals (SDG), such as SDG2 (Zero Hunger and Improved Nutrition) and SDG 6 (Clean Water and Sanitation).

Collectively, by combining the experiences, stories and recipes of the communities on the SuChos platform through machine learning-driven technologies, SuChos aspires towards encouraging communities (producers and consumers) to align their lifestyles with the SDGs and have a positive impact on their health and environment.

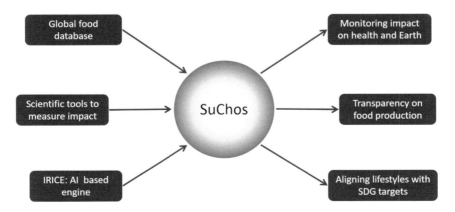

Figure 28.2 The pathway to impact for the developed platform SuChos.

Recommendations

Such a breadth and quantity of publicly available data is now available to support decisions globally on sustainable food systems. However, such data are not currently integrated into an easily accessible format for consumers to make informed choices to guide their own behaviour. The availability of indicators and state of art technologies are integrated on the SuChos platform to calculate and monitor nutritional and environmental considerations of our food systems. We are not aware of any comparable application that can rapidly make such information available to individuals to make their own decisions on how to support sustainable and nutritious food systems that respect our planetary boundaries.

Abbreviations

AI   artificial intelligence
DALYs   disability adjusted life years
FSA-NPS   Food Standards Agency Nutrient Profiling System
IPCC   Intergovernmental Panel on Climate Change
IRICE   Intelligence Recommendation, Identification and Categorisation Engine
SDGs   Sustainable Development Goals

References

Arno, A., and Thomas, S. (2016). The efficacy of nudge theory strategies in influencing adult dietary behaviour: a systematic review and meta-analysis. *BMC Public Health*, 16, 676.

Baker, P., and Friel, S. (2016). Food systems transformations, ultra-processed food markets and the nutrition transition in Asia. *Global Health*, 12, 80.

Clune, S., Crossin, E., and Verghese, K. (2016). Systematic review of greenhouse gas emissions for different fresh food categories. *Journal of Cleaner Production*, 140, 766–783.

Economist. 2008. Water for farming: running dry. *The Economist*. Retrieved from www.economist.com/international/2008/09/18/running-dry.

FAO. (2011). The state of the world's land and water resources for food and agriculture—managing systems at risk. Retrieved from www.fao.org/docrep/017/i1688e/i1688e.pdf.

Fern, E. B., Watzke, H., Barclay, D. V., Roulin, A., and Drewnowski, A. (2015). The nutrient balance concept: a new quality metric for composite meals and diets. *PLOS One*, 10(7), e0130491.

Foley, J. A., DeFries, R., Asner, G. P., Barford, C., Bonan, G., Carpenter, C. R. et al., (2005). Global consequences of land use. *Science*, 22(309) (5734), 570–574.

Forouzanfar, M. H., Alexander, L., Anderson, H. R., Bachman, B. F., Biryukov, S., Brauer, M. et al., (2015). Global, regional and national comparative risk assessment of 79 behavioural, environmental and occupational and metabolic risks or clusters of risks in 188 countries, 1990–2013: a systematic analysis for the Global Burden of Disease Study 2013. *Lancet*, 386, 2287–2323.

FSIN. (2019). Global report on food crises. Retrieved from www.fsinplatform.org/sites/default/files/resources/files/GRFC_2019-Full_Report.pdf.

Godecke, T., Stein, A. J., and Qaim, M. (2018). The global burden of chronic and hidden hunger: trends and determinants. *Global Food Security*, 17, 21–29.

He, X., Liao, L., Zhang, H., Nie, L., Hu, X., and Chua, T. S. (2017). Neural collaborative filtering. In *Proceedings of the 26th International Conference on World Wide Web* (pp. 173–182). International World Wide Web Conferences Steering Committee.

Herforth, A., Arimond, M., Alvarez-Sanchez, C., Coates, J., Christianson, K., and Muehlhoff, E. (2019). A global review of food-based dietary guidelines. *Advances in Nutrition*, 10(4), 590–605.

Herforth, A., and Ahmed, S. (2015). The food environment, its effects on dietary consumption, and potential for measurement within agriculture-nutrition interventions. *Food Security*, 7, 505–520.

IPCC. (2019). *Climate change and land: an IPCC special report on climate change, desertification, land degradation, sustainable land management, food security, and greenhouse gas fluxes in terrestrial ecosystems*. IPCC, Geneva.

Julia, C., and Hercberg, S. (2017). Nutri-Score: evidence of the effectiveness of the French front-of-pack nutrition label. *Ernahrungs Umschau*, 64, 181–187.

Lops, P., De Gemmis, M., and Semeraro, G. (2011). Content-based recommender systems: state of the art and trends. In *Recommender systems handbook* (pp. 73–105). Springer, Boston, MA.

Mabhaudhi, T., Chibarabada, T. P., Chimonyo, V. G. P., Murugani, V. G., Pereira, L. M., Sobratee, N., Govender, L., Slotow, R. and Modi, A. T. (2019). Mainstreaming indigenous crops into food systems: a South African perspective. *Sustainability*, 11, 172.

Mekonnen, M. M., and Hoekstra, A. Y. (2014). Water footprint benchmarks for crop production: a first global assessment. *Ecological Indicators*, 46, 214–223.

Mustafa, M. A., Mateva, K., and Massawe, F. (2019). Sustainable crop production for environmental and human health – the future of agriculture. *Annual Plant Reviews*, 2, 1117–1140.

Naether, F. (2019). *New deities and new habits. a companion to Greco-Roman and Late Antique Egypt*, 439–447.

NamZ. (2018). Together we can tackle the nutritional paradox. Retrieved from http://nutritionalparadox.com.

Nisbett, N., van den Bold, M., Gillespie, S., Menon, P., Davis, P., Roopnaraine, T. et al., (2017). Community-level perceptions of drivers of change in nutrition: evidence from South Asia and sub-Saharan Africa. *Global Food Security*, 13, 74–82.

Nyathi, M. K., Mabhaudhi, T., Halsema, G. E., van Annandale, J. G., and Struik, P. C. (2019). Benchmarking nutritional water productivity of twenty vegetables – a review. *Agricultural Water Management*, 221, 248–259.

Rockström, J., W. Steffen, K. Noone, A. Persson, F. S. Chapin, III, E. Lambin, T. M. Lenton, M. Scheffer, C. Folke, H. Schellnhuber, B. Nykvist, C. A. De Wit, T. Hughes, S. van der Leeuw, H. Rodhe, S. Sorlin, P. K. Snyder, R. Costanza, U. Svedin, M. Falkenmark, L. Karlberg, R. W. Corell, V. J. Fabry, J. Hansen, B. Walker, D. Liverman, K. Richardson, P. Crutzen, and J. Foley. (2009). Planetary boundaries: exploring the safe operating space for humanity. *Ecology and Society*, 14, 32.

Russakovsky, O., Deng, J., Su, H., Krause, J., Satheesh, S., Ma, S. et al., (2015). Imagenet large scale visual recognition challenge. *International Journal of Computer Vision*, 115, 211–252.

Sokolow, J., Kennedy, G., and Attwood, S. (2019). Managing Crop tradeoffs: A methodology for comparing the water footprint and nutrient density of crops for food system sustainability. *Journal of Cleaner Production*, 225, 913–927.

Tilman, D., and Clarke, M. (2014). Global diets link environmental sustainability and human health. *Nature*, 515, 518–522.

Willet, W., Rockström, J., Loken, B., Springmann, M., Lang, T., Vermeulen, S. et al., (2019). Commission food in the Anthropocene: the EAT-Lancet Commission on Healthy Diets from Sustainable Food Systems. *The Lancet*, 393, 10170, 447–492.

You, Y., Zhang, Z., Hsieh, C. J., Demmel, J., and Keutzer, K. (2018). Imagenet training in minutes. In *Proceedings of the 47th International Conference on Parallel Processing* (p. 1). ACM.

29 Environmental systems innovation in ancient India with Factor X components as revealed in old Tamil Manuscripts

Kannan Narayanan

Introduction

The post-industrial revolution has changed our paths, personalities, lifestyle and perspectives on a global scale. As a result, we have forgotten our roots and our civilisational continuity. There is a quick search for solutions to a world in disorder. Our present-day market economy has ultimately changed humans into gregarious consumers who are tilting the balance of nature, exhausting resources by exceeding its replenishing capacity. Our habitat has been changed, life forms (flora and fauna) have been exterminated, food chain has been poisoned, and the world has been polluted with anthropogenic hazardous materials (El-Haggar 2007). Part of the problem is that the global system is so massive that we could not comprehend the cause but the aftermath can be seen and felt globally. Climate crisis is an excellent example which has altered seasonal monsoons everywhere, affecting our food production leading to poverty (O'Connor 2019). Monocultural practice in agriculture has placed humanity in peril. If an epidemic on the few principle crops that sustain us occurs, it will be a disaster. Biodiversity has been reduced through landscaping and cash crop agriculture. What we are witnessing on a global scale, could be just the tip of the iceberg. The ramifications of such a catastrophe have not yet been completely understood.

Though planet earth functions as an enclosed ecosystem in unison with its components, people who inhabit it are not in harmony with nature, but divisive in thinking and antagonistic to each other and nature. Their politics, economy and local governance are disruptive. It was only in the '60s that an interdisciplinary field called Ecology was introduced in university education, to understand how nature works. Realisation soon followed that our ecosystem was in trouble and human activities were the cause for it. Rachel Carson's *Silent Spring* broke the 'God's in His heaven, all is right with the world' lull. (Mann 2018). This was largely due to our misconstruction that (a) earth's resources are limitless and renewable, (b) our actions in polluting the waters, air and land are local and hence will not have far-reaching effects, (c) the belief that man is special and everything else 'out there' is of no concern to him. These wrong beliefs led to indifference and apathy, which in turn are the main reasons for his present existential crisis.

The current global crisis is new to humanity. However, it has seen civilisational declines due to environmental disaster or mismanagement of local resources. For example, the Mayan civilisation collapsed due to overpopulation and overuse of the land, endemic warfare and drought. Some researchers point out that the loss of topsoil was a principle factor in the collapse of Mayan agriculture which, led to famine and the ultimate destruction (History.com 2019). 'The medieval Khmer were confronted with a period of climatic instability that they had no experience of, and which fully changed the rules of the game that they had been playing for hundreds of years,' said Dan Penny, an expert in environmental history who has studied the Angkor civilisation for many years (Lovgren 2019). A similar scale of challenge is now confronting contemporary communities, as the climate begins to change.

If Factor X stands for savings in natural resources and resource efficiency improvements, then one finds examples in ancient Tamil texts as explained below. It is indeed comforting to realise that humanity has thought about it earlier. The nexus perspective emphasises the inter-relatedness and interdependencies of these environmental resources and their transitions and fluxes across spatial scales and between compartments. Surprisingly, these principles were well understood and addressed in ancient times. United Nations has produced a set of universal goals that meet the urgent environmental, political and economic challenges facing our world. Centuries ago, the wise people of southern India had addressed these Sustainable Development Goals (SDGs 2019). Observing nature's connectivity, they came up with concepts of circular economy as well. Thus, this

Figure 29.1 Stone inscriptions in Tamil (11 CE).
Source: Wikipedia

article attempts to remind scholars of an ancient past voicing the same concerns of the current world (Jackson 2017).

Methodology

The ancient wisdom of Tamil culture, an integral part of Indian civilisation, was understood relatively recently, after the arrival of Europeans to India along with the introduction of modern press (Encyclopaedia Britannica 2017). Printing technology encouraged Tamil scholars to transfer ancient knowledge from an older media to a newer one. There was a hunt for palm leaf manuscripts that carried ancient wisdom to be transformed into print media. Publication, reproduction and distribution of these were factors that encouraged Tamil scholars in early 20th century to read, undertake discourse analysis and publish ancient knowledge to an emerging modern world. Unfortunately, those who are familiar with classical Tamil are getting scarce these days. Additionally, there are not that many among the scholars who can understand those ancient scripts and interpret them in Factor X and Nexus perspective. The author of this manuscript whose speciality is environmental sciences and whose mother tongue is Tamil however, manages to link the ancient wisdom and modern nexus perspective. Fortunately, most of the ancient Tamil texts are available in the web which has helped the author to collect those poems from cyberspace. Interactive social media have enabled the author to interact with other Tamil scholars to verify the meaning and perspective of those ancient Tamil voices. While Thirukkural, a well-known treatise in Tamil, reflecting the ancient wisdom of the land had been translated into English by early European scholars such as Rev. G.U. Pope (Tirukkural 1886), most of the other poems in this article have no published translations.

Figure 29.2 The Tiruvalangadu copper plates of Rajendra Chola (reign: 1018–1048), which records his gift of the Palaiyanur village to the Tiruvalangadu Siva temple.
Source: photo by R. Shivaji Rao.

Results and discussion

Human conflicts have severed man's links with ancient wisdom and a lifestyle that was originally eco-friendly and eco-centric. Browsing through the ancient manuscripts of an older civilisation in the southern part of India where people speak one of the oldest languages of the world, namely, Tamil, one gets an idea of how those people discovered the planetary boundaries, ecological limitations and attempted to live a lifestyle that was pro-environmental. Nature was at the centre of their life, whether in love, business, agriculture, tribal governance or travel. Their correct understanding of the natural system in which they lived, made them an integral part of a unifying universe. This is completely different from a Judeo-Christian perspective that placed man at the centre of the universe. This naturally led to the assumption that nature is for them to exploit. An eventual development was a growing apathy towards nature and a complete indifference towards it to treat the earth as a dust bin for his trash (Denig 1985).

However, discussions in recent years on a global level, about sustainable use of natural resources and the implementation of resource efficiency improvements, have picked up considerable speed and shaped the environmental debate. In 2017, there was a decision to establish a G20 Resource Efficiency Dialogue to make efficient and sustainable use of natural resources, a core element of future.

While these efforts look modern and timely, it may come as a surprise to know that sustainability principles were elucidated by ancient Tamil scholars, particularly in this case as an advice to the king who ruled their land (Pisiranthaiyar 2019). A poem, written roughly about 400 years before the Christian era, speaks eloquently about sustainability and renewability. This poem was quoted recently (2019 Union Budget) in the Indian parliament by Nirmala Seetharaman, the Finance minister of Union of India. The poem reads:

காய்நெல்அறுத்துக்கவளங்கொளினே,
மாநிறைவுஇல்லதும்பன்னாட்குஆகும்,
நூறுசெறுஆயினும்தமித்துப்புக்குஉணினே,
வாய்புகுவதனினும்கால்பெரிதுகெடுக்கும்,
அறிவுடைவேந்தன்நெறிஅறிந்துகொளினே,
கோடியாத்துநாடுபெரிதுநந்தும்,
மெல்லியன்கிழவன்ஆகிவைகலும்
வரிசைஅறியாக்கல்லென்சுற்றமொடு
பரிவுதபஎடுக்கும்பிண்டம்நச்சின்,
யானைபுக்கபுலம்போலத்,
தானும்உண்ணான், உலகமும்கெடுமே

The author Pisiranthaiyar explains the principles of sustainability using paddy field and elephant as an example. If paddy cultivation is allowed to fruition, the harvested rice can feed an elephant for months. On the contrary, if one allows the elephant to feed on its own, most of the yield will be trampled and wasted. A king should know the principles of sustainability and govern his land accordingly. Instead, if he is driven by greed and by wrong advisers, he will not only destroy it but will cause suffering on a large-scale. The poet talks about natural resources and resource-efficiency improvements through good practice or best practice in line with the modern understanding of Factor X.

In another incident, a piece of advice was given to the king by a scholar named Kudapulaviyanar (2019) which is as follows:

நீர்இன்றுஅமையாயாக்கைக்குஎல்லாம்
உண்டிகொடுத்தோர்உயிர்கொடுத்தோரே;
உண்டிமுதற்றேஉணவின்பிண்டம்;
உணவுஎனப்படுவதுநிலத்தொடுநீரே;
நீரும்நிலனும்புணரியோர்ஈண்டு
உடம்பும்உயிரும்படைத்திசினோரே;
வித்திவான்நோக்கும்புன்புலம்கண்அகன்
வைப்பிற்றுஆயினும், நண்ணிஆளும்
இறைவன்தாட்குஉதவாதே; அதனால்,
அடுபோர்ச்செழிய! இகழாதுவல்லே
நிலன்நெளிமருங்கில்நீர்நிலைபெருகத்
தட்டோர்அம்ம, இவண்தட்டோரே;
தள்ளாதோர்இவண்தள்ளாதோரே

This author had a clear understanding of planet earth and its functions. He explains the intrinsic bond of water to planet earth and its intricate link to life. He states that food is a combination of soil and water. Watering the land is giving life to it. Therefore it is most advisable to harvest rainwater and manage water resources efficiently. It is astounding how these ancient voices speak about modern SDGs such as poverty (SDG 1), zero hunger (SDG 2), clean water (SDG 6), climate action (SDG 13), life on land (SDG 15), peace, justice and strong institutions (SDG 16) in their poems.

Similarly, Valluvar, who is said to have lived between 300 BCE to 5th century CE, and is the author of a celebrated collection of couplets called Thirukkural, reflects on the importance of water:

வான்நின்றுஉலகம்வழங்கிவருதலால்
தான்அமிழ்தம்என்றுணரற்பாற்று

[The world its course maintains through life that rain unfailing gives; thus rain is known as the true ambrosial food of all that lives. It is the bounty of rain, that preserves the world. It is, therefore, worthy of being called ambrosia.]

This poem understands life as immortal, and for that rain is essential, and hence, rain should be called ambrosia or nectar of life (SDG 7). Life on planet earth is manifold. Individual life is mortal but life as a collective process is immortal. This immortality is bestowed by rain. This sophisticated understanding that life depends on rain for its survival, is 'thought-provoking'. From a system's approach, he explains further that rain is essential not only for maintaining life on land but also in the sea (SDG 14).

நெடுங்கடலும்தன்நீர்மைகுன்றும்தடிந்தெழிலி
தான்நல்காதாகிவிடின்

[If clouds restrain their gifts and grant no rain, the treasures fail in the ocean's vast domain. Even the wealth of the vast sea will be diminished if the cloud that has drawn (its waters) up gives them not back again (as rain).]

Figure 29.3 Tamil texts in palm leaves.
Source: own photograph.

This couplet explains that the sea will lose its vitality if rain fails and there is no circulation of water. A detailed understanding of the hydrologic cycle is necessary to compose a poem like this.

நீர்இன்றுஅமையாதுஉலகெனின்யார்யார்க்கும்
வான்இன்றுஅமையாதுஒழுக்கு

[When water fails, functions of nature cease, you say; thus when rain fails, no men can walk in 'duty's ordered way'. If it is said that no one can discharge the duties of life without water, for without rain, there is no life.]

He further elucidates that our world cannot function and civilisation will collapse without rain. Water conservation on land is often discussed yet rarely understood. One may wonder why one should bother when 71% of the Earth is covered in water, but according to the US Department of Interior's Bureau of Reclamation (2019), ninety-seven per cent of all water on earth is salt water, not suitable for drinking. Only 3% of water on earth is fresh water, and only 0.5% of that is available for drinking. The other 2.5% of fresh water is locked in ice caps, glaciers, the atmosphere, soil, under the earth's surface, or is too polluted for consumption. Further, there is a real fear, a warming planet may lead to 'water wars'. Water is central to all human activities, including food production, no state can allow its water resources to be compromised (Mancosu et al. 2015). Therefore, in a world squeezed dry of water supply, states would go to war to protect their access to water (Levy & Sidel 2011). At its core, the 'water wars' hypothesis expresses our deepest anxieties about a drought-laden future, wherein desperately thirsty societies take up arms against one another. This is expressed lucidly in the above-mentioned poem of Thiruvaluvar that the order of the society will collapse if water scarcity appears (SDG 16). Knowing the significance of this couplet, Prime Minister of India Mr Narendra Modi quoted this poem in Indian Parliament (Union Budget 2019).

If a civilisation could view water as holy, one has an inkling of the sanctity with which it must have viewed all living beings. Thiruvalluvar (Tirukkural 1886) insists on equal rights for all beings on planet earth in one phrase பிறப்பொக்கும் எல்லா உயிர்க்கும் (all beings are equal) and consequently, speaks out against the indiscriminate killing of life forms through over-fishing, large scale farming and finally biological extinction.

பகுத்துண்டுபல்லுயிர்ஓம்புதல்நூலோர்
தொகுத்தவற்றுள்எல்லாம்தலை

[Let those that need to partake your meal guard every-thing that lives; this the chief and sum of lore that hoarded wisdom gives. The chief of all (the virtues), which authors have summed up, is the partaking of food that has been shared with others, and the preservation of the manifold life of other creatures.]

Figure 29.4 An image of Thiruvalluvar in gold coin commissioned by Thomas Scott-Ellis, Collector, British India.

He says that sharing of resources among all beings is considered the best of all virtues (SDG 12).

Probably Thiruvalluvar's voice was the first authentic SDG on hunger (SDG 2). He had the audacity to curse the creator.

இரந்தும்உயிர்வாழ்தல்வேண்டின்பரந்து
கெடுகஉலகியற்றியான்

[If He that shaped the world desires that men should go begging, through life's long course, let him a wanderer be and perish so. If the Creator of the world has decreed even begging as a means of livelihood, may he too go abegging and perish.]

The ancient Tamils treated flora and fauna as equals and were aware of the inter-species connectivity, and its significance. In a poem in the collection Narrinai (2019), a lover hurried to meet his girl under a tree, but she was not to be found there. Questioning her friend on it, the truth comes out that it was a tree that the girl had accidentally planted, then seeing it sprout, had fed and nourished it like a sibling and watched it grow. Now, she feels embarrassed to meet her lover under the watchful eyes of a sibling. The tree that has been mentioned is called Punnai in Tamil (Ballnut in English). This poem in Tamil reads like this:

Factor X components in old Tamil Manuscripts 355

விளையாடுஆயமொடுவெண்மணல்அழுத்தி

மறந்தனம்துறந்தகான்முளை

ஆகையநெய்பெய்தீம்பால்பெய்தினிது

வளர்ப்பநும்மினும்சிறந்ததுநுவ்வை

ஆகுமென்றுஅன்னைகூறினள்

புன்னையதுசிறப்பேஅம்ம!!

நாணுதும்நும்மொடுநகையே!

This is just a sampling of ancient Tamil poems and their insistence on sensitivity, sensibility and connectivity to nature and a call for universal brotherhood. This is clearly a nexus perspective emphasising the inter-relatedness and interdependencies of environmental resources and their transitions and fluxes across spatial scales and between compartments.

The ancient Tamil lifestyle was designed in an ecocentric way, and everything, including their gods, are an extension of time and space surrounding them. This concept was called 'Ainthinai' (David 2011) in Tamil (Ecotype/Biotype/Ecozone). Here the planetary boundaries are clearly defined. For example, ecotypes are characterised by typical flora, fauna, and the tribes living on it. Since an ecosystem essentially defines a way of living, each ecotype has its mood, music and a typical psychological factor called 'deity' or God. This applies to the essential four ecotypes, namely, 'Mullai' (forest ecotype), 'Kurunji (mountain ecozone) 'Marudham' (Agricultural ecozone) and 'Neythal' (Coastal zone). This concept binds all beings in an ecosystem through complex relationships. God, in this concept, is a psychological extension of the ecosystem or a metaphor. This is revealed when the question of a suitable god was sought for a new ecotype called 'Palai or the desert' that appeared several centuries later due to extensive landscaping. It has been explained in literature that Mullai and Kurunji through deforestation led to Palai the desert. The original concept of the four ecotypes was explained in 'Tholkappiam' (David 2011; it has been dated variously between the 3rd century BCE and the 5th century CE). However, a need appeared later to define desert ecosystem with its typical flora, fauna, tribes and a God. This systems innovation approach was certainly a Factor X attempt.

The Tamils had something to say on a circular economy as well. A lady poet called Auvaiyar explains the interconnectivity of ecosystem components clearly in her poem. It reads like this:

வரப்புயர, நீர் உயரும்

நீர் உயர, நெல் உயரும்

நெல் உயர, குடி உயரும்

குடி உயர, கோல் உயரும்

கோல் உயர, கோன் உயர்வான்.

Auvaiyar (2019) observes that if the bund of a rice field rises, the water level in the field will rise. When the water level is right for paddy, the plant grows well and yields well. When there is a good harvest people are fed and they are happy. When people are happy, they pay taxes and hence the King becomes powerful. This regenerative approach of Auvaiyar reflects indeed a circular economy, which is in contrast to linear economy, that is a 'take, make, dispose' model.

Key findings

It is clearly evident that these ancient Tamil texts were forerunners of the modern concept of sustainability, environmental systems innovation, circular economy, nexus approach, an ancient attempt or a model for a society on X Factor principles.

Recommendation

By reading those ancient texts, one may wonder how an eco-centric lifestyle has changed so drastically, over the years to a recklessly consuming society, contributing to poverty, environmental degradation and ultimately collapse of ethics and values. Modern India has made great advances through science and technology but simultaneously has been made poorer by losing values which had once sustained it. The objectives of SDGs were to produce a set of universal goals that meet the urgent environmental, political and economic challenges facing our world. Ancient India had all of them. However, not practising them has led to the present sad status. There were debates in India after the end of European colonisation whether India's progress should take the line of decentralisation, sustainability and self-reliance backed by Mohandas Karamchand Gandhi or western style of modernisation backed by Jawarhal Nehru. Gandhi being an ardent believer of ancient wisdom of India based his arguments on universal values that would sustain everyone. His succinct words 'there is enough on Earth for everybody's need, but not enough for everybody's greed' have been proved right. There is no greater truth!

References

Auvaiyar (2019). [Title in Tamil.] Retrieved from https://ta.wikisource.org/wiki/%E0%AE%AA%E0%AE%95%E0%AF%8D%E0%AE%95%E0%AE%AE%E0%AF%8D:%E0%AE%A4%E0%AE%AE%E0%AE%BF%E0%AE%B4%E0%AF%8D_%E0%AE%A8%E0%AF%82%E0%AE%B2%E0%AF%8D_%E0%AE%85%E0%AE%B1%E0%AE%BF%E0%AE%AE%E0%AF%81%E0%AE%95%E0%AE%AE%E0%AF%8D.pdf/268 (accessed 12 September 2019).

David, H. (2011). Ainthinai: The Five Regions of the Tamil Country. Traditional Knowledge Systems. Retrieved from https://is.muni.cz/el/1423/podzim2011/HEN612/um/26486599/TEK-CHAP2.pdf (accessed 12 September 2019).

Denig, N. (1985). 'On Values' Revisited: A Judeo-Christian Theology of Man and Nature. *Landscape Journal*, *4*(2), 96–105. Retrieved from www.jstor.org/stable/43323106 (accessed 12 September 2019).

El-Haggar, S. M. (2007). *Sustainable Industrial Design and Waste Management: Cradle-to-Cradle for Sustainable Development*. Burlington, MA: Elsevier Academic Press.

Encyclopaedia Britannica (2017). Tamil. Retrieved from www.britannica.com/topic/Tamil (accessed 12 September 2019).

History.com (2019). Maya. Retrieved from www.history.com/topics/ancient-americas/maya (accessed 12 September 2019).

Jackson, A. (2017). The 10 Most Serious Problems in the World, According to Millennials. Retrieved from www.businessinsider.my/world-problems-most-serious-according-to-millennials-2017-8/?r=US&IR=T#2-large-scale-conflict-wars-389-9 (accessed 12 September 2019).

Kudapulaviyanar (2019). Purananuru Collections. Retrieved from www.tamilvu.org/library/l1280/html/l1280f09.htm (accessed 12 September 2019).

Levy, B. S. & Sidel, V. W. (2011). Water Rights and Water Fights: Preventing and Resolving Conflicts Before They Boil Over. *American Journal of Public Health*, *101*(5), 778–780.

Lovgren, S. (2019). Angkor Wat's Collapse from Climate Change Has Lessons for Today. Retrieved from www.nationalgeographic.com/news/2017/04/angkor-wat-civilization-collapsed-floods-drought-climate-change/ (accessed 12 September 2019).

Mancosu, N., Snyder, R. L., Kyriakakis, G. & Spano, D. (2015). Water Scarcity and Future Challenges for Food Production. *Water*, 7, 975–992.

Mann, C. C. (2018). 'Silent Spring & Other Writings' Review: The Right and Wrong of Rachel Carson. *The Wall Street Journal*, 26 April. Retrieved from www.wsj.com/articles/silent-spring-other-writings-review-the-right-and-wrong-of-rachel-carson-1524777762 (accessed 12 September 2019).

Narrinai (2019). [Title in Tamil.] Retrieved from www.tamilvu.org/library/l1210/html/l12106bd.htm (accessed 12 September 2019).

O'Connor, L. (2019). Changing Monsoons and Climate: What's the Rain Forecast? Retrieved from https://medium.com/uncclearn/changing-monsoons-and-climate-whats-the-rain-forecast-8a56c51d6de0 (accessed 12 September 2019).

Pisiranthaiyar (2019). Yanai pukka nilam, Retrieved from http://puram400.blogspot.com/2010/09/184.html (accessed 12 September 2019).

SDGs (2019). Sustainable Development Goals. Retrieved from www.undp.org/content/undp/en/home/sustainable-development-goals.html (accessed 12 September 2019).

Tirukkural (1886). *Tirukkural*. English translation and commentary by Rev. Dr G.U. Pope, Rev. W. H. Drew, Rev. John Lazarus and Mr F. W. Ellis. London: W. H. Allen & Co.

US Department of Interior's Bureau of Reclamation (2019). Water Facts – Worldwide Water Supply. Retrieved from www.usbr.gov/mp/arwec/water-facts-ww-water-sup.html (accessed 12 September 2019).

Index

Note: Page locators in *italic* refer to figures and in **bold** refer to tables.

Agenda 21 92
agriculture: alternatives for business-as-usual scenario 115–116; battle of interests 119–120; environment and health nexus 337, *338*; monocultural practice 347; need for major reforms 9; organic farming 116–118, *117*; testing sustainable resource output 230–231, 231–232, *233*; water reuse 71–72, 74; wrong memes 115, 116, 119, 120; *see also* food production
air travel 139
Aldi 279
aluminium 150, 178, 262, 265, 266
Ameli, N. 265
Anthropocene 90, 182–183; need for urgent action 3–10; thinking 183–185, 187, 190
Anthropogenic stock of materials 106; recycling and 107–108, *108*
antibiotic resistance 331, 333
artificial intelligence (AI) 187, 188–189; Intelligence Recommendation, Identification and Categorisation Engine (IRICE) 342
automobile industry; *see* electric vehicles
Auvaiyar 355–356
aviation fuel 296, *297*
avoidance 7
awards 126–127

Bahn-Walkowiak, B. 159, 161, 164
battery-powered mobility; *see* electric vehicles
Benefit Return On Investment (BeROI) 14, 19
'Best Available Technologies' (BAT) 126

bicycle: couriers 310; lanes 59
biodiversity: conservation and marginal land 291, 298; declines in 135, 289, 330; indicators 232, 234
biogenic waste and residues 292–293; in Germany 293–296, **293**, *294*
biomass in a defossilised world 288–301; biogenic waste and residues in Germany 293–296, **293**, *294*; evaluating technologies for conversion to energy 295–296; feedstock cultivated on surplus land 291–292, 298; feedstock cultivated on unused land 290–291; with low risk for land-use change 289–290; matching bioenergy supply and energy demand in Germany 296, *297*; pathways for use in heat sector 295–296; potentials from biogenic waste and residues 292; residual forest wood 292–293, 294, 295, 298; role in forward-looking scenarios 296–297, 298; types of biogenic waste and residues 292–293
biomass production, environmental assessment of; *see* sustainable resource output (SRO) to assess biomass production
biomass use, Green scenarios for 143, *143*
biomethane 296
Bleischwitz, R. 81, 206, 268
Böttcher, H. 230, 231, 232
Brand, U. 43, 44, 49
Brazil 80, 81, 127, 128; *see also* hydropower, water-energy nexus of Brazil's
Bromley, D.W. 220
Brundtland Report 91, 205
Buhl, J. 252, 253, 254, *254*, 257, 258, 265
building materials 8, 126, 143, 149

Index 359

building standard, Israeli green 59
Burivalova, Z. 280

car-sharing vehicles 265
carbon sinks 9, 138
Carson, R. 91, 347
catering at Kirchentag Festival 309–310
Caucci, S. 70, 72, 74
causal loop diagrams 105; nexus of greenhouse gas emissions and material use 105–110, *106*
CE Delft 333, 334, 335
Centre for Resource Efficiency (VDI ZRE) 160, 166
Cerutti, P.O. 281
chemical industry 296, 297
China 125, 125–126, 127, 129
circular economy 9, 143, 151, 155; ancient Tamil texts speaking of 355–356; international policy approaches to 129–130
circular economy in metals sector 263–269; digitalisation 268–269; role of eco-design 264–267, 270; role of indicators 267–268; role of metal industry 263–264
Clean Development Mechanism (CDM) 291, 292
Climate Act, Netherlands 194–195, 199
climate change: adaptation of big events to 312–313; assessments for different energy scenarios *22*, 23; evaporation projections in Brazil 83–85, *84*, 86; externalisation and discourse on 49; food production and 330, 332, 333, 340, 347; increase in wealth and 115, 147; link between raw materials' use and 37; precipitation projections in Brazil 83–84; temperature projections in Brazil 83; water footprint projections in Brazil 85–86, *85*
CMU (Circular Material Use rate) 267–268
CO2: primary metal production 262; scenario for global energy-related 173; transport sector 42
cobalt 19, 46, 47, 144, 177
Cochrane, J.A. 220
Combined Cooling, Heat and Power (CCHP) instalments 62
common goods, natural resources as 205–225; combining of individual approaches and concepts 217–218; control beyond national borders 219–220; definitions 206–209; design principles for assessment of management

approaches 211–220; development of common good management concept 209–211; relationship between social cohesion and management of commons 217, *217*; various approaches to 205–206; Water Framework Directive 220–223
common resource pools 207, *207*, 208–209
commons, definition of 207–209
commons of energy 188
competition 185–186; market 187–188
complexity theory 320
composting toilets *311*, 312
consumption: international policy approaches to 127–128, 130; and production loops 105, 110, *111*, 112; purchasing decisions and influence on 96
critical infrastructure 182–183; Anthropocene thinking 183–185, 187; artificial intelligence (AI) 187, 188–189; beyond 189–190; choosing futures 186–188; commons of energy 188; good governance 185–186; privatisation 187–188
cybernetics 184
cycle: couriers 310; lanes 59

Dasgupta, S. 280
'Data on the Environment' report 32
Delors Report 93
Democratic Republic of Congo 46, 47
'development by doing' 322–323
Deventer; *see* energy transition in Deventer
dietary deficiencies 339
diets, sustainable 138, 139, 143, 330; defining 337–338; SuChos app to encourage choices for healthy 341–342, 343
digitalisation 115, 340; Industry 4.0 240–241, 242; and metal management 268–269; to support resource efficiency; *see* Effizienz-Agentur NRW (EFA) consulting offer for greater resource efficiency
Dittrich, M. 140, 144, 148, 150, 151
Durance-Verdon basin 72–73, 74

Earth Index 341–342
Earth Summit 92, 94, 238
eco-design 264–267, 270
Eco Design Directive 266, 267
eco-labelling and certification 128
Eco-Management and Audit Scheme (EMAS) 307, 308, 313–314

360   *Index*

economy: approach to resource management 90; consumption and production 105, 110, *111*, 112; environmental degradation and link with growth of 91–92; Resource Report and role of 36, *36*

ecosystem services 67, 68–69, 227; need to integrate within nexus assessments 69–70, 75

ecosystems, entrepreneurial; *see* entrepreneurial ecosystems, study of Kwawu

ecotypes, ancient Tamil 355

education: furthering sustainable development 95–97; role in understanding need for sustainable development 92–94

Education for Sustainable Development (ESD) 92–94, 95, 96

Effizienz-Agentur NRW (EFA) consulting offer for greater resource efficiency 238–251; background 238–239; calculation 244; conservation of resources and digitisation 240–241; future of company 244–245; initial consultation 240; metal industry company consultancy case studies 247–250; need for action 239; operational areas of activity 242–245, *242*; order clarification 242–243; order processing 243–244; plastics company consultancy case study 246–247; Resource Efficiency 4.0 and digitalisation as a tool 241–242; solutions 240; summary 250–251

Eilat 57–58, 59, 61

electric vehicles 42–54; analysis of transition towards 48–50; automobile industry and resistance to switch to 115, 118, 119, 120; drivers for transition to 47–48; externalities of 42–43, 46–47; in Green scenarios 138, 153; promotion in Kfar Saba 58; scenarios for 118–119, *120*; shortage of materials for 19; wrong memes 118, 119, 120

emotional efficacy 114–115

employment, training and preparation for sustainable 95–96

'Energiewende' policy *22*, 23, **24**, 111

energy: commons of sharing 188; and declining demand in Green scenarios 151–152, *152*; demands of metal industry 296; efficiency and Green scenarios 137–138; and emissions at Kirchentag

Festival 310–311, 314; and material extraction 19, *21*; technologies for converting biomass to 295–296; *see also* fossil fuels; greenhouse gas (GHG) emissions, modelling nexus of material use in energy sector and; hydropower, water-energy nexus of Brazil's; renewable energy; renewable energy, increasing resource efficiency of

Energy Return On Investment (EROI) 19, *21*

energy transition in Deventer 193–202; action framework for potential solar park constructors 201–202; calculating energy demand and supply 200, **200**; capacity of electricity network 202; delays in developing plans for wind turbines 202; 'Fossil Free and Affordable Homes' project 194, 196, 197; heat supply transition 194, 196–199; history 193; land use 200–201, **201**, *201*; National Climate Agreement and local goals 194–195; political debate on wind turbines and solar parks 199; production of sustainable electricity 195, 199–202; responsibility for energy market 197–198; selecting heat source 197; sustainability policies since 2007 193–194; Transform and financing of energy transition 198

entrepreneurial ecosystems, study of Kwawu 317–328; adapting 323; adopting 323; complexity systems and entrepreneurship 320; contributions to sustainable management and development theory and practice 325; 'development by doing' 322–323; enabling entrepreneurial culture 321–322; interdependent learning cycle 322–325; Kwawu people of Ghana 318; literature review 318–320; mentoring 322; methodology 320–321; observing 322; replication 324; resilience and ecosystems 319; social inclusion 324–325; Spiritors 324

environment, agriculture and health nexus 337, *338*

Environmental Economic Accounting (UGR) 33, 34, 38

EOL-RIR (End-of-life recycling input rates) 267

ESD for 2030 Framework 94

European Commission 47, 48, 90, 263,

267, 295; Circular Economy Action Plan 30, 122; Roadmap to a Resource Efficient Europe 30, 122

European Environment Agency (EEA) 30, 123, 159, 234, 265, 266

European Union (EU): biofuel targets 289; Eco-Management and Audit Scheme (EMAS) 307, 308, 313–314; externalities of agriculture in 332; sustainable development policy 263; Water Framework Directive 220–223; White Paper on Integrated Product Policy (IPP) 264

events, big; *see* Kirchentag Festival

EXIOBASE 33, 34

externalisation: analysis of transition towards 48–50; electric vehicles and 46–48; failure of efforts to overcome 50

externalisation society 42–43, 43–44

FABio (Forestry and Agriculture Biomass Model) 231

'Factor X' 30–31, 348; ancient understanding of principles of 348; understanding in ancient times of principles of 351, 355, 356

Faulstich, M. 270

Faure Report 93

Fehrenbach, H. 292, 293, 294, 295, 296, 297

First Solar 178

food and catering at Kirchentag Festival 309–310

food database, global 341

food production: antibiotic use in 331, 333; climate change and 330, 332, 333, 340, 347; energy consumption 68, 288; livestock production 138, 139, 230–231, 330, 332; mitigating trade-offs between sustainable resource management and 68–69; population growth and increasing demand for 291, 298, 329–330, 338; resource management 68; water usage and 331, 332, 339–340; worsening conditions for 331; *see also* agriculture; *see also* meat

food scarcity 339; ancient Tamil texts speaking of 354

Food Standards Agency Nutrient Profiling System (FSA-NPS) 341

food systems, sustainability in 337–346, *338*; defining sustainable diets 337–338;

Earth Index 341–342; environmental demands 339–340; global food database 341; Health Index 341; integration of technologies 341–342, 343; Intelligence Recommendation, Identification and Categorisation Engine (IRICE) 342; nutritional demands 339; pathway to sustainable impact 343, *343*; recommendations 344; societal demands 340; SuChos app 341–342, 343

food waste 117, *117*, 139

forest management 138; testing sustainable resource output in 230, 231, 232, 232–233, *233*

Forest Stewardship Council (FSC) 275–287; assessing impact of 279–281, *280*; certification 275–276, 280–281; certification dilemma 282–283; certification dilemma, solutions to 283–286; -certified materials mixed with non-certified materials 277–278; COC certification 277; company procurement policies 278–279; concept 276–277; consumer perceptions of sustainable production and labelled products 281–282; Controlled Wood (CW) 277; labelling 275–276, 281, 282, 286; social and environmental standards in processing and trade 277–278; social impact of certification in Congo basin study 281, *281*; standards 276–277; support in Germany for brand and products 278

Forrester, J. 12, 13

'Fossil Free and Affordable Homes' project 194, 196, 197

fossil fuels: climate change assessment in phasing out *22*, 23; Green scenarios for replacement with renewable energies 136, 137, 138, 141, 149, 151–152, *152*; loss of materials in energy production 106; substituting new energy technologies for 19, 103–104, 118–119

France 72–73, 74

Futures of Education 94

games 186, 189

Gandhi, M. 356

GAP (Global Action Programme on Education for Sustainable Development 2015–2019) 93

Geels, F.W. 43, 44, 45

GEE(R) (Globale Erneuerbare Energien in

362 *Index*

Abhängigkeit von Ressourcen) model
118–119, 120, *120*
German federal system structure 159–160
German Resource Report 2018 34–38;
contrasting carbon and material footprint
37; data harmonisation 38; domestic raw
material extraction 34–35, *35*; future
reporting 38; goals 37–38; raw materials
for consumption 36–37; role of economy
36, *36*; share in global raw material
trade 35–36
Ghana; *see* entrepreneurial ecosystems,
study of Kwawu
global commons 208–209; lack of
regulation of 218–219; multilateral
political approach to 220
global food database 341
governance: of common goods 209;
governing good 185–186
'Great Transformation' 3–4
Green Credit Card 128
GreenEe1 and Ee2 energy-efficiency
137–138
greenhouse gas (GHG) emissions 3, 135;
derived from agricultural activities 340;
in Germany 172; under Green scenarios
140–141, *142*; in Israeli cities 59; at
Kirchentag Festival 310–311, 314; land
use key to reducing 9, 330;
see also RESCUE (Resource-efficient
Pathways towards Greenhouse-Gas-
Neutrality) study
greenhouse gas (GHG) emissions,
modelling nexus of material use in energy
sector and 103–113; Anthropogenic
stock and recycling 106, 107–108, *108*;
balancing and reinforcing loops 107;
causal loop diagram of system 105–107,
106; consequences for policy design
107–108, 110–112; consumption and
production 105, 110, *111*, 112; energy
demand 105–106, *106*; loss of materials
106–107; nexus between energy and
resource use 108–110, *109*, 110–112;
systemic approaches 104–105; use of raw
materials 106
GreenLate (late transition) 138
GreenLife (lifestyle changes) 139
GreenMe (material efficiency) 138–139
GreenSupreme 139–140
Greiff, K. 252, 253, 266, 270
gross domestic product (GDP) 140;
assumptions in RESCUE study 91, 140;

energy and materials extraction 19, *21*;
growth in combined 90
Group of Seven (G7) 30, 122
Group of Twenty (G20) 122, 350
Guatemala 72
Günther, J. 3, 140, 142, 143, 297

Haifa 61–62
health: agriculture and environment nexus
337, *338*; meat consumption and adverse
impacts on 331, 333–334
Health Index 341
healthy eating: habits leading to reduced
production of livestock 138, 139, 143,
330; SuChos app to encourage
sustainable 341–342, 343
heating systems: industrial 296, *297*;
pathways for use of biomass in
295–296, *297*; transition to new 194,
196–199
housing 139, 149
Hülsmann, S. 67, 69, 70, 74
hydropower, water-energy nexus of Brazil's
80–89; analysis with IDA3 energy-water-
land model 86; annual evaporation
projections 83–85, *84*, 86; call for overhaul
of electricity system 87–88; evidence base
81; future planning 86–88; importance of
seasonality 83, 86, 86–87; increasing water
footprints 85–86, *85*; precipitation
projections 83–84; regional disparities
86–87; temperature projections 83; water
system and water budget analysis 81–83
hypervalue 186

IDA3 energy-water-land model 86
IKEA 279
imperial mode of living 44; externalisation
as stabilising 49–50
India 124, 125, 130, 356; *see also* Tamil
texts, ancient
Indian Resource Panel 125
indirect land-use change (iLUC) 289,
291, 298
Indonesia 126–127
industrial heating 296, *297*
Industry 4.0 240–241, 242
integral theory 184, 185, 186
Integrated Product Policy (IPP) White
Paper 264
Intelligence Recommendation,
Identification and Categorisation Engine
(IRICE) 342

Intergovernmental Panel on Climate Change (IPCC) 42, 48, 82, 83, 135, 141, 262, 340
International Energy Agency (IEA) 172–173
International Resource Panel (IRP) 29–30, 33, 38, 122, 135, 143, 147, 153, 155
international resource policies, monitoring; *see* MoniRess ('Monitoring international resource policies')
internet of things 60
iron 129, 149–150, 152, 153, 265
Israel; *see* smart cities, study of Israeli

Jahns, P. 238, 239

Kfar Saba 58, 61
Kirchentag Festival 305–316; adapting to climate-change weather extremes 312–313; catering 309–310; composting toilets *311*, 312; costs 306; eco-controlling exercise 307; Eco-Management and Audit Scheme (EMAS) 307, 308, 313–314; employee training on environmental measures 312; energy and emissions 310–311, 314; environmental management framework 306–307; environmental management principles 307–308; environmental standards 313; future recommendations 314–315; implementation of environmental measures 308–313; indicators for environmental achievements 313–314; methodology 306; mobility to and at *309*, 310; preparation 306; sustainable procurement of products and services 311; volunteers 306; waste reduction and recycling 311–312, 314; water consumption 312, 314
Klein, L. 182, 183, 184, 186
Korber, S. 319
Kudapulaviyanar 351
Kwawu of Ghana; *see* entrepreneurial ecosystems, study of Kwawu

labelling 7–8, 128, 267; Forest Stewardship Council (FSC) 275–276, 281, 282, 286; German Blue Angel 281
land degradation 331, 332
land take for transport and settlements 138, 139
land use: biomass and low risk for change in 289–290; biomass feedstock cultivated on surplus land 291–292, 298; biomass

feedstock cultivated on unused land 290–291, 298; biomass production and 227; dedicated to livestock and livestock food production 330; demand for bioenergy and change in 288–289; in Deventer 200–201, **201**, *201*; key to reducing greenhouse gas emissions 9, 330
land use, land-use change and forestry (LULUCF) model 116–118, *117*
leasing models 265
legislation, resource 47
Lehmann, H. 5, 31, 56, 144
Lessenich, S. 43, 44
Lettenmeier, M. 252, 253, 257
Lidl 279
Liedtke, C. 238, 252, 253, 254, 257, 263, 265, 266, 268
lifestyle 6, 94; 8-tonne 252; GreenLife changes to 139; *see also* material footprints for German households, monitoring sustainable
lithium: production hazards 46, 47; supply and demand 19, *20*, 46, 118–119, *120*, 144, 153
livestock: antibiotic resistance 331, 333; production 138, 139, 230–231, 330, 332
living space 138, 139, 148
lock-in effect 50, 112, 114
Lorenz, U. 13, 23, 107, 110

Mabhaudhi, T. 338
MAGIC project 290
malnutrition 339
Manstein, C. 31
manufacturers: recycling obligations 264–265; sustainability behaviour 285–286
material added tax (MAT) 8
material databases 266–267
material efficiency: in photovoltaics 175–176; RESCUE study scenarios 138–139, 150–151; *see also* resource efficiency
Material Flow Analysis (MFA) 29–30
material footprints for German households, monitoring sustainable 252–261; background 252–253; challenges of existing approaches 255; data requirements for environmental data 257–258; describing different types of household footprints 252–253; online survey investigating predictors for resource use 254, *254*; panel approach

364   *Index*

and advantages 255–257; pilot study 258–259; potential to integrate digital data 257; previous studies 252, 253–254; providing numerous applications for sustainability research 259–260

Mayan civilisation 348

McNaughton, R.B. 319

Meadows, D.H. 12, 13, 14, 91, 184

meat 329–336; adverse health impacts of eating 331, 333–334; calculating real cost of 329, 332–334, **333**; the problem 329–331; taxation 329, 334–335

media 276, 286, 349

memes 114, 115; counter arguments against battery-powered electric mobility 118, 119, 120; counter arguments against organic farming 115, 116, 119, 120

metals: company EFA consultancy case studies 247–250; consumption in Green pathways 152–154, *152*, 154–155; consumption in Green pathways, German share of global 153, *154*, 155; consumption predictions in Germany 143, 144; dissipation 264–265, 269; economic availability 262; German metal industry 263–264, 269–270; industry energy demands 262, 296; product life cycle and resource-efficient management 270, **271**; recycling 129, 149–150, 152, 177–178, 262; requirements for circular management 263–269; secondary 152, 177–178, 262, 264, 268–269, 269–270; substitution rate indicators 267–268, 270; supply and demand in new technologies for energy production 19, *20*, 153, 173, **174**, 263; *see also* rare earth elements

Mexico 72, 126

Modi, N. 353

modular design 266

MoniRess ('Monitoring international resource policies') 122–134; actors in enforcing resource efficiency 125; awards for innovative companies 126–127; awareness campaigns 128; construction sector 126; on consumption 127–128, 130; fostering cooperation between companies 127; future research 131; monitoring approach 123–124; objectives 123; packaging sector 126; on production 125–127, 130; on recycling and circular economy 129–130; relevance of resource efficiency 122–123; reporting scheme 123–124, *124*; resource

efficiency policies 124–125, 130; training and technical advice 127

multi-level perspective (MLP) approach 44–46, *45*

multinational corporations (MNCs) 96

Mustafa, M.A. 337, 339

Narrinai 354

National Climate Agreement, Netherlands 194, 195, 199, 202

National Platform for Resource Efficiency (NaRess), 160, 165, 167

National Sustainability Strategy, Germany 31, 238

natural resources: contemporary economic approach to 90; definition 206–207; depletion 68–69, 91–92, 338; SDGs covering 29; sustainable development and use of 29–30; sustainable use by households 252; treatment in World3 and WORLD7 14; *see also* common goods, natural resources as; raw materials

nature: ancient Tamil understanding of 350, 353–354, 354–355; Tamil vs. Judeo-Christian perspective on humans' place in 350

neodymium 177, 263, 268

Netanya 58, 59

Netherlands: calculating possibilities and impact of a meat tax 334–335; Climate Act 194–195, 199; National Climate Agreement 194, 195, 199, 202; real price of meat 333, **333**; *see also* energy transition in Deventer

Neumann, K. 105, 114

nitrogen compounds and livestock production 332

non-governmental organisations 283, 286

North Rhine-Westphalia 238; *see also* Effizienz-Agentur NRW (EFA) consulting offer for greater resource efficiency

nutrition 339

obesity 339

OECD (Organisation for Economic Co-operation and Development) 30, 33

Olafsdottir, A.H. 17, 19

organic farming 116–118, *117*

Ostrom, E. 208, 210, 211, 212, 216

packaging sector, resource efficiency in 126

paper industry 150, 279, 282
Paris Agreement 3, 135, 141, 172
participation: public 169; stakeholder 70–71, 75
Patzelt, H. 320
Pavel, C.C. 177
Pisiranthaiyar 350–351
planetary boundaries 135, 226, 262, 338; ancient Tamil 350, 355
planning policy, challenging central Israeli 61–62
Plast GmbH & Co 246–247
plastics 61, 128, 150
population 90; Green scenarios' prediction of decline in 148; growth and increasing demand for food 291, 298, 329–330, 338
power to liquid (PtL) 5, 136, 298
precipitation: as ambrosia of life 352; projections, Brazil 83–84
privatisation of critical infrastructure 187–188
procurement 128, 278–279, 285, 311
ProgRess (Resource Efficiency Programme) 31, 124, 158–171; background 168; construction of German federal system 159–160; content advancement 167–168; content and representation 165–166; deficits and potential of vertical structure 164–166; definition of natural resources 207; evaluation 161; implementation mechanisms 160–161, 166; implications for European policy development 169; improving structural integration 167; increasing awareness level 168; länder responsibilities and influence 162, 165, 166; municipality responsibilities and influence 162–164, 163; policy development process 164–165; public participation 169; recommendations for better vertical integration 167; structure 159, 160, 161; Waste Prevention Programme 165
public goods 208
Putzier Oberflächentechnik GmbH 247–249

qualitative modelling 105

rare earth elements: demand for 46, 173, 176–177, 263, 265; mining of 42, 46, 47
raw materials: availability and use of 106–107; in building renewable energy infrastructure 103–104, 106, 109–110, 109; competition for 173; for

consumption in Germany 3, 36–37, 158; consumption towards GHG neutrality 137–138, 140, 141–144, 143; energy transformation process and demand for 172–175, 174; fostering cooperation between companies using 127; German extraction 34–35, 35; German productivity 36, 36; German share in global trade in 35–36; GHGs as a result of extraction and processing of 135; increase in usage 3, 122; increased prices 8, 175; international policies and efficiency in use of 124–128; shortages 5–6; supply and demand in new energy technologies 19, 20, 173, 174, 263, 265; usage calculations 8; worldwide extraction 122; see also greenhouse gas (GHG) emissions, modelling nexus of material use in energy sector and; metals; rare earth elements
recycling: Anthropogenic stock and 107–108, 108; awareness campaigns 128; closed-loop process 178–179; Green scenarios and 149–150, 155; metals 129, 149–150, 152, 177–178, 262; MoniRess study of approaches to 129–130; obligations of product manufacturers 264–265; smartphones 266; solar panels 178, 179; and waste reduction at Kirchentag Festival 311–312, 314; wind turbines 178, 179
renewable energy: biomass contribution to 289; GEE(R) (Globale Erneuerbare Energien in Abhängigkeit von Ressourcen) model 118; Green scenarios for replacement of fossil fuels with 136, 137, 138, 141, 149, 151–152, 152; projects in Eilat 57–58; supply and demand for metals in 19, 20, 153, 173, 174, 263, 265; use of raw materials in building infrastructure 103–104, 106, 109–110, 109; see also energy transition in Deventer
renewable energy, increasing resource efficiency of 172–181; material efficiency measures in PV 175–176; novel concepts 176; rare earth elements in wind turbines 176–177; recycling to reduce material demand 177–178; towards a sustainable system with efficient resource utilisation 178–180; transformation process and demand for raw materials 172–175, 174
repairs 8–9
Republic of Korea 124, 125, 128

366 *Index*

RESCUE (Resource-efficient Pathways towards Greenhouse-Gas-Neutrality) study 3, 5–6, 135–146, 147–157; assumptions of similar policies outside Germany 148–149; declining population prediction 148; economic growth prediction 148; GDP 140; GHG emission results under Green scenarios 140–141, *142*; GreenEe1 and Ee2 energy-efficiency 137–138; GreenLate (late transition) 138; GreenLife (lifestyle changes) 139; GreenMe (material efficiency) 138–139; GreenSupreme 139–140; material efficiency 138–139, 150–151; metal consumption 152–154, *152*, 154–155; methodology 140; raw material consumption 140, 141–144, *143*, 148–154, *152*, 154–155; recommendations 144; recycling 149–150, 155; six scenarios 136–140; strategies to reduce resource use 148–154; substitution of renewable energy for fossil fuels 136, 137, 138, 141, 149, 151–152, *152*

reservoirs: management case study 72–73, 74; *see also* hydropower, water–energy nexus of Brazil's

resonance, theories of 184–185

resource efficiency: limits to concept of 226–228; policies in Germany 30–31; Roadmap to a Resource Efficient Europe 30, 122; SRO expanding concept of 233–234, 235; *see also* Effizienz-Agentur NRW (EFA) consulting offer for greater resource efficiency; MoniRess ('Monitoring international resource policies'); ProgRess (Resource Efficiency Programme); renewable energy, increasing resource efficiency of; RESCUE (Resource-efficient Pathways towards Greenhouse-Gas-Neutrality) study

Resource Efficiency 4.0: digitalisation and resource conservation 240–241, 251; digitalisation as a tool 241–242; fields of activity 242–245, *242*

Resource Efficiency Network (NeRess) 161

Resource Efficiency Programme (ProgRess); *see* ProgRess (Resource Efficiency Programme)

Resource-efficient Pathways towards Greenhouse-Gas-Neutrality (RESCUE)

study; *see* RESCUE (Resource-efficient Pathways towards Greenhouse-Gas-Neutrality) study

resource management, water–energy–food (WEF) nexus approach to 67–79; challenges and limitations 67–68; future recommendations 75; integrating ecosystem service modelling 69–70, 75; reservoir management case study 72–73, 74; social and environmental dimensions 74–75; stakeholder participation 70–71, 75; water reuse case study 71–72, 74; WEF-E approach 67, 68–69; WEF nexus 67–68

resource use: efficiency policies in Germany 30–31; externalities of resource exploitation 46–47; Green scenarios and strategies to reduce 148–154, *152*, 154–155; per-capita in Germany and Europe 158; reporting in Germany 31–41; setting usage targets 7; sustainable development and 29–30

Ressourcenkostenrechnung, RKR, Resource Cost Accounting 248, 250

'Ressourcewende' policy 23, **24**

Rio de Janeiro Summit 92, 94, 238

Roundy, P.T. 317, 318, 319, 320

Russia 126, 129

Schmees 249–250

Schmidt-Bleek, F xii–xiii, 6, 30, 31, 227, 252

Schwärzel, K. 68, 74

secondary materials: Anthropogenic stock of 106, 107–108, *108*; consumption in Green scenarios 151–152, *152*; digitalisation and increased information on 268–269; Green scenarios and increasing 149–150; metals 152, 177–178, 262, 264, 268–269, 269–270

security issues and reliance on IT/ICT 60–61

SEEMLA project 290

Semertzidis, T. 80, 82, 84, 85, 87

SHARE concept 73

sharing economy 9, 265

Shepherd, D.A. 320

silicon heterojunction (SHJ) solar cells 176

silver 154, 173, 177, 178, 178–179

SludgeTec 71–72

small to medium-sized enterprises (SMEs) 96; in North Rhine-Westphalia 238; *see also* Effizienz-Agentur NRW (EFA) consulting offer for greater resource efficiency

Smart and Sustainable Cities Index 56

smart cities, study of Israeli 55–66; challenges of fast adoption of IT/ICT 59–61, 62–63; challenging central planning and policies 61–62; cities as instigators for change 61–62; development and technology 56–57; Eilat 57–58, 59, 61; feasibility of smart solutions for more sustainable cities 58–59; government support for tech companies 57; Haifa 61–62; Kfar Saba 58, 61; methodology 56; Netanya 58, 59; race to get 'smart' 57–58; Tel-Aviv-Yafo 57, 58, 59, 62

smartphones 266

social systems, IT/ICT and fragmentation of 60

societal maturity and integration 185–186

socio-technical regimes 44, 48–50

socio-technical transitions 43; multi-level perspective on 44–46, 45

solar panels 61, 138–139, 172, 179; material efficiency measures 175–176, 179; predicted cumulative installed capacity 173; raw materials, supply and demand 19, 20, 173, **174**, 263; recycling 178, 179

solar parks: in Deventer 199, 200, **200**, 201–202; use of marginal land for 291

South Africa 124, 127, 129–130

South Korea 124, 125, 128

Spataru, C 86

'Special Report on Renewable Energy Sources and Climate Change Mitigation' 82

Springmann, M. 331, 333, 334

Stadler, K. 33, 34, 253

stakeholder participation in WEF nexus approach 70–71, 75

steel production 149–150, 153, 264; Putzier Oberflächentechnik GmbH 247–249; Schmees 249–250

straw 295, 298

substitution 7, 8; in Green scenarios 149, 151–152, 152; lack of, for many natural resources 91; of materials in solar cells 175, 176, 179; of new energy technologies for fossil fuels 19, 103–104, 118–119; rate indicators for metals 267–268, 270; in wind turbines 177

Suchos 337

SuChos app 341–343, 343

Sustainable Consumption and Production Hotspots Analysis Tool (SCP-HAT) 30

Sustainable Development Goals (SDGs) 29, 67, 93, 158, 173; ancient Tamil texts speaking of 351, 352, 353, 354, 356; Education for Sustainable Development and implementation of 93–94; entrepreneurial ecosystem to achieve 317–328; German adoption and monitoring of 31–32; as a possible forecaster of economy 95; Responsible Consumption and Production 252, 258, 259–260; SuChos app to inspire alignment of lifestyles with 343; water-energy nexus and 80; water-energy-food (WEF) nexus and 67–68, 70, 71, 74

Sustainable Development Scenarios (SDS) 173

sustainable resource output (SRO) to assess biomass production 226–237; assessing in agriculture and forestry biomass production 230–231; expanding concept of resource efficiency 233–234, 235; limits to concept of resource efficiency 226–228; methods 228–229, 228; need for monitoring of biomass use 226; results and interpretation 232–235, 233; scenario development in agriculture and forestry 231–232; selection of indicators 234

SUWA (Safe Use of Wastewater in Agriculture) 71–72

Sverdrup, U. 11, 13, 15, 17, 19, 109

system analysis 104

system-policies 6–9

systems sciences 184

Tamil texts, ancient 347–357, 348; 'Ainthinai' concept 355; on circular economy 355–356; ecotypes 355; on equal rights for all living beings 353–354; on hunger 354; on importance and management of water 351–353; on inter-species connectivity 354–355; methodology 349; nature at centre of life 350; nexus perspective in 349, 355; in palm leaves 349, 352; on principles of sustainability 350–351; rain as ambrosia 352; speaking of SDGs 351, 352, 353, 354, 356

tax on meat 329, 334–335

techno-scientific knowledge 49–50

technology 187; see also smart cities, study of Israeli

Tel-Aviv-Yafo 57, 58, 59, 62

368　*Index*

tellurium 263
temperature: global average 135; projections, Brazil 83
Teubler, J. 252, 253, 254, 257, 258, 263
theories of resonance 184–185
Thirukkural 349, 351–354
Tholkappiam 355
Tragedy of the Commons 208
Transform 198
transport: alternatives for business as usual scenario 116; CO2 emissions 42; GreenEe1 and Ee2 scenario 137–138; GreenLate scenario 138; GreenLife scenario 139; Kirchentag Festival *309*, 310; land take for settlements and 138, 139; smart mobility in Israel 57, 58, 59; *see also* bicycle; electric vehicles

UNESCO 93–94, 95
United Nations Environment Programme (UNEP) 206–207
United Nations Environment (UNE) 29–30
United Nations Framework Convention on Climate Change (UNFCCC) 3, 135, 141, 172
United Nations International Resource Panel (IRP) 29–30, 33, 38, 122, 135, 143, 147, 153, 155
United Nations Program on Sustainable Consumption and Production (SCP) 127
United States of America 47, 125, 127, 128
UNU-FLORES 71, 72

Valluvar 351
Verbücheln, M. 161, 163, 164
'Vertical integration of the national resource efficiency programme ProgRess (VertRess)' 159
Viebahn, P. 174, 177

waste: attitude to 9; food 117, *117*, 139; reduction and recycling at Kirchentag Festival 311–312, 314
Waste Electrical and Electronic Equipment (WEEE) Directive 178
Waste Prevention Programme 165
Waste Recycling Action Program (WRAP) 128

water: ancient Tamil text on importance and management of 351–353; application of a WEF nexus approach to reuse 71–72, 74; consumption at Kirchentag Festival 312, 314; food production and use of 331, 332, 339–340; footprint of crops 340; fresh drinking 353; per capita use 339; 'wars' 353
Water Framework Directive (WFD) 220–223
water-energy nexus of Brazil's hydropower; *see* hydropower, water-energy nexus of Brazil's
water-energy-food (WEF) nexus; *see* resource management, water-energy-food (WEF) nexus approach to
water-energy-food-ecosystem (WEF-E) nexus 67, 68–69
wealth: and consumer choices 96; increase of 12, 115, 147
well-being 96–97
wind turbines 172; demand for raw materials 173, **174**, 263, 265; in Deventer 199, 200, **200**, 202; predicted cumulative installed capacity 173; recycling 178, 179; reducing demand for rare earth elements 176–177; substitution measures 177, 179
Wissen, M. 43, 44, 50
wood: construction 143, 149; residual forest 292–293, 294, 295, 298
workforce education for a sustainable future 95–96
World Business Council for Sustainable Development 317
World Energy Outlook (WEO) 172–173, *174*
World3 model 13, 14, 15
WORLD6 model 13
WORLD7 model 11–28; approach to global problems and challenges 23–26; description 17–18, *18*; development methodology 12–16; economics 14; model methodology 16, *16*; natural resources 14; other policies tested with 23, **24**; pollution 14–15; purpose 12; results 19–23; scope and objectives 11–12; social aspects 15
Zhang, L. 68, 74